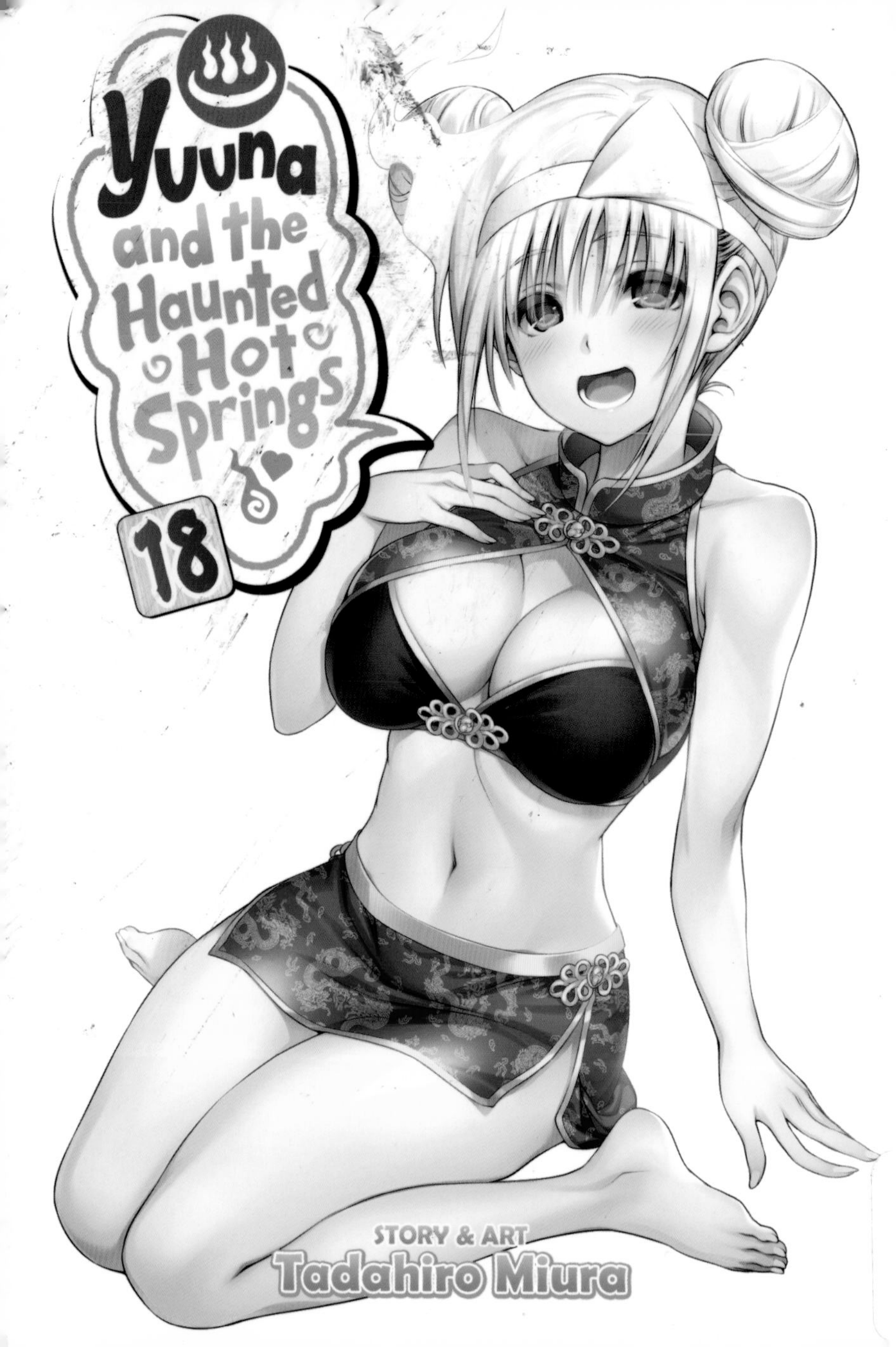
Yuuna and the Haunted Hot Springs
18
STORY & ART
Tadahiro Miura

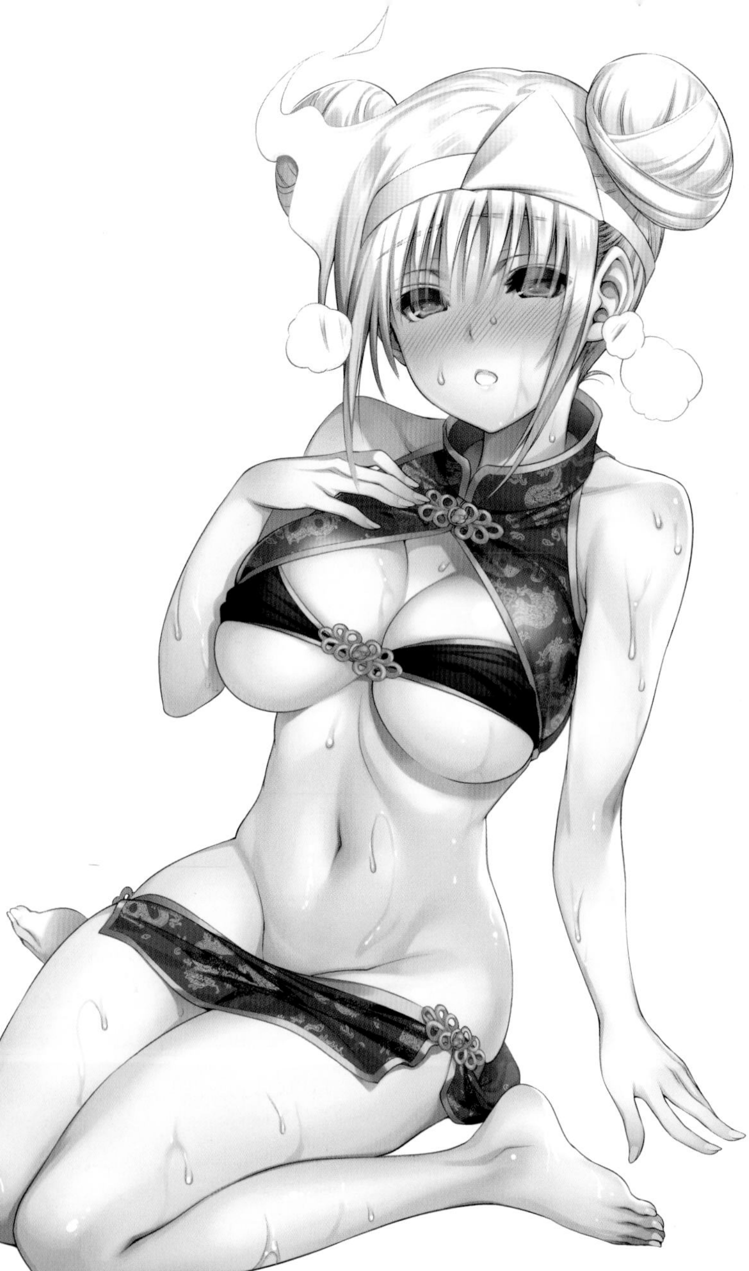

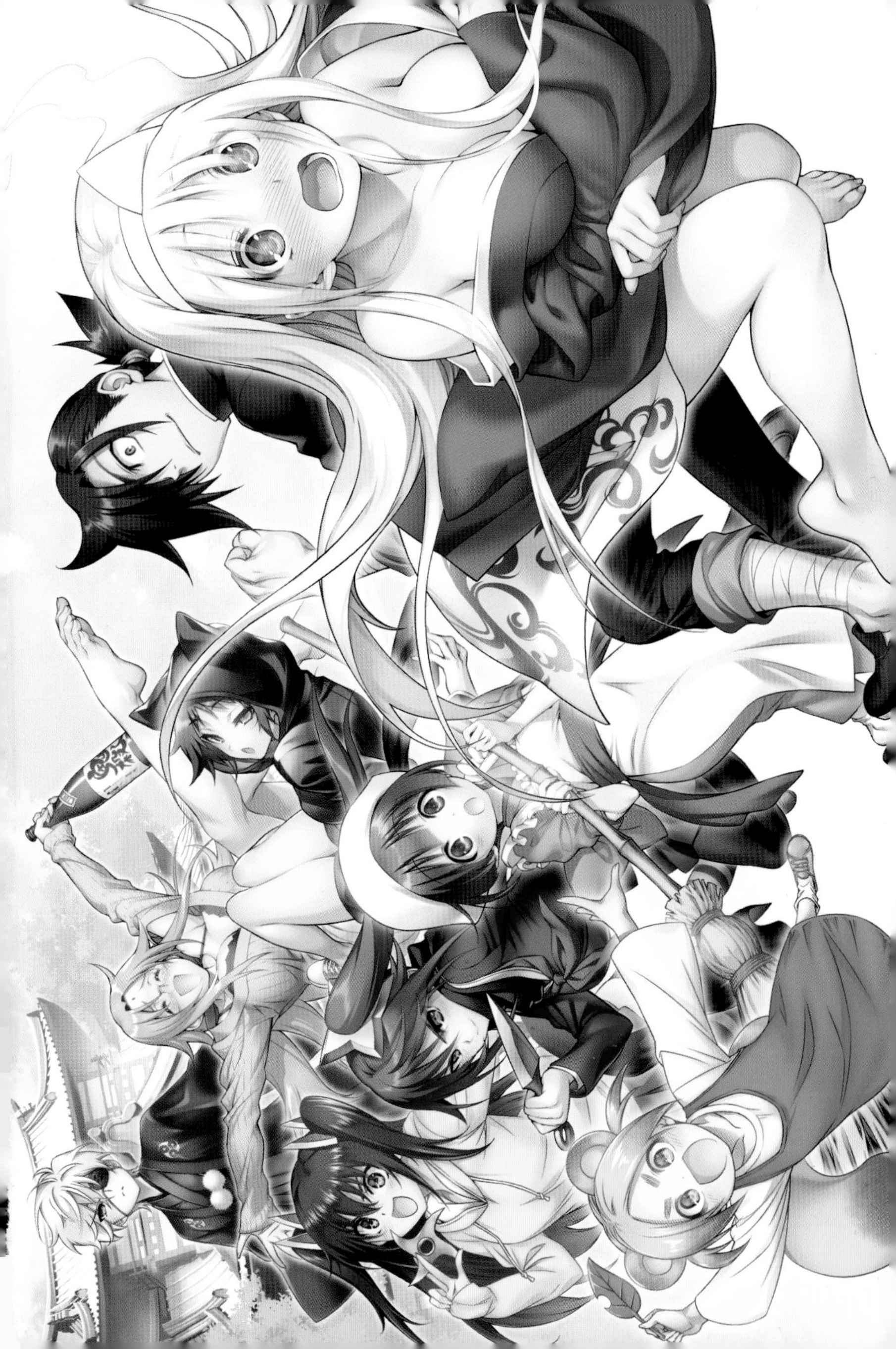

Yuuna and the Haunted Hot Springs

18

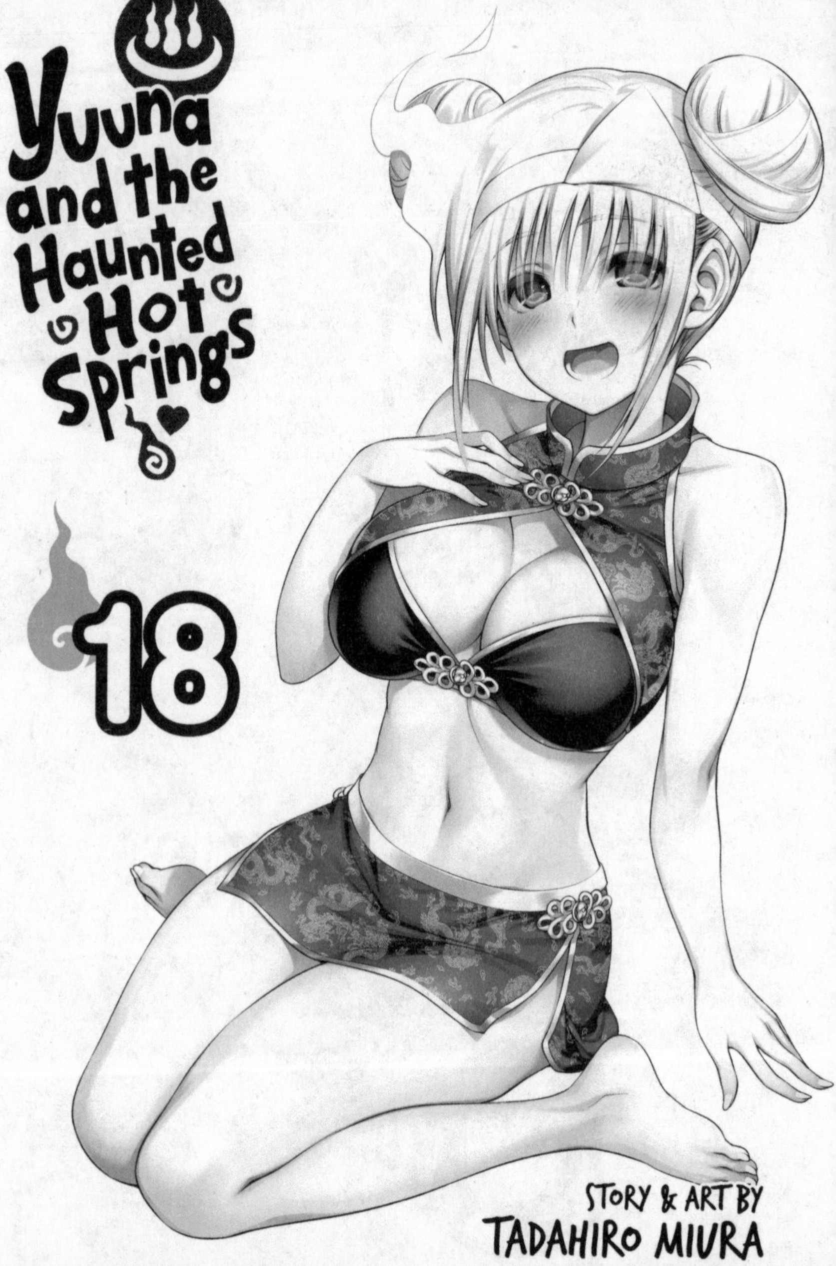

STORY & ART BY
TADAHIRO MIURA

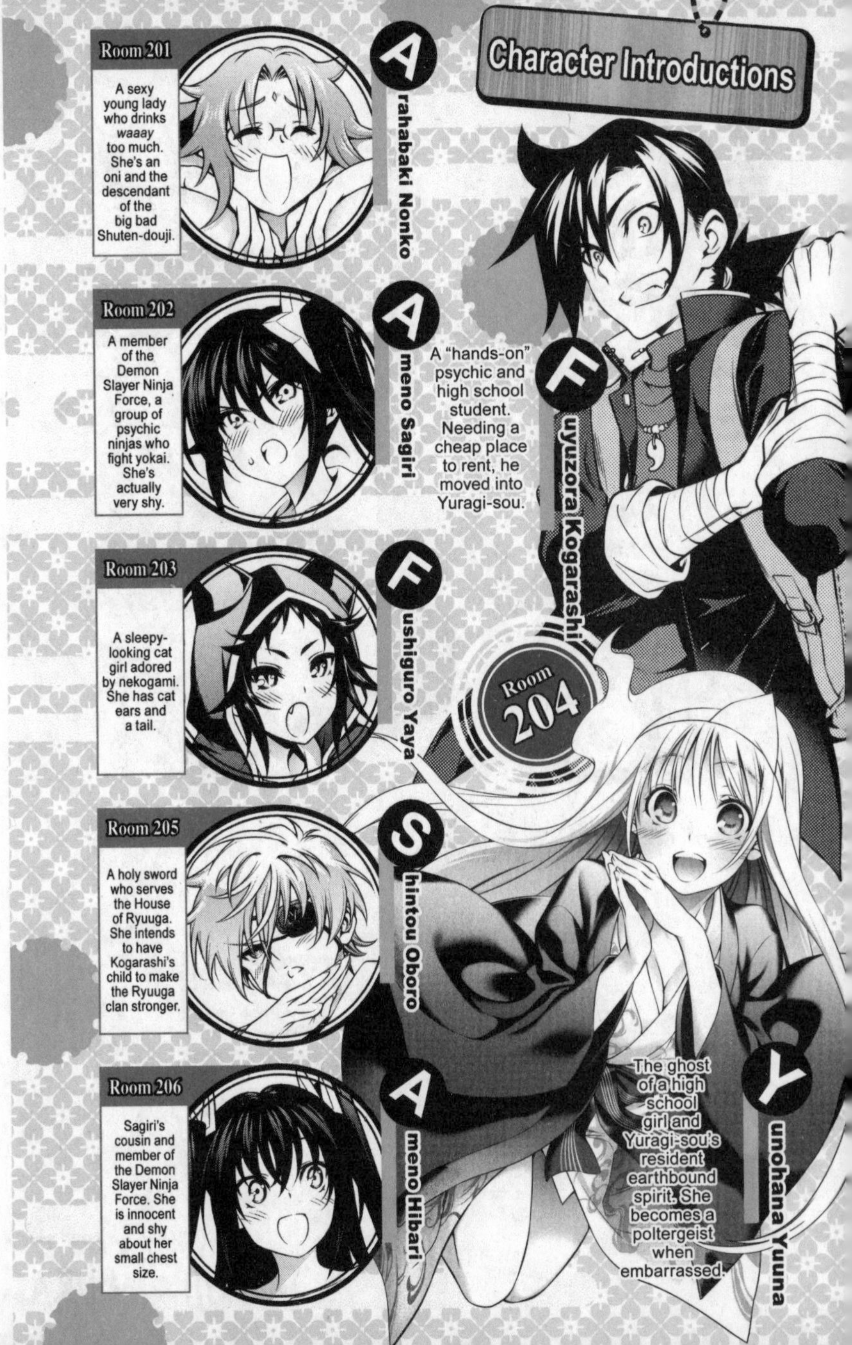
Character Introductions
Room 201
A sexy young lady who drinks *waaay* too much. She's an oni and the descendant of the big bad Shuten-douji.
Arahabaki Nonko
Room 202
A member of the Demon Slayer Ninja Force, a group of psychic ninjas who fight yokai. She's actually very shy.
Ameno Sagiri
A "hands-on" psychic and high school student. Needing a cheap place to rent, he moved into Yuragi-sou.
Fuyuzora Kogarashi
Room 203
A sleepy-looking cat girl adored by nekogami. She has cat ears and a tail.
Fushiguro Yaya
Room 204
Room 205
A holy sword who serves the House of Ryuuga. She intends to have Kogarashi's child to make the Ryuuga clan stronger.
Shintou Oboro
Room 206
Sagiri's cousin and member of the Demon Slayer Ninja Force. She is innocent and shy about her small chest size.
Ameno Hibari
The ghost of a high school girl and Yuragi-sou's resident earthbound spirit. She becomes a poltergeist when embarrassed.
Yunohana Yuuna

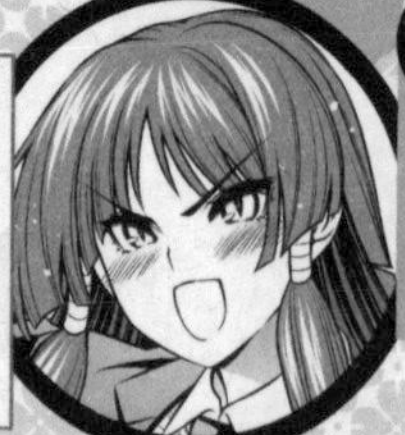

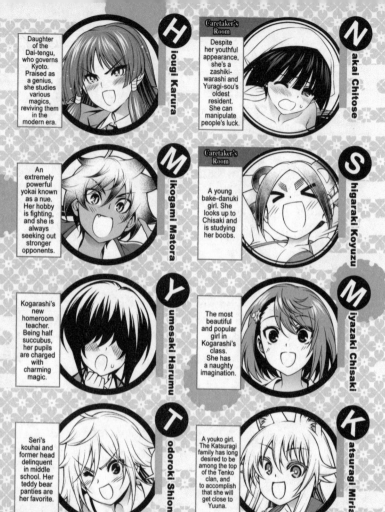

Hiougi Karura

Daughter of the Dai-tengu, who governs Kyoto. Praised as a genius, she studies various magics, reviving them in the modern era.

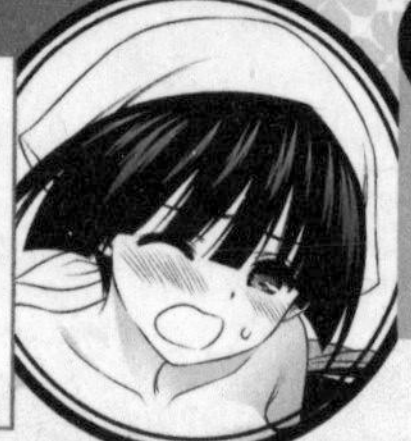

Nakai Chitose

Caretaker's Room

Despite her youthful appearance, she's a zashiki-warashi and Yuragi-sou's oldest resident. She can manipulate people's luck.

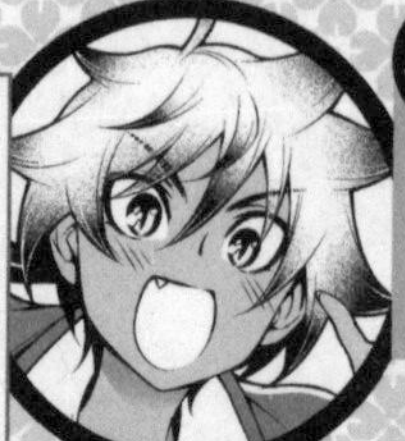

Mikogami Matora

An extremely powerful yokai known as a nue. Her hobby is fighting, and she is always seeking out stronger opponents.

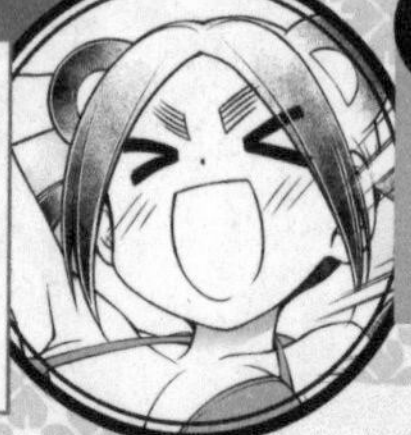

Shigaraki Koyuzu

Caretaker's Room

A young bake-danuki girl. She looks up to Chisaki and is studying her boobs.

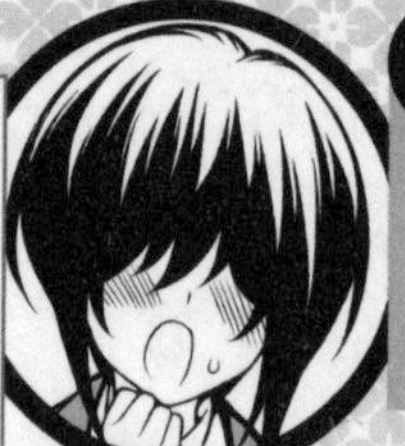

Yumesaki Harumu

Kogarashi's new homeroom teacher. Being half succubus, her pupils are charged with charming magic.

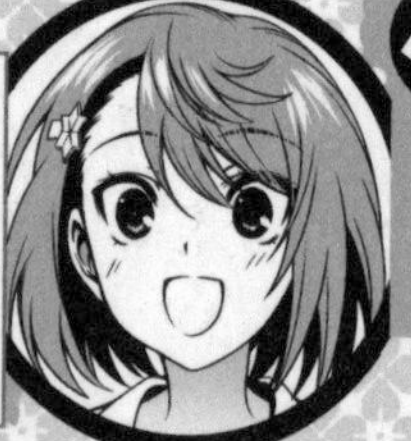

Miyazaki Chisaki

The most beautiful and popular girl in Kogarashi's class. She has a naughty imagination.

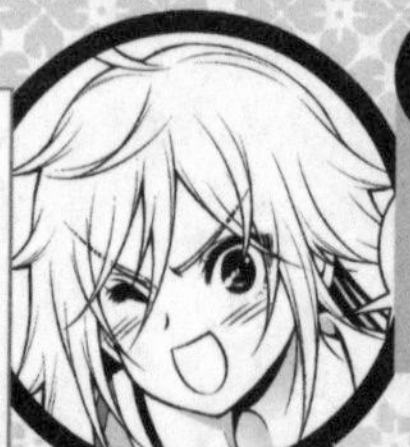

Todoroki Shion

Seri's kouhai and former head delinquent in middle school. Her teddy bear panties are her favorite.

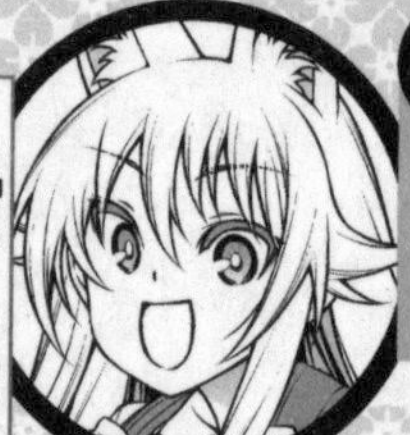

Katsuragi Miria

A youko girl. The Katsuragi family has long desired to be among the top of the Tenko clan, and to accomplish that she will get close to Yuuna.

Summary

While living in Yuragi-sou, a hot spring inn-turned-boardinghouse with an unusual history, “hands-on” psychic Fuyuzora Kogarashi promised Yuuna, the earthbound spirit of a high school girl, that he would make her happy and help her pass on. The members of Yuragi-sou visited Kyoto on a school trip. In her dream, Chisaki experiences a happy future in which she lives with Kogarashi. However, when she learns about the war between East and West that took place in the future, Chisaki realizes that the cause of the war stems from the school trip. Chisaki then sacrifices the future to save everyone.

152 Oboro-san's Proposal

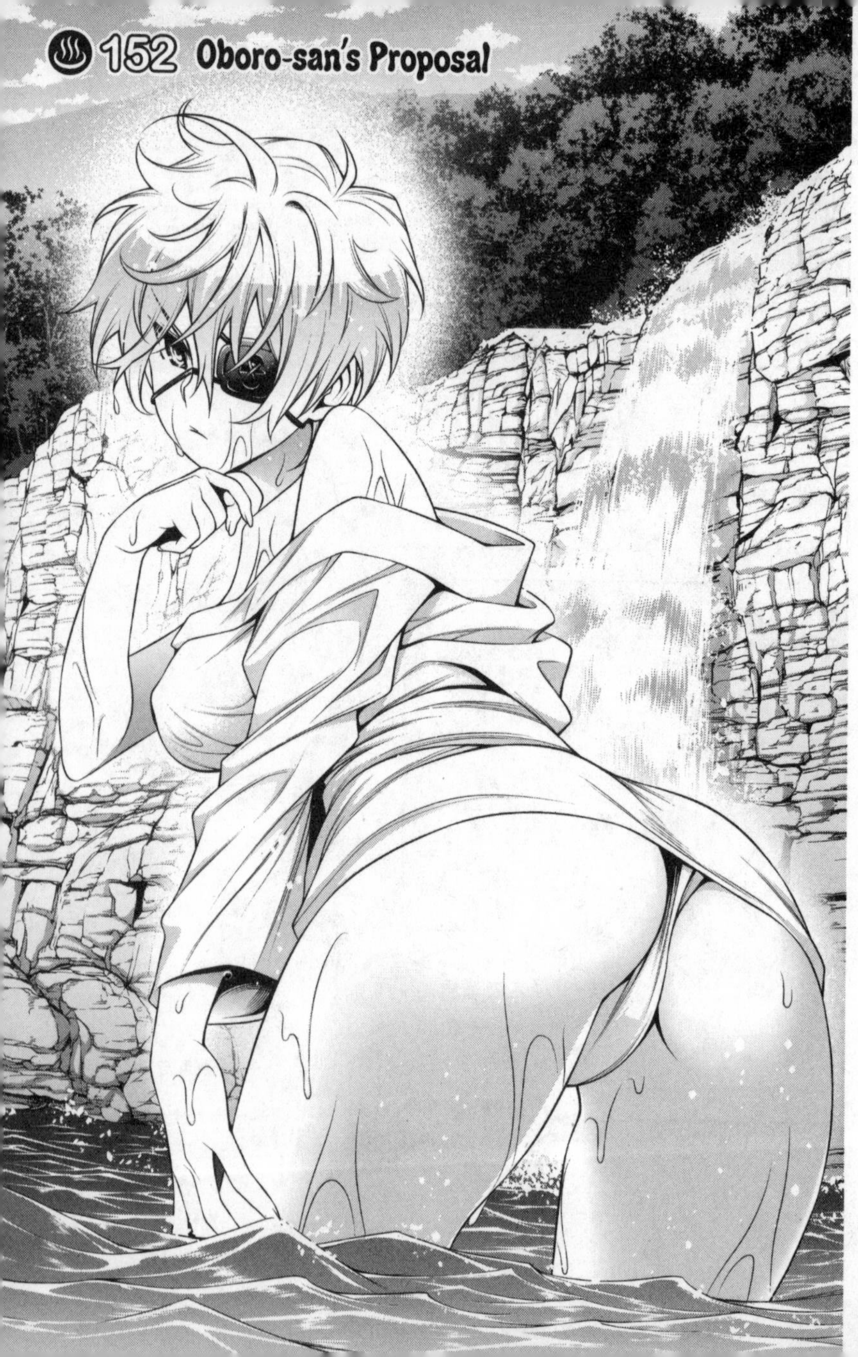

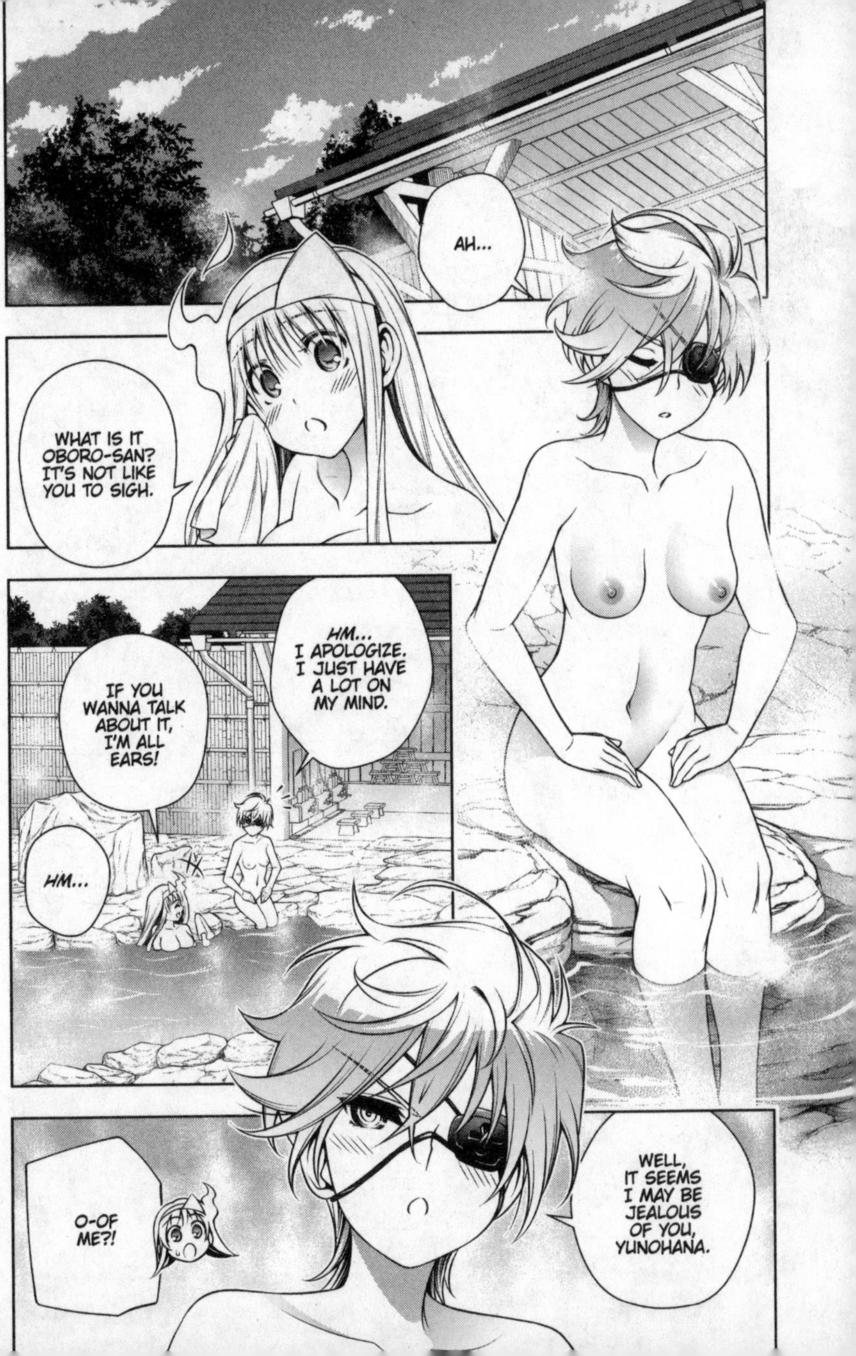
AH...
WHAT IS IT OBORO-SAN? IT'S NOT LIKE YOU TO SIGH.
HM... I APOLOGIZE. I JUST HAVE A LOT ON MY MIND.
IF YOU WANNA TALK ABOUT IT, I'M ALL EARS!
HM...
WELL, IT SEEMS I MAY BE JEALOUS OF YOU, YUNOHANA.
O-OF ME?!

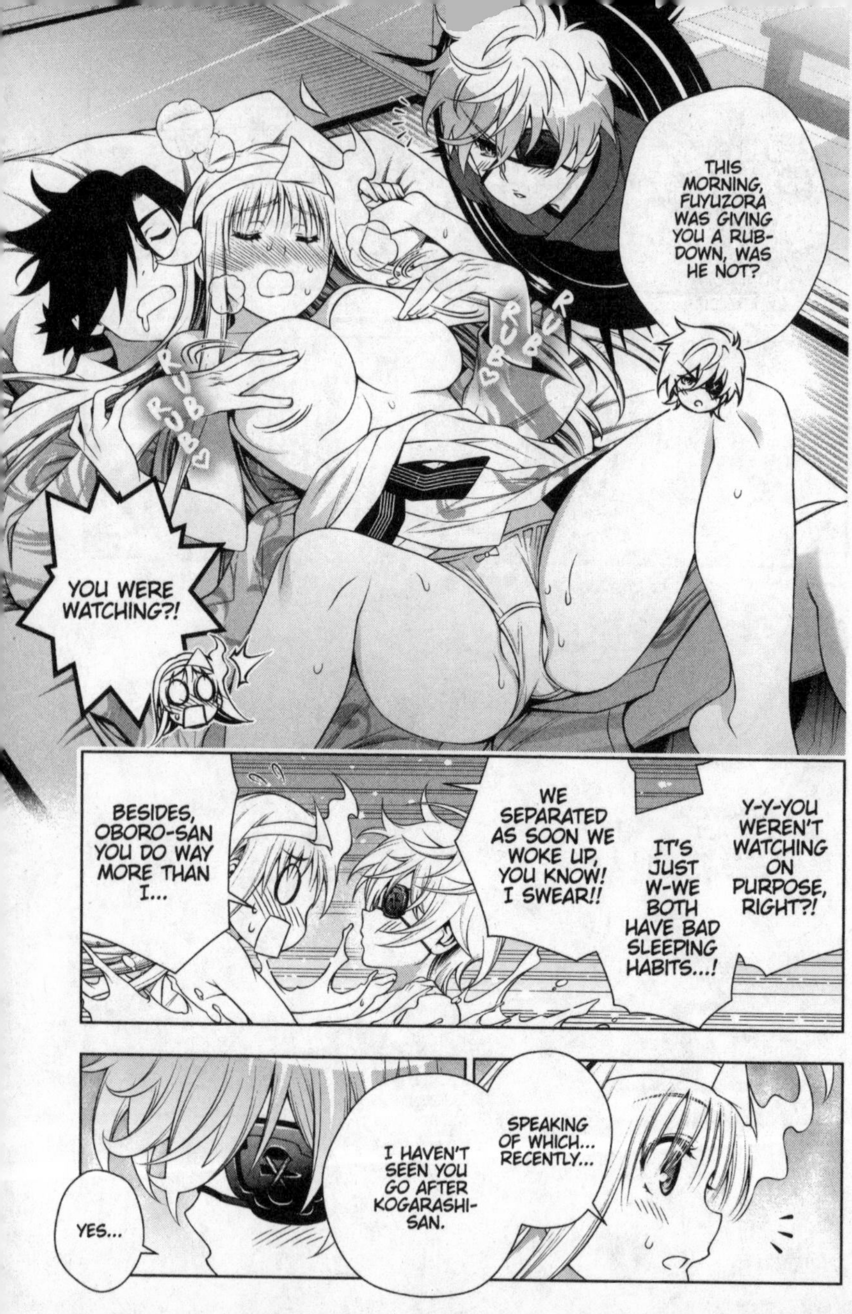
THIS MORNING, FUYUZORA WAS GIVING YOU A RUB-DOWN, WAS HE NOT?
RUB RUB♡
RUB RUB♡
YOU WERE WATCHING?!
Y-Y-YOU WEREN'T WATCHING ON PURPOSE, RIGHT?!
IT'S JUST W-WE BOTH HAVE BAD SLEEPING HABITS...!
WE SEPARATED AS SOON WE WOKE UP, YOU KNOW! I SWEAR!!
BESIDES, OBORO-SAN YOU DO WAY MORE THAN I...
SPEAKING OF WHICH... RECENTLY...
I HAVEN'T SEEN YOU GO AFTER KOGARASHI-SAN.
YES...

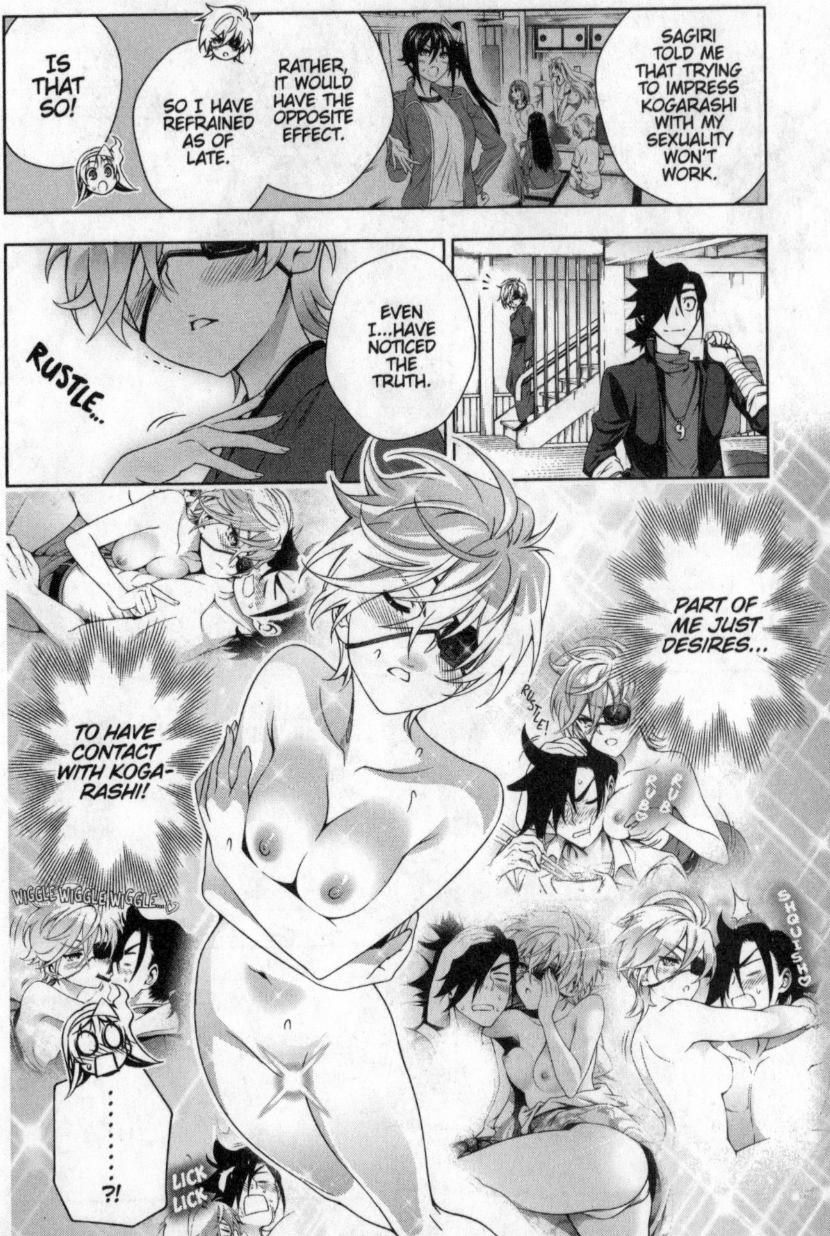
SAGIRI TOLD ME THAT TRYING TO IMPRESS KOGARASHI WITH MY SEXUALITY WON'T WORK.
RATHER, IT WOULD HAVE THE OPPOSITE EFFECT.
SO I HAVE REFRAINED AS OF LATE.
IS THAT SO!
EVEN I...HAVE NOTICED THE TRUTH.
RUSTLE...
PART OF ME JUST DESIRES...
TO HAVE CONTACT WITH KOGA-RASHI!
RUSTLE!
RUB RUB
SHQUISH
WIGGLE WIGGLE WIGGLE...
......
?!
LICK LICK

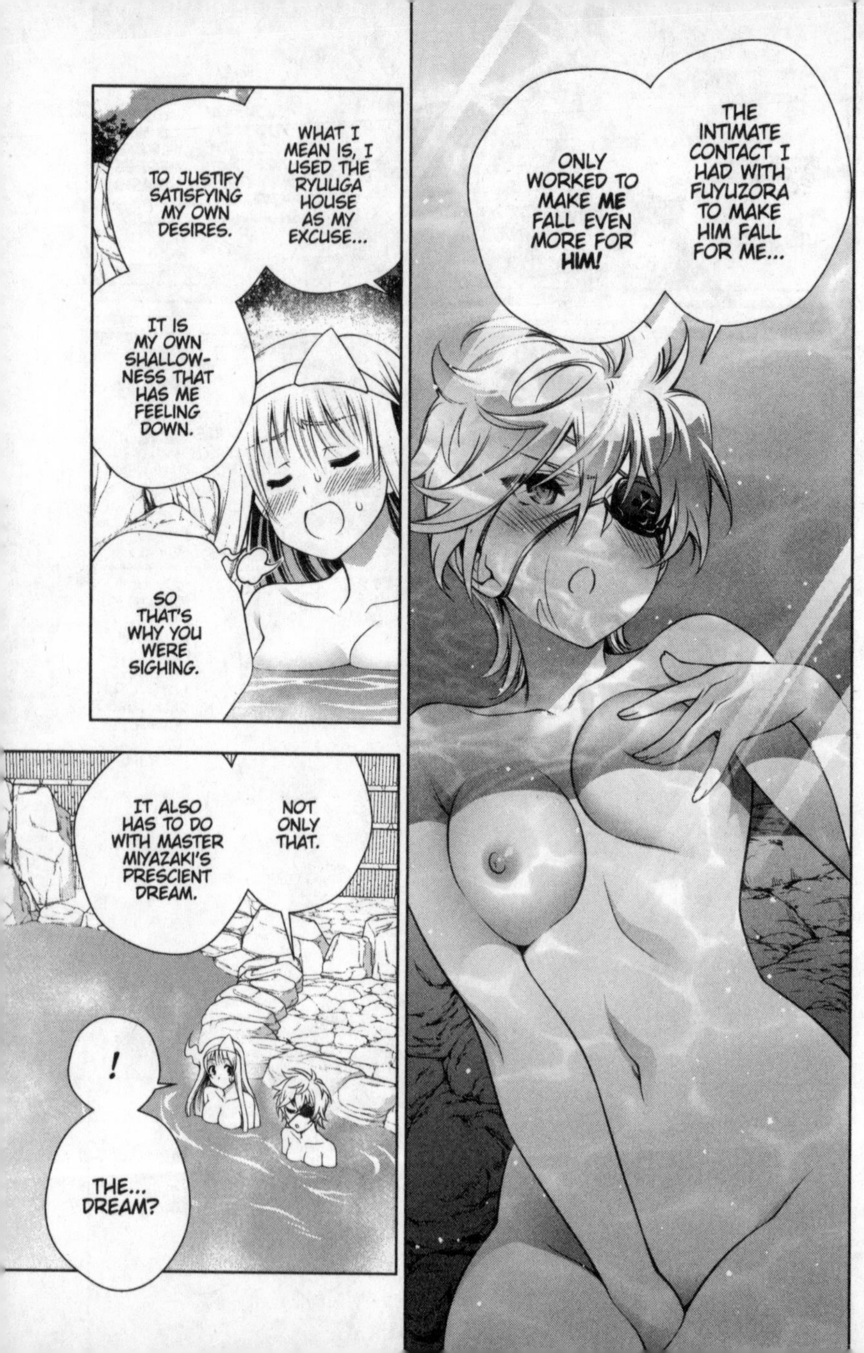
THE INTIMATE CONTACT I HAD WITH FUYUZORA TO MAKE HIM FALL FOR ME...
ONLY WORKED TO MAKE ME FALL EVEN MORE FOR HIM!
WHAT I MEAN IS, I USED THE RYUUGA HOUSE AS MY EXCUSE...
TO JUSTIFY SATISFYING MY OWN DESIRES.
IT IS MY OWN SHALLOWNESS THAT HAS ME FEELING DOWN.
SO THAT'S WHY YOU WERE SIGHING.
NOT ONLY THAT.
IT ALSO HAS TO DO WITH MASTER MIYAZAKI'S PRESCIENT DREAM.
!
THE... DREAM?

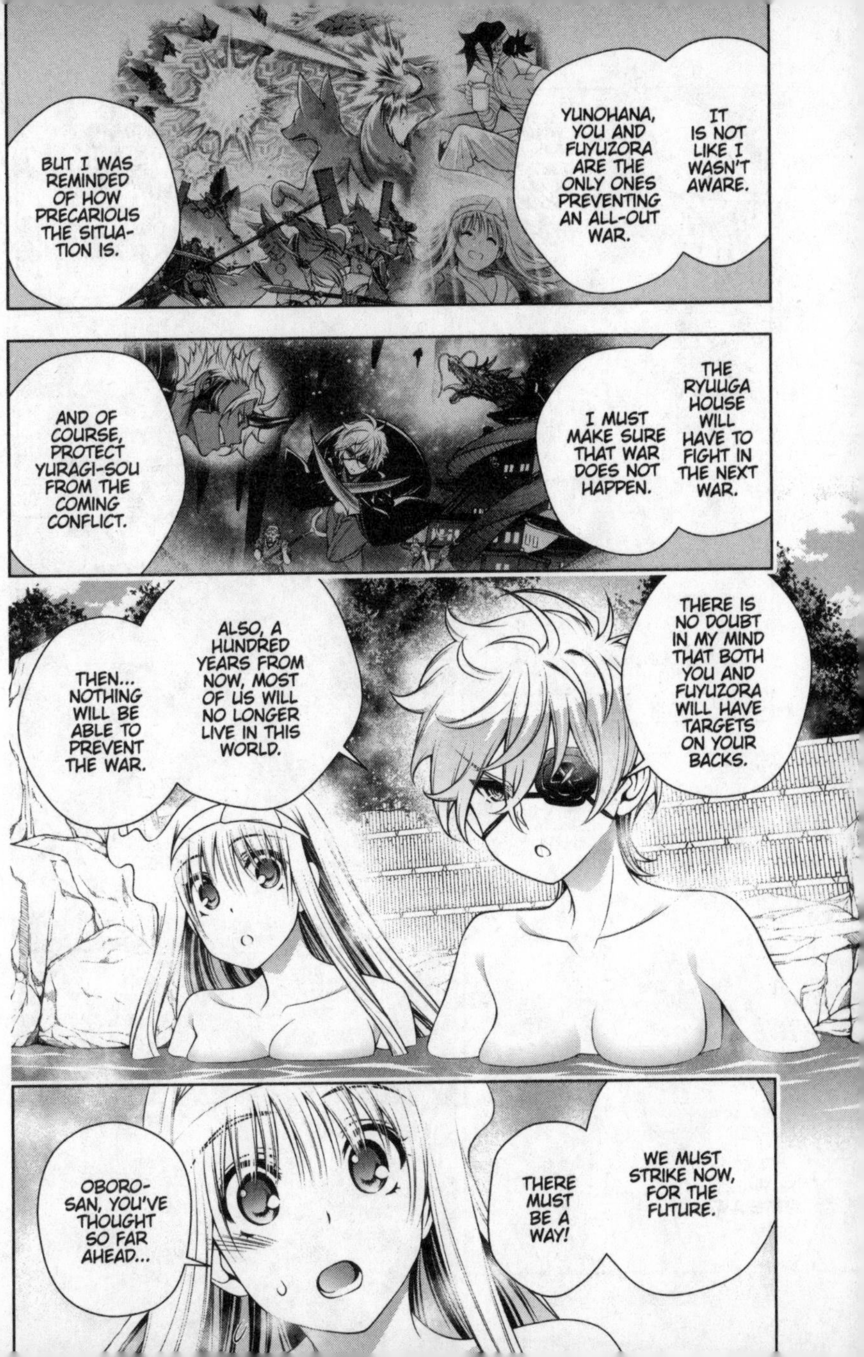
IT IS NOT LIKE I WASN'T AWARE.
YUNOHANA, YOU AND FUYUZORA ARE THE ONLY ONES PREVENTING AN ALL-OUT WAR.
BUT I WAS REMINDED OF HOW PRECARIOUS THE SITUA-TION IS.
THE RYUUGA HOUSE WILL HAVE TO FIGHT IN THE NEXT WAR.
I MUST MAKE SURE THAT WAR DOES NOT HAPPEN.
AND OF COURSE, PROTECT YURAGI-SOU FROM THE COMING CONFLICT.
THERE IS NO DOUBT IN MY MIND THAT BOTH YOU AND FUYUZORA WILL HAVE TARGETS ON YOUR BACKS.
ALSO, A HUNDRED YEARS FROM NOW, MOST OF US WILL NO LONGER LIVE IN THIS WORLD.
THEN... NOTHING WILL BE ABLE TO PREVENT THE WAR.
WE MUST STRIKE NOW, FOR THE FUTURE.
THERE MUST BE A WAY!
OBORO-SAN, YOU'VE THOUGHT SO FAR AHEAD...

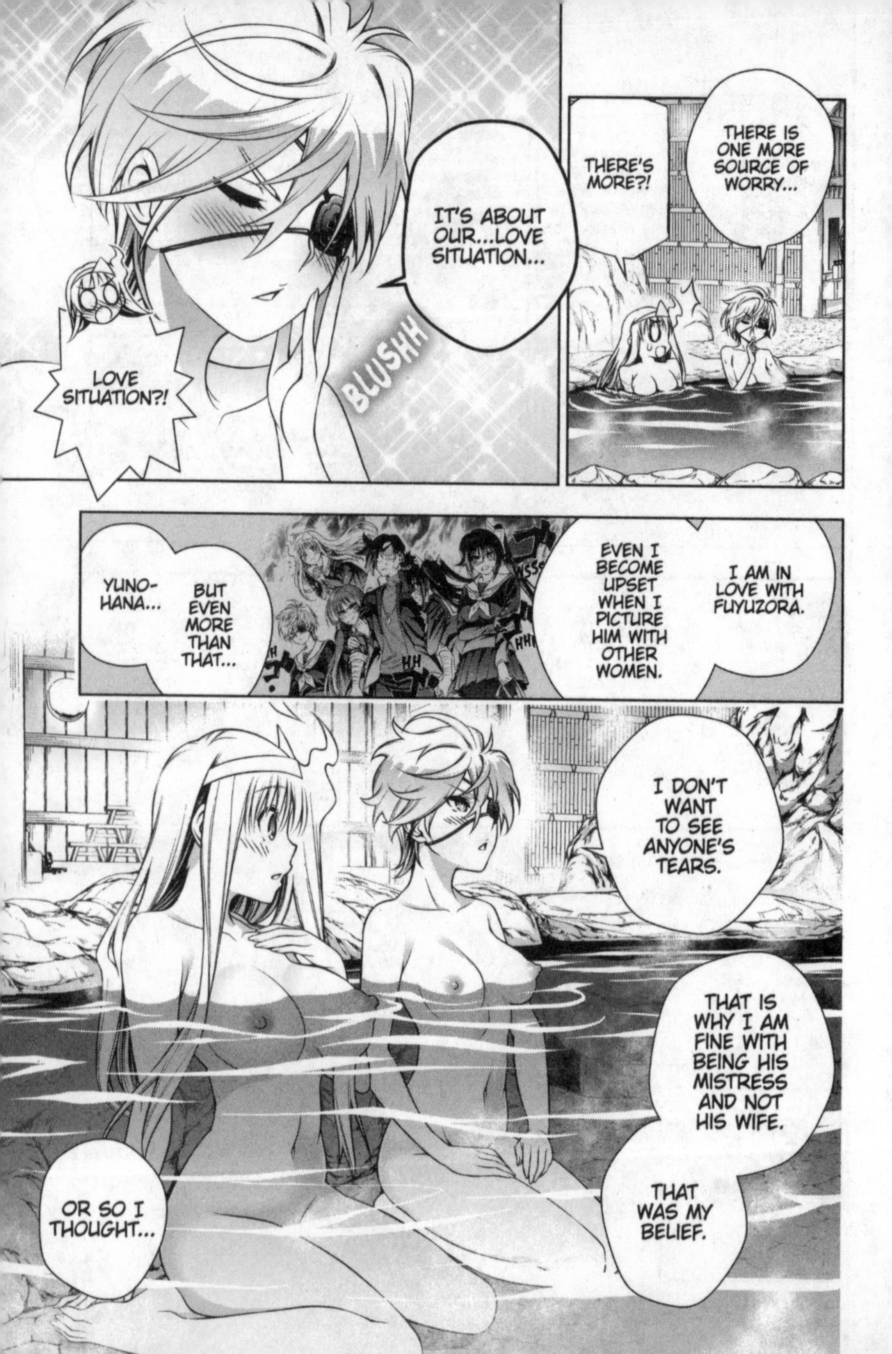
THERE IS ONE MORE SOURCE OF WORRY...
THERE'S MORE?!
IT'S ABOUT OUR...LOVE SITUATION...
BLUSHH
LOVE SITUATION?!
I AM IN LOVE WITH FUYUZORA.
EVEN I BECOME UPSET WHEN I PICTURE HIM WITH OTHER WOMEN.
BUT EVEN MORE THAN THAT...
YUNO-HANA...
I DON'T WANT TO SEE ANYONE'S TEARS.
THAT IS WHY I AM FINE WITH BEING HIS MISTRESS AND NOT HIS WIFE.
THAT WAS MY BELIEF.
OR SO I THOUGHT...

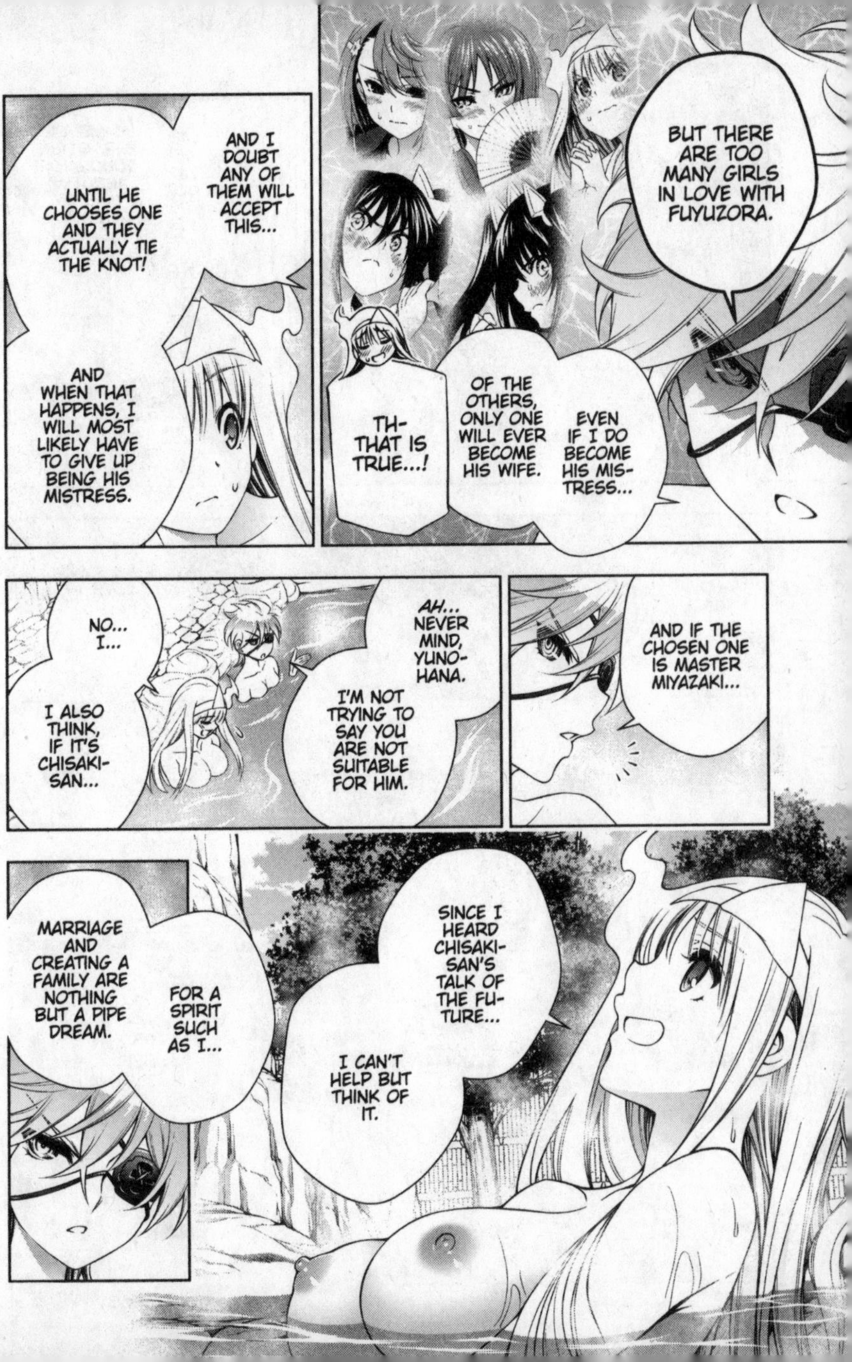
BUT THERE ARE TOO MANY GIRLS IN LOVE WITH FUYUZORA.
EVEN IF I DO BECOME HIS MISTRESS...
OF THE OTHERS, ONLY ONE WILL EVER BECOME HIS WIFE.
TH-THAT IS TRUE...!
AND I DOUBT ANY OF THEM WILL ACCEPT THIS...
UNTIL HE CHOOSES ONE AND THEY ACTUALLY TIE THE KNOT!
AND WHEN THAT HAPPENS, I WILL MOST LIKELY HAVE TO GIVE UP BEING HIS MISTRESS.
AND IF THE CHOSEN ONE IS MASTER MIYAZAKI...
AH... NEVER MIND, YUNOHANA.
I'M NOT TRYING TO SAY YOU ARE NOT SUITABLE FOR HIM.
NO... I...
I ALSO THINK, IF IT'S CHISAKI-SAN...
SINCE I HEARD CHISAKI-SAN'S TALK OF THE FUTURE...
I CAN'T HELP BUT THINK OF IT.
FOR A SPIRIT SUCH AS I...
MARRIAGE AND CREATING A FAMILY ARE NOTHING BUT A PIPE DREAM.

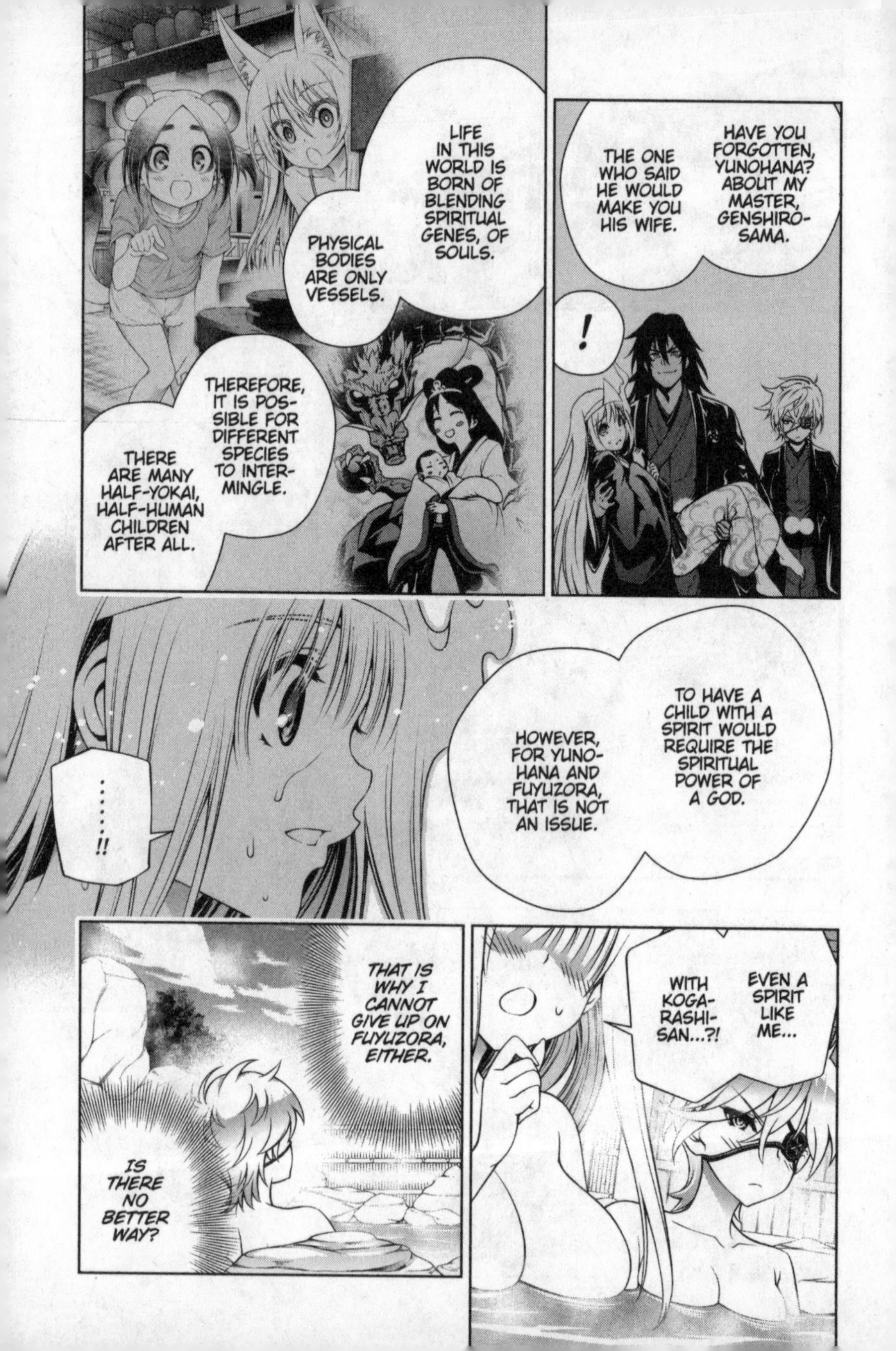
HAVE YOU FORGOTTEN, YUNOHANA? ABOUT MY MASTER, GENSHIRO-SAMA.
THE ONE WHO SAID HE WOULD MAKE YOU HIS WIFE.
!
LIFE IN THIS WORLD IS BORN OF BLENDING SPIRITUAL GENES, OF SOULS.
PHYSICAL BODIES ARE ONLY VESSELS.
THEREFORE, IT IS POSSIBLE FOR DIFFERENT SPECIES TO INTERMINGLE.
THERE ARE MANY HALF-YOKAI, HALF-HUMAN CHILDREN AFTER ALL.
TO HAVE A CHILD WITH A SPIRIT WOULD REQUIRE THE SPIRITUAL POWER OF A GOD.
HOWEVER, FOR YUNOHANA AND FUYUZORA, THAT IS NOT AN ISSUE.
......!!
EVEN A SPIRIT LIKE ME...
WITH KOGARASHI-SAN...?!
THAT IS WHY I CANNOT GIVE UP ON FUYUZORA, EITHER.
IS THERE NO BETTER WAY?

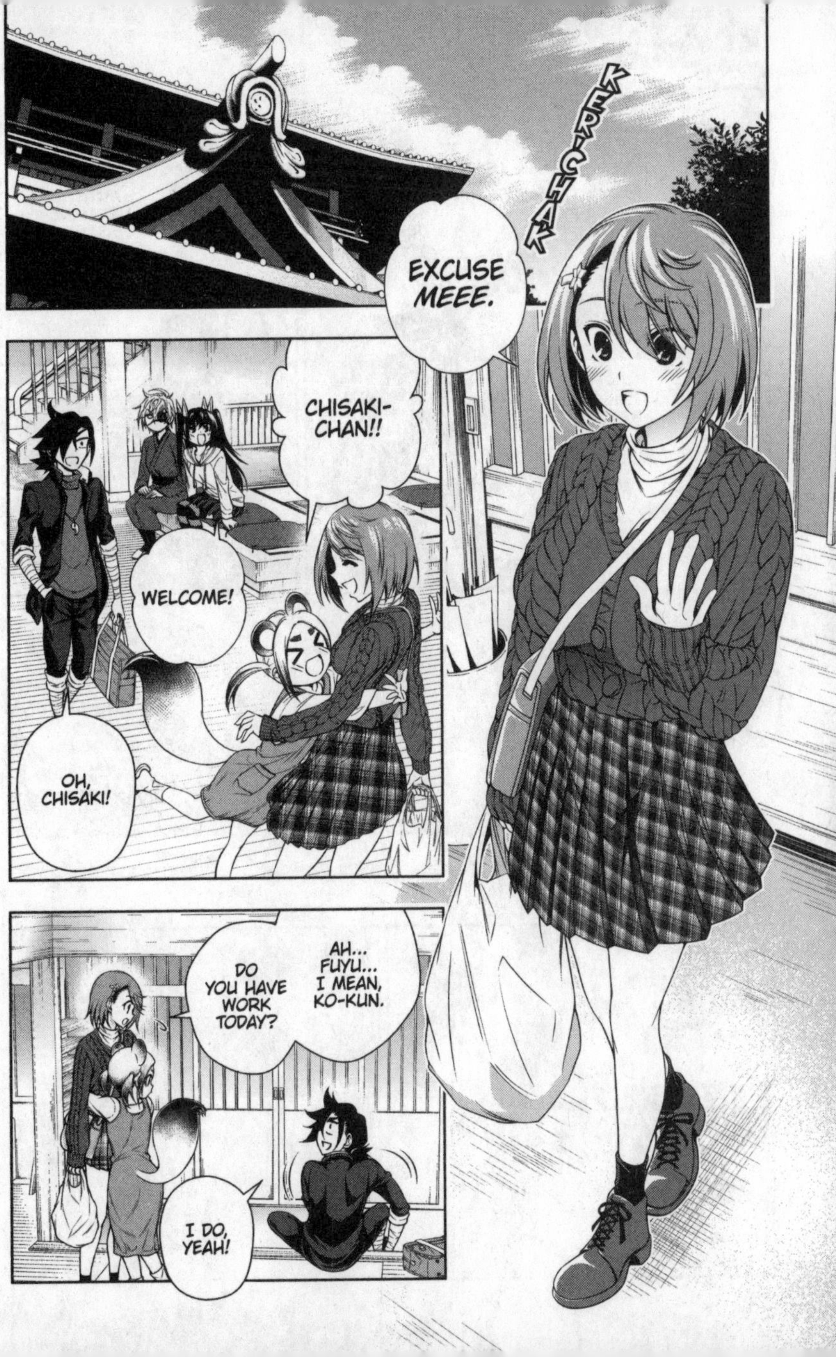
KERI-CHAK
EXCUSE MEEE.
CHISAKI-CHAN!!
WELCOME!
OH, CHISAKI!
AH... FUYU... I MEAN, KO-KUN.
DO YOU HAVE WORK TODAY?
I DO, YEAH!

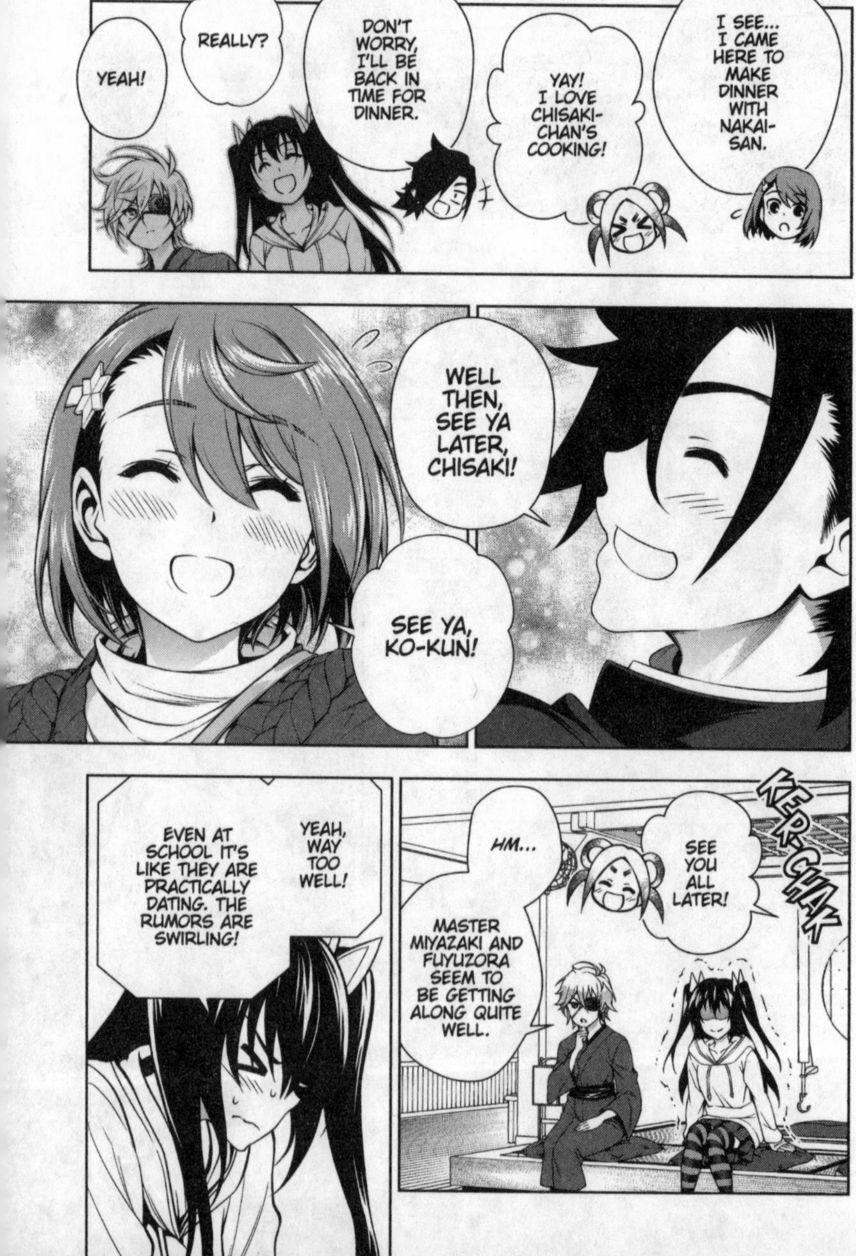
I SEE... I CAME HERE TO MAKE DINNER WITH NAKAI-SAN.
YAY! I LOVE CHISAKI-CHAN'S COOKING!
DON'T WORRY, I'LL BE BACK IN TIME FOR DINNER.
REALLY?
YEAH!
WELL THEN, SEE YA LATER, CHISAKI!
SEE YA, KO-KUN!
KER-CHAK
SEE YOU ALL LATER!
HM...
MASTER MIYAZAKI AND FUYUZORA SEEM TO BE GETTING ALONG QUITE WELL.
YEAH, WAY TOO WELL!
EVEN AT SCHOOL IT'S LIKE THEY ARE PRACTICALLY DATING. THE RUMORS ARE SWIRLING!

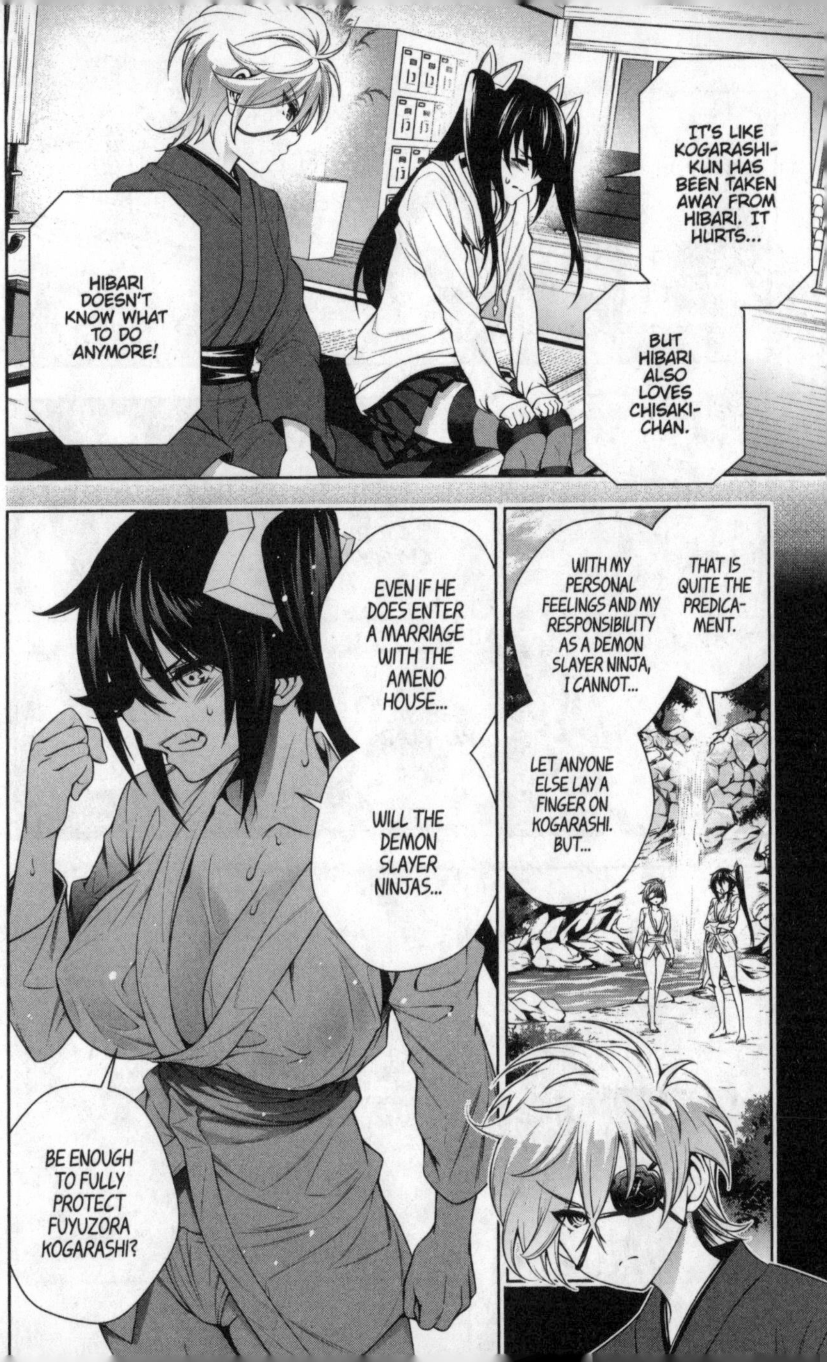
IT'S LIKE KOGARASHI-KUN HAS BEEN TAKEN AWAY FROM HIBARI. IT HURTS...
BUT HIBARI ALSO LOVES CHISAKI-CHAN.
HIBARI DOESN'T KNOW WHAT TO DO ANYMORE!
THAT IS QUITE THE PREDICA-MENT.
WITH MY PERSONAL FEELINGS AND MY RESPONSIBILITY AS A DEMON SLAYER NINJA, I CANNOT...
LET ANYONE ELSE LAY A FINGER ON KOGARASHI. BUT...
EVEN IF HE DOES ENTER A MARRIAGE WITH THE AMENO HOUSE...
WILL THE DEMON SLAYER NINJAS...
BE ENOUGH TO FULLY PROTECT FUYUZORA KOGARASHI?

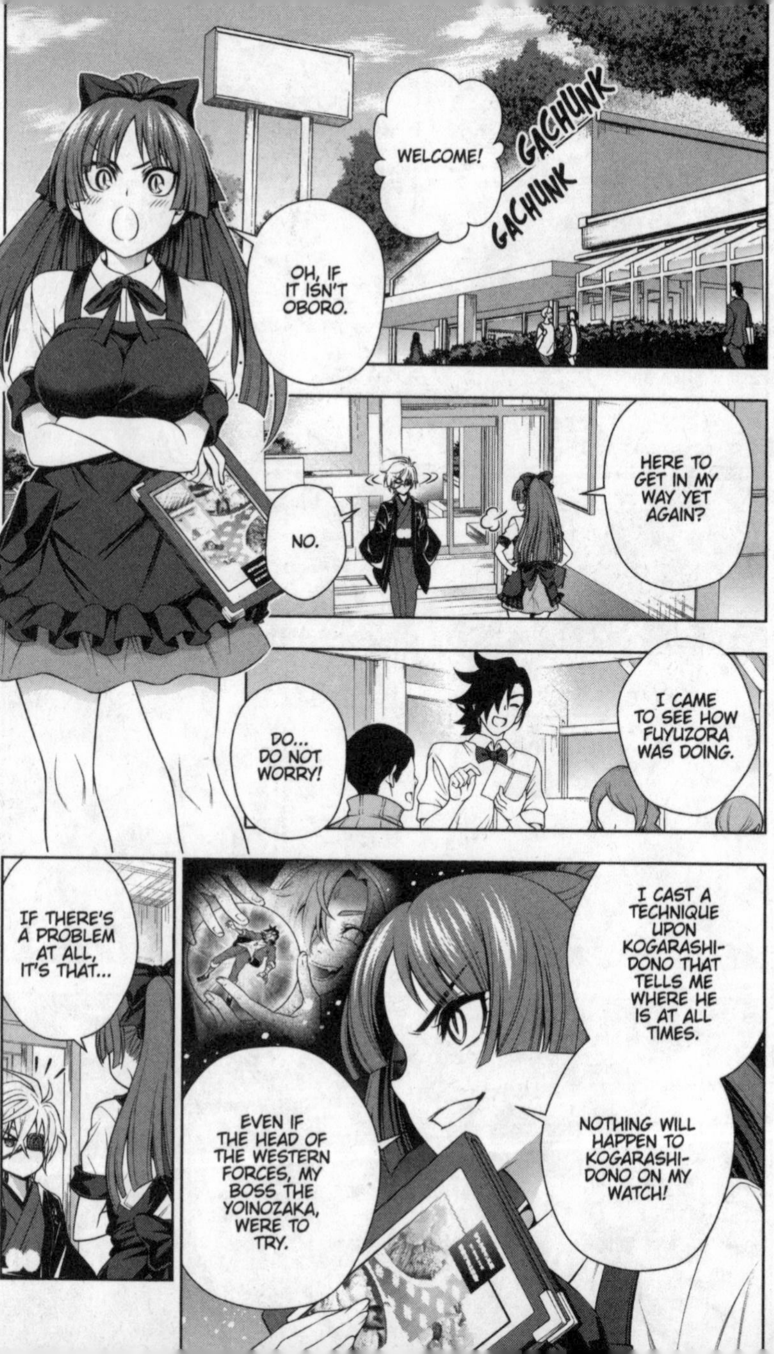
WELCOME!
GACHUNK
GACHUNK
OH, IF IT ISN'T OBORO.
HERE TO GET IN MY WAY YET AGAIN?
NO.
I CAME TO SEE HOW FUYUZORA WAS DOING.
DO... DO NOT WORRY!
I CAST A TECHNIQUE UPON KOGARASHI-DONO THAT TELLS ME WHERE HE IS AT ALL TIMES.
NOTHING WILL HAPPEN TO KOGARASHI-DONO ON MY WATCH!
EVEN IF THE HEAD OF THE WESTERN FORCES, MY BOSS THE YOINOZAKA, WERE TO TRY.
IF THERE'S A PROBLEM AT ALL, IT'S THAT...

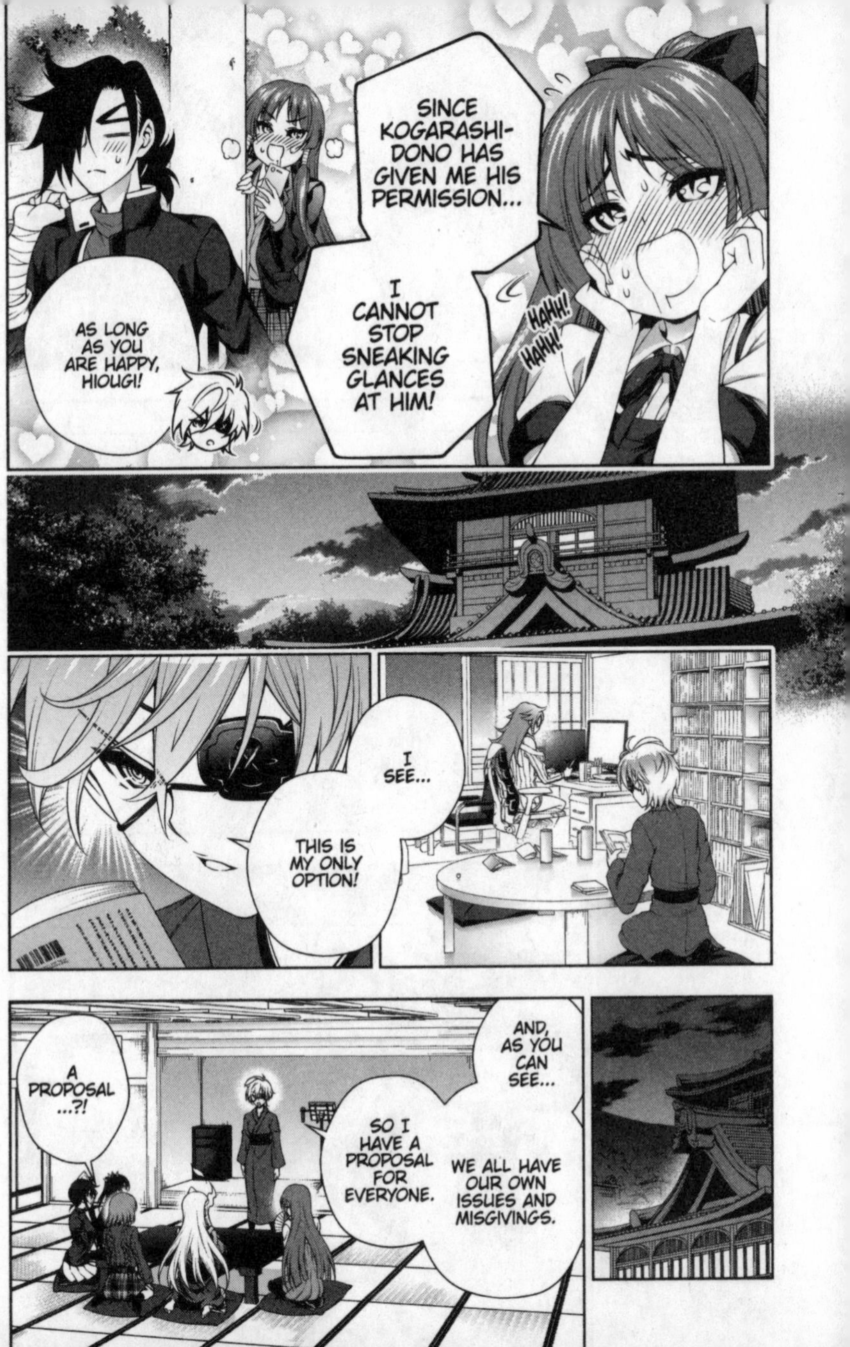
SINCE KOGARASHI-DONO HAS GIVEN ME HIS PERMISSION...
I CANNOT STOP SNEAKING GLANCES AT HIM!
HAHH! HAHH!
AS LONG AS YOU ARE HAPPY, HIOUGI!
I SEE...
THIS IS MY ONLY OPTION!
AND, AS YOU CAN SEE...
WE ALL HAVE OUR OWN ISSUES AND MISGIVINGS.
SO I HAVE A PROPOSAL FOR EVERYONE.
A PROPOSAL ...?!

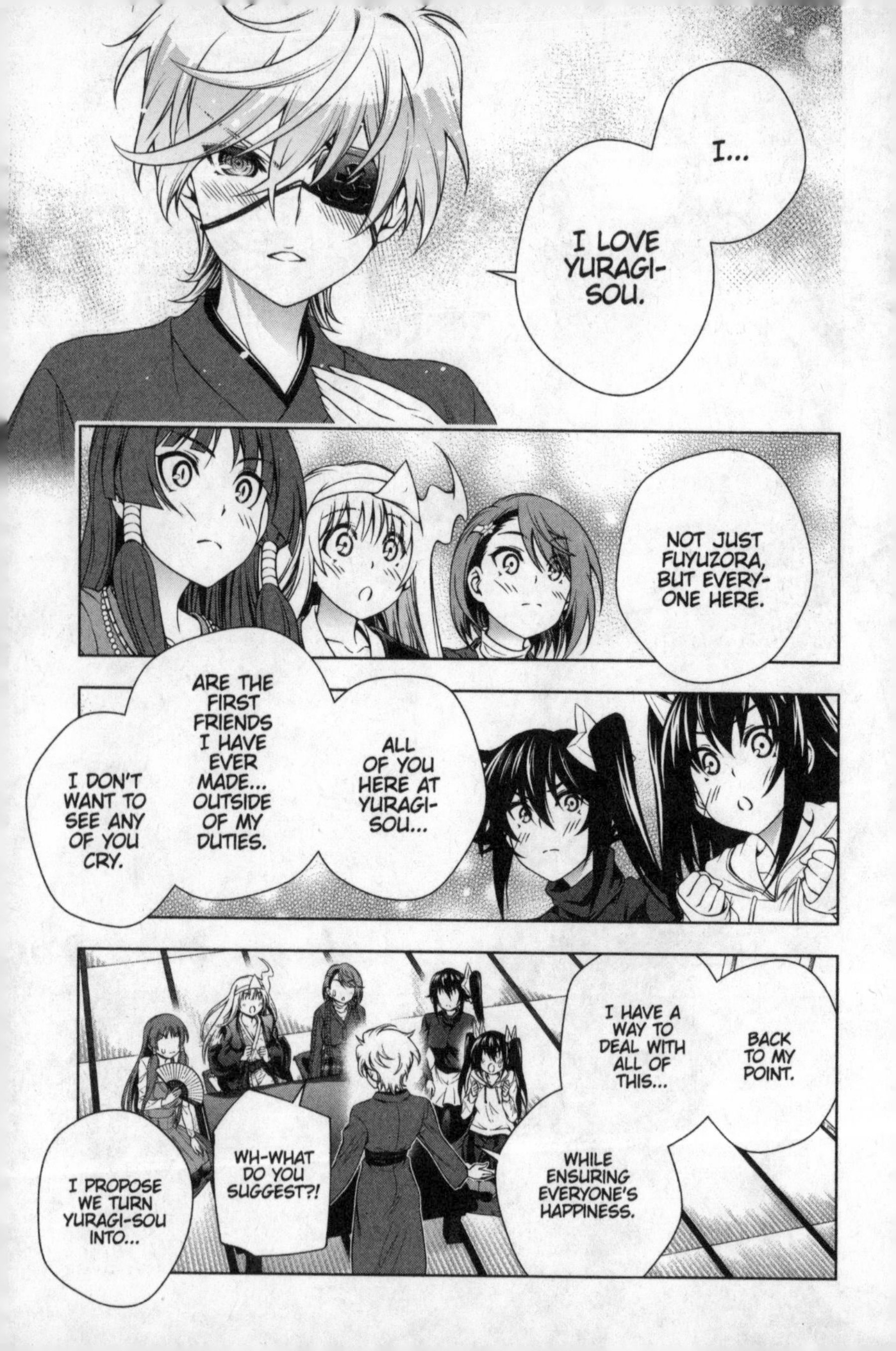
I...
I LOVE YURAGI-SOU.
NOT JUST FUYUZORA, BUT EVERYONE HERE.
ALL OF YOU HERE AT YURAGI-SOU...
ARE THE FIRST FRIENDS I HAVE EVER MADE... OUTSIDE OF MY DUTIES.
I DON'T WANT TO SEE ANY OF YOU CRY.
BACK TO MY POINT.
I HAVE A WAY TO DEAL WITH ALL OF THIS...
WHILE ENSURING EVERYONE'S HAPPINESS.
WH-WHAT DO YOU SUGGEST?!
I PROPOSE WE TURN YURAGI-SOU INTO...

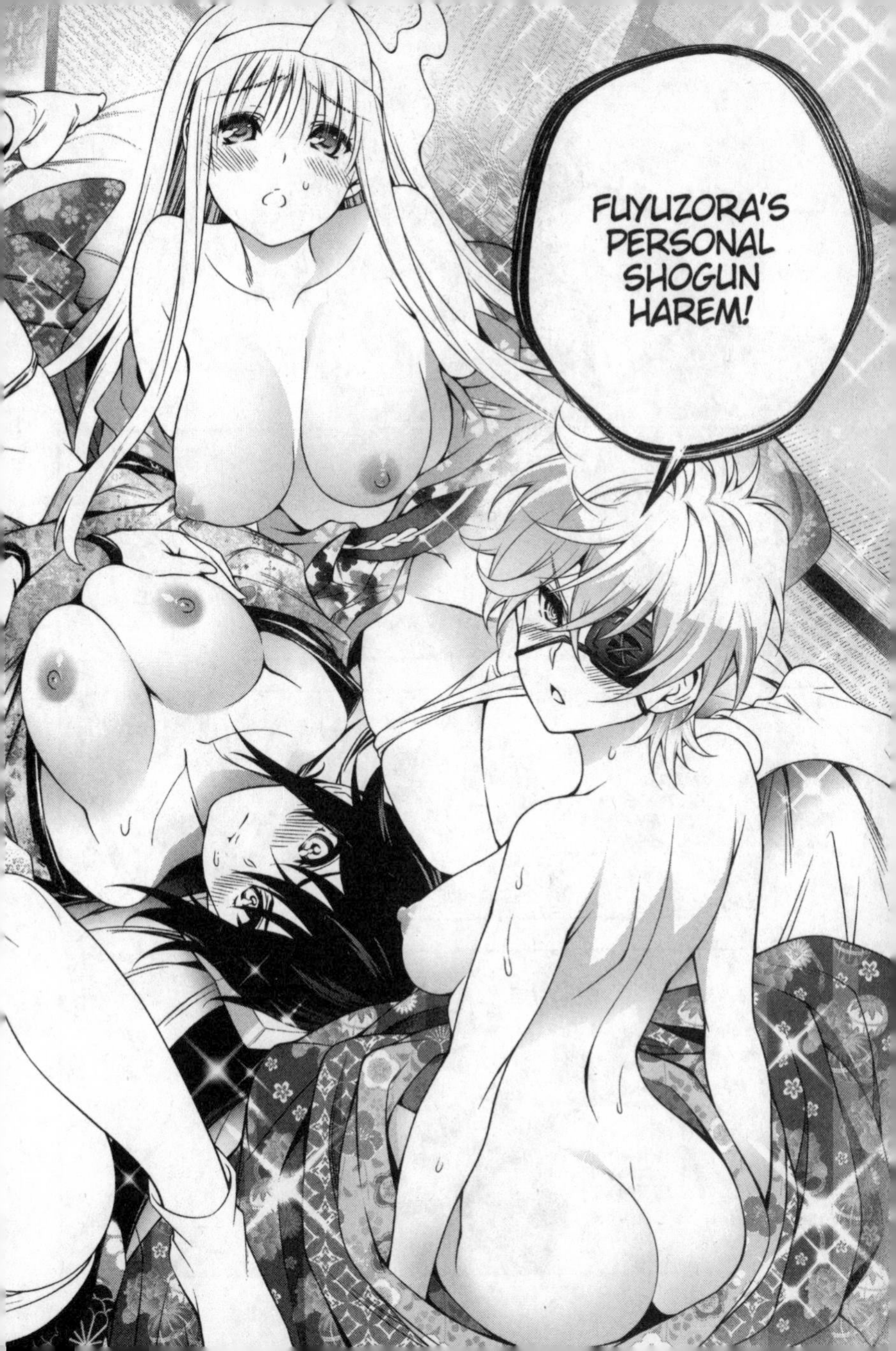
FUYUZORA'S PERSONAL SHOGUN HAREM!

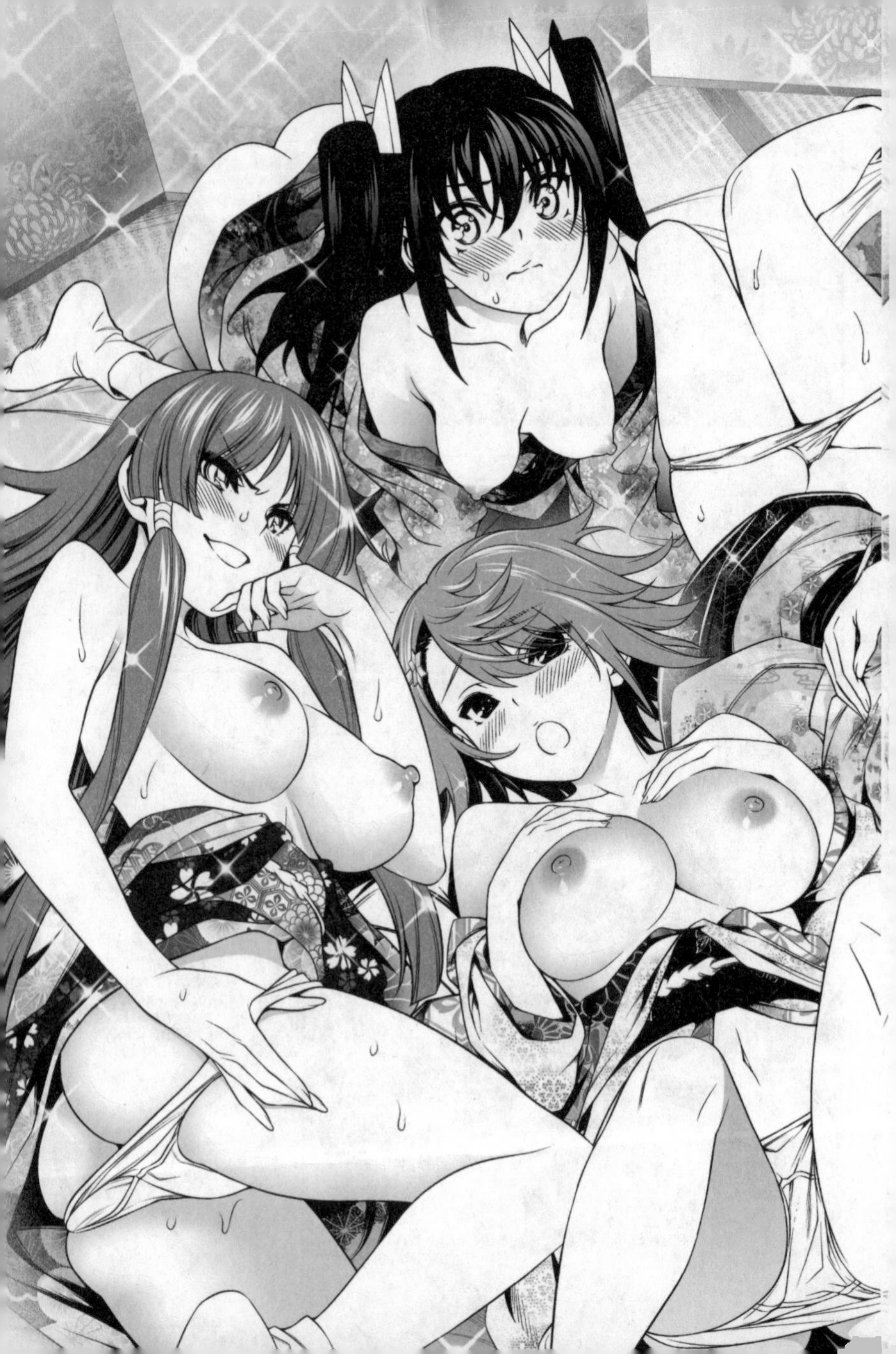

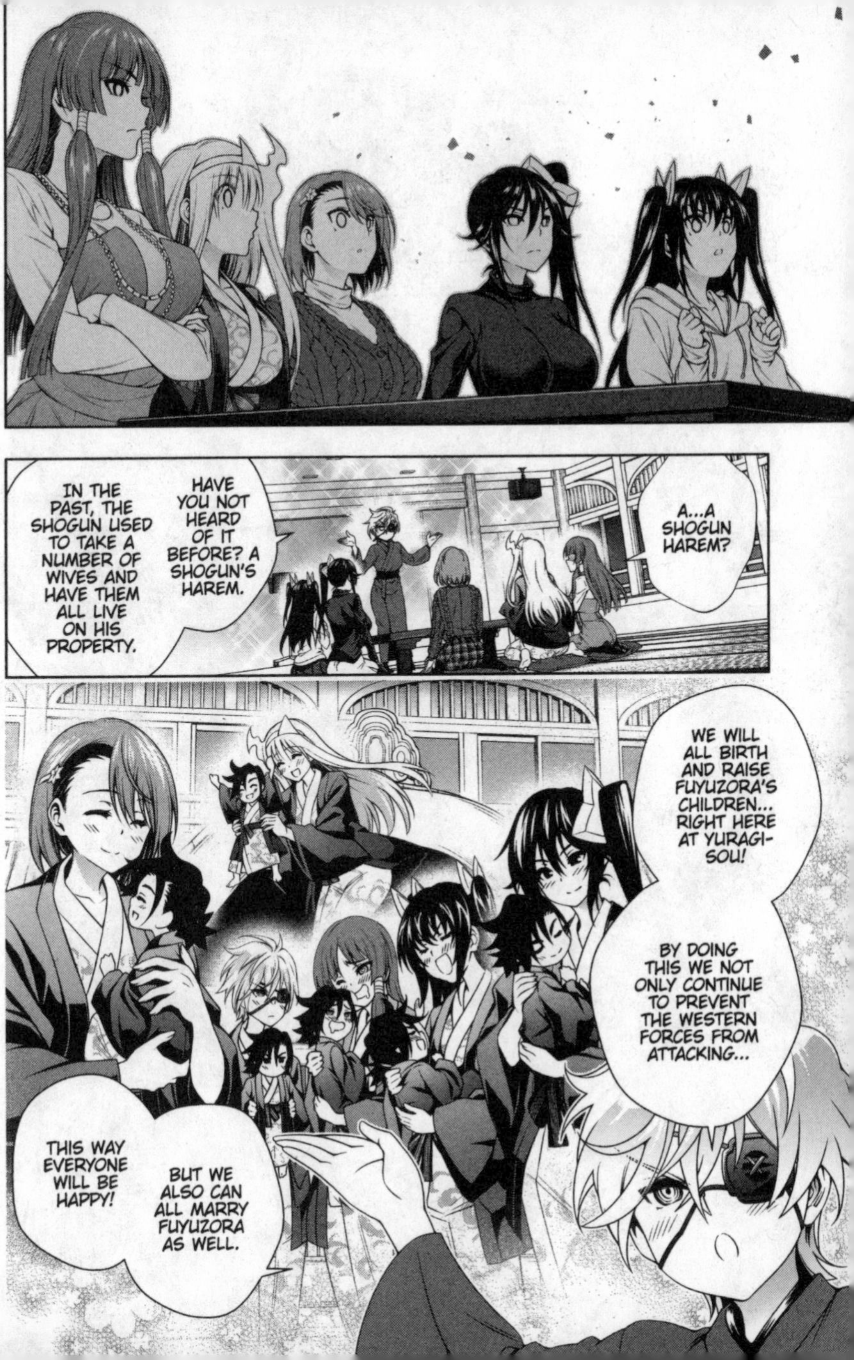
A...A SHOGUN HAREM?
HAVE YOU NOT HEARD OF IT BEFORE? A SHOGUN'S HAREM.
IN THE PAST, THE SHOGUN USED TO TAKE A NUMBER OF WIVES AND HAVE THEM ALL LIVE ON HIS PROPERTY.
WE WILL ALL BIRTH AND RAISE FUYUZORA'S CHILDREN... RIGHT HERE AT YURAGI-SOU!
BY DOING THIS WE NOT ONLY CONTINUE TO PREVENT THE WESTERN FORCES FROM ATTACKING...
BUT WE ALSO CAN ALL MARRY FUYUZORA AS WELL.
THIS WAY EVERYONE WILL BE HAPPY!

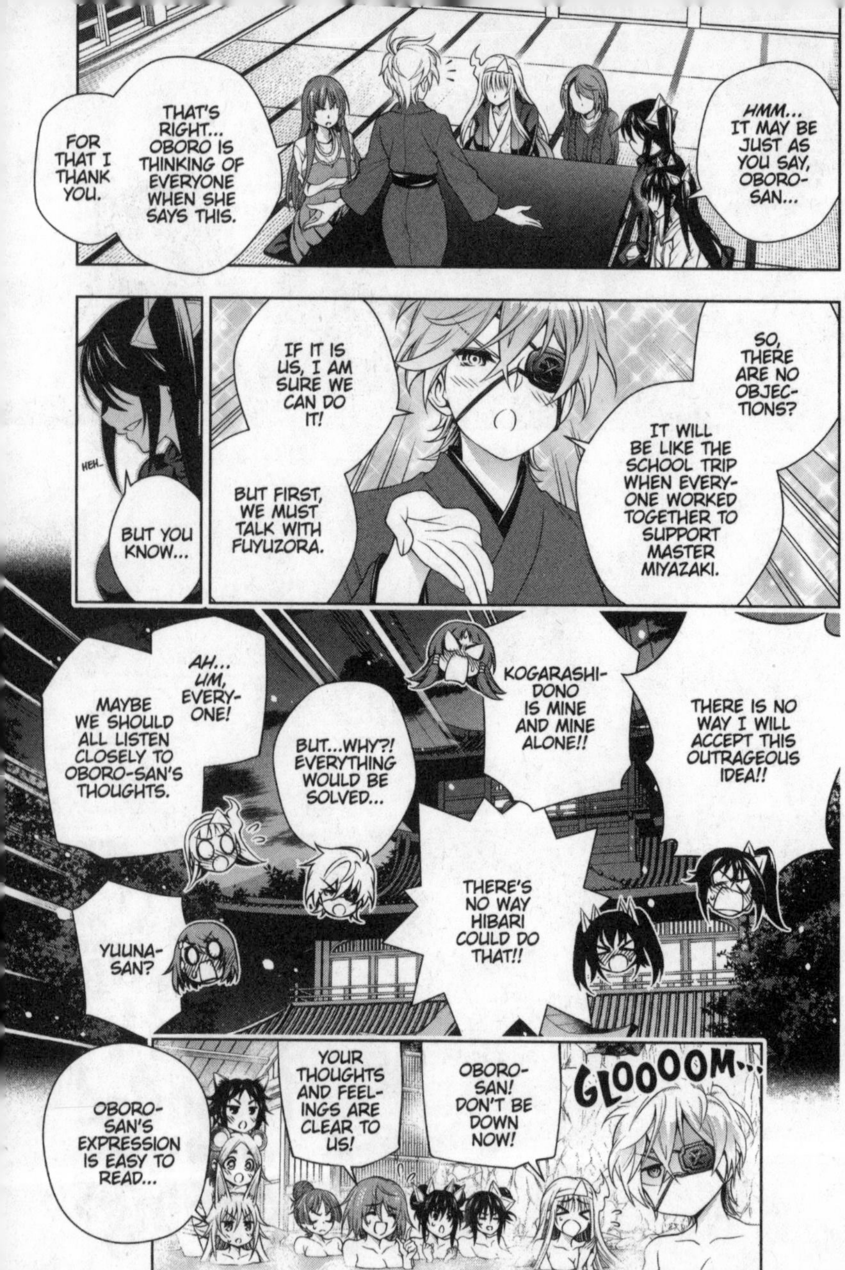
HMM... IT MAY BE JUST AS YOU SAY, OBORO-SAN...
THAT'S RIGHT... OBORO IS THINKING OF EVERYONE WHEN SHE SAYS THIS.
FOR THAT I THANK YOU.
SO, THERE ARE NO OBJECTIONS?
IT WILL BE LIKE THE SCHOOL TRIP WHEN EVERYONE WORKED TOGETHER TO SUPPORT MASTER MIYAZAKI.
IF IT IS US, I AM SURE WE CAN DO IT!
BUT FIRST, WE MUST TALK WITH FUYUZORA.
HEH...
BUT YOU KNOW...
THERE IS NO WAY I WILL ACCEPT THIS OUTRAGEOUS IDEA!!
KOGARASHI-DONO IS MINE AND MINE ALONE!!
THERE'S NO WAY HIBARI COULD DO THAT!!
BUT...WHY?! EVERYTHING WOULD BE SOLVED...
AH... UM, EVERYONE!
MAYBE WE SHOULD ALL LISTEN CLOSELY TO OBORO-SAN'S THOUGHTS.
YUUNA-SAN?
GLOOOOM...
OBORO-SAN! DON'T BE DOWN NOW!
YOUR THOUGHTS AND FEELINGS ARE CLEAR TO US!
OBORO-SAN'S EXPRESSION IS EASY TO READ...

Yuuna and the Haunted Hot Springs

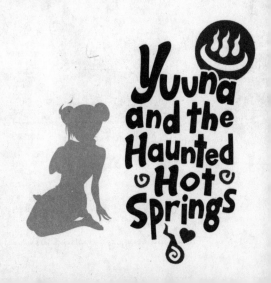

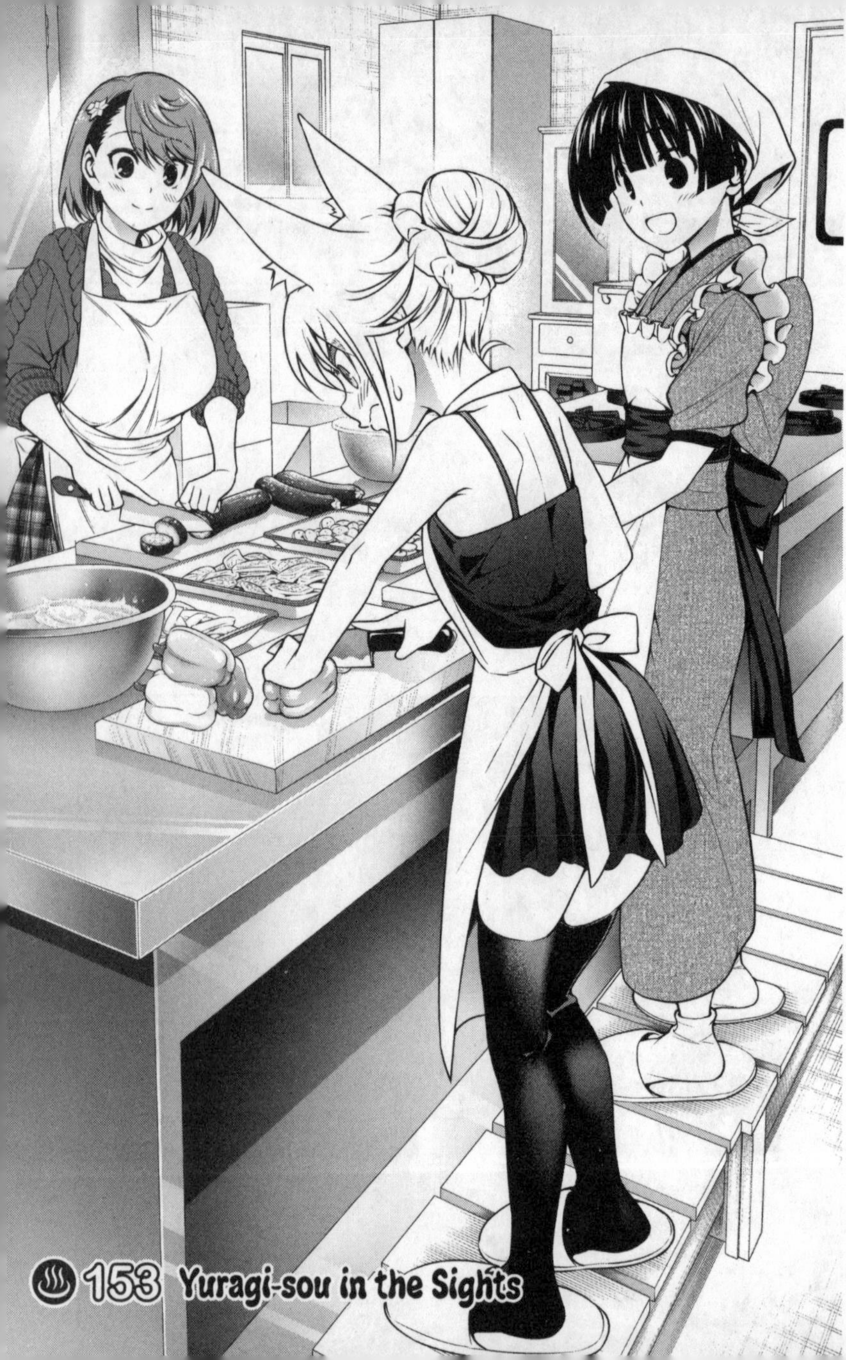
153 Yuragi-sou in the Sights

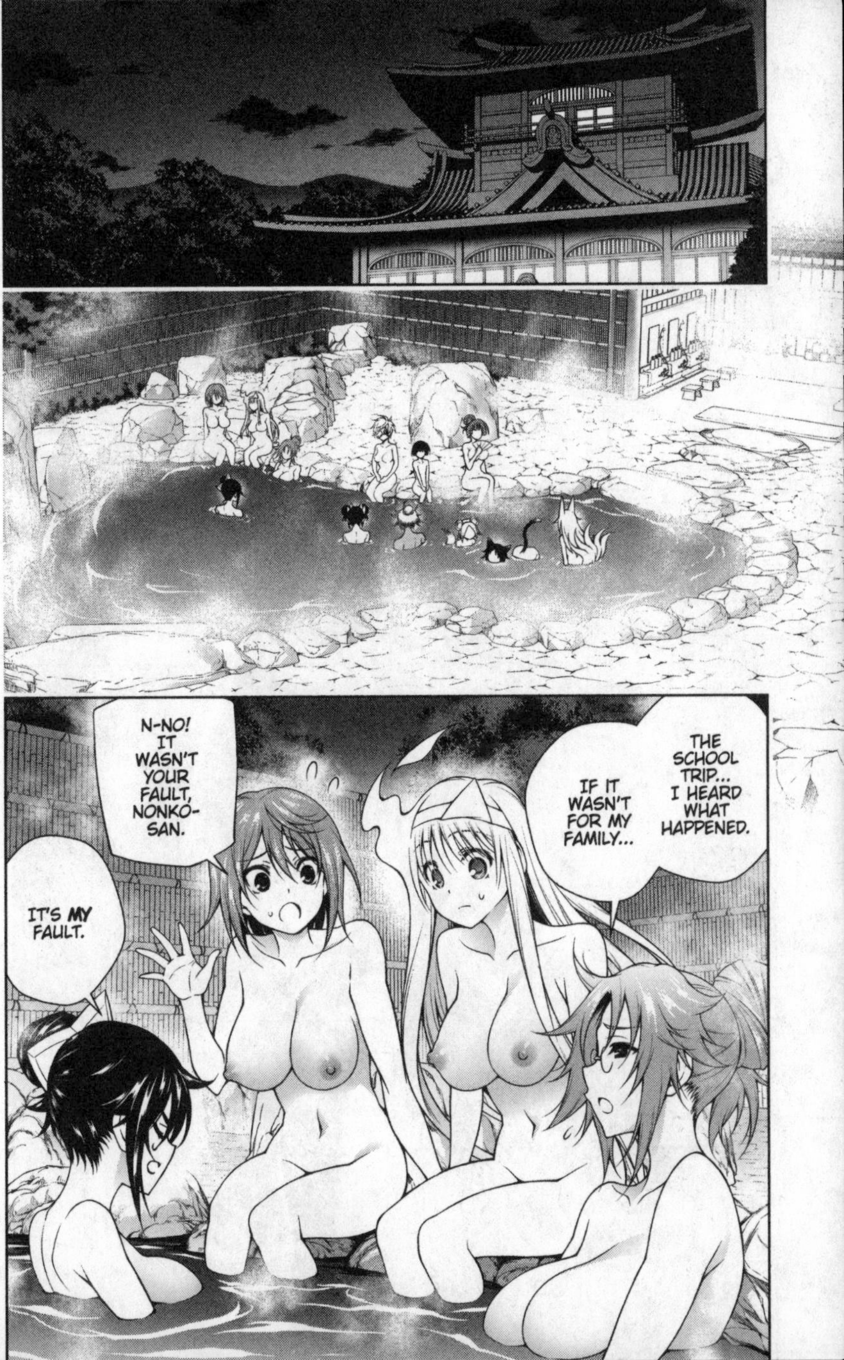
THE SCHOOL TRIP... I HEARD WHAT HAPPENED.
IF IT WASN'T FOR MY FAMILY...
N-NO! IT WASN'T YOUR FAULT, NONKO-SAN.
IT'S MY FAULT.

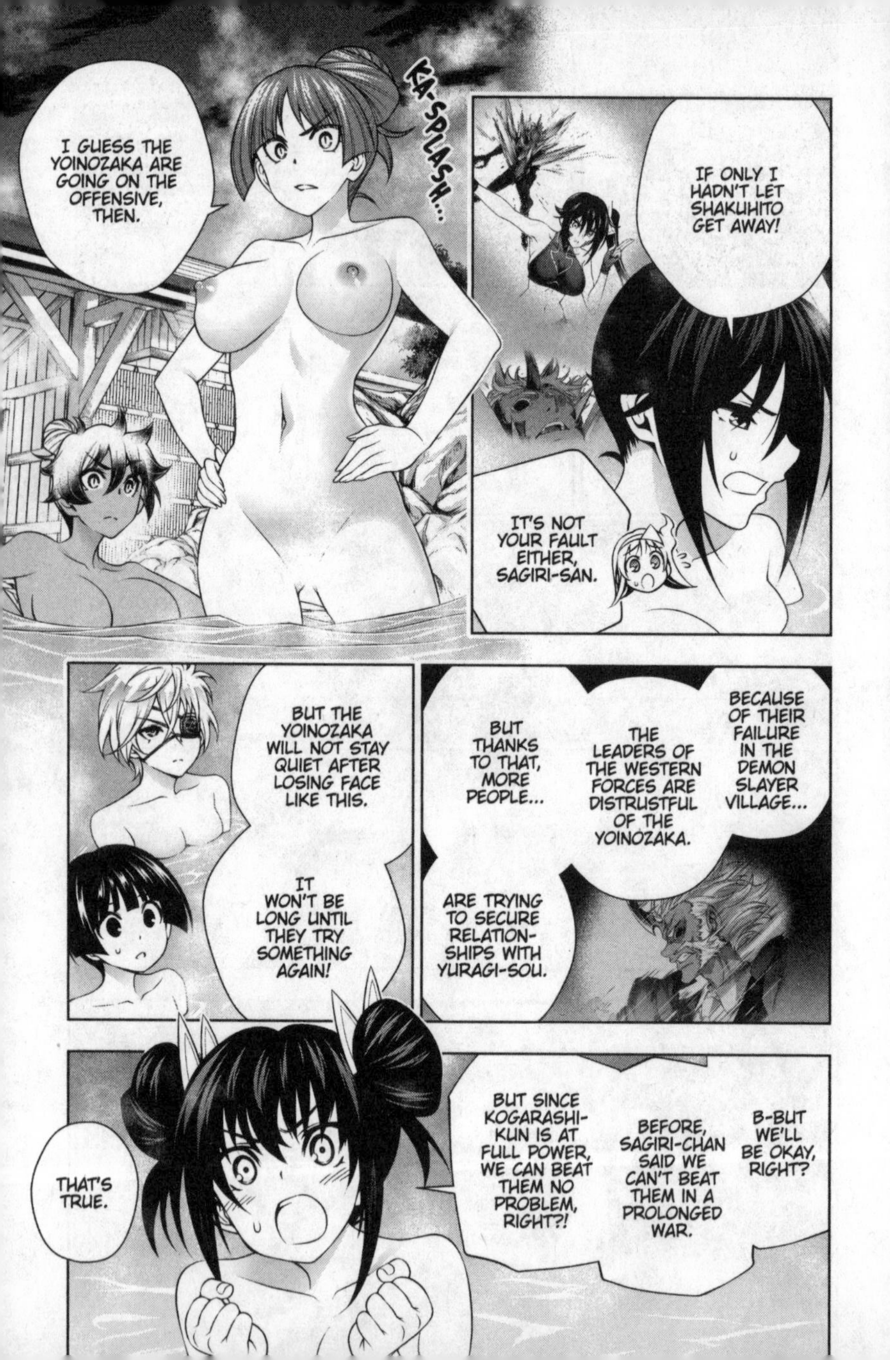

IF ONLY I HADN'T LET SHAKUHITO GET AWAY!
IT'S NOT YOUR FAULT EITHER, SAGIRI-SAN.
KA-SPLASH...
I GUESS THE YOINOZAKA ARE GOING ON THE OFFENSIVE, THEN.
BECAUSE OF THEIR FAILURE IN THE DEMON SLAYER VILLAGE...
THE LEADERS OF THE WESTERN FORCES ARE DISTRUSTFUL OF THE YOINOZAKA.
BUT THANKS TO THAT, MORE PEOPLE...
ARE TRYING TO SECURE RELATION-SHIPS WITH YURAGI-SOU.
BUT THE YOINOZAKA WILL NOT STAY QUIET AFTER LOSING FACE LIKE THIS.
IT WON'T BE LONG UNTIL THEY TRY SOMETHING AGAIN!
B-BUT WE'LL BE OKAY, RIGHT?
BEFORE, SAGIRI-CHAN SAID WE CAN'T BEAT THEM IN A PROLONGED WAR.
BUT SINCE KOGARASHI-KUN IS AT FULL POWER, WE CAN BEAT THEM NO PROBLEM, RIGHT?!
THAT'S TRUE.

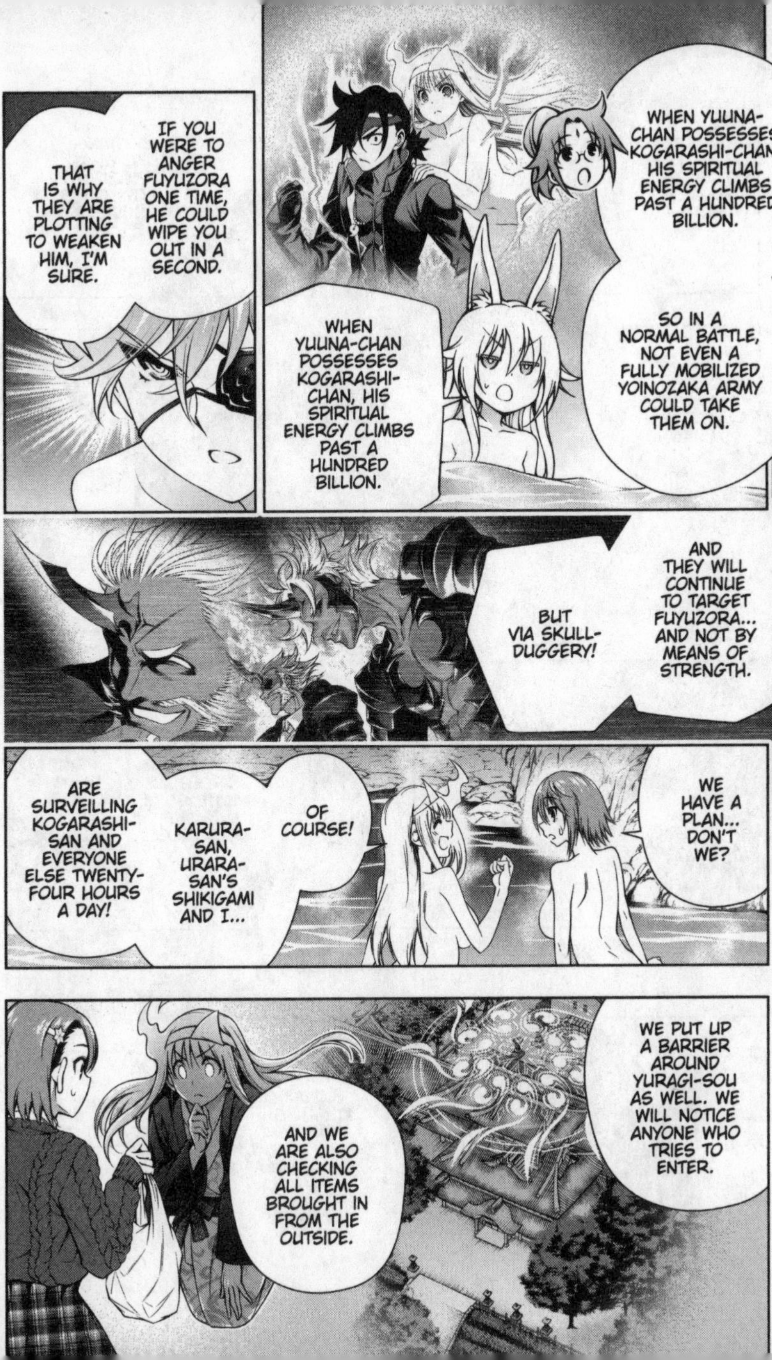
WHEN YUUNA-CHAN POSSESSES KOGARASHI-CHAN, HIS SPIRITUAL ENERGY CLIMBS PAST A HUNDRED BILLION.
SO IN A NORMAL BATTLE, NOT EVEN A FULLY MOBILIZED YOINOZAKA ARMY COULD TAKE THEM ON.
WHEN YUUNA-CHAN POSSESSES KOGARASHI-CHAN, HIS SPIRITUAL ENERGY CLIMBS PAST A HUNDRED BILLION.
IF YOU WERE TO ANGER FUYUZORA ONE TIME, HE COULD WIPE YOU OUT IN A SECOND.
THAT IS WHY THEY ARE PLOTTING TO WEAKEN HIM, I'M SURE.
AND THEY WILL CONTINUE TO TARGET FUYUZORA... AND NOT BY MEANS OF STRENGTH.
BUT VIA SKULL-DUGGERY!
WE HAVE A PLAN... DON'T WE?
OF COURSE!
KARURA-SAN, URARA-SAN'S SHIKIGAMI AND I...
ARE SURVEILLING KOGARASHI-SAN AND EVERYONE ELSE TWENTY-FOUR HOURS A DAY!
WE PUT UP A BARRIER AROUND YURAGI-SOU AS WELL. WE WILL NOTICE ANYONE WHO TRIES TO ENTER.
AND WE ARE ALSO CHECKING ALL ITEMS BROUGHT IN FROM THE OUTSIDE.

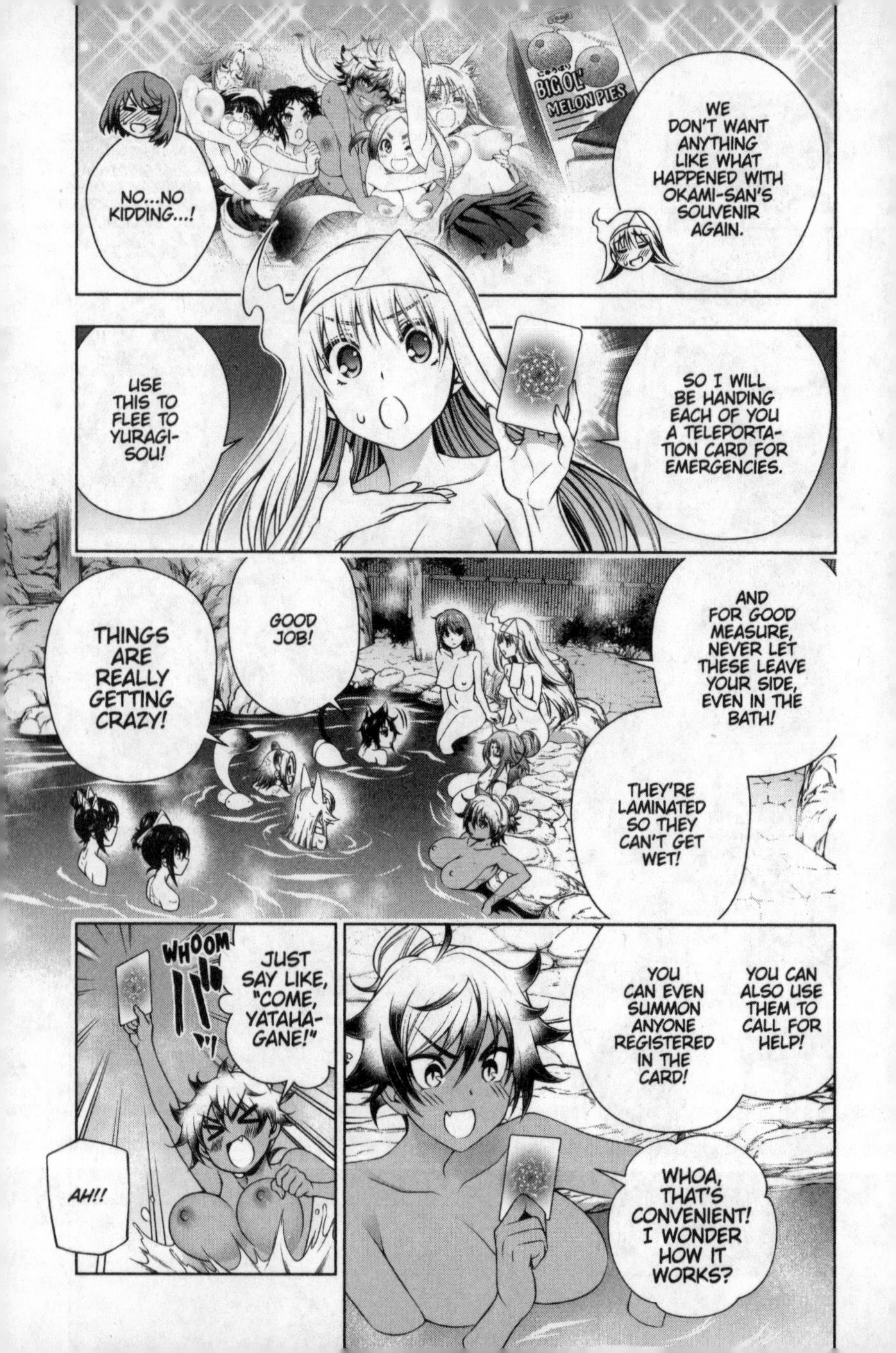
BIG OL' MELON PIES
WE DON'T WANT ANYTHING LIKE WHAT HAPPENED WITH OKAMI-SAN'S SOUVENIR AGAIN.
NO...NO KIDDING...!
SO I WILL BE HANDING EACH OF YOU A TELEPORTATION CARD FOR EMERGENCIES.
USE THIS TO FLEE TO YURAGI-SOU!
AND FOR GOOD MEASURE, NEVER LET THESE LEAVE YOUR SIDE, EVEN IN THE BATH!
THEY'RE LAMINATED SO THEY CAN'T GET WET!
GOOD JOB!
THINGS ARE REALLY GETTING CRAZY!
YOU CAN ALSO USE THEM TO CALL FOR HELP!
YOU CAN EVEN SUMMON ANYONE REGISTERED IN THE CARD!
WHOA, THAT'S CONVENIENT! I WONDER HOW IT WORKS?
JUST SAY LIKE, "COME, YATAHA-GANE!"
WHOOM
AH!!

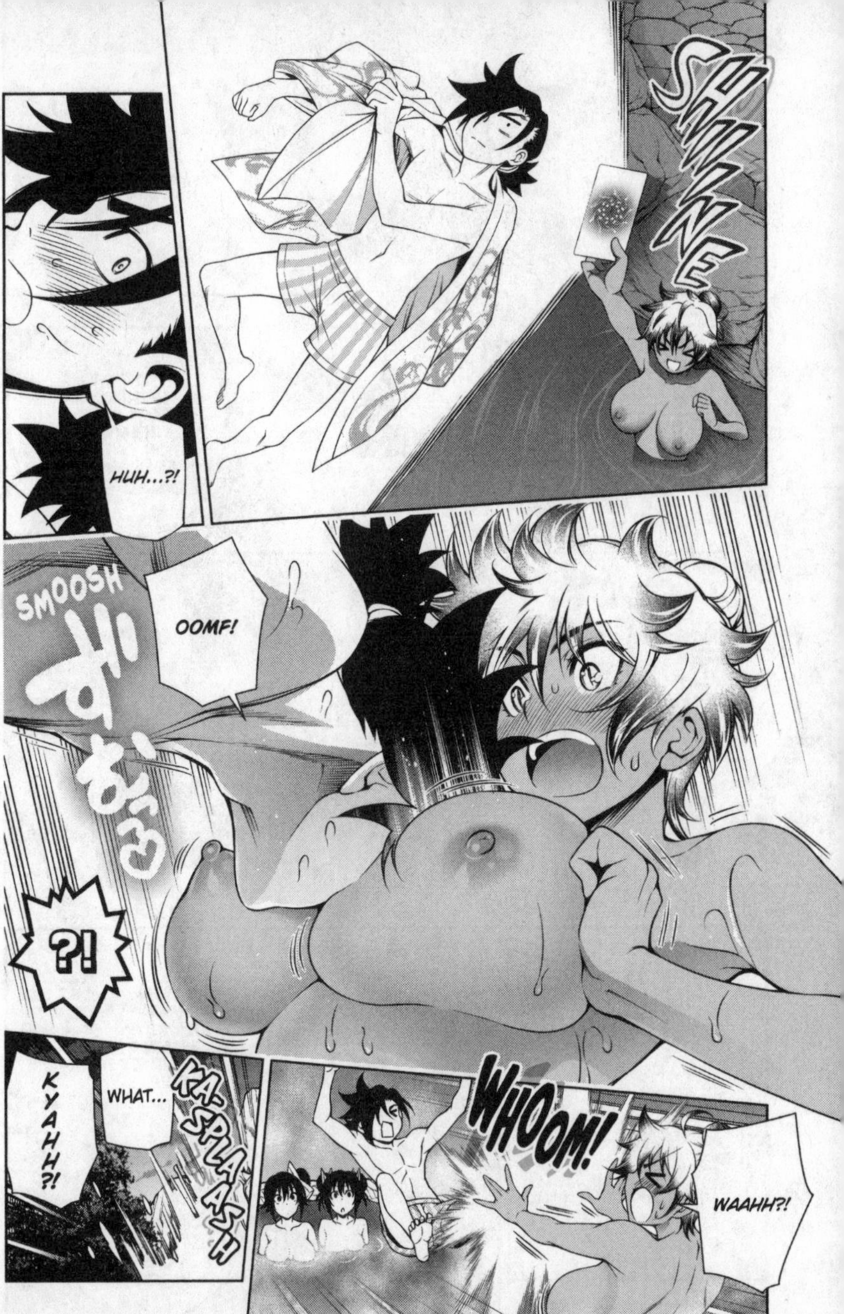
SHIIINE
HUH...?!
SMOOSH
OOMF!
?!
WHOOM!
WAAHH?!
KA-SPLASH
WHAT...
KYAHH?!

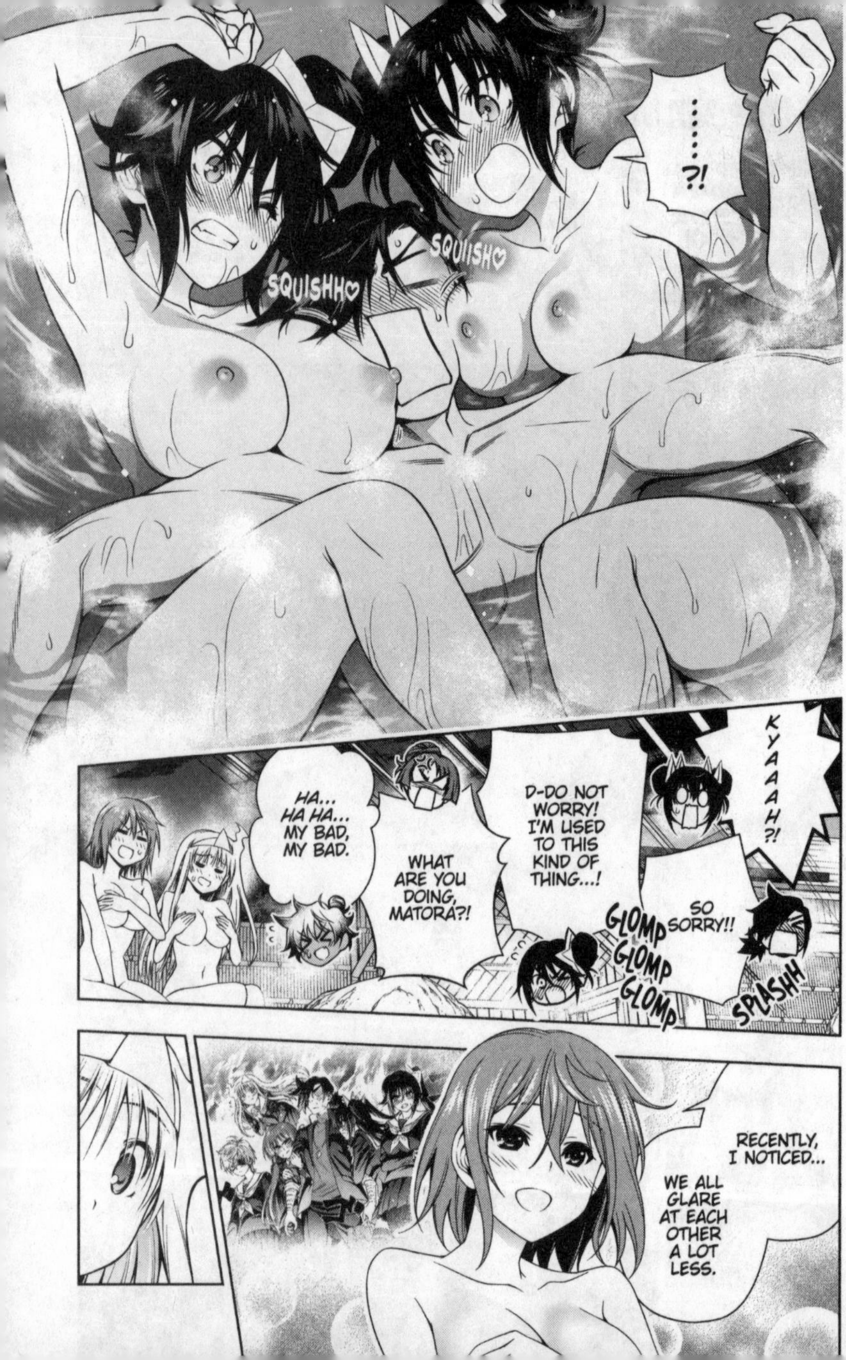
......?!
SQUIISH♡
SQUISHH♡
KYAAAH?!
SO SORRY!!
SPLASHH
GLOMP GLOMP GLOMP
D-DO NOT WORRY! I'M USED TO THIS KIND OF THING...!
WHAT ARE YOU DOING, MATORA?!
HA... HA HA... MY BAD, MY BAD.
RECENTLY, I NOTICED...
WE ALL GLARE AT EACH OTHER A LOT LESS.

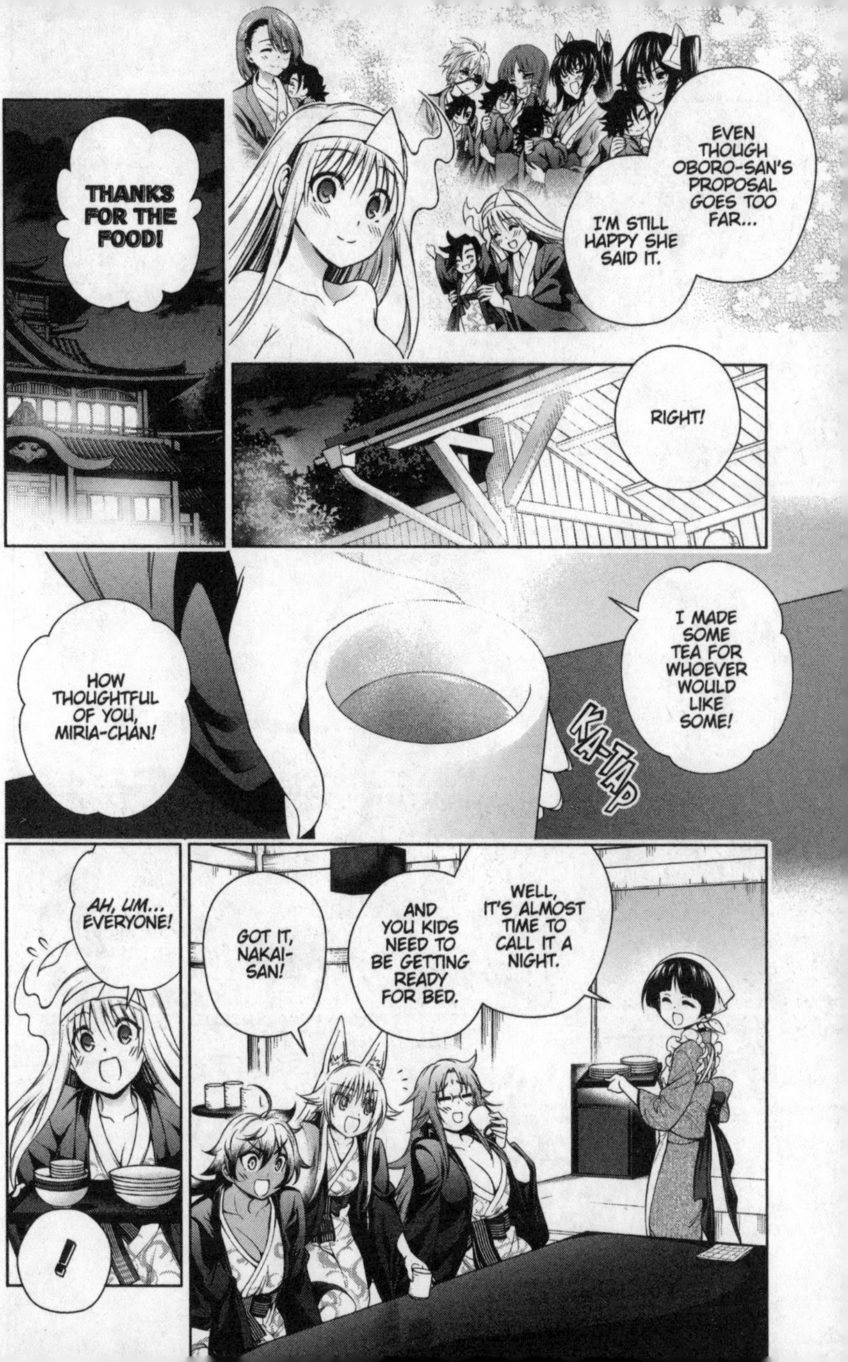
EVEN THOUGH OBORO-SAN'S PROPOSAL GOES TOO FAR...
I'M STILL HAPPY SHE SAID IT.
THANKS FOR THE FOOD!
RIGHT!
I MADE SOME TEA FOR WHOEVER WOULD LIKE SOME!
KA-TAP
HOW THOUGHTFUL OF YOU, MIRIA-CHAN!
WELL, IT'S ALMOST TIME TO CALL IT A NIGHT.
AND YOU KIDS NEED TO BE GETTING READY FOR BED.
GOT IT, NAKAI-SAN!
AH, UM... EVERYONE!
!

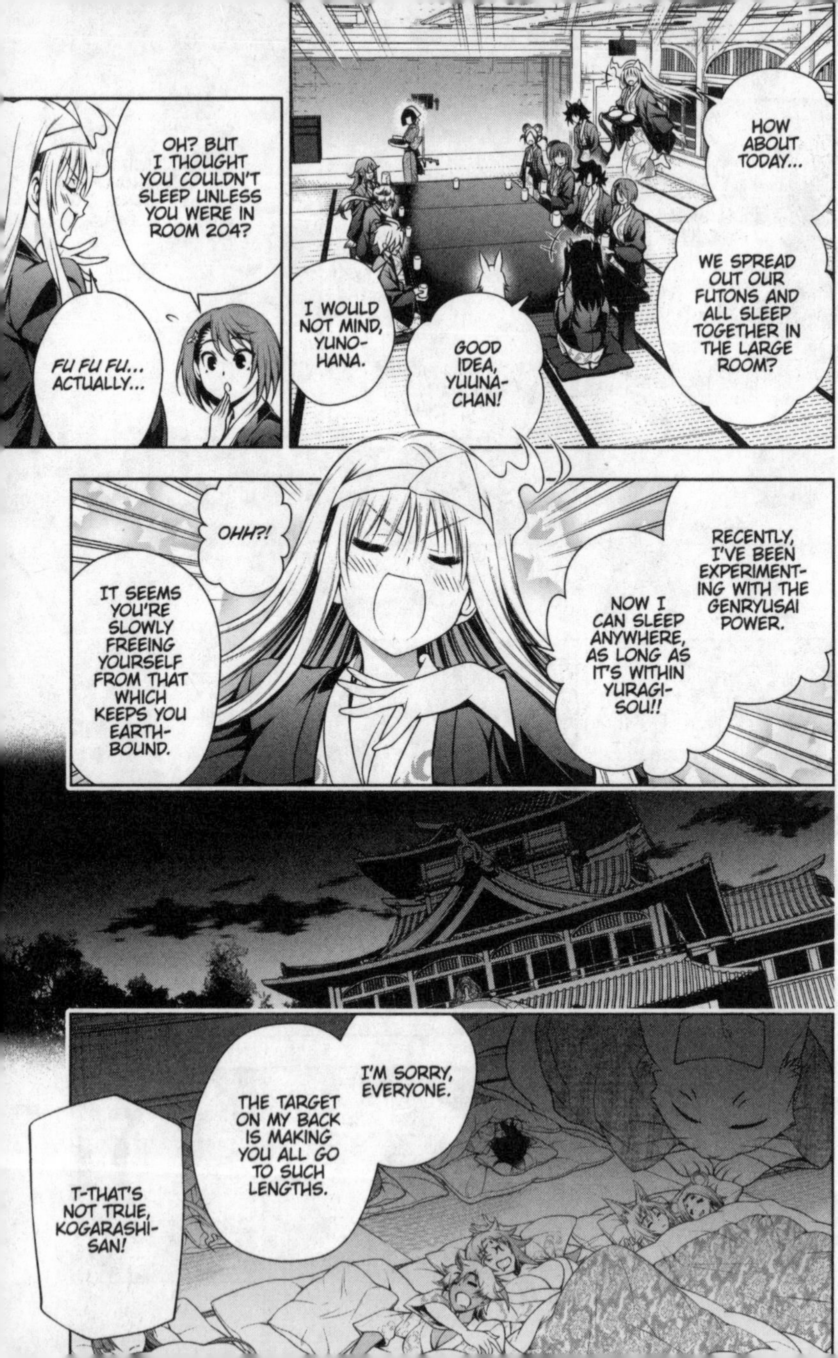
HOW ABOUT TODAY...
WE SPREAD OUT OUR FUTONS AND ALL SLEEP TOGETHER IN THE LARGE ROOM?
GOOD IDEA, YUUNA-CHAN!
I WOULD NOT MIND, YUNO-HANA.
OH? BUT I THOUGHT YOU COULDN'T SLEEP UNLESS YOU WERE IN ROOM 204?
FU FU FU... ACTUALLY...
RECENTLY, I'VE BEEN EXPERIMENTING WITH THE GENRYUSAI POWER.
NOW I CAN SLEEP ANYWHERE, AS LONG AS IT'S WITHIN YURAGI-SOU!!
OHH?!
IT SEEMS YOU'RE SLOWLY FREEING YOURSELF FROM THAT WHICH KEEPS YOU EARTHBOUND.
I'M SORRY, EVERYONE.
THE TARGET ON MY BACK IS MAKING YOU ALL GO TO SUCH LENGTHS.
T-THAT'S NOT TRUE, KOGARASHI-SAN!

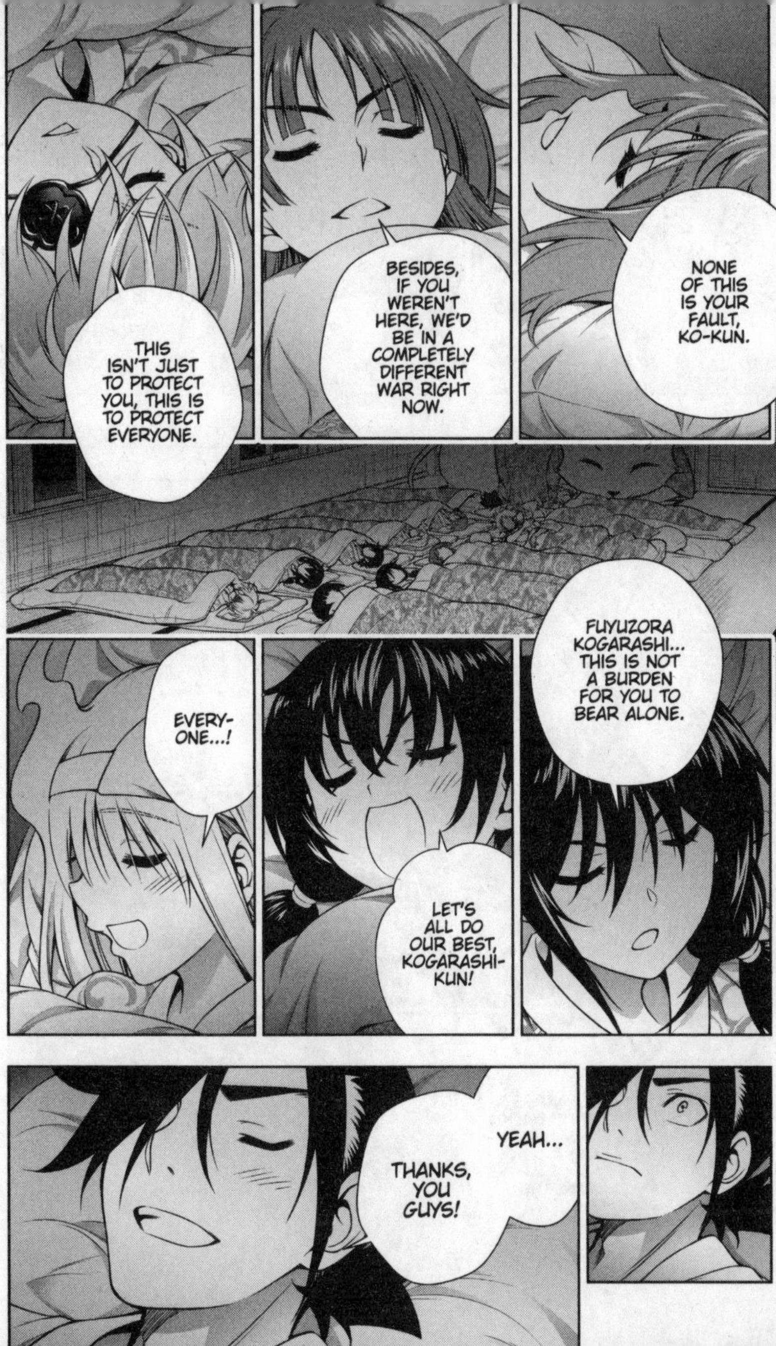
NONE OF THIS IS YOUR FAULT, KO-KUN.
BESIDES, IF YOU WEREN'T HERE, WE'D BE IN A COMPLETELY DIFFERENT WAR RIGHT NOW.
THIS ISN'T JUST TO PROTECT YOU, THIS IS TO PROTECT EVERYONE.
FUYUZORA KOGARASHI... THIS IS NOT A BURDEN FOR YOU TO BEAR ALONE.
LET'S ALL DO OUR BEST, KOGARASHI-KUN!
EVERY-ONE...!
YEAH...
THANKS, YOU GUYS!

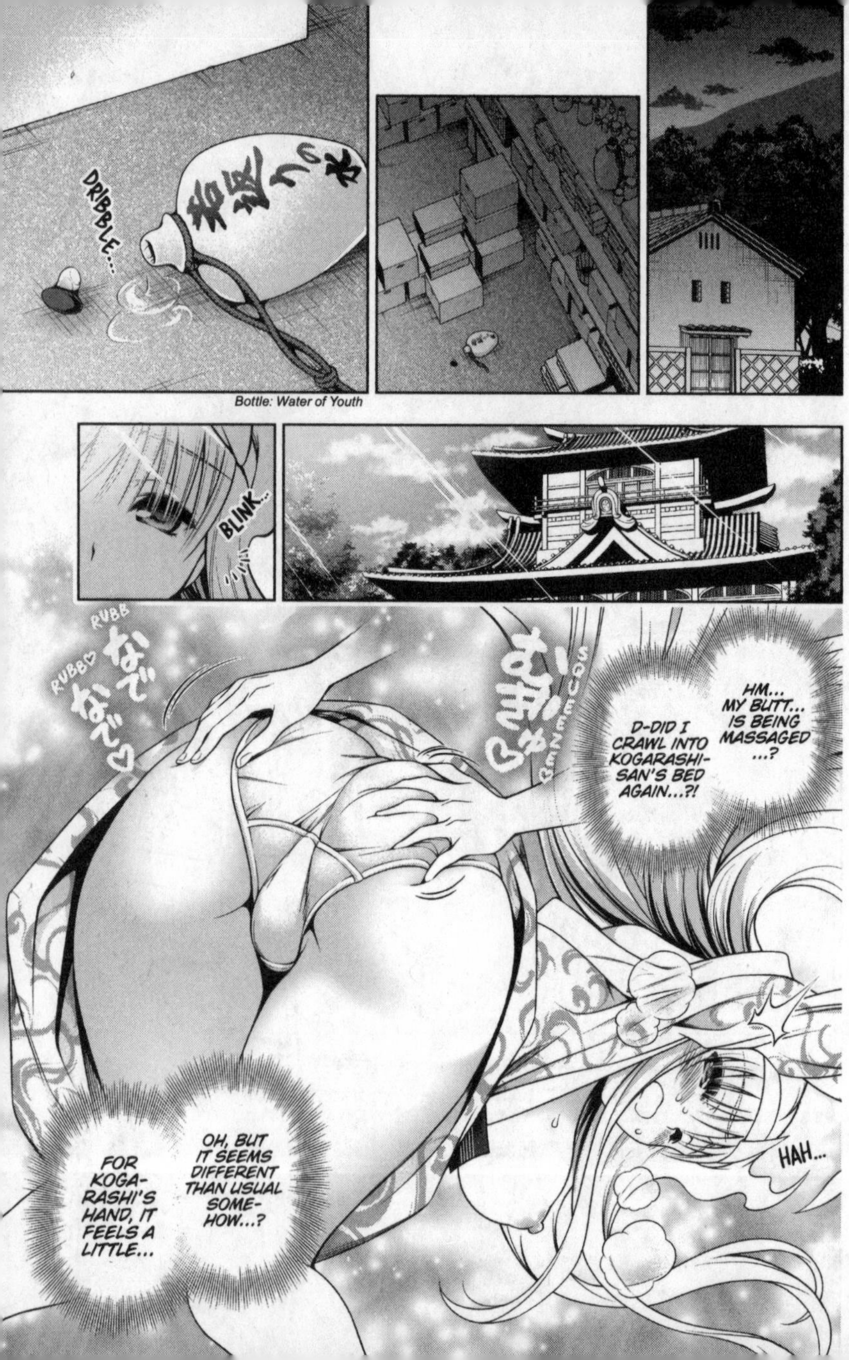
DRIBBLE...
Bottle: Water of Youth
BLINK...
HM... MY BUTT... IS BEING MASSAGED...?
D-DID I CRAWL INTO KOGARASHI-SAN'S BED AGAIN...?!
RUBB RUBB♡
なでなで♡
HAH...
OH, BUT IT SEEMS DIFFERENT THAN USUAL SOME-HOW...?
FOR KOGA-RASHI'S HAND, IT FEELS A LITTLE...

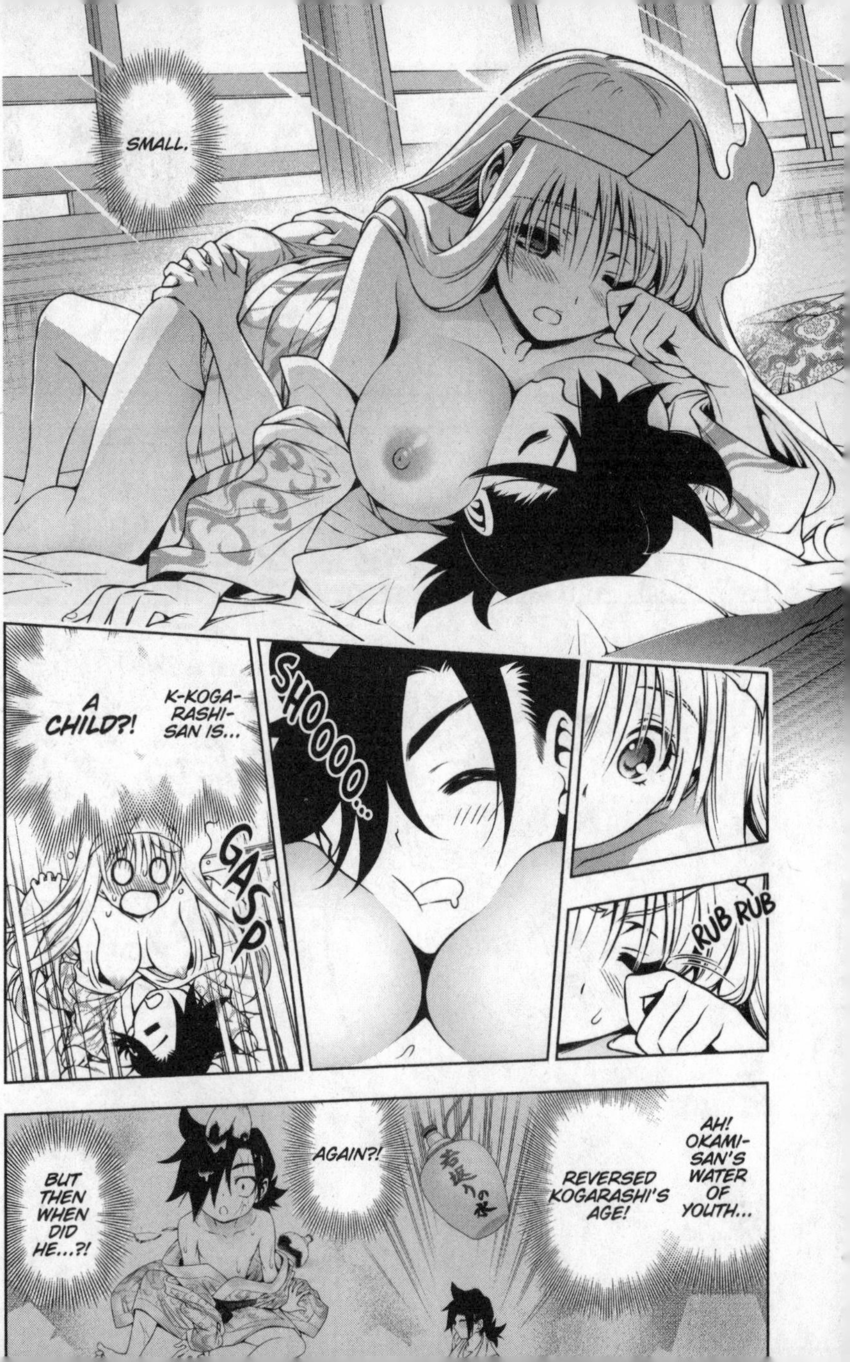
SMALL.
RUB RUB
SHOOOO...
GASP
K-KOGARASHI-SAN IS...
A CHILD?!
AH! OKAMI-SAN'S WATER OF YOUTH...
REVERSED KOGARASHI'S AGE!
AGAIN?!
BUT THEN WHEN DID HE...?!

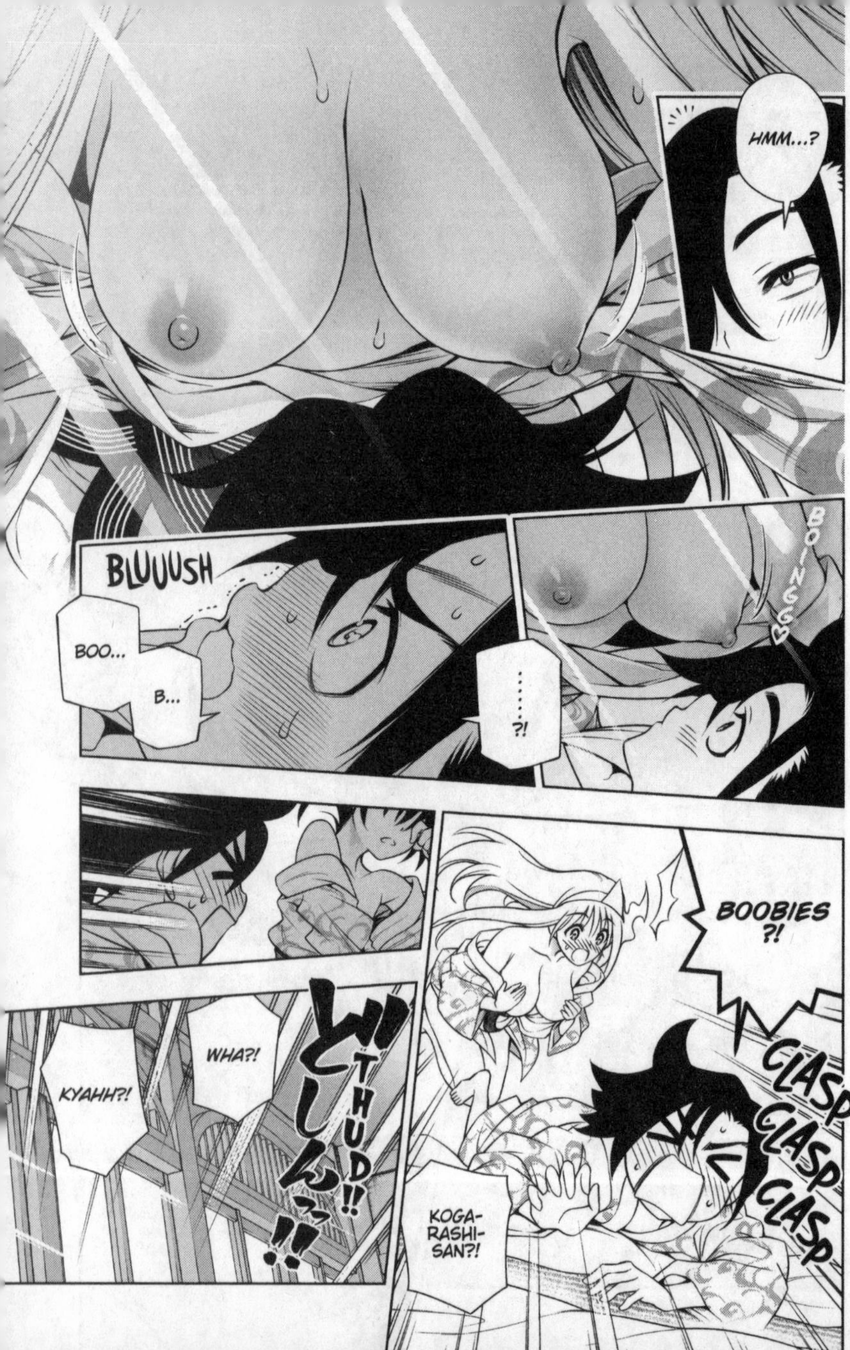
HMM...?
BOINGG
......?!
BLUUUSH
BOO...
B...
BOOBIES ?!
CLASP CLASP CLASP
KOGA-RASHI-SAN?!
WHA?!
KYAHH?!
どしんっ!!
THUD!!

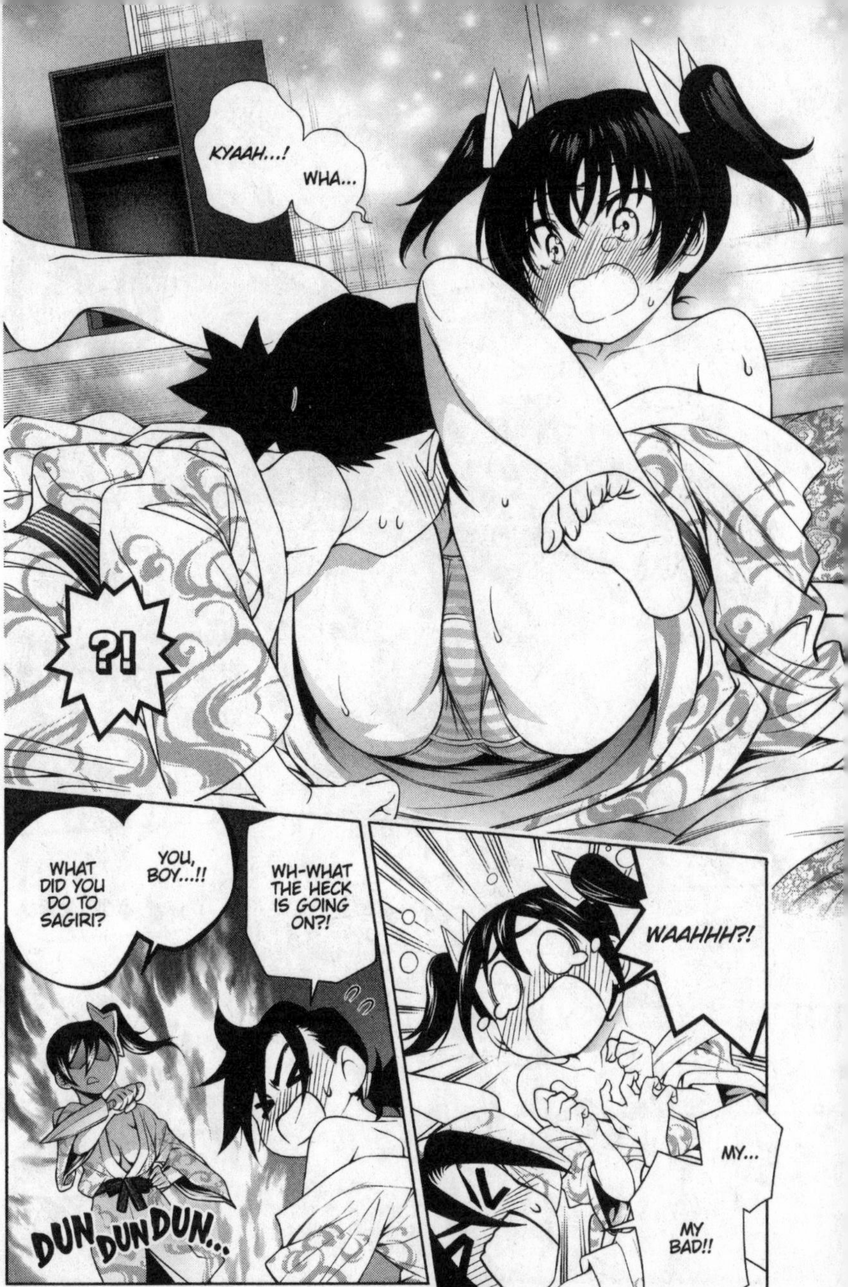
KYAAH...!
WHA...
?!
WAAHHH?!
MY...
MY BAD!!
WH-WHAT THE HECK IS GOING ON?!
YOU, BOY...!!
WHAT DID YOU DO TO SAGIRI?
DUN DUN DUN...

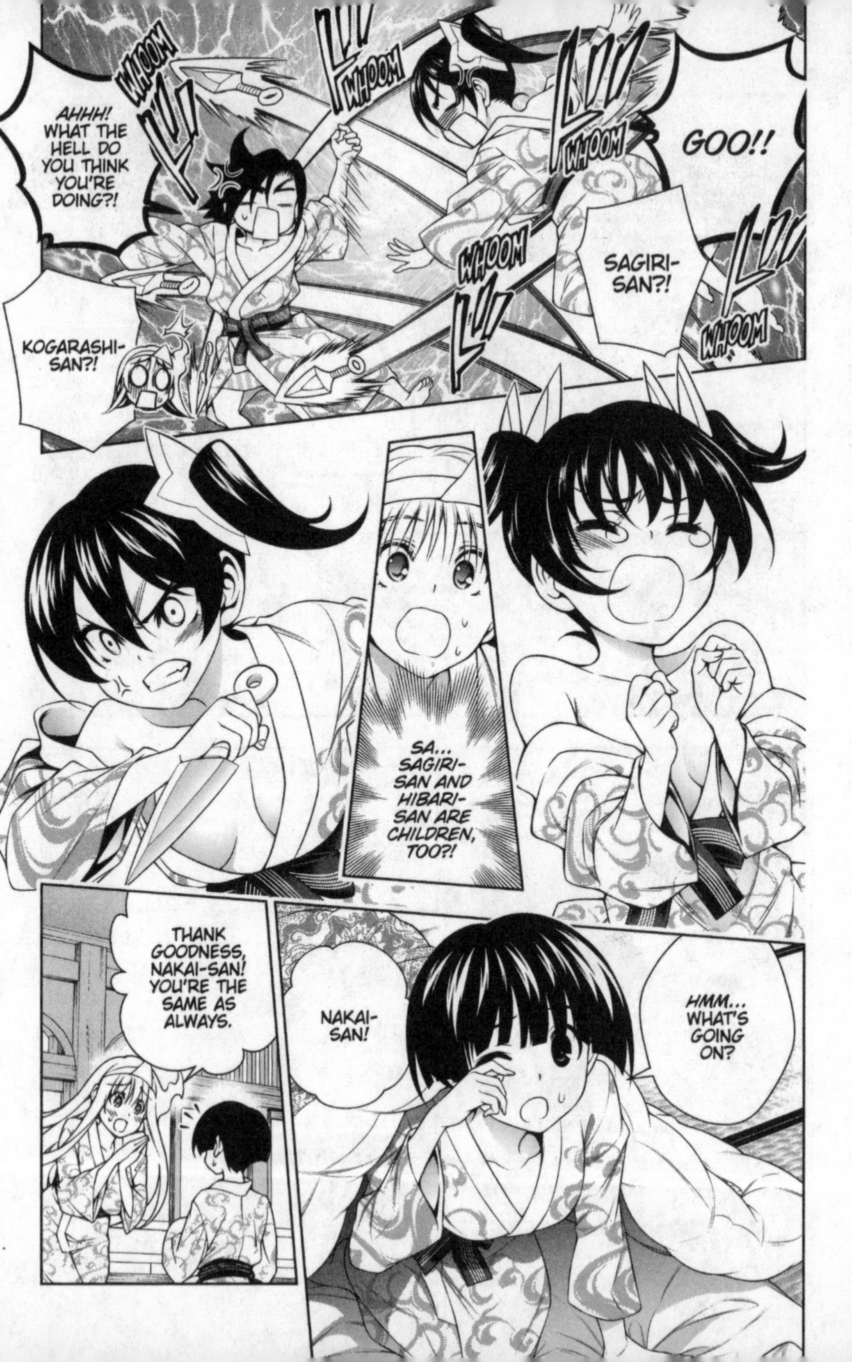

GOO!!
WHOOM
WHOOM
SAGIRI-SAN?!
WHOOM
WHOOM
WHOOM
AHHH! WHAT THE HELL DO YOU THINK YOU'RE DOING?!
KOGARASHI-SAN?!
SA... SAGIRI-SAN AND HIBARI-SAN ARE CHILDREN, TOO?!
HMM... WHAT'S GOING ON?
NAKAI-SAN!
THANK GOODNESS, NAKAI-SAN! YOU'RE THE SAME AS ALWAYS.

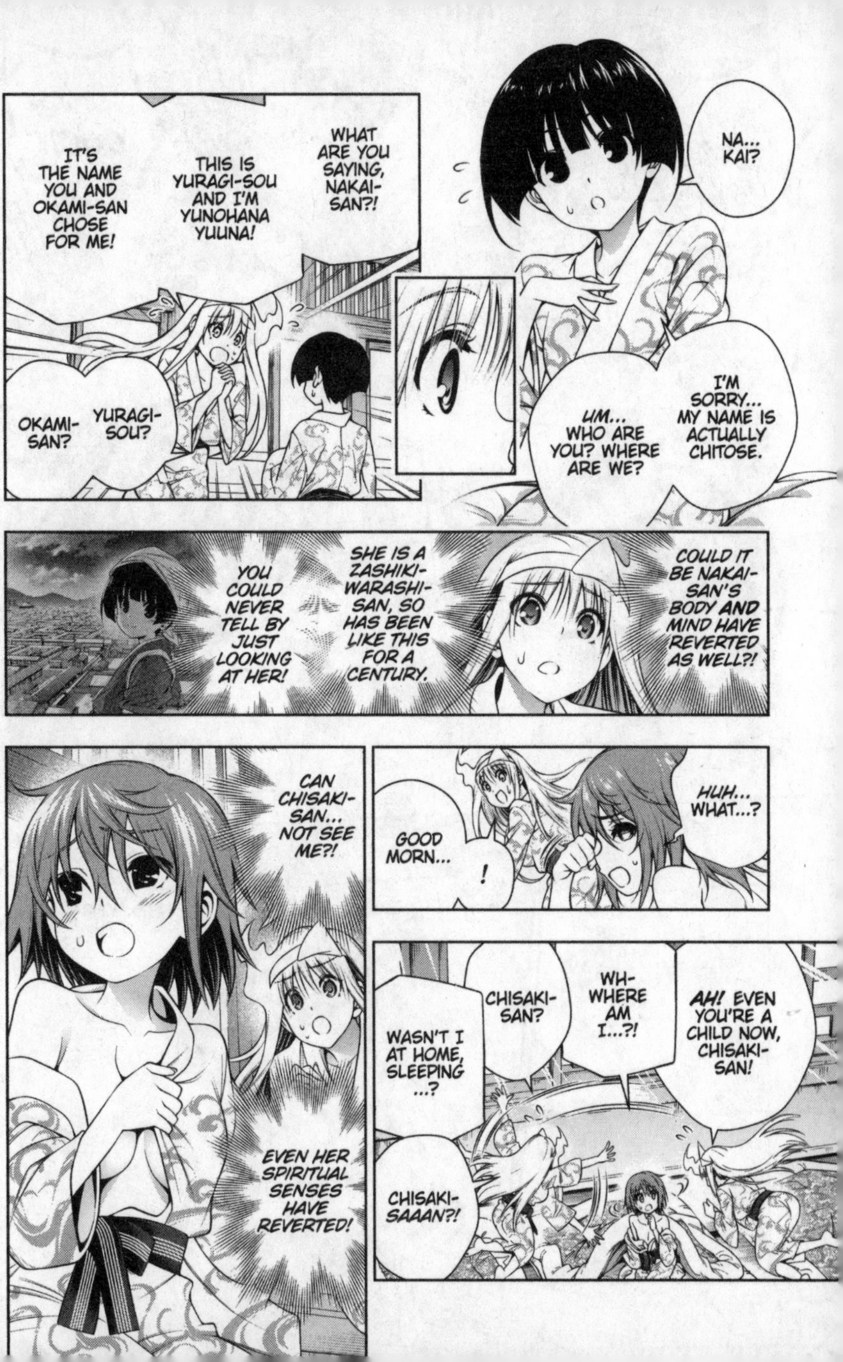

NA... KAI?
I'M SORRY... MY NAME IS ACTUALLY CHITOSE.
UM... WHO ARE YOU? WHERE ARE WE?
WHAT ARE YOU SAYING, NAKAI-SAN?!
THIS IS YURAGI-SOU AND I'M YUNOHANA YUUNA!
IT'S THE NAME YOU AND OKAMI-SAN CHOSE FOR ME!
YURAGI-SOU?
OKAMI-SAN?
COULD IT BE NAKAI-SAN'S BODY AND MIND HAVE REVERTED AS WELL?!
SHE IS A ZASHIKI-WARASHI-SAN, SO HAS BEEN LIKE THIS FOR A CENTURY.
YOU COULD NEVER TELL BY JUST LOOKING AT HER!
HUH... WHAT...?
GOOD MORN... !
AH! EVEN YOU'RE A CHILD NOW, CHISAKI-SAN!
WH-WHERE AM I...?!
CHISAKI-SAN?
WASN'T I AT HOME, SLEEPING ...?
CHISAKI-SAAAN?!
CAN CHISAKI-SAN... NOT SEE ME?!
EVEN HER SPIRITUAL SENSES HAVE REVERTED!

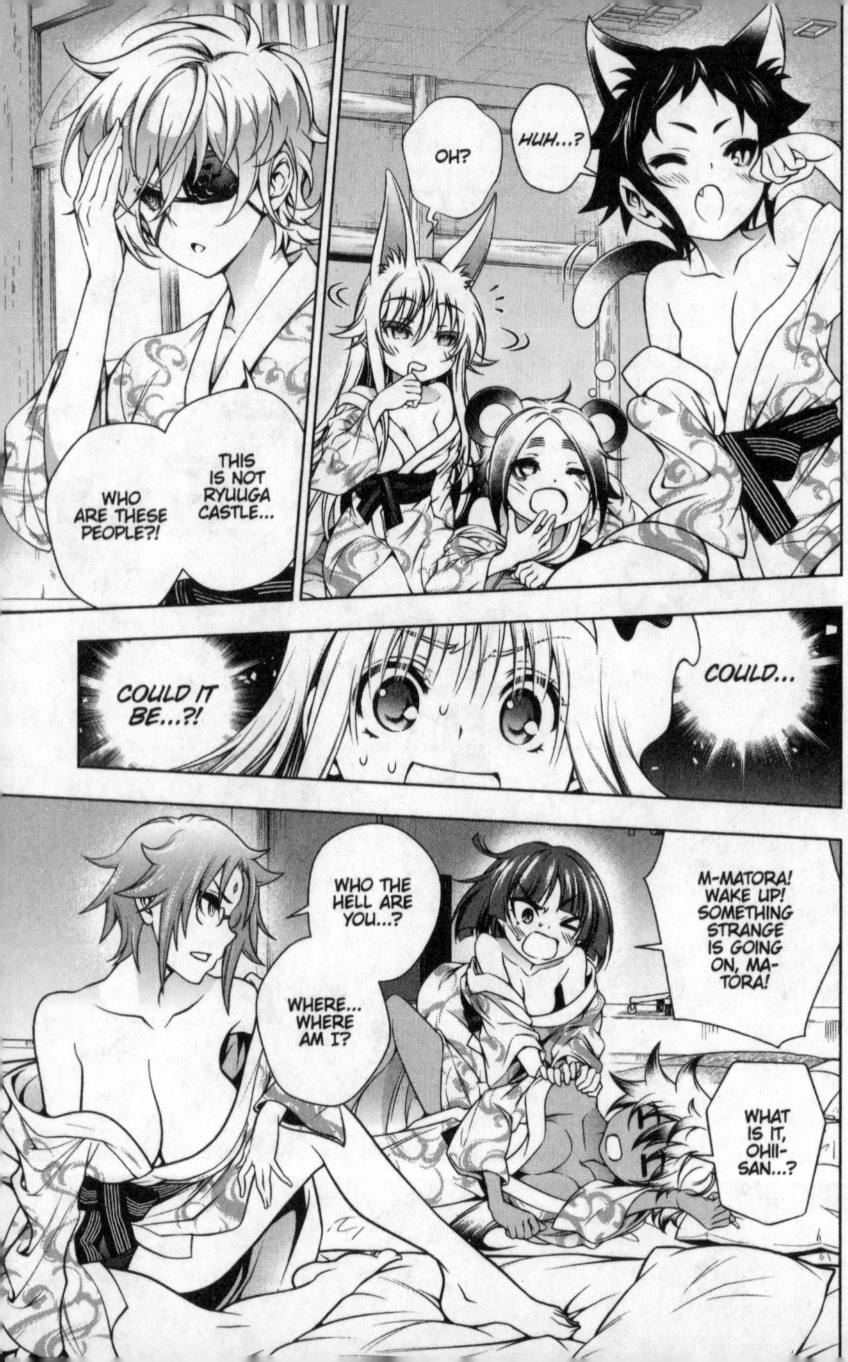

HUH...?
OH?
THIS IS NOT RYUUGA CASTLE...
WHO ARE THESE PEOPLE?!
COULD...
COULD IT BE...?!
M-MATORA! WAKE UP! SOMETHING STRANGE IS GOING ON, MATORA!
WHAT IS IT, OHII-SAN...?
WHO THE HELL ARE YOU...?
WHERE... WHERE AM I?

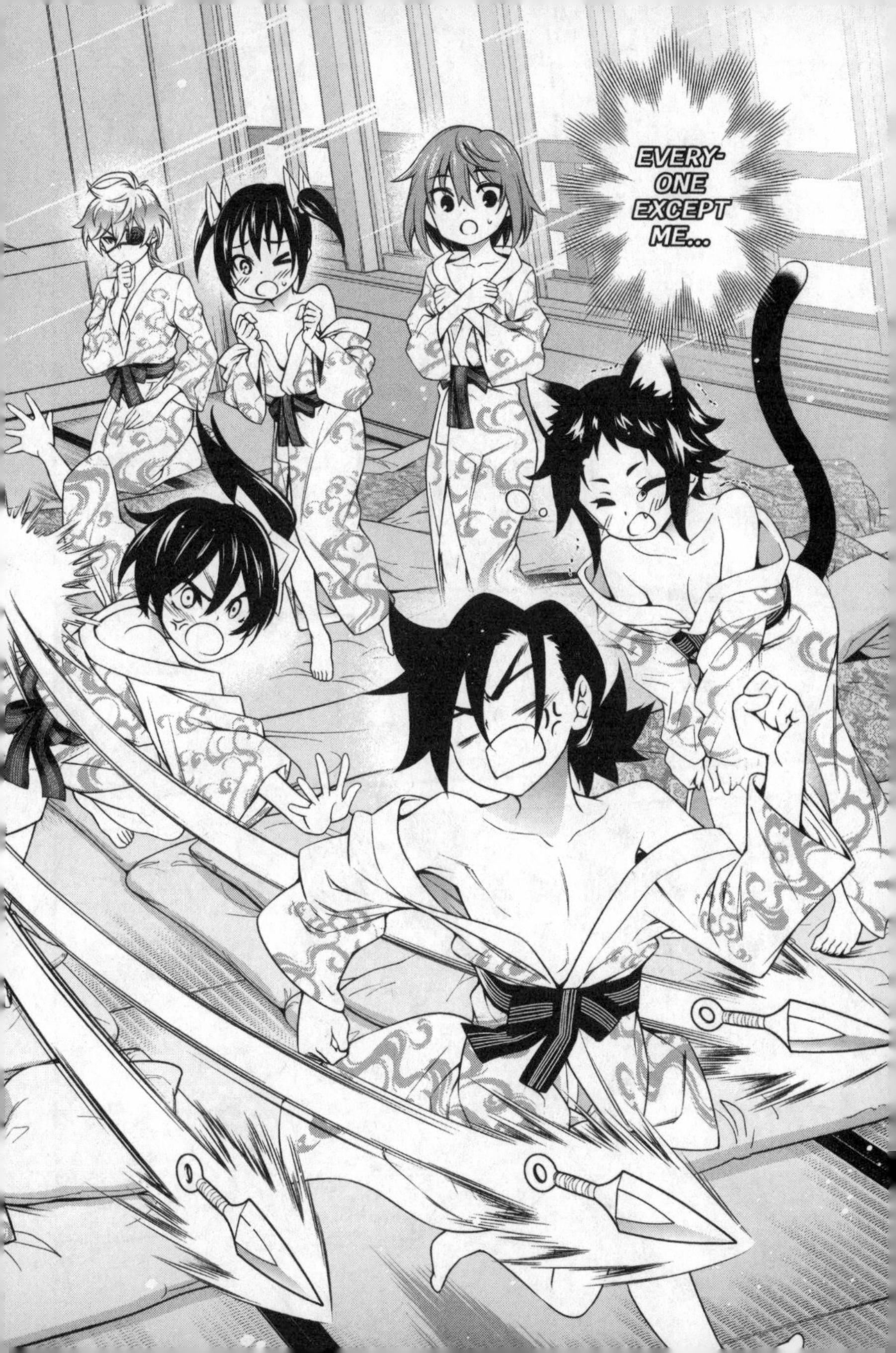
EVERY-ONE EXCEPT ME...

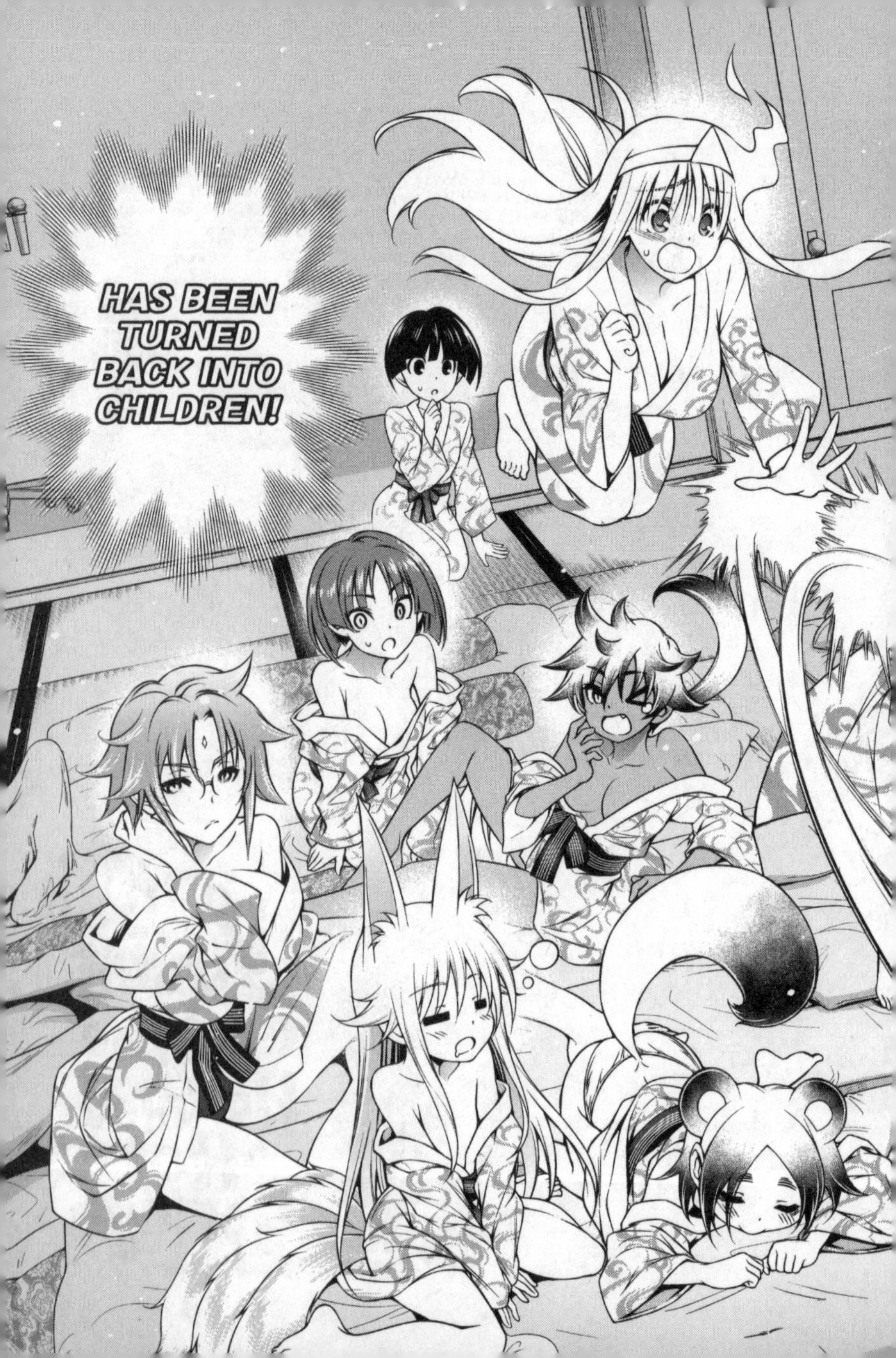
HAS BEEN TURNED BACK INTO CHILDREN!

Yuuna and the Haunted Hot Springs

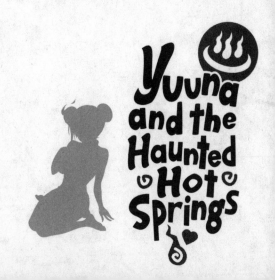

♨154 Everyone's Small

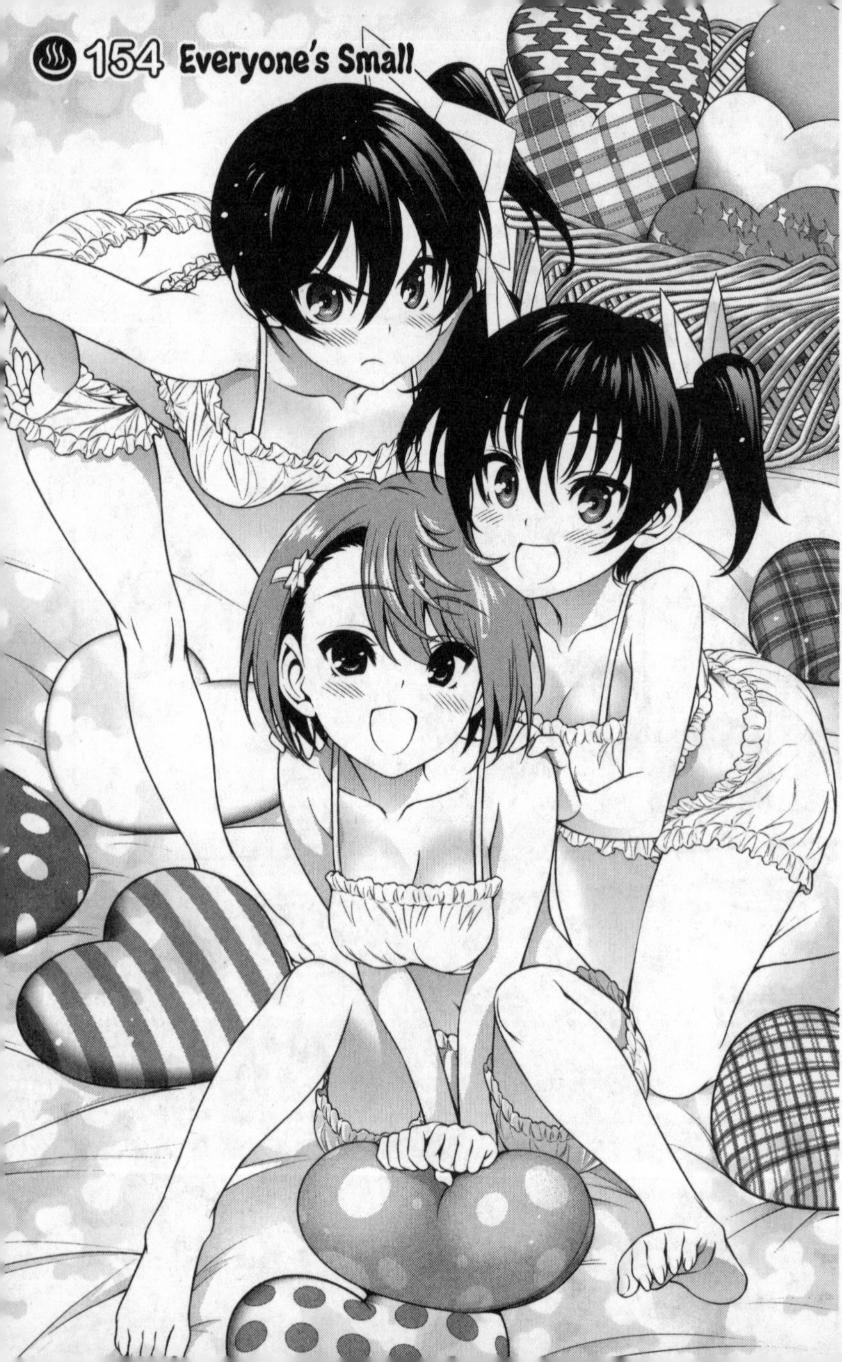

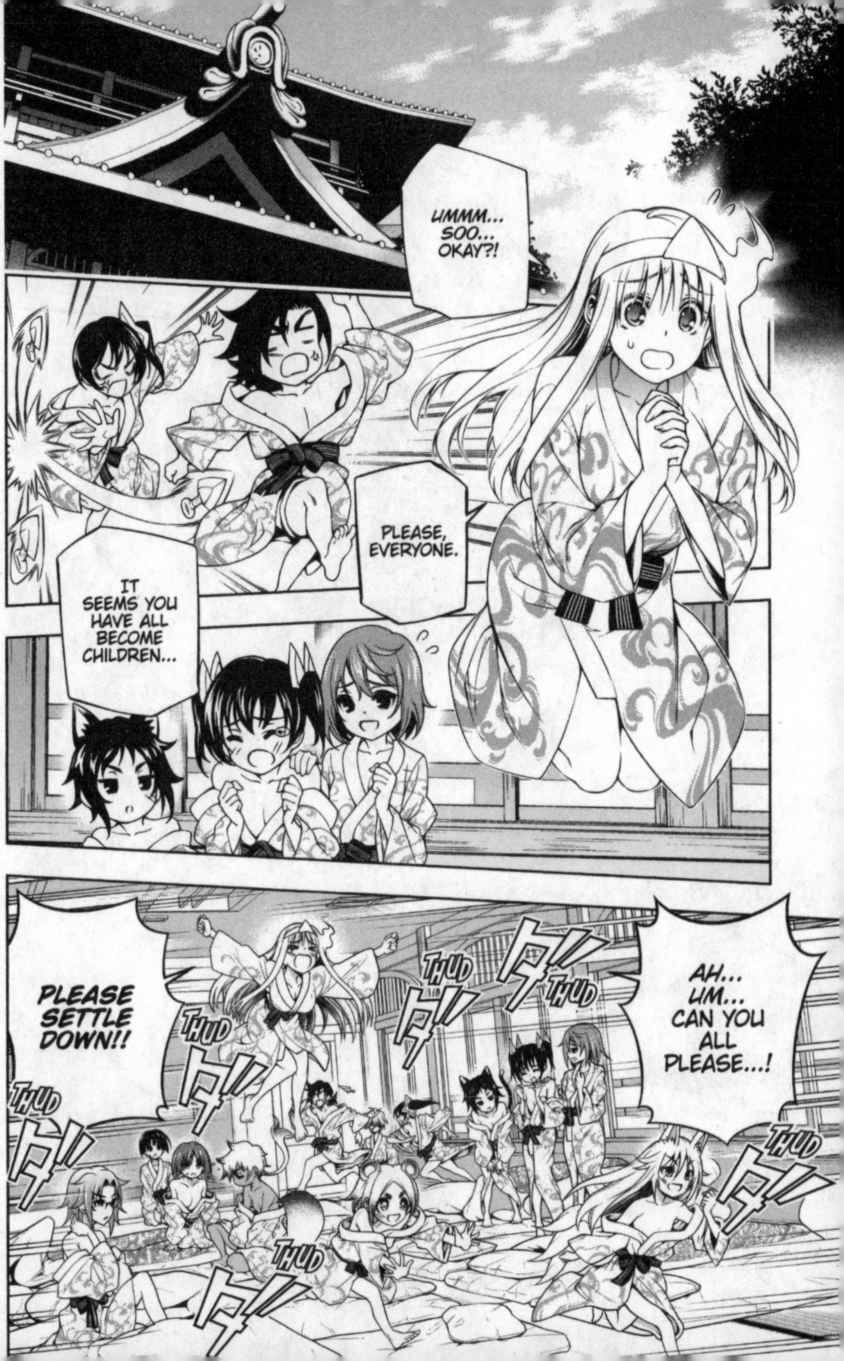
UMMM... SOO... OKAY?!
PLEASE, EVERYONE.
IT SEEMS YOU HAVE ALL BECOME CHILDREN...
AH... UM... CAN YOU ALL PLEASE...!
THUD
THUD
PLEASE SETTLE DOWN!!
THUD
THUD
THUD
THUD

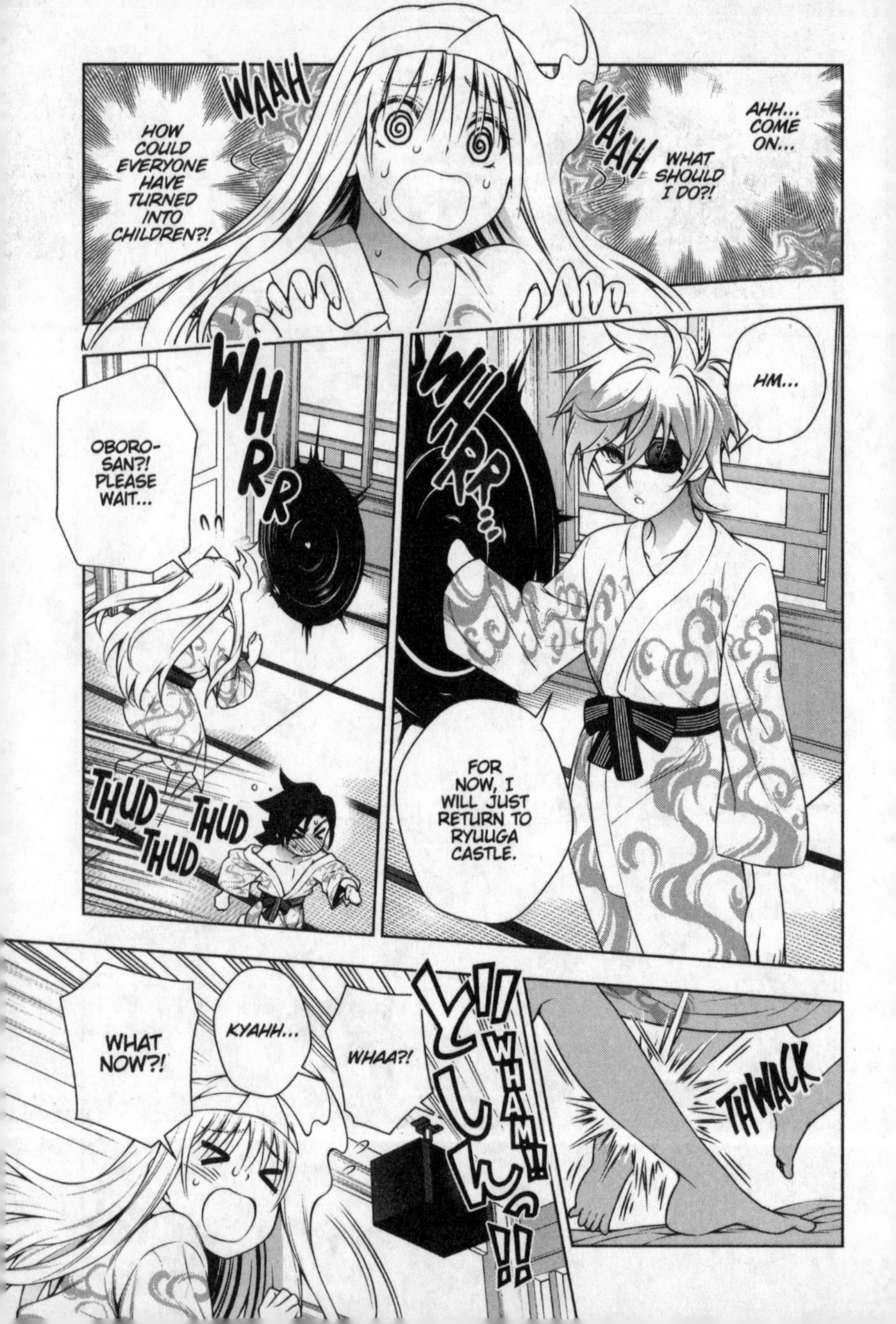

AHH... COME ON...
WHAT SHOULD I DO?!
WAAH
WAAH
HOW COULD EVERYONE HAVE TURNED INTO CHILDREN?!
HM...
WHRR...
FOR NOW, I WILL JUST RETURN TO RYUUGA CASTLE.
WHRR
OBORO-SAN?! PLEASE WAIT...
THUD THUD THUD
THWACK
WHAM!!
どしん!!
WHAA?!
KYAHH...
WHAT NOW?!

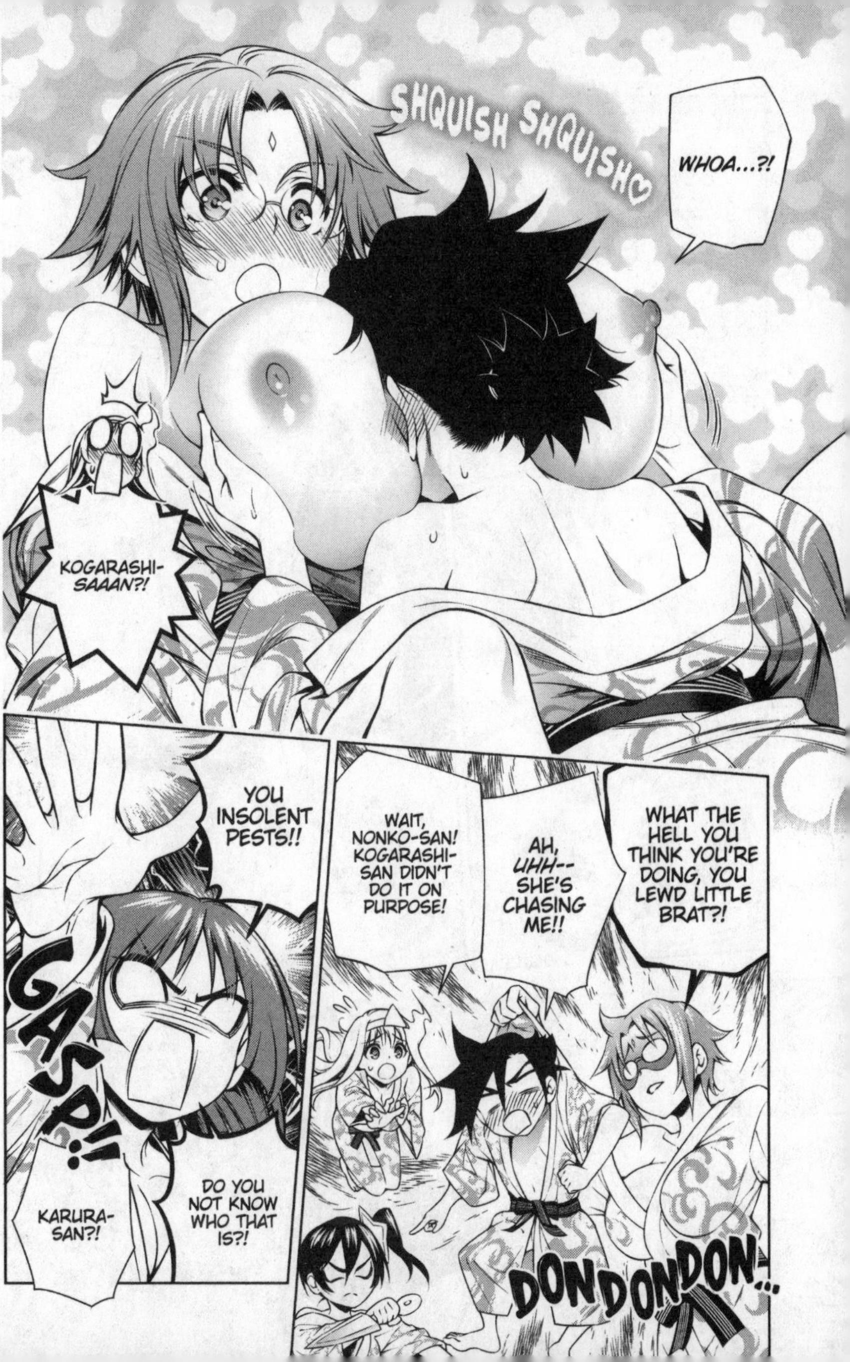
SHQUISH SHQUISH♡
WHOA...?!
KOGARASHI-SAAAN?!
WHAT THE HELL YOU THINK YOU'RE DOING, YOU LEWD LITTLE BRAT?!
AH, UHH-- SHE'S CHASING ME!!
WAIT, NONKO-SAN! KOGARASHI-SAN DIDN'T DO IT ON PURPOSE!
DONDONDON...
YOU INSOLENT PESTS!!
GASP!!
DO YOU NOT KNOW WHO THAT IS?!
KARURA-SAN?!

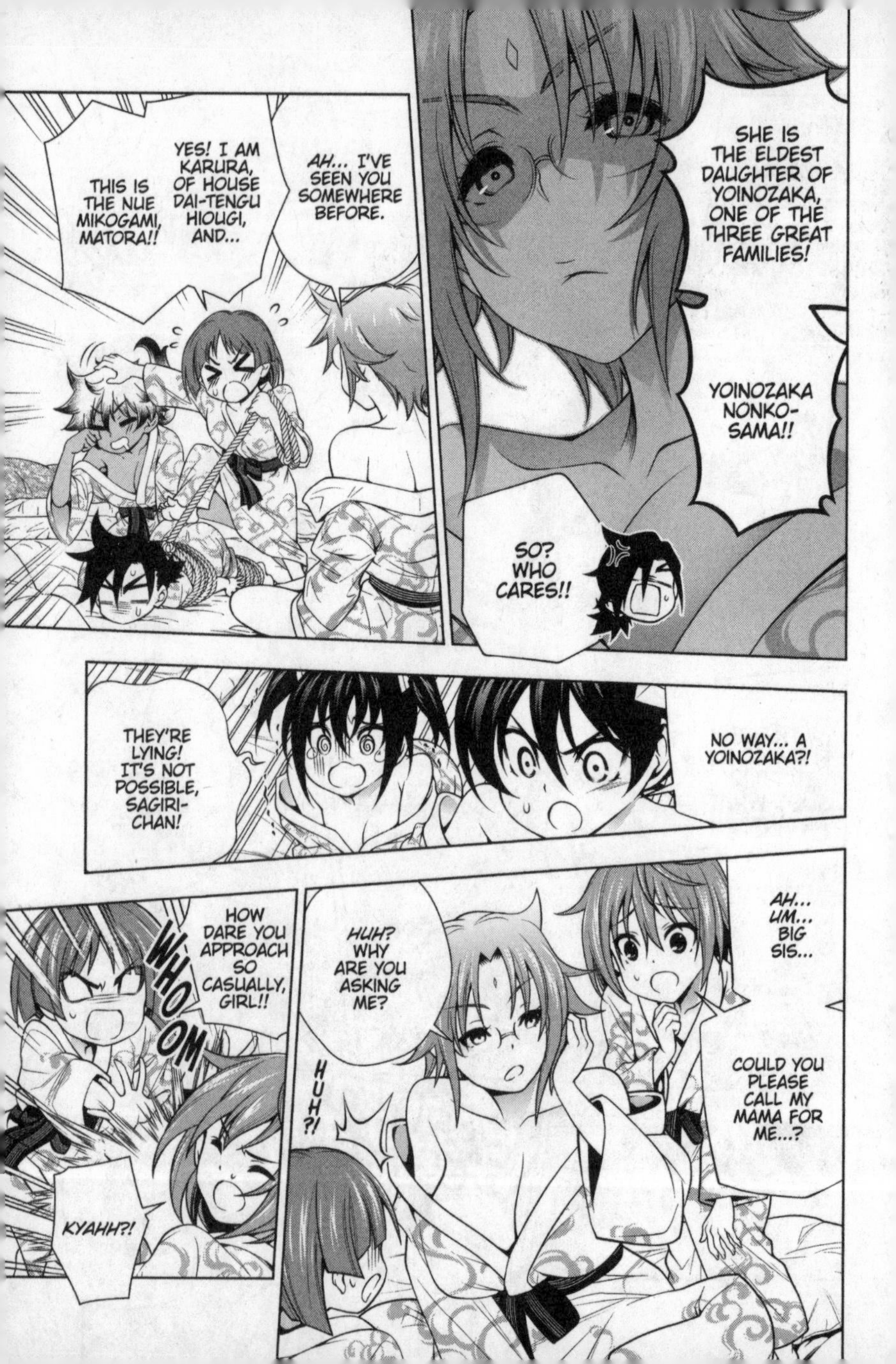
SHE IS THE ELDEST DAUGHTER OF YOINOZAKA, ONE OF THE THREE GREAT FAMILIES!
YOINOZAKA NONKO-SAMA!!
SO? WHO CARES!!
AH... I'VE SEEN YOU SOMEWHERE BEFORE.
YES! I AM KARURA, OF HOUSE DAI-TENGU HIOUGI, AND...
THIS IS THE NUE MIKOGAMI, MATORA!!
NO WAY... A YOINOZAKA?!
THEY'RE LYING! IT'S NOT POSSIBLE, SAGIRI-CHAN!
AH... UM... BIG SIS...
COULD YOU PLEASE CALL MY MAMA FOR ME...?
HUH? WHY ARE YOU ASKING ME?
HUH?!
HOW DARE YOU APPROACH SO CASUALLY, GIRL!!
WHOOM
KYAHH?!

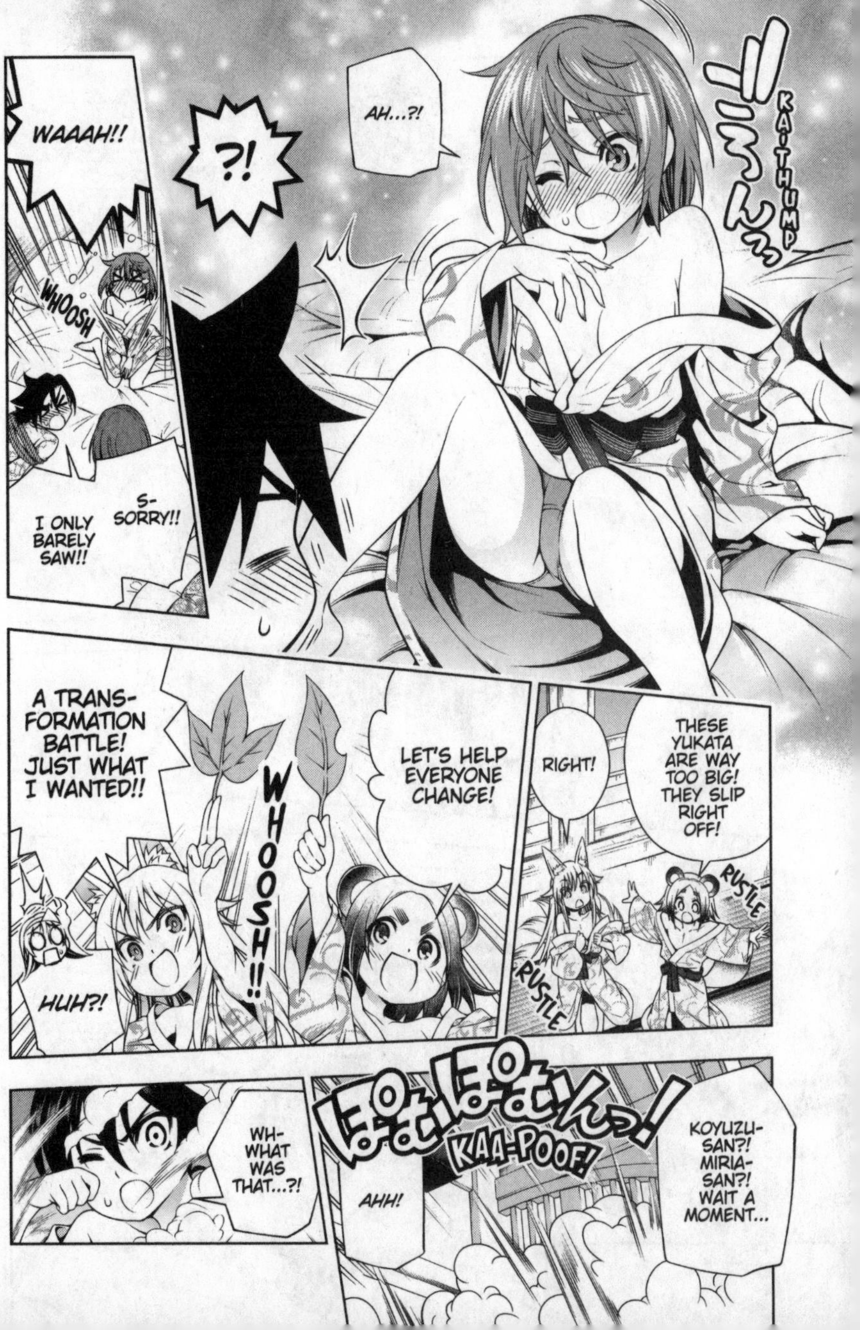
ごろんっ
KAITHUMP
AH...?!
?!
WAAAH!!
WHOOSH
S-SORRY!!
I ONLY BARELY SAW!!
THESE YUKATA ARE WAY TOO BIG! THEY SLIP RIGHT OFF!
RIGHT!
RUSTLE
RUSTLE
LET'S HELP EVERYONE CHANGE!
WHOOSH!!
A TRANS-FORMATION BATTLE! JUST WHAT I WANTED!!
HUH?!
KOYUZU-SAN?! MIRIA-SAN?! WAIT A MOMENT...
ぽむぽむんっ!
KAA-POOF!
AHH!
WH-WHAT WAS THAT...?!

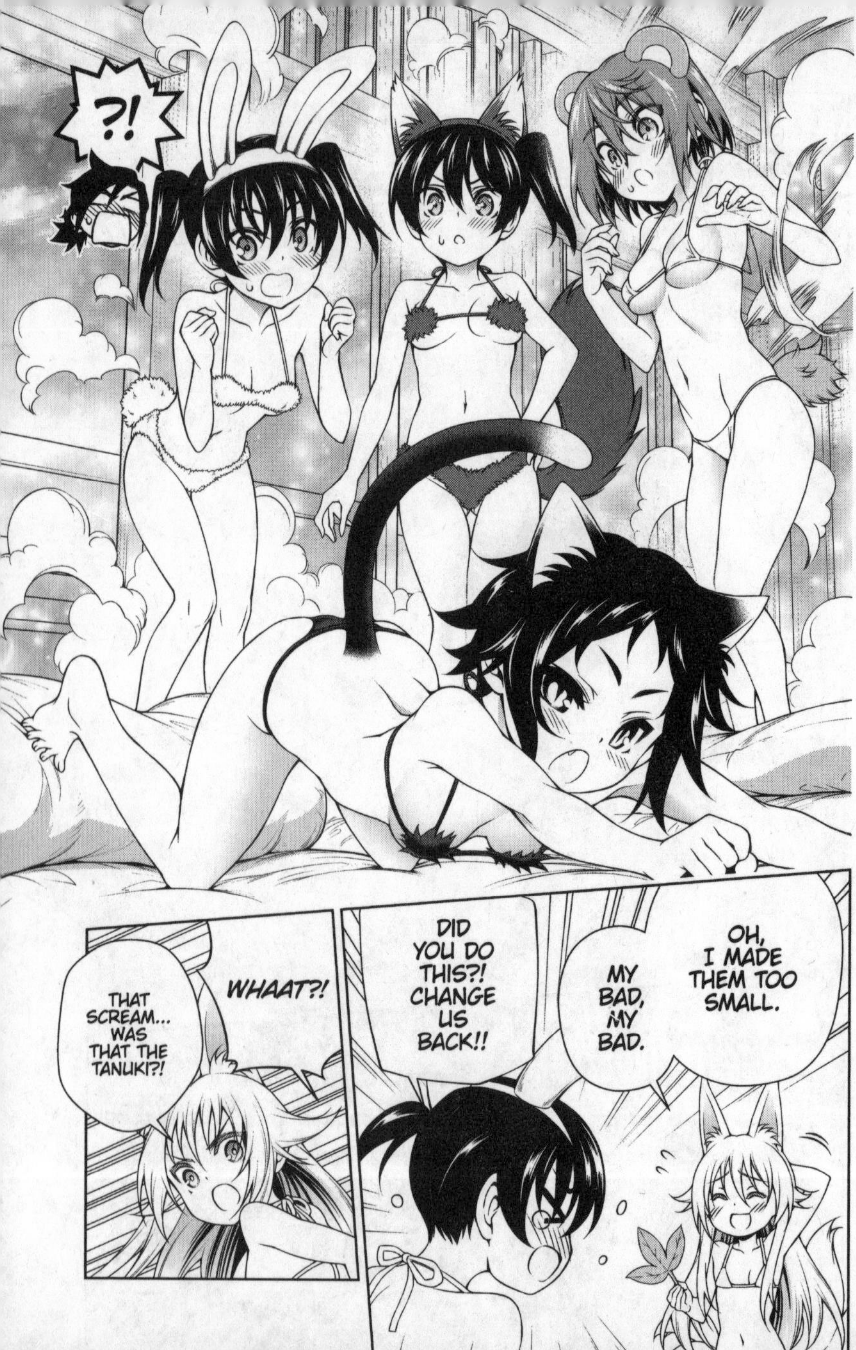

?!
OH, I MADE THEM TOO SMALL.
MY BAD, MY BAD.
DID YOU DO THIS?! CHANGE US BACK!!
WHAAT?!
THAT SCREAM... WAS THAT THE TANUKI?!

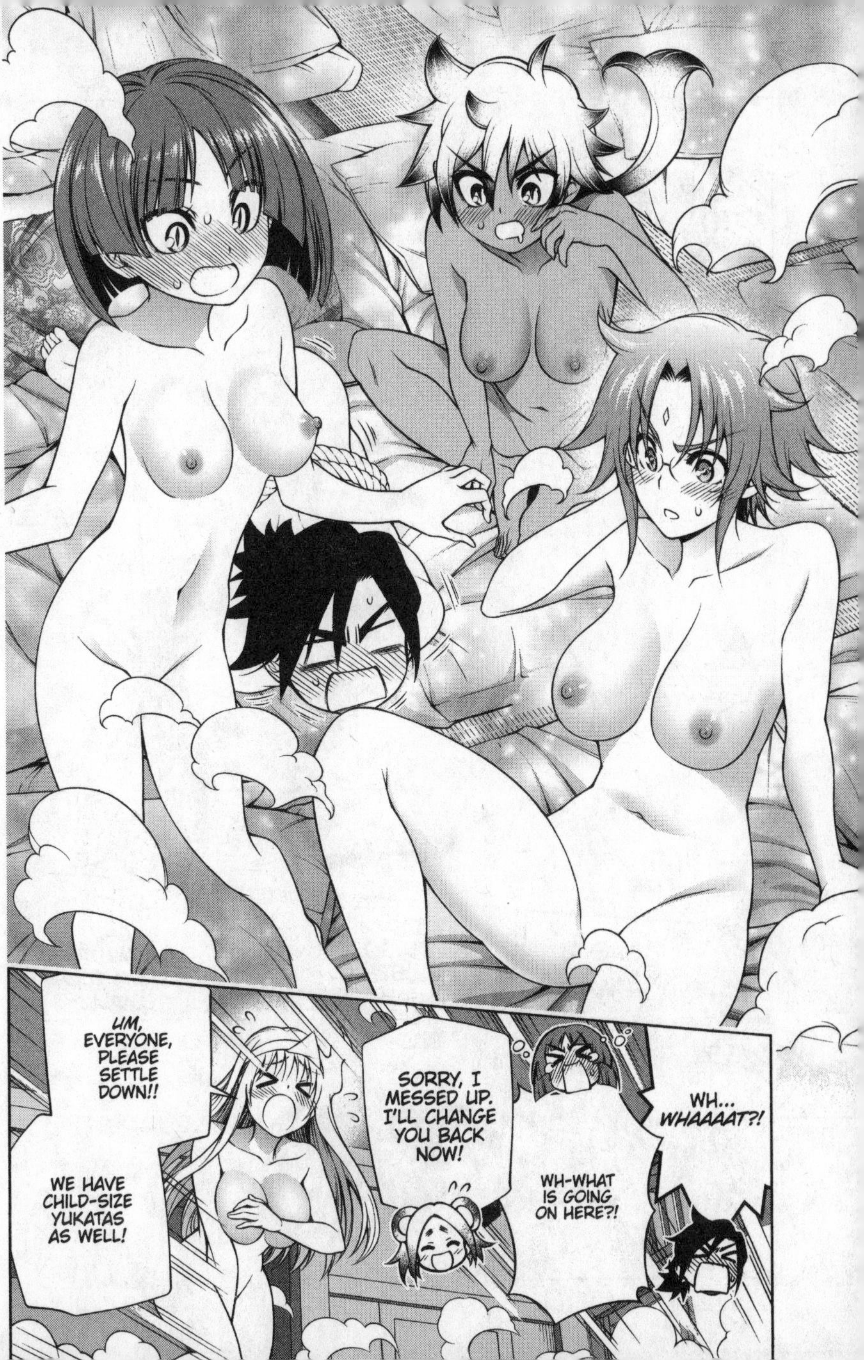
WH... WHAAAAT?!
WH-WHAT IS GOING ON HERE?!
SORRY, I MESSED UP. I'LL CHANGE YOU BACK NOW!
UM, EVERYONE, PLEASE SETTLE DOWN!!
WE HAVE CHILD-SIZE YUKATAS AS WELL!

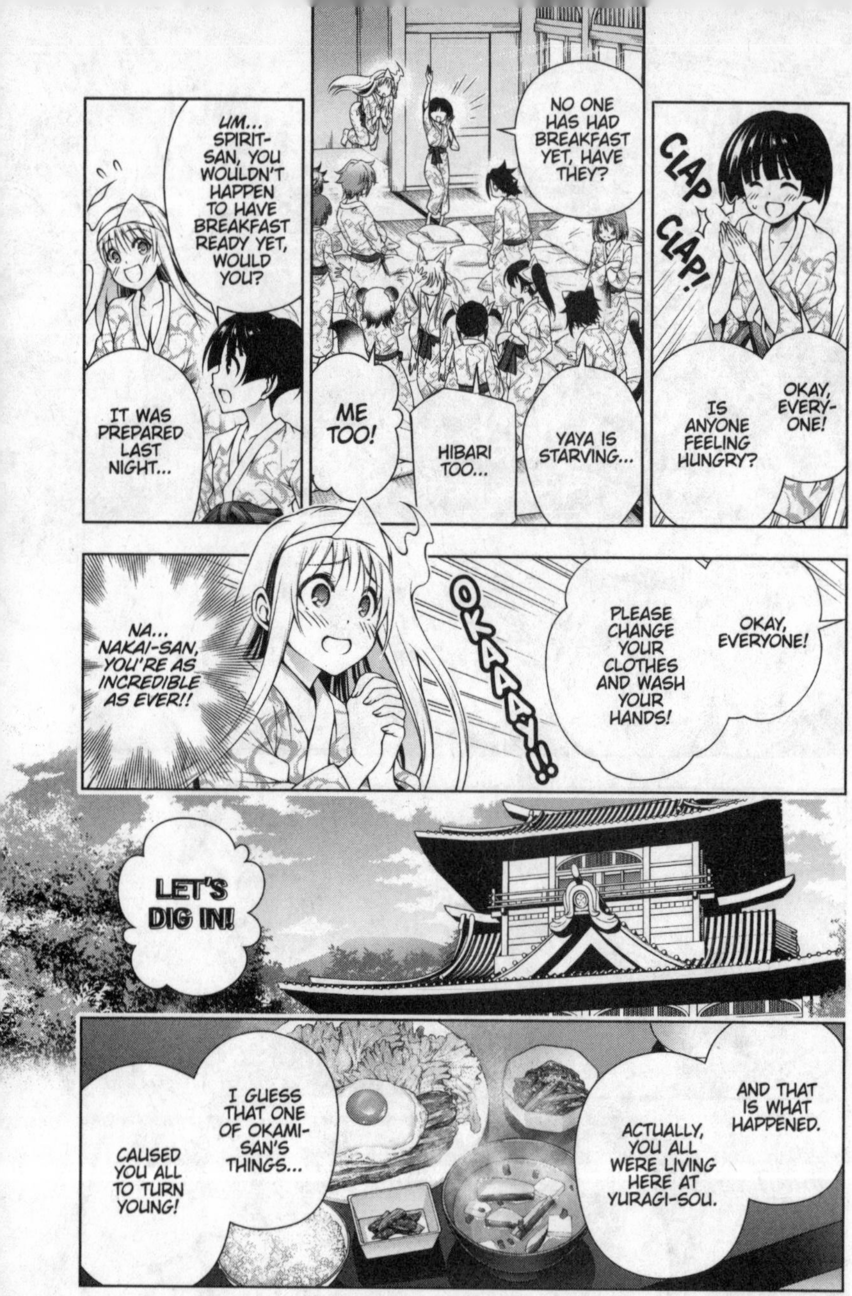
CLAP CLAP!
OKAY, EVERYONE!
IS ANYONE FEELING HUNGRY?
NO ONE HAS HAD BREAKFAST YET, HAVE THEY?
YAYA IS STARVING...
HIBARI TOO...
ME TOO!
UM... SPIRIT-SAN, YOU WOULDN'T HAPPEN TO HAVE BREAKFAST READY YET, WOULD YOU?
IT WAS PREPARED LAST NIGHT...
OKAY, EVERYONE!
PLEASE CHANGE YOUR CLOTHES AND WASH YOUR HANDS!
OKAAAAY!!
NA... NAKAI-SAN, YOU'RE AS INCREDIBLE AS EVER!!
LET'S DIG IN!
AND THAT IS WHAT HAPPENED.
ACTUALLY, YOU ALL WERE LIVING HERE AT YURAGI-SOU.
I GUESS THAT ONE OF OKAMI-SAN'S THINGS...
CAUSED YOU ALL TO TURN YOUNG!

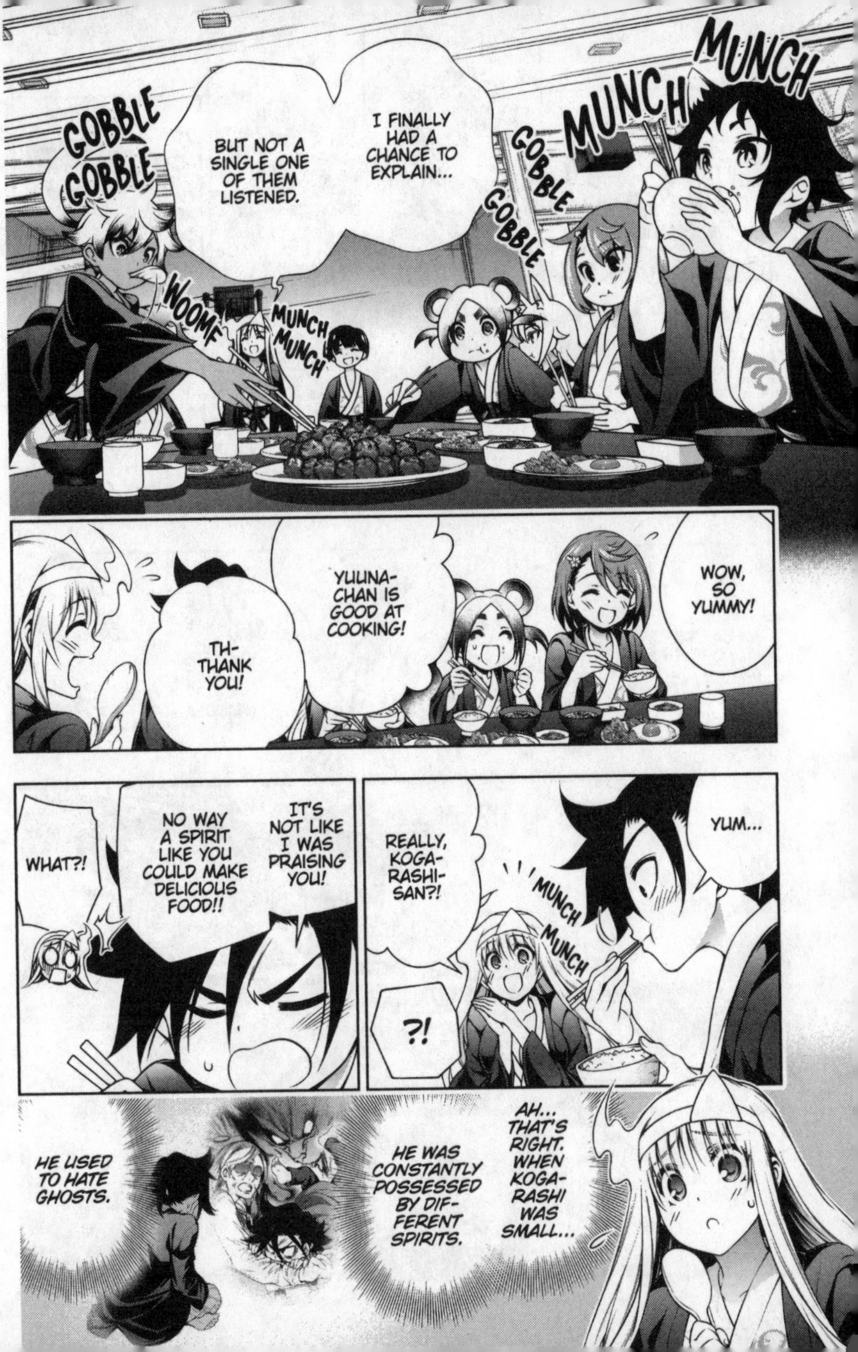
MUNCH MUNCH
GOBBLE GOBBLE
I FINALLY HAD A CHANCE TO EXPLAIN...
BUT NOT A SINGLE ONE OF THEM LISTENED.
GOBBLE GOBBLE
MUNCH MUNCH
WOOMF
WOW, SO YUMMY!
YUUNA-CHAN IS GOOD AT COOKING!
TH-THANK YOU!
YUM...
MUNCH MUNCH
REALLY, KOGA-RASHI-SAN?!
?!
IT'S NOT LIKE I WAS PRAISING YOU!
NO WAY A SPIRIT LIKE YOU COULD MAKE DELICIOUS FOOD!!
WHAT?!
AH... THAT'S RIGHT. WHEN KOGA-RASHI WAS SMALL...
HE WAS CONSTANTLY POSSESSED BY DIF-FERENT SPIRITS.
HE USED TO HATE GHOSTS.

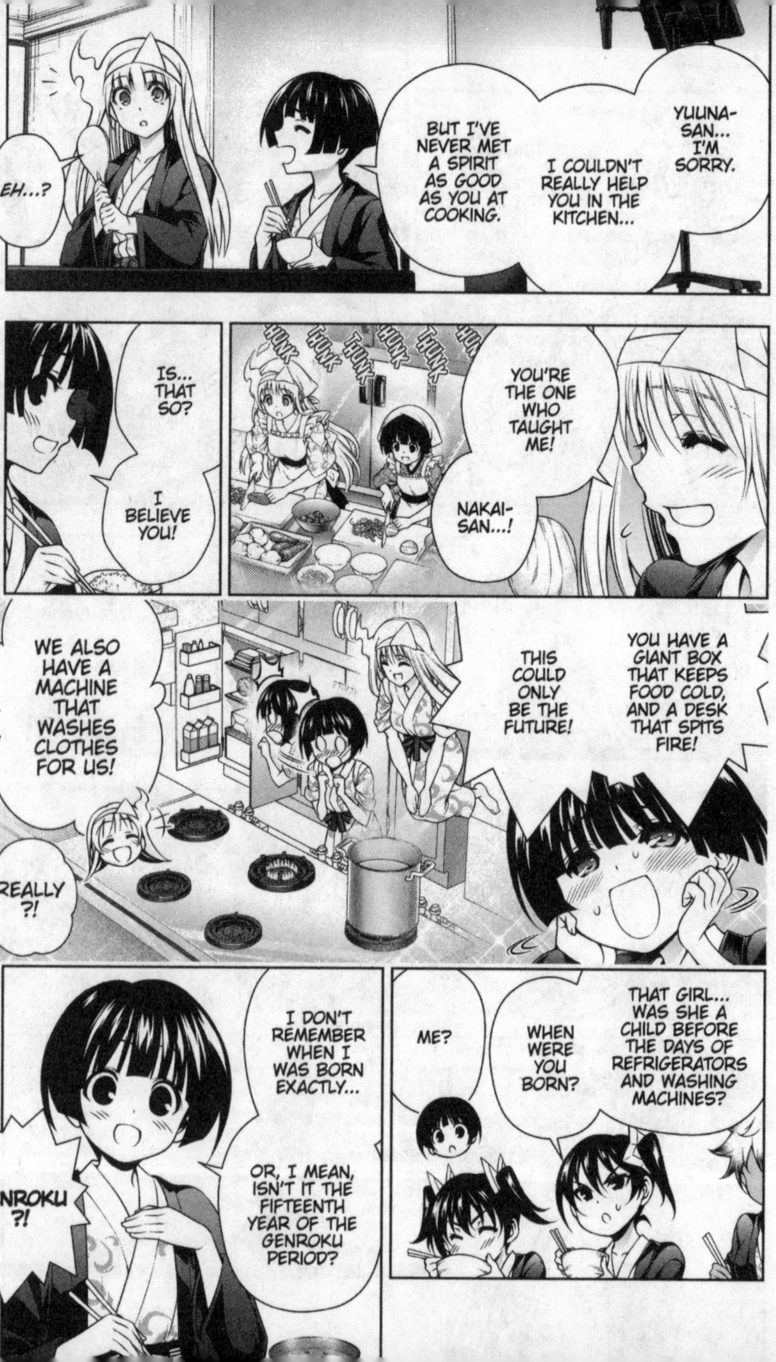
YUUNA-SAN... I'M SORRY.
I COULDN'T REALLY HELP YOU IN THE KITCHEN...
BUT I'VE NEVER MET A SPIRIT AS GOOD AS YOU AT COOKING.
EH...?
YOU'RE THE ONE WHO TAUGHT ME!
NAKAI-SAN...!
THUNK THUNK THUNK THUNK THUNK THUNK
IS... THAT SO?
I BELIEVE YOU!
YOU HAVE A GIANT BOX THAT KEEPS FOOD COLD, AND A DESK THAT SPITS FIRE!
THIS COULD ONLY BE THE FUTURE!
WE ALSO HAVE A MACHINE THAT WASHES CLOTHES FOR US!
REALLY ?!
THAT GIRL... WAS SHE A CHILD BEFORE THE DAYS OF REFRIGERATORS AND WASHING MACHINES?
WHEN WERE YOU BORN?
ME?
I DON'T REMEMBER WHEN I WAS BORN EXACTLY...
OR, I MEAN, ISN'T IT THE FIFTEENTH YEAR OF THE GENROKU PERIOD?
GENROKU ?!

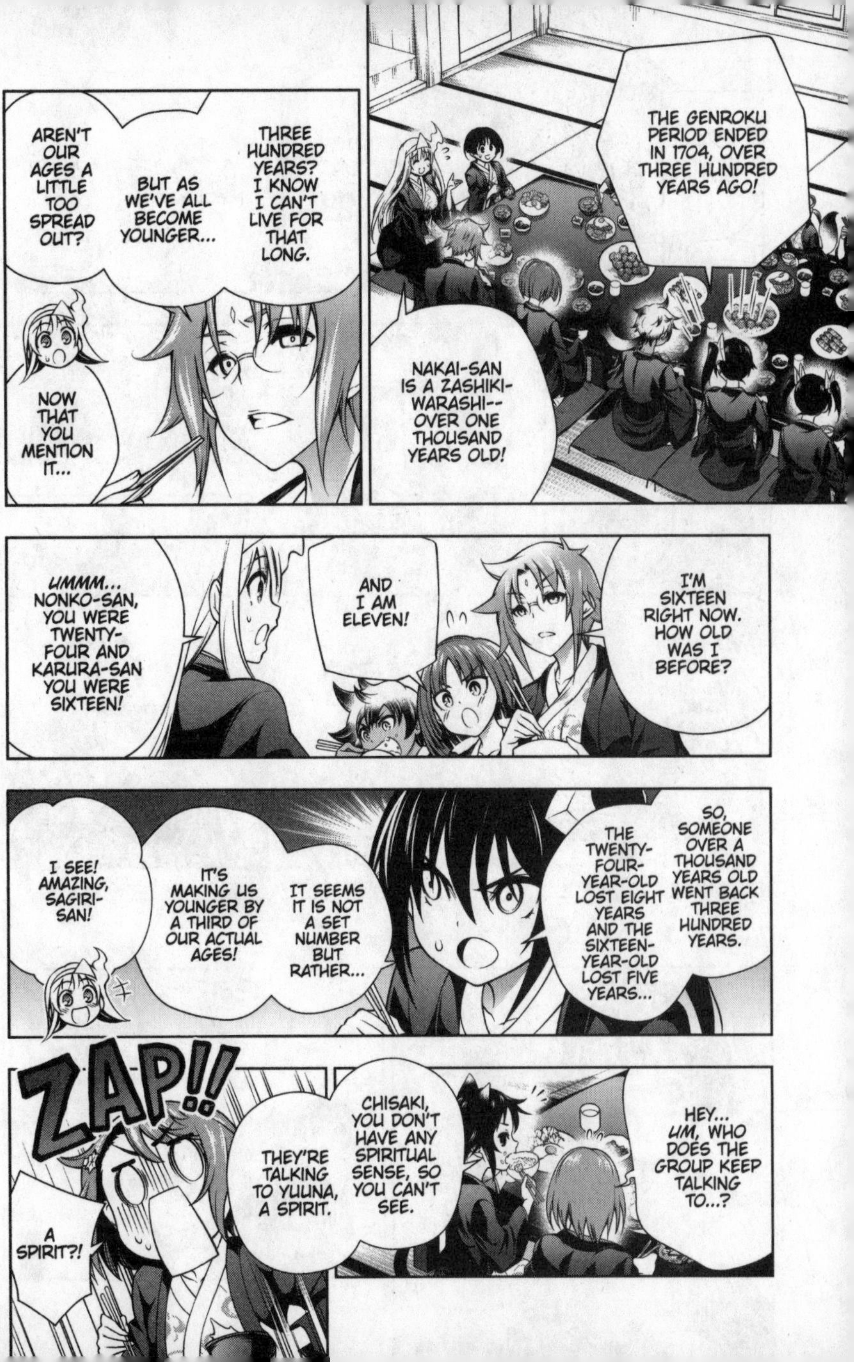
THE GENROKU PERIOD ENDED IN 1704, OVER THREE HUNDRED YEARS AGO!
NAKAI-SAN IS A ZASHIKI-WARASHI-- OVER ONE THOUSAND YEARS OLD!
THREE HUNDRED YEARS? I KNOW I CAN'T LIVE FOR THAT LONG.
BUT AS WE'VE ALL BECOME YOUNGER...
AREN'T OUR AGES A LITTLE TOO SPREAD OUT?
NOW THAT YOU MENTION IT...
I'M SIXTEEN RIGHT NOW. HOW OLD WAS I BEFORE?
AND I AM ELEVEN!
UMMM... NONKO-SAN, YOU WERE TWENTY-FOUR AND KARURA-SAN YOU WERE SIXTEEN!
SO, SOMEONE OVER A THOUSAND YEARS OLD WENT BACK THREE HUNDRED YEARS.
THE TWENTY-FOUR-YEAR-OLD LOST EIGHT YEARS AND THE SIXTEEN-YEAR-OLD LOST FIVE YEARS...
IT SEEMS IT IS NOT A SET NUMBER BUT RATHER...
IT'S MAKING US YOUNGER BY A THIRD OF OUR ACTUAL AGES!
I SEE! AMAZING, SAGIRI-SAN!
HEY... UM, WHO DOES THE GROUP KEEP TALKING TO...?
CHISAKI, YOU DON'T HAVE ANY SPIRITUAL SENSE, SO YOU CAN'T SEE.
THEY'RE TALKING TO YUUNA, A SPIRIT.
ZAP!!
A SPIRIT?!

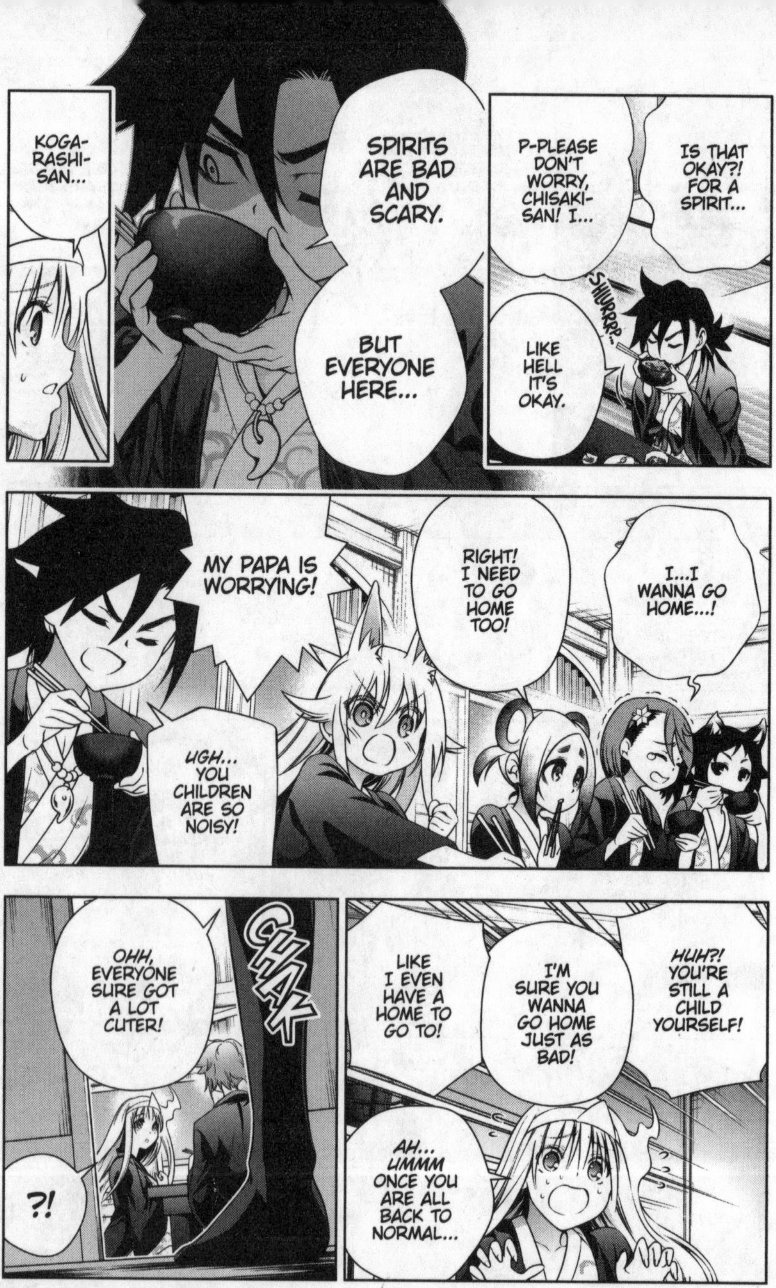
IS THAT OKAY?! FOR A SPIRIT...
SHURRP...
LIKE HELL IT'S OKAY.
P-PLEASE DON'T WORRY, CHISAKI-SAN! I...
SPIRITS ARE BAD AND SCARY.
BUT EVERYONE HERE...
KOGA-RASHI-SAN...
I...I WANNA GO HOME...!
RIGHT! I NEED TO GO HOME TOO!
MY PAPA IS WORRYING!
UGH... YOU CHILDREN ARE SO NOISY!
HUH?! YOU'RE STILL A CHILD YOURSELF!
I'M SURE YOU WANNA GO HOME JUST AS BAD!
LIKE I EVEN HAVE A HOME TO GO TO!
AH... UMMM ONCE YOU ARE ALL BACK TO NORMAL...
CHAK
OHH, EVERYONE SURE GOT A LOT CUTER!
?!

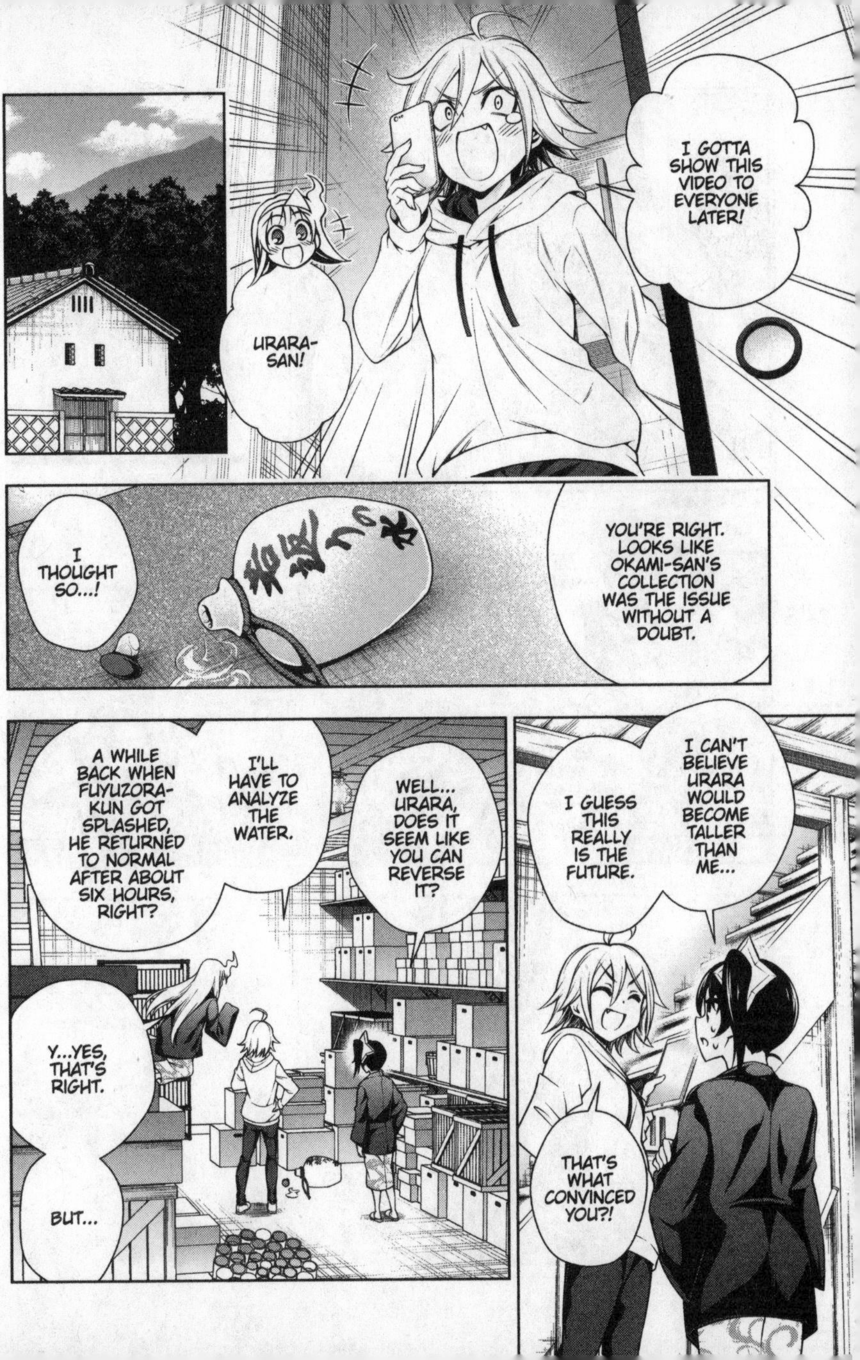
I GOTTA SHOW THIS VIDEO TO EVERYONE LATER!
URARA-SAN!
YOU'RE RIGHT. LOOKS LIKE OKAMI-SAN'S COLLECTION WAS THE ISSUE WITHOUT A DOUBT.
I THOUGHT SO...!
I CAN'T BELIEVE URARA WOULD BECOME TALLER THAN ME...
I GUESS THIS REALLY IS THE FUTURE.
THAT'S WHAT CONVINCED YOU?!
WELL... URARA, DOES IT SEEM LIKE YOU CAN REVERSE IT?
I'LL HAVE TO ANALYZE THE WATER.
A WHILE BACK WHEN FUYUZORA-KUN GOT SPLASHED, HE RETURNED TO NORMAL AFTER ABOUT SIX HOURS, RIGHT?
Y...YES, THAT'S RIGHT.
BUT...

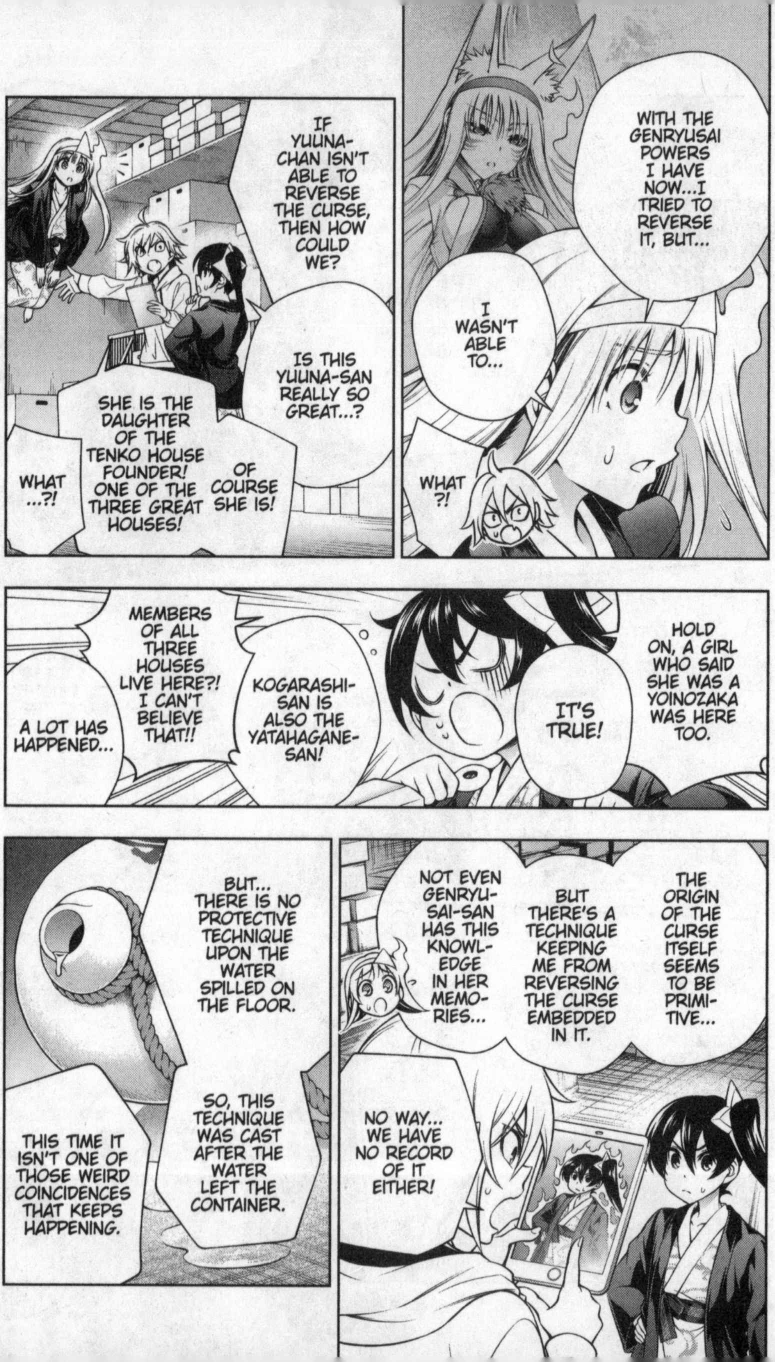
WITH THE GENRYUSAI POWERS I HAVE NOW...I TRIED TO REVERSE IT, BUT...
I WASN'T ABLE TO...
WHAT ?!
IF YUUNA-CHAN ISN'T ABLE TO REVERSE THE CURSE, THEN HOW COULD WE?
IS THIS YUUNA-SAN REALLY SO GREAT...?
OF COURSE SHE IS!
SHE IS THE DAUGHTER OF THE TENKO HOUSE FOUNDER! ONE OF THE THREE GREAT HOUSES!
WHAT ...?!
HOLD ON, A GIRL WHO SAID SHE WAS A YOINOZAKA WAS HERE TOO.
IT'S TRUE!
KOGARASHI-SAN IS ALSO THE YATAHAGANE-SAN!
MEMBERS OF ALL THREE HOUSES LIVE HERE?! I CAN'T BELIEVE THAT!!
A LOT HAS HAPPENED...
THE ORIGIN OF THE CURSE ITSELF SEEMS TO BE PRIMI-TIVE...
BUT THERE'S A TECHNIQUE KEEPING ME FROM REVERSING THE CURSE EMBEDDED IN IT.
NOT EVEN GENRYU-SAI-SAN HAS THIS KNOWL-EDGE IN HER MEMO-RIES...
NO WAY... WE HAVE NO RECORD OF IT EITHER!
BUT... THERE IS NO PROTECTIVE TECHNIQUE UPON THE WATER SPILLED ON THE FLOOR.
SO, THIS TECHNIQUE WAS CAST AFTER THE WATER LEFT THE CONTAINER.
THIS TIME IT ISN'T ONE OF THOSE WEIRD COINCIDENCES THAT KEEPS HAPPENING.

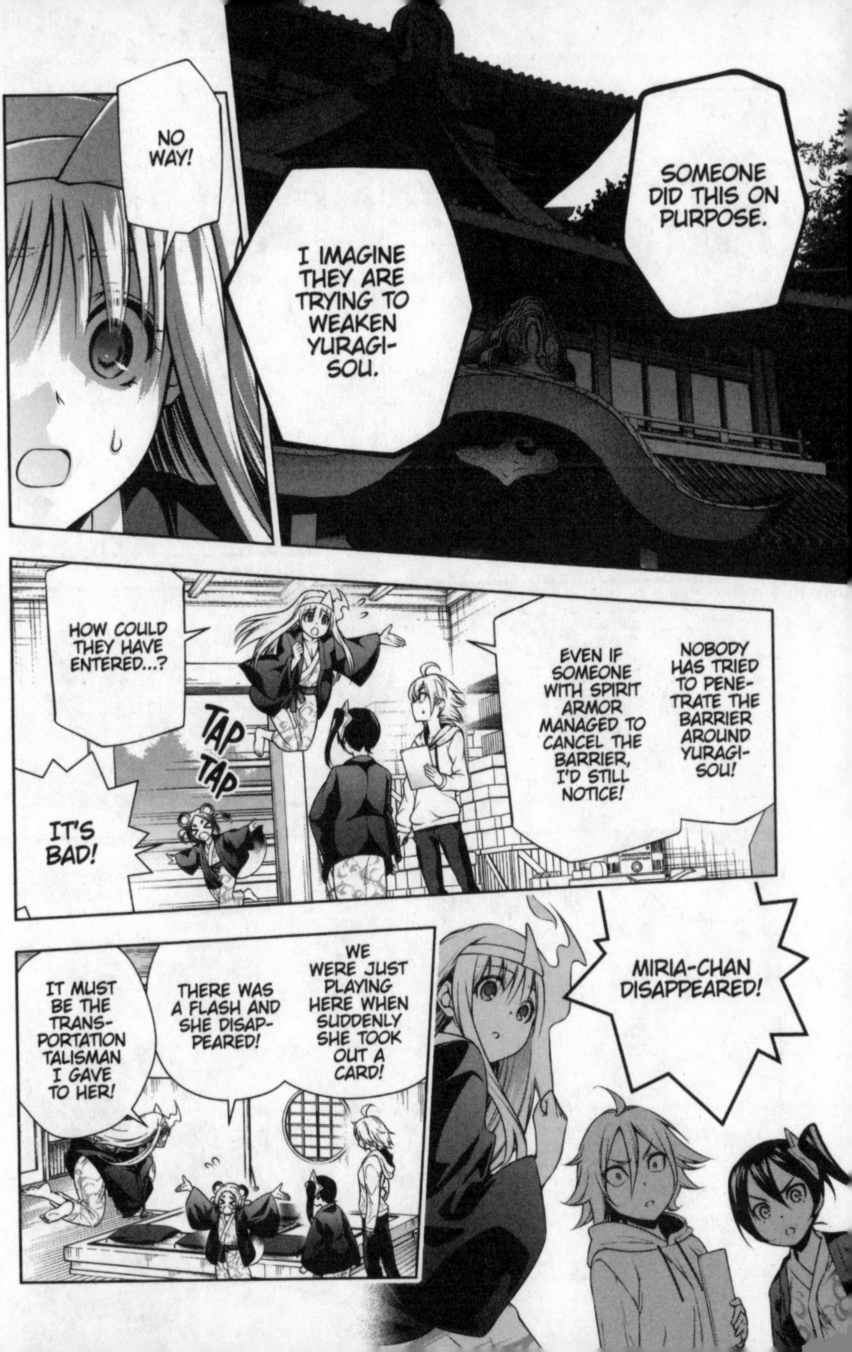
SOMEONE DID THIS ON PURPOSE.
I IMAGINE THEY ARE TRYING TO WEAKEN YURAGI-SOU.
NO WAY!
NOBODY HAS TRIED TO PENE-TRATE THE BARRIER AROUND YURAGI-SOU!
EVEN IF SOMEONE WITH SPIRIT ARMOR MANAGED TO CANCEL THE BARRIER, I'D STILL NOTICE!
HOW COULD THEY HAVE ENTERED...?
TAP TAP
IT'S BAD!
MIRIA-CHAN DISAPPEARED!
WE WERE JUST PLAYING HERE WHEN SUDDENLY SHE TOOK OUT A CARD!
THERE WAS A FLASH AND SHE DISAP-PEARED!
IT MUST BE THE TRANS-PORTATION TALISMAN I GAVE TO HER!

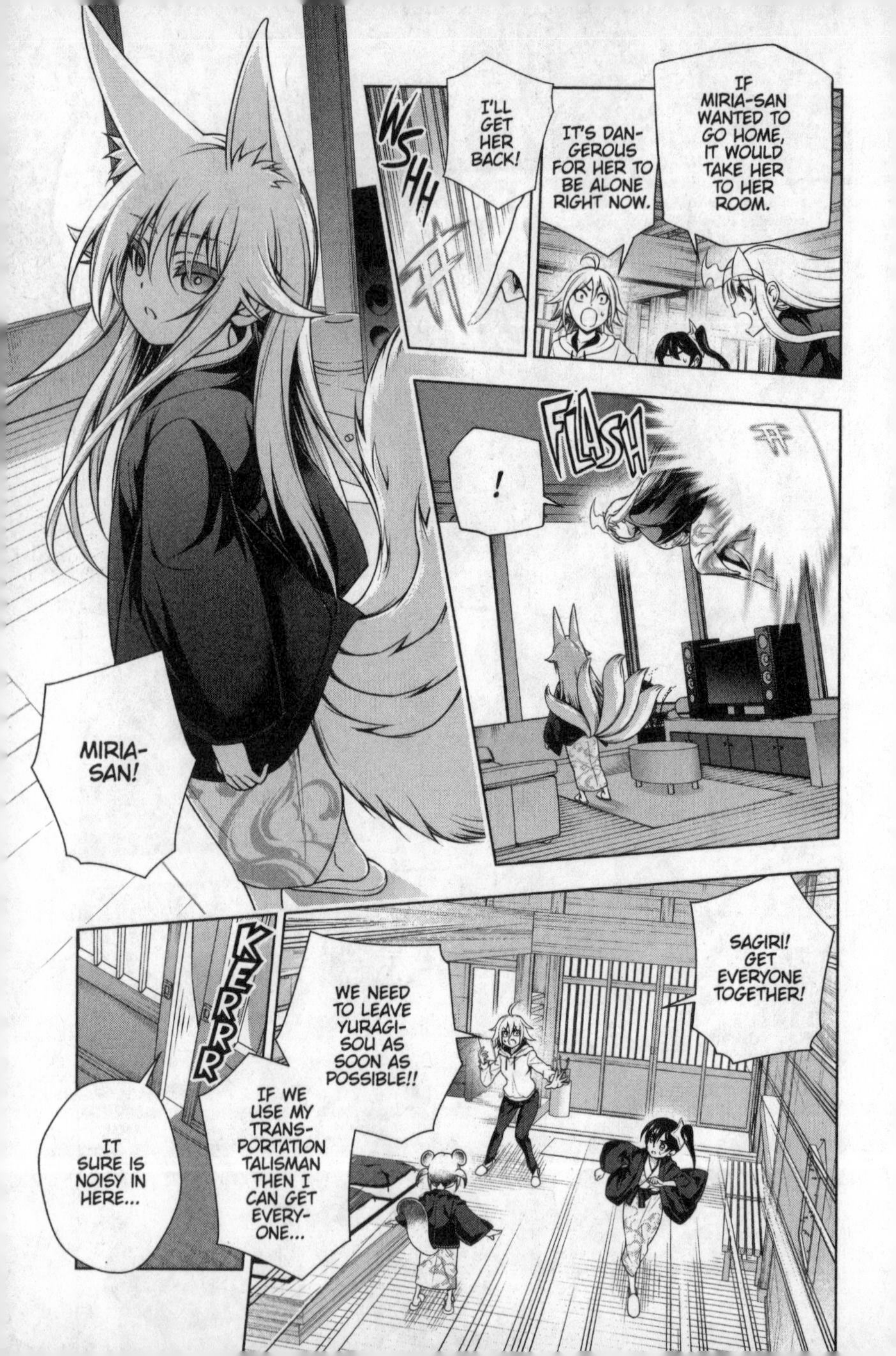
IF MIRIA-SAN WANTED TO GO HOME, IT WOULD TAKE HER TO HER ROOM.
IT'S DAN-GEROUS FOR HER TO BE ALONE RIGHT NOW.
WSHH
I'LL GET HER BACK!
FLASH
!
MIRIA-SAN!
SAGIRI! GET EVERYONE TOGETHER!
WE NEED TO LEAVE YURAGI-SOU AS SOON AS POSSIBLE!!
IF WE USE MY TRANS-PORTATION TALISMAN THEN I CAN GET EVERY-ONE...
KERRRR
IT SURE IS NOISY IN HERE...

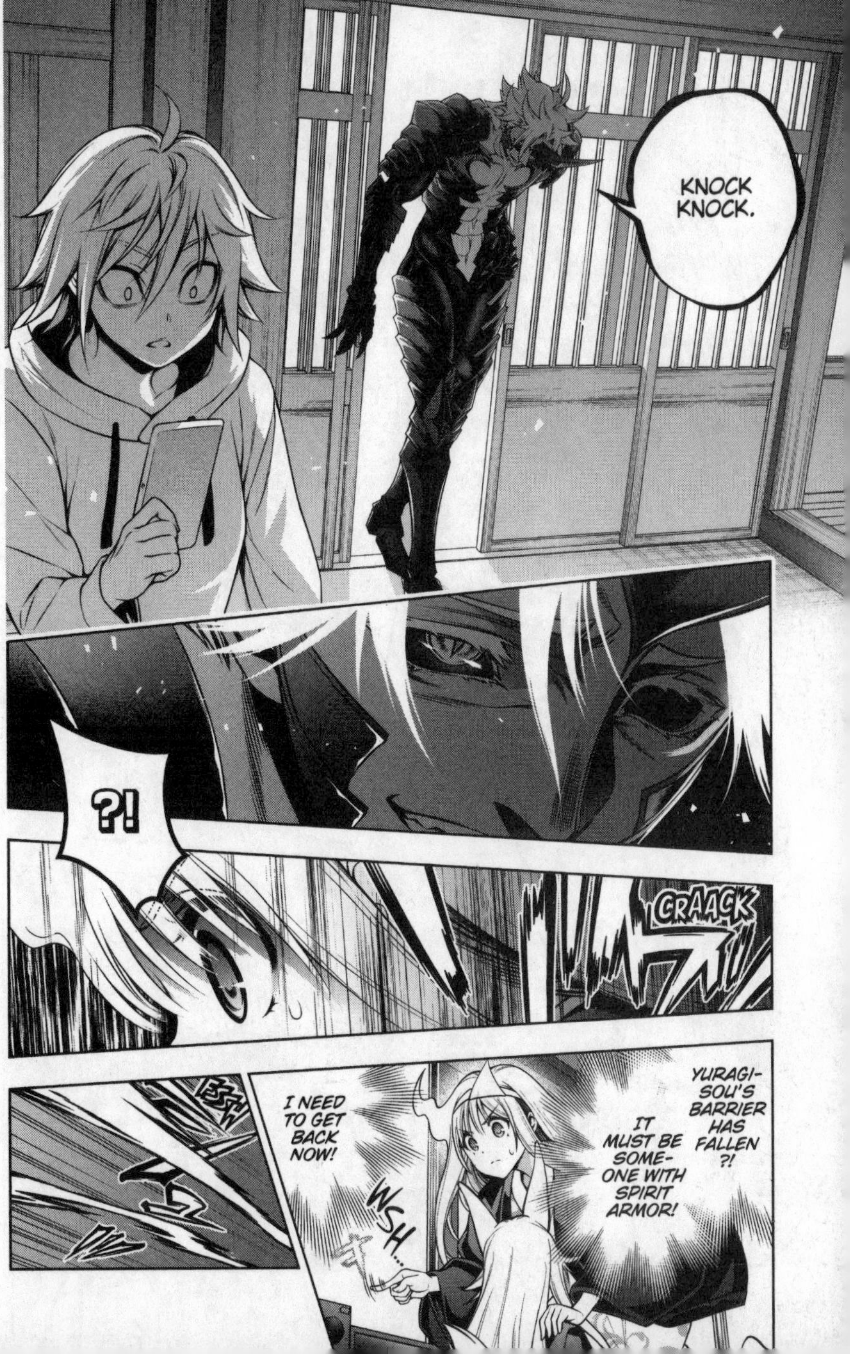
KNOCK KNOCK.
?!
CRAACK
YURAGI-SOU'S BARRIER HAS FALLEN ?!
IT MUST BE SOME-ONE WITH SPIRIT ARMOR!
I NEED TO GET BACK NOW!
WSH...

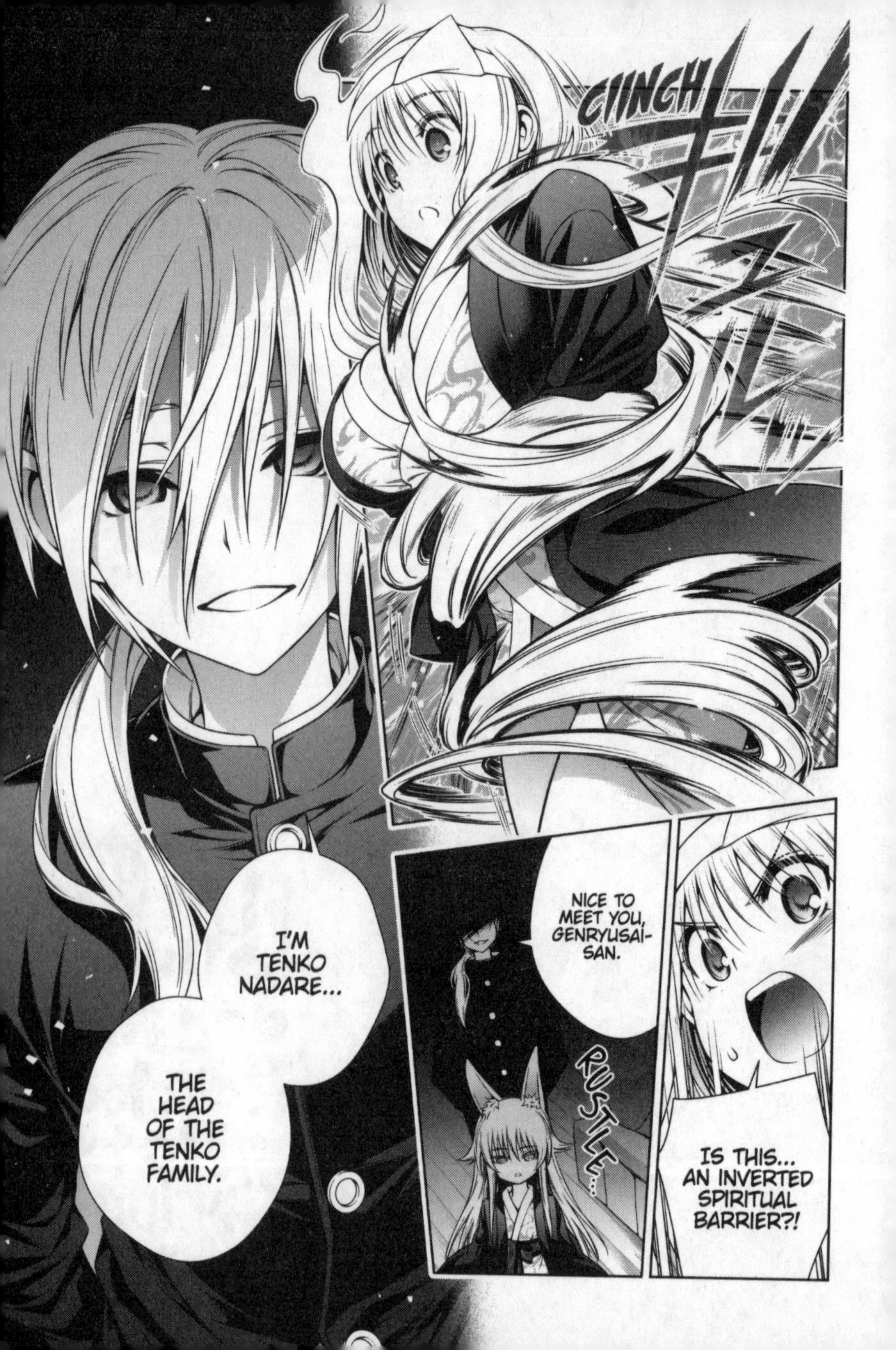
CIINCH
IS THIS... AN INVERTED SPIRITUAL BARRIER?!
RUSTLE...
NICE TO MEET YOU, GENRYUSAI-SAN.
I'M TENKO NADARE...
THE HEAD OF THE TENKO FAMILY.

Yuuna and the Haunted Hot Springs

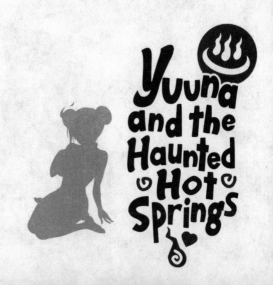

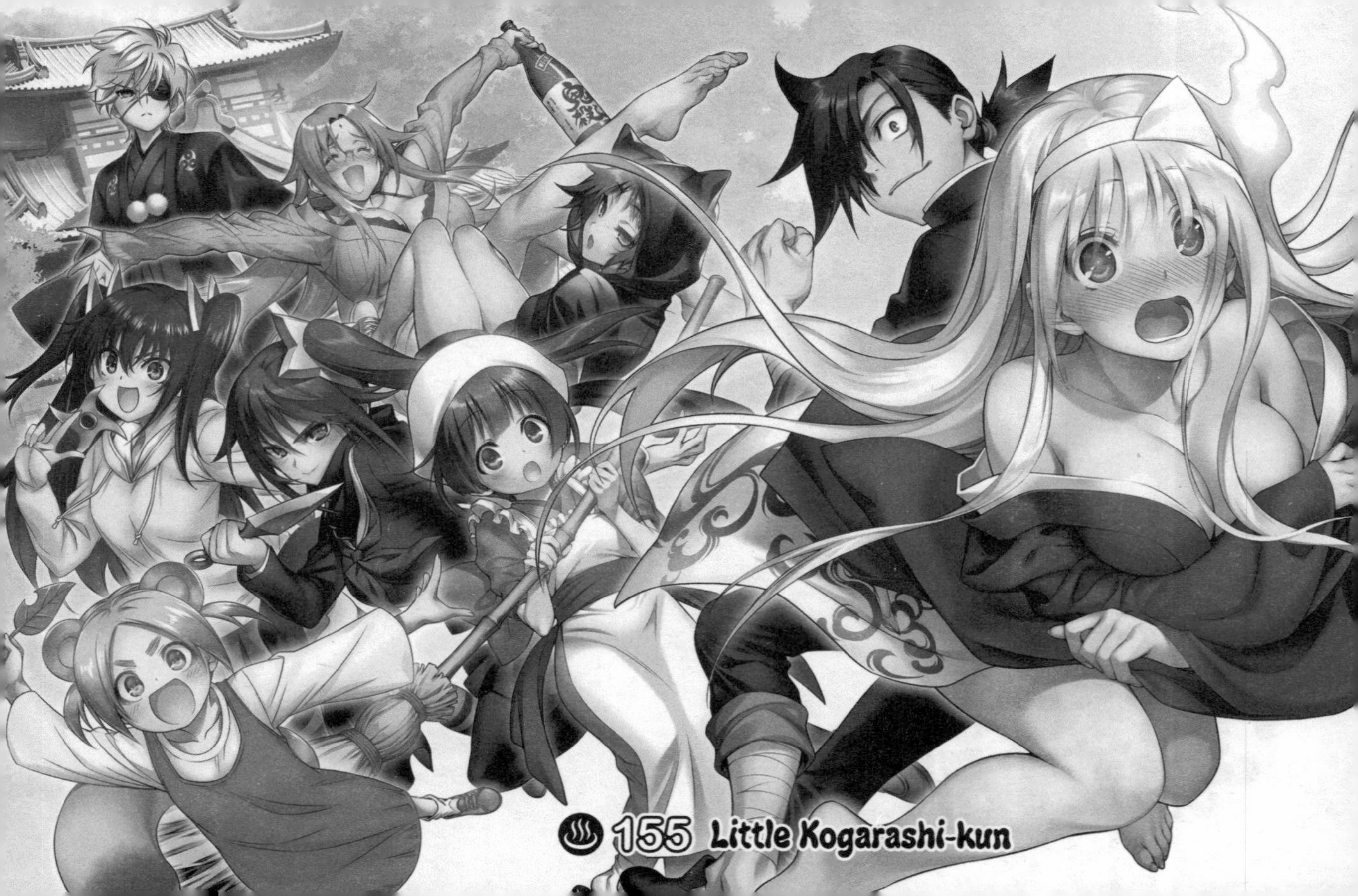
155 Little Kogarashi-kun

Yuuna and the Haunted Hot Springs

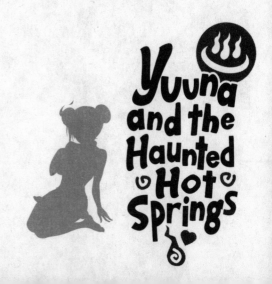

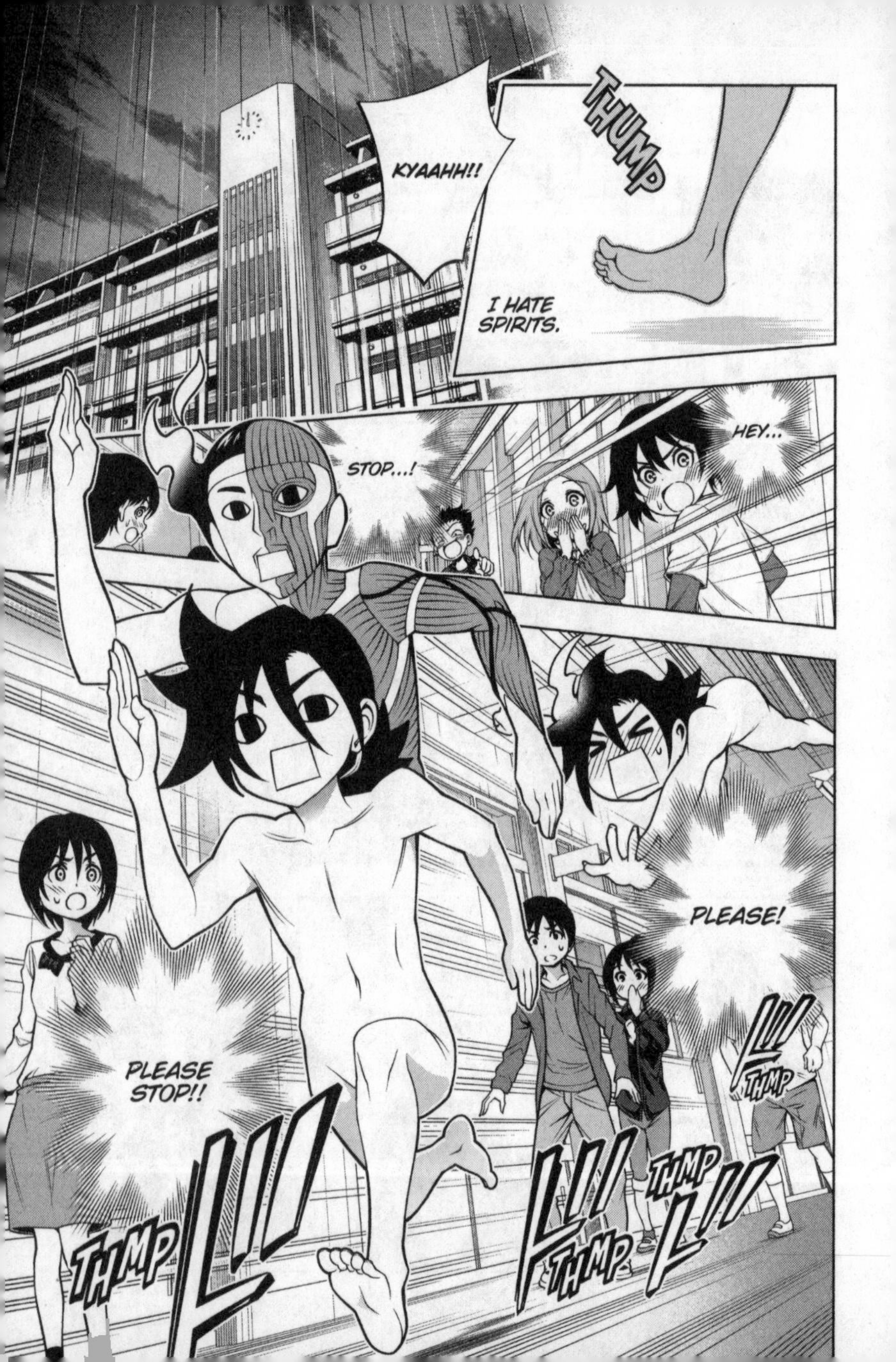
THUMP
I HATE SPIRITS.
KYAAHH!!
HEY...
STOP...!
PLEASE!
THMP
THMP
THMP
PLEASE STOP!!
THMP

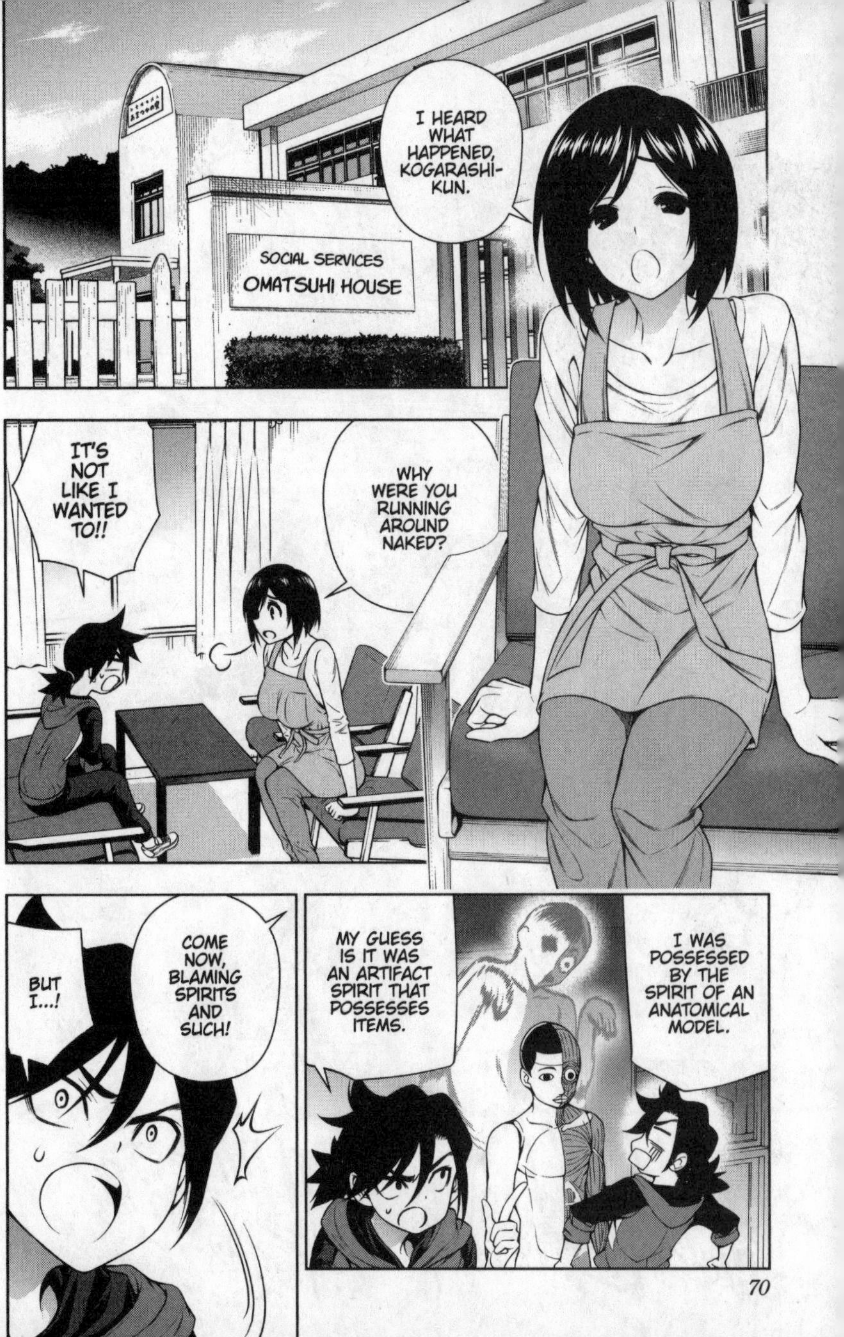
SOCIAL SERVICES
OMATSUHI HOUSE
I HEARD WHAT HAPPENED, KOGARASHI-KUN.
WHY WERE YOU RUNNING AROUND NAKED?
IT'S NOT LIKE I WANTED TO!!
I WAS POSSESSED BY THE SPIRIT OF AN ANATOMICAL MODEL.
MY GUESS IS IT WAS AN ARTIFACT SPIRIT THAT POSSESSES ITEMS.
COME NOW, BLAMING SPIRITS AND SUCH!
BUT I...!

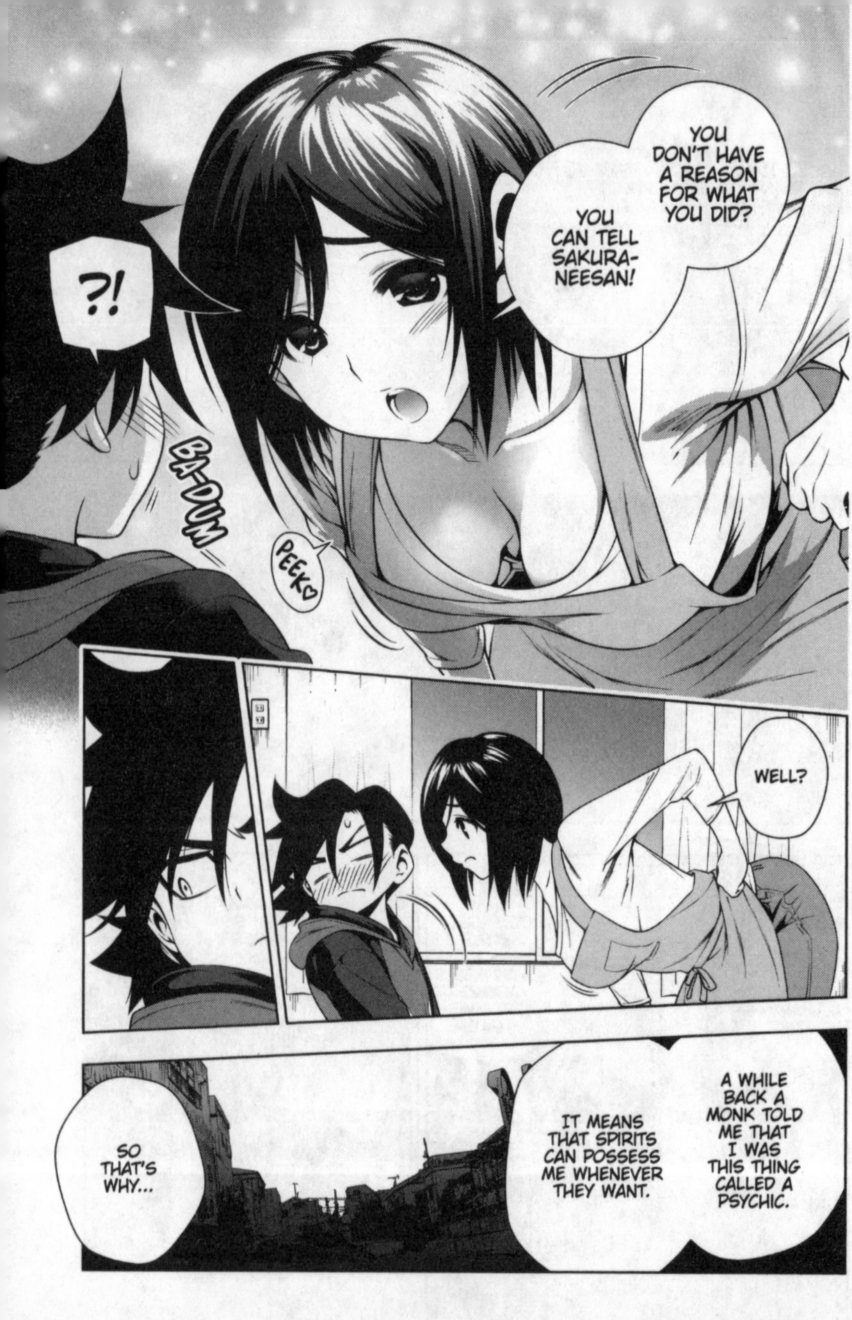
YOU DON'T HAVE A REASON FOR WHAT YOU DID?
YOU CAN TELL SAKURA-NEESAN!
?!
BA-DUM
PEEK♡
WELL?
A WHILE BACK A MONK TOLD ME THAT I WAS THIS THING CALLED A PSYCHIC.
IT MEANS THAT SPIRITS CAN POSSESS ME WHENEVER THEY WANT.
SO THAT'S WHY...

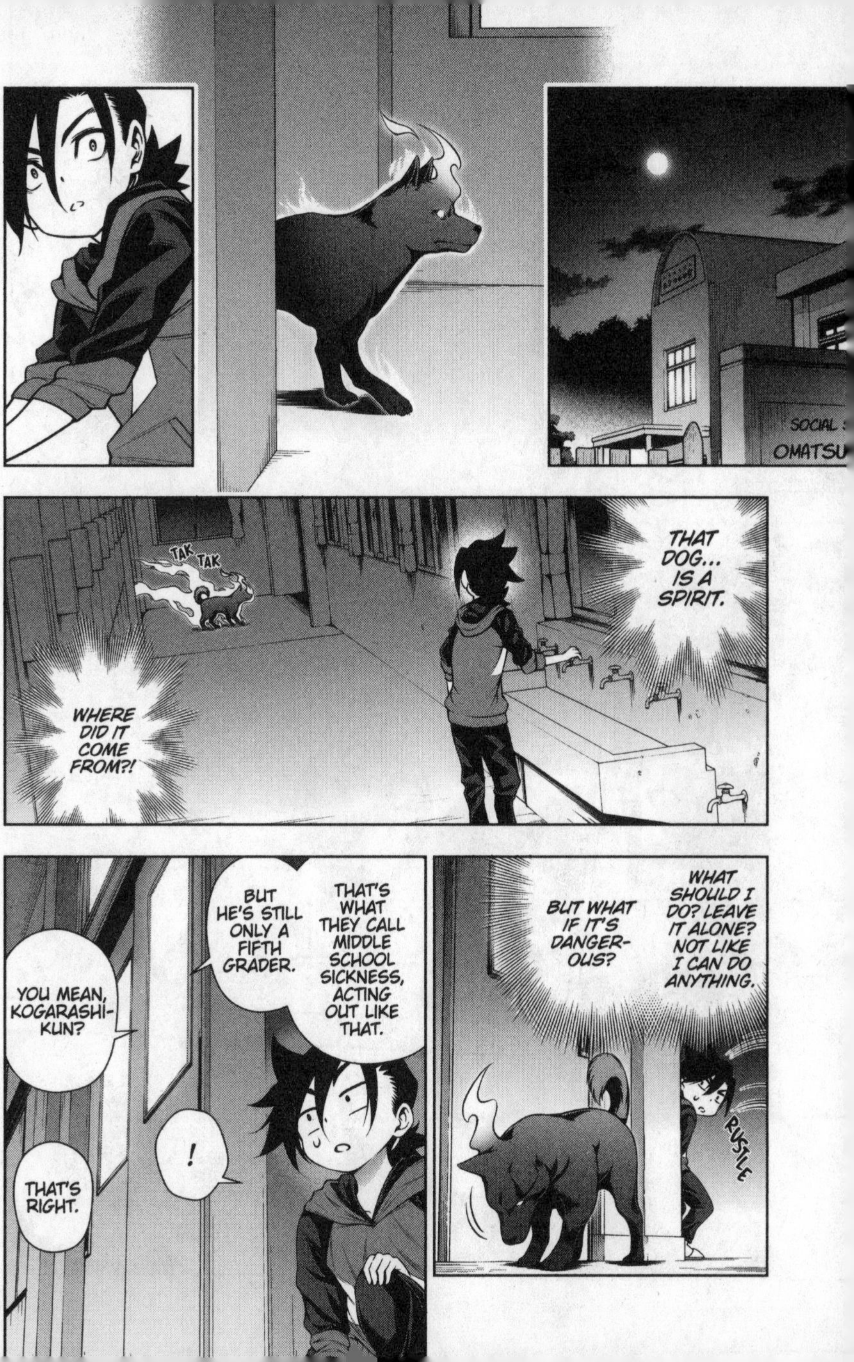
SOCIAL :
OMATSU
THAT DOG... IS A SPIRIT.
TAK TAK
WHERE DID IT COME FROM?!
WHAT SHOULD I DO? LEAVE IT ALONE? NOT LIKE I CAN DO ANYTHING.
BUT WHAT IF IT'S DANGER-OUS?
RUSTLE
THAT'S WHAT THEY CALL MIDDLE SCHOOL SICKNESS, ACTING OUT LIKE THAT.
BUT HE'S STILL ONLY A FIFTH GRADER.
YOU MEAN, KOGARASHI-KUN?
!
THAT'S RIGHT.

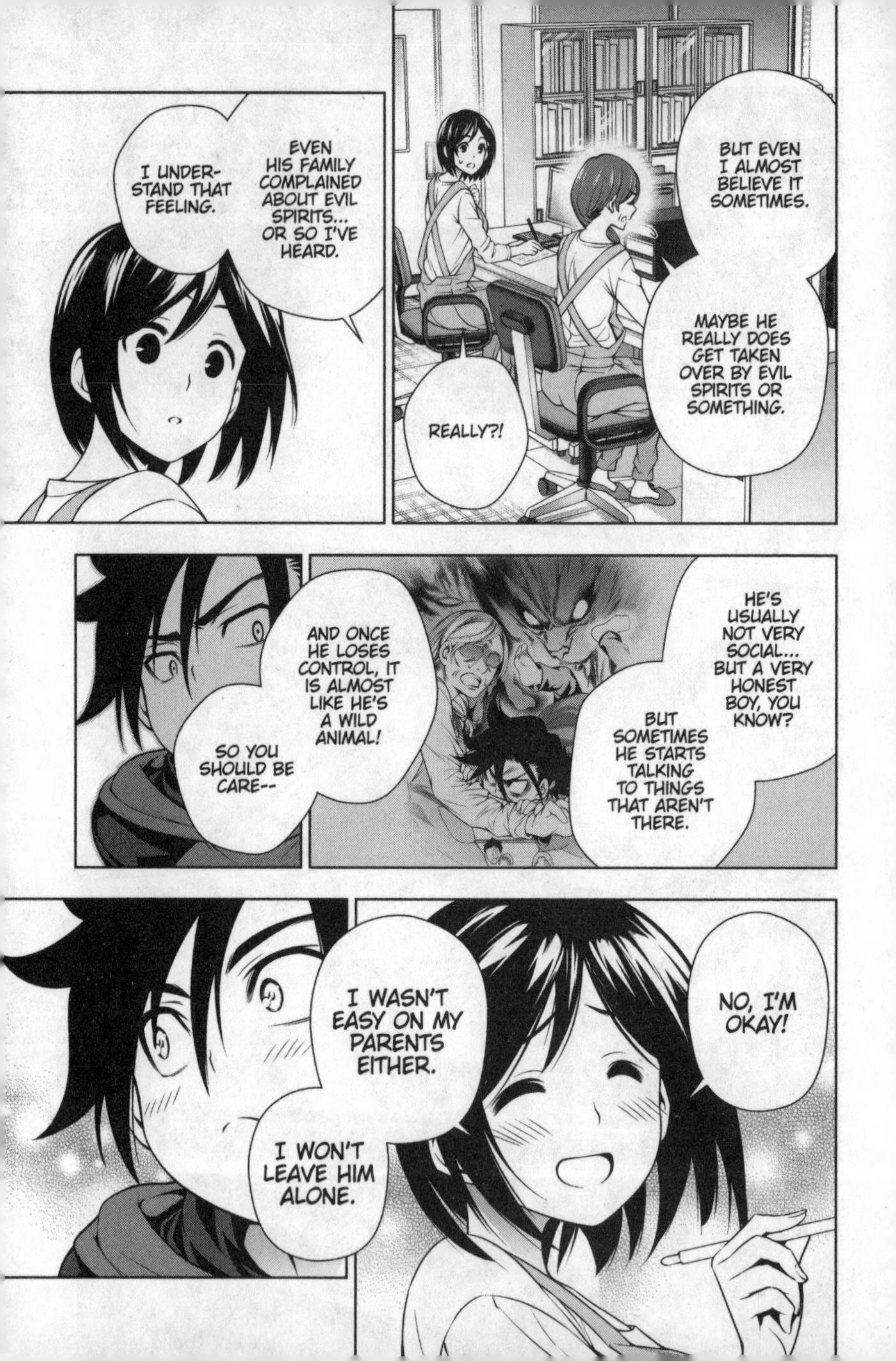
BUT EVEN I ALMOST BELIEVE IT SOMETIMES.
MAYBE HE REALLY DOES GET TAKEN OVER BY EVIL SPIRITS OR SOMETHING.
REALLY?!
EVEN HIS FAMILY COMPLAINED ABOUT EVIL SPIRITS... OR SO I'VE HEARD.
I UNDER-STAND THAT FEELING.
HE'S USUALLY NOT VERY SOCIAL... BUT A VERY HONEST BOY, YOU KNOW?
BUT SOMETIMES HE STARTS TALKING TO THINGS THAT AREN'T THERE.
AND ONCE HE LOSES CONTROL, IT IS ALMOST LIKE HE'S A WILD ANIMAL!
SO YOU SHOULD BE CARE--
NO, I'M OKAY!
I WASN'T EASY ON MY PARENTS EITHER.
I WON'T LEAVE HIM ALONE.

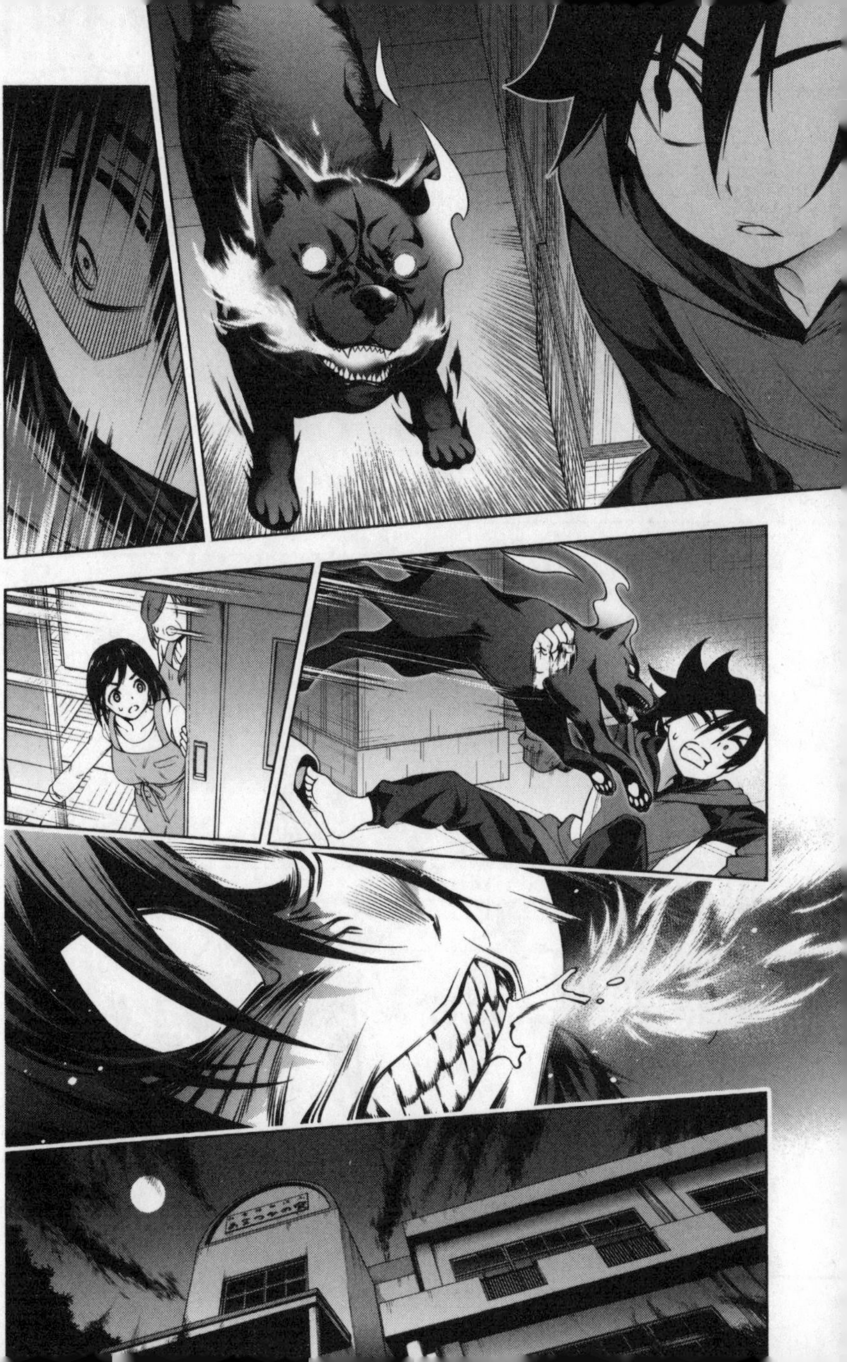

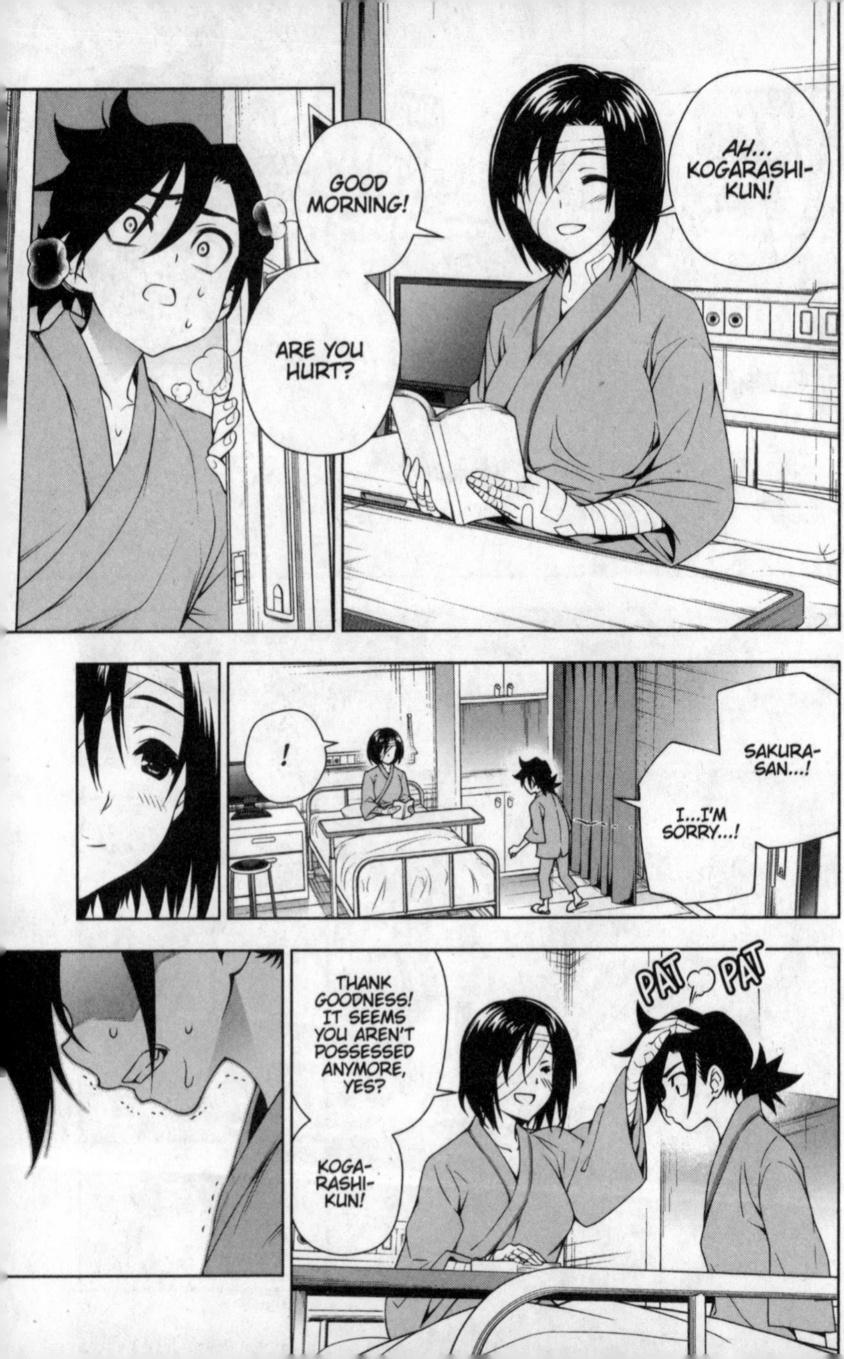
AH... KOGARASHI-KUN!
GOOD MORNING!
ARE YOU HURT?
SAKURA-SAN...!
I...I'M SORRY...!
!
PAT PAT
THANK GOODNESS! IT SEEMS YOU AREN'T POSSESSED ANYMORE, YES?
KOGA-RASHI-KUN!

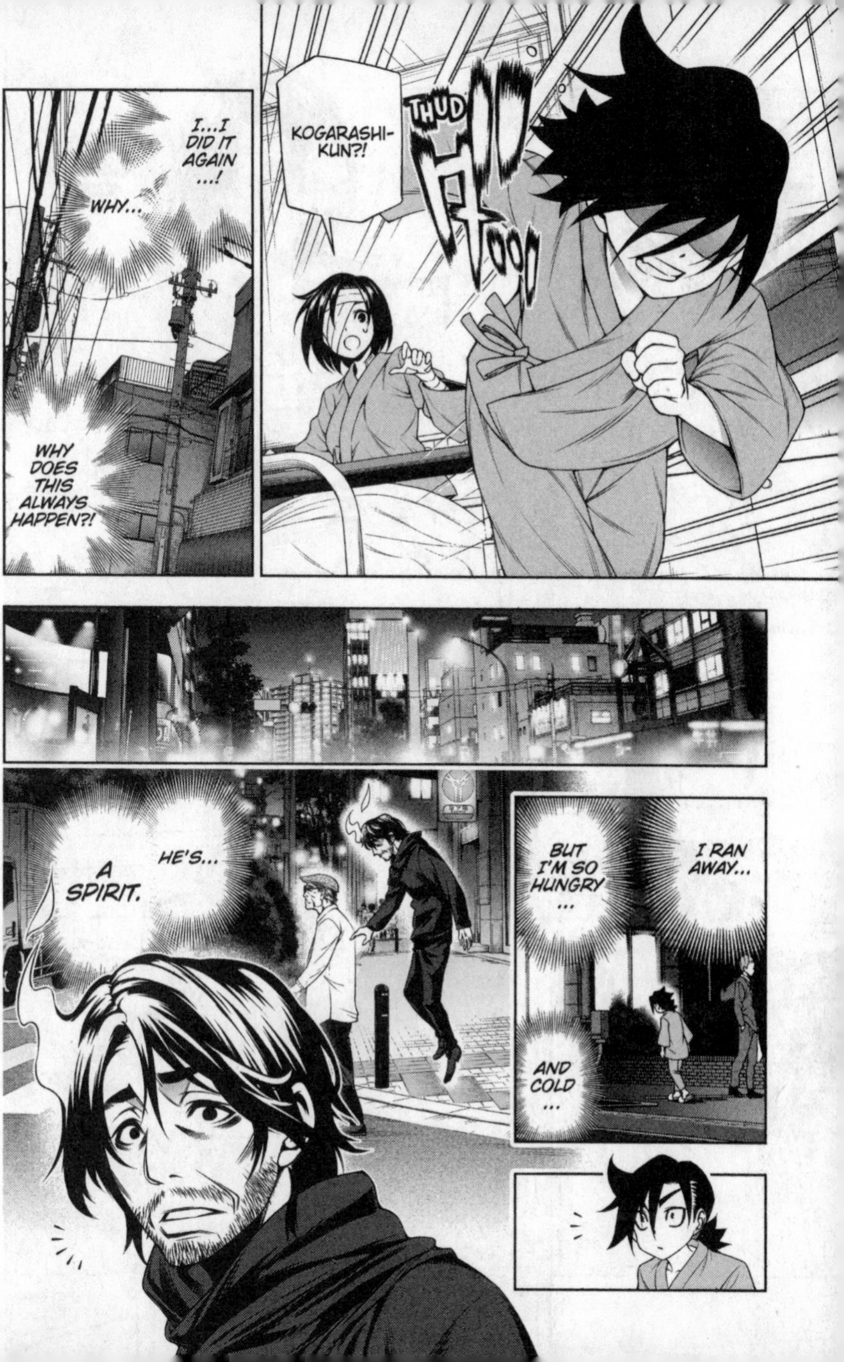
THUD
KOGARASHI-KUN?!
I...I DID IT AGAIN ...!
WHY...
WHY DOES THIS ALWAYS HAPPEN?!
I RAN AWAY...
BUT I'M SO HUNGRY ...
AND COLD ...
HE'S...
A SPIRIT.

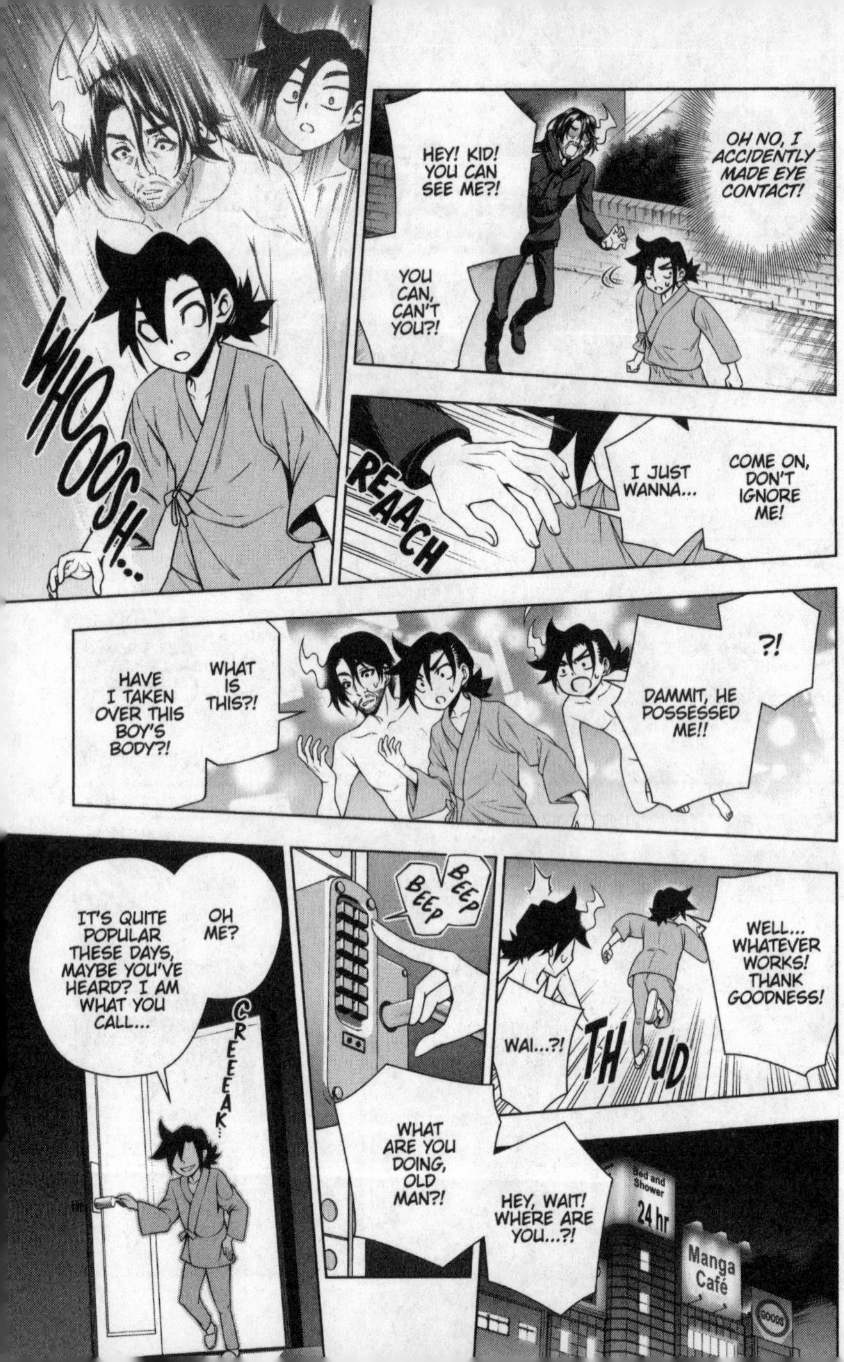
OH NO, I ACCIDENTLY MADE EYE CONTACT!
HEY! KID! YOU CAN SEE ME?!
YOU CAN, CAN'T YOU?!
COME ON, DON'T IGNORE ME!
I JUST WANNA...
REAACH
WHOOOSH...
?!
DAMMIT, HE POSSESSED ME!!
WHAT IS THIS?!
HAVE I TAKEN OVER THIS BOY'S BODY?!
WELL... WHATEVER WORKS! THANK GOODNESS!
THUD
WAI...?!
BEEP BEEP
WHAT ARE YOU DOING, OLD MAN?!
Bed and Shower
24 hr
Manga Café
HEY, WAIT! WHERE ARE YOU...?!
OH ME?
IT'S QUITE POPULAR THESE DAYS, MAYBE YOU'VE HEARD? I AM WHAT YOU CALL...
CREEEAK...

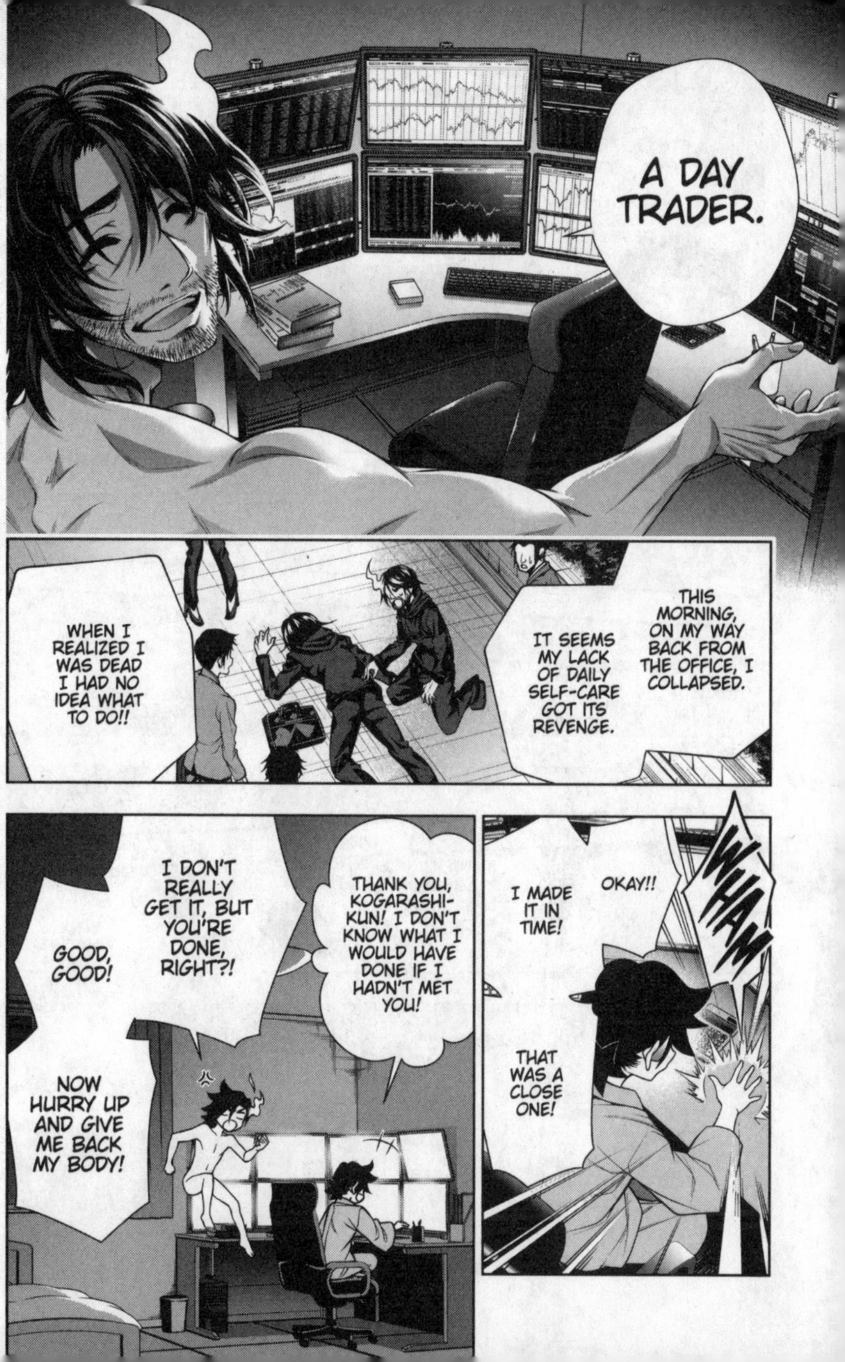
A DAY TRADER.
THIS MORNING, ON MY WAY BACK FROM THE OFFICE, I COLLAPSED.
IT SEEMS MY LACK OF DAILY SELF-CARE GOT ITS REVENGE.
WHEN I REALIZED I WAS DEAD I HAD NO IDEA WHAT TO DO!!
WHAM
OKAY!!
I MADE IT IN TIME!
THAT WAS A CLOSE ONE!
THANK YOU, KOGARASHI-KUN! I DON'T KNOW WHAT I WOULD HAVE DONE IF I HADN'T MET YOU!
I DON'T REALLY GET IT, BUT YOU'RE DONE, RIGHT?!
GOOD, GOOD!
NOW HURRY UP AND GIVE ME BACK MY BODY!

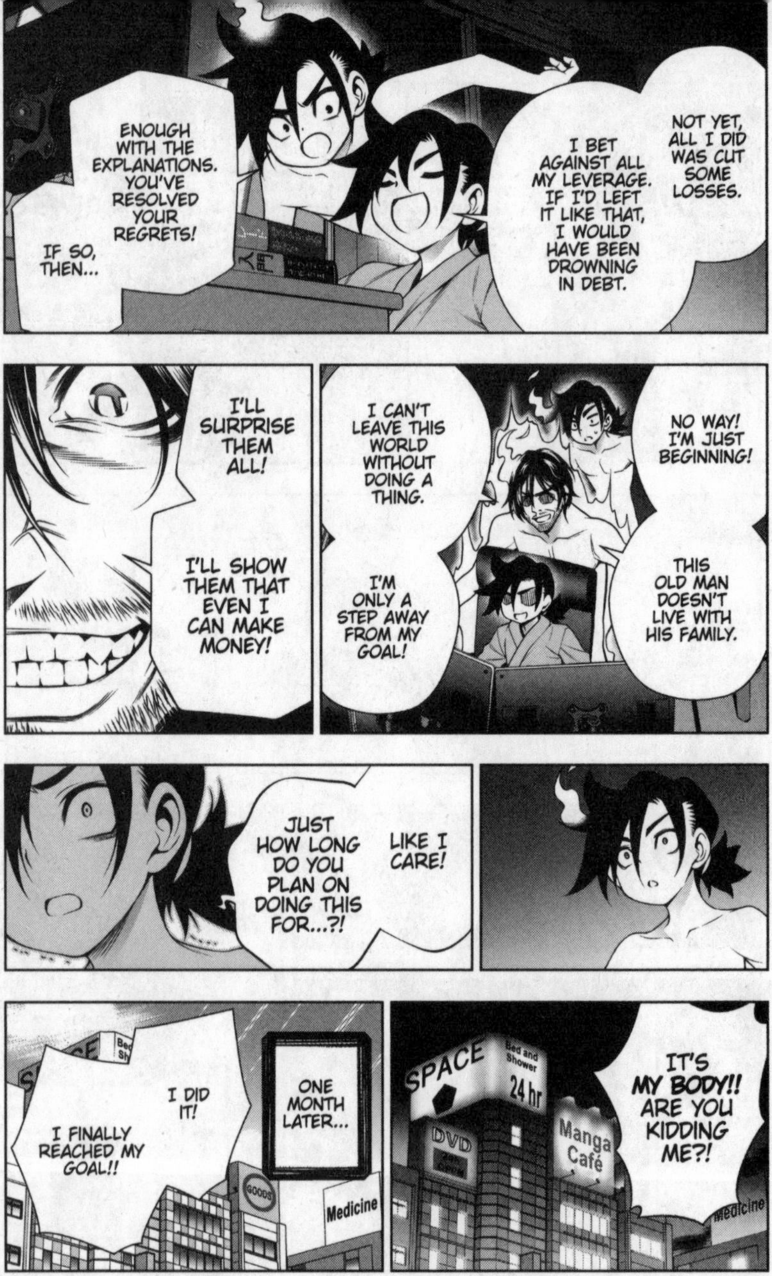
NOT YET, ALL I DID WAS CUT SOME LOSSES.
I BET AGAINST ALL MY LEVERAGE. IF I'D LEFT IT LIKE THAT, I WOULD HAVE BEEN DROWNING IN DEBT.
ENOUGH WITH THE EXPLANATIONS. YOU'VE RESOLVED YOUR REGRETS!
IF SO, THEN...
NO WAY! I'M JUST BEGINNING!
THIS OLD MAN DOESN'T LIVE WITH HIS FAMILY.
I CAN'T LEAVE THIS WORLD WITHOUT DOING A THING.
I'M ONLY A STEP AWAY FROM MY GOAL!
I'LL SURPRISE THEM ALL!
I'LL SHOW THEM THAT EVEN I CAN MAKE MONEY!
LIKE I CARE!
JUST HOW LONG DO YOU PLAN ON DOING THIS FOR...?!
IT'S MY BODY!! ARE YOU KIDDING ME?!
SPACE
Bed and Shower
24 hr
DVD
Manga Café
Medicine
ONE MONTH LATER...
I DID IT!
I FINALLY REACHED MY GOAL!!
GOODS
Medicine

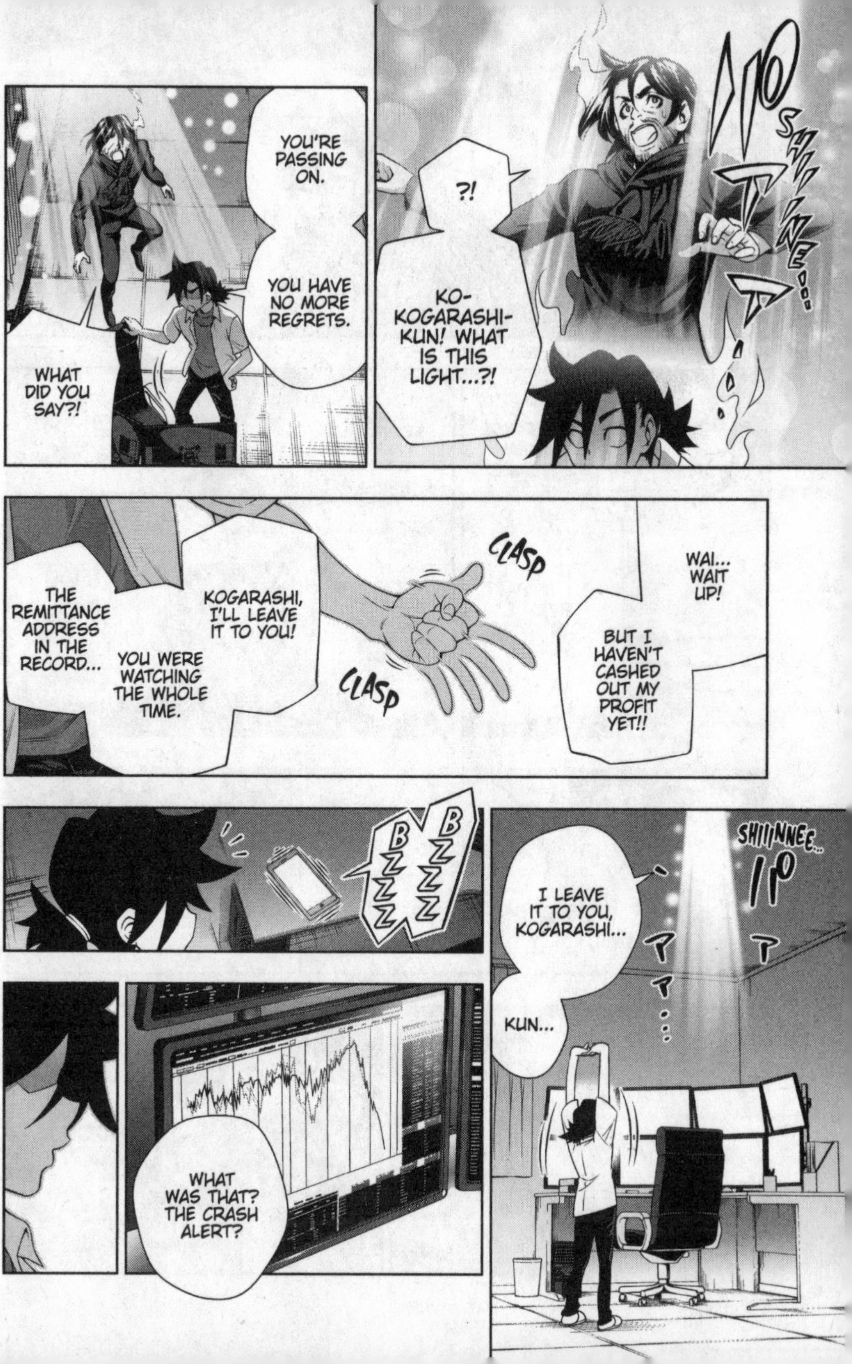
SHIIINE...
?!
KO-KOGARASHI-KUN! WHAT IS THIS LIGHT...?!
YOU'RE PASSING ON.
YOU HAVE NO MORE REGRETS.
WHAT DID YOU SAY?!
WAI... WAIT UP!
BUT I HAVEN'T CASHED OUT MY PROFIT YET!!
CLASP
CLASP
KOGARASHI, I'LL LEAVE IT TO YOU!
YOU WERE WATCHING THE WHOLE TIME.
THE REMITTANCE ADDRESS IN THE RECORD...
SHIIINNEE...
I LEAVE IT TO YOU, KOGARASHI...
KUN...
BZZZ
BZZZ
WHAT WAS THAT? THE CRASH ALERT?

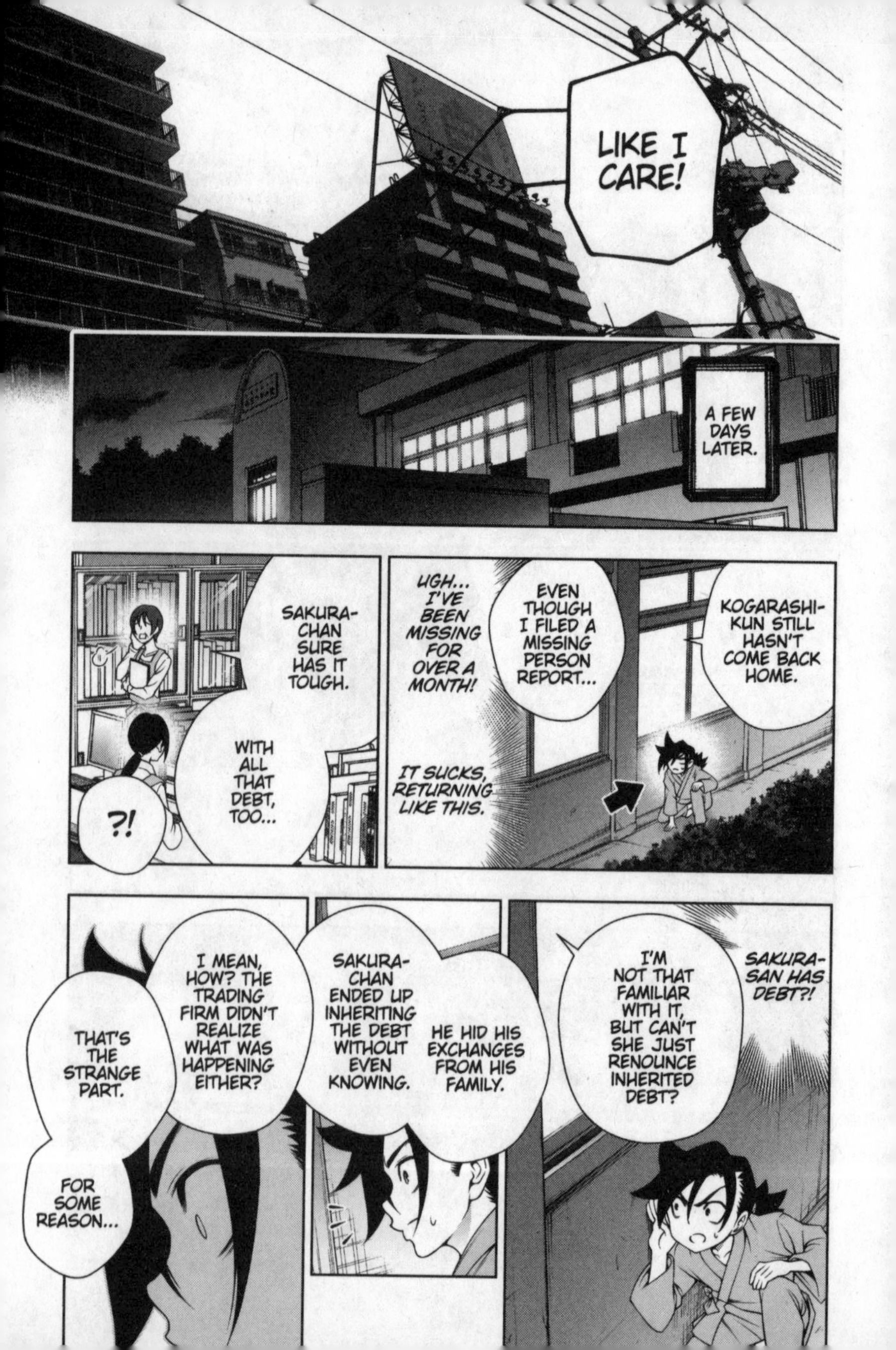

LIKE I CARE!
A FEW DAYS LATER.
KOGARASHI-KUN STILL HASN'T COME BACK HOME.
EVEN THOUGH I FILED A MISSING PERSON REPORT...
UGH... I'VE BEEN MISSING FOR OVER A MONTH!
IT SUCKS, RETURNING LIKE THIS.
SAKURA-CHAN SURE HAS IT TOUGH.
WITH ALL THAT DEBT, TOO...
?!
SAKURA-SAN HAS DEBT?!
I'M NOT THAT FAMILIAR WITH IT, BUT CAN'T SHE JUST RENOUNCE INHERITED DEBT?
HE HID HIS EXCHANGES FROM HIS FAMILY.
SAKURA-CHAN ENDED UP INHERITING THE DEBT WITHOUT EVEN KNOWING.
I MEAN, HOW? THE TRADING FIRM DIDN'T REALIZE WHAT WAS HAPPENING EITHER?
THAT'S THE STRANGE PART.
FOR SOME REASON...

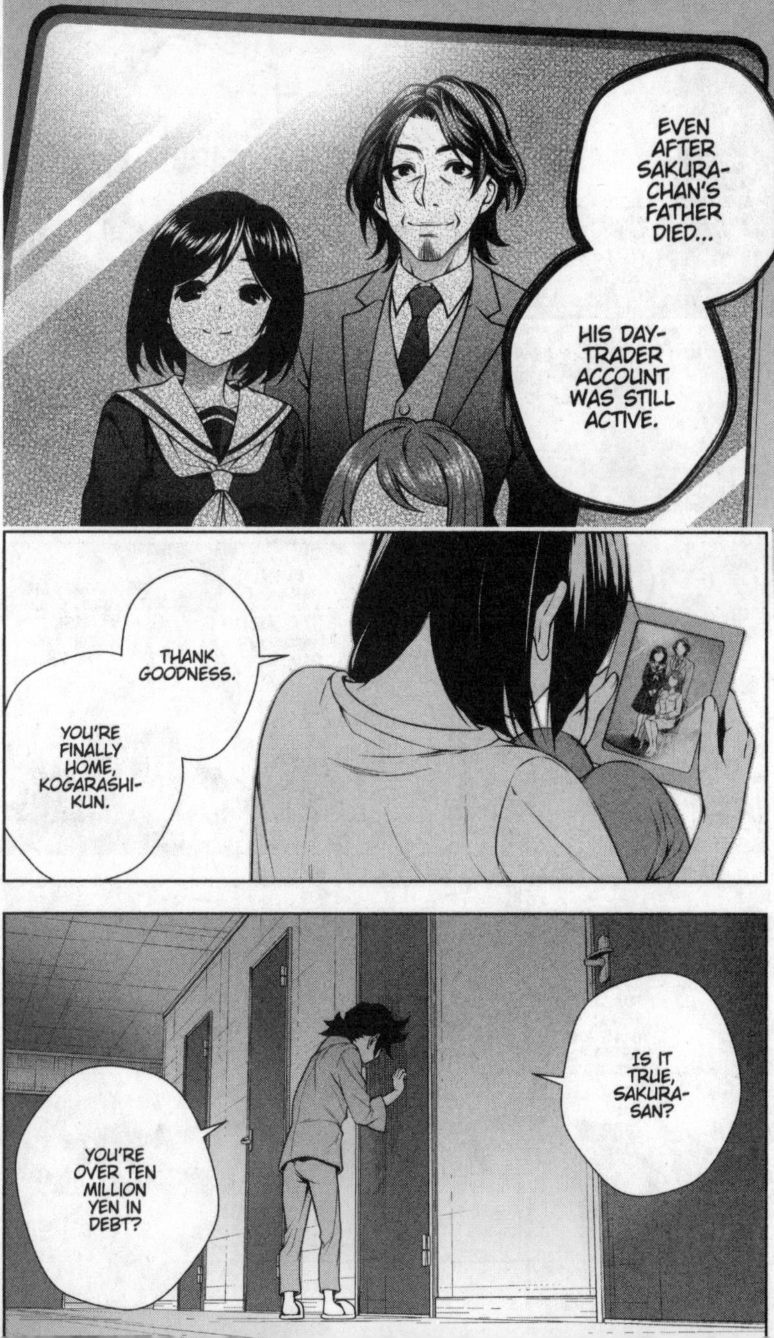
EVEN AFTER SAKURA-CHAN'S FATHER DIED...
HIS DAY-TRADER ACCOUNT WAS STILL ACTIVE.
THANK GOODNESS.
YOU'RE FINALLY HOME, KOGARASHI-KUN.
IS IT TRUE, SAKURA-SAN?
YOU'RE OVER TEN MILLION YEN IN DEBT?

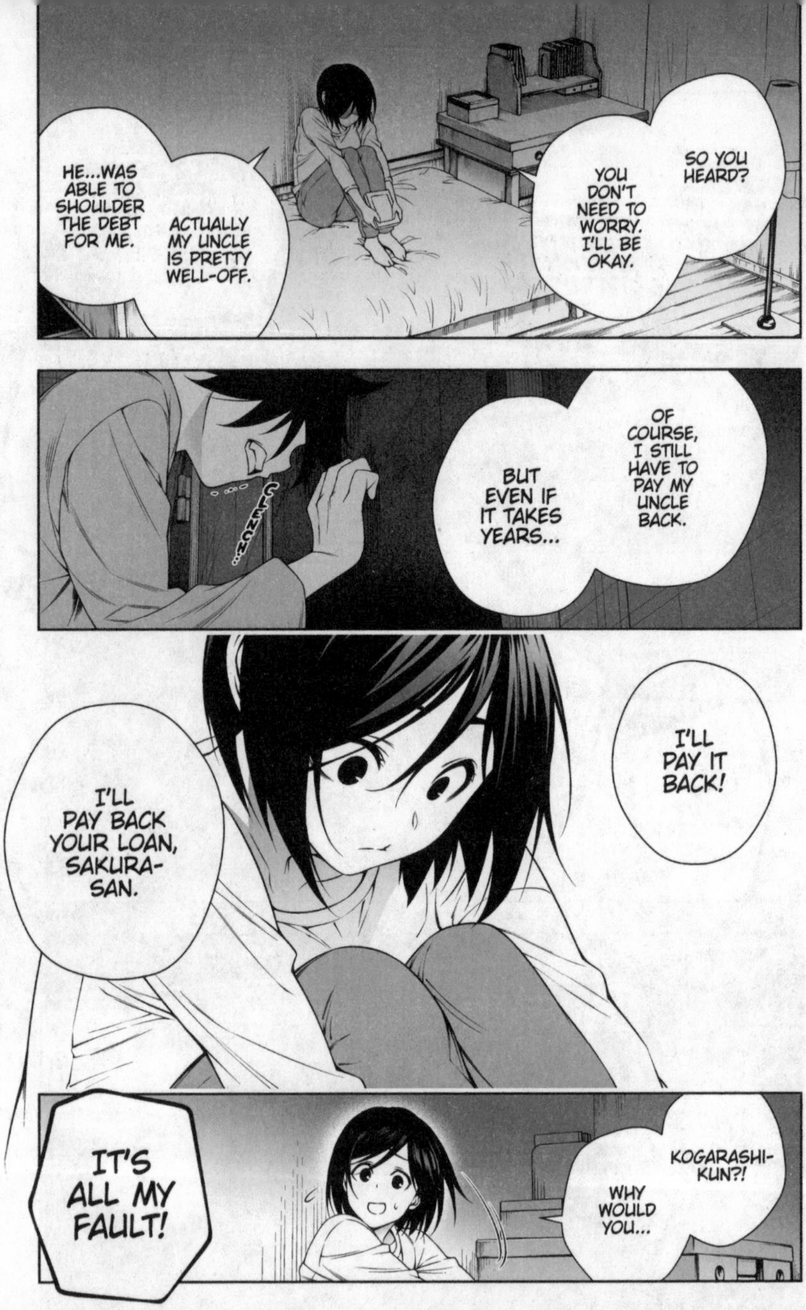
SO YOU HEARD?
YOU DON'T NEED TO WORRY. I'LL BE OKAY.
ACTUALLY MY UNCLE IS PRETTY WELL-OFF.
HE...WAS ABLE TO SHOULDER THE DEBT FOR ME.
OF COURSE, I STILL HAVE TO PAY MY UNCLE BACK.
BUT EVEN IF IT TAKES YEARS...
CLENCH...
I'LL PAY IT BACK!
I'LL PAY BACK YOUR LOAN, SAKURA-SAN.
KOGARASHI-KUN?!
WHY WOULD YOU...
IT'S ALL MY FAULT!

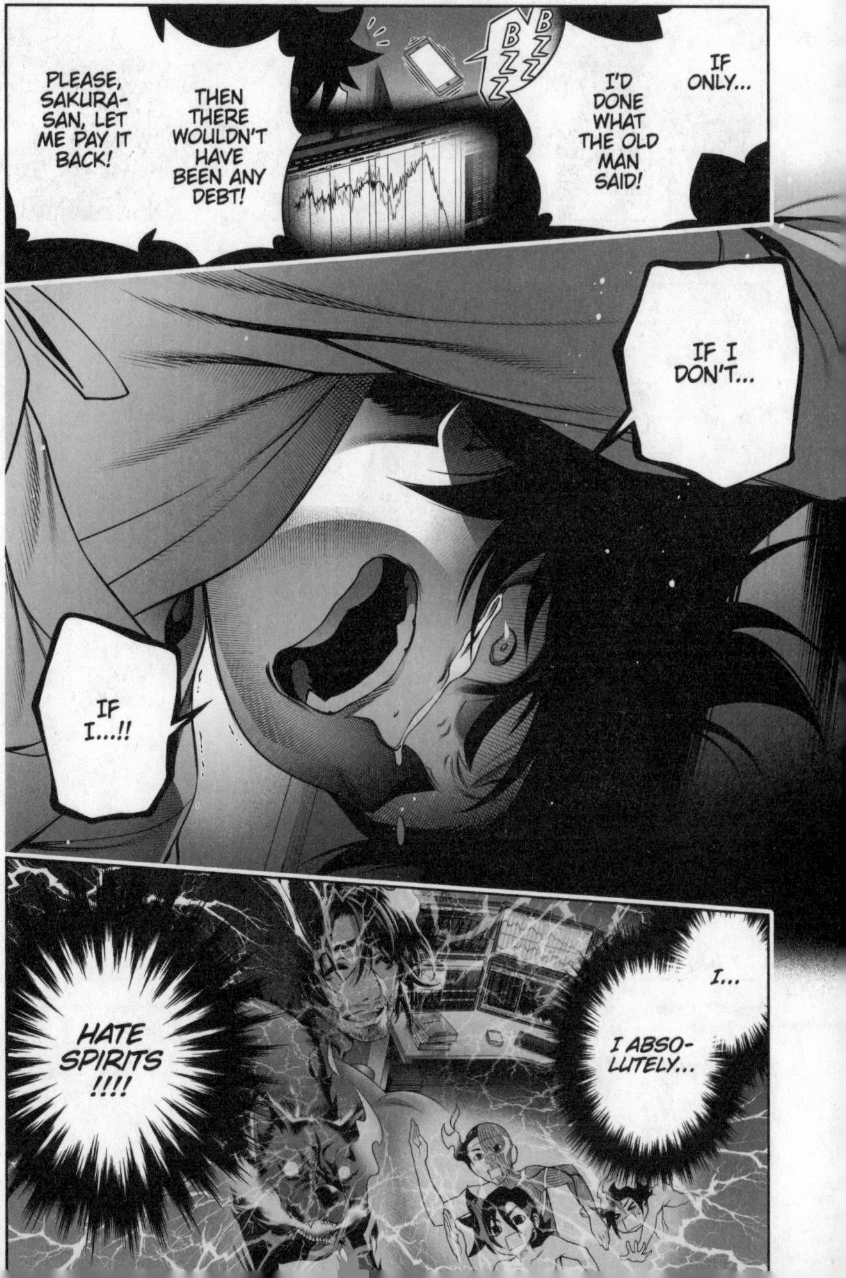
IF ONLY...
I'D DONE WHAT THE OLD MAN SAID!
BZZZ BZZZ
THEN THERE WOULDN'T HAVE BEEN ANY DEBT!
PLEASE, SAKURA-SAN, LET ME PAY IT BACK!
IF I DON'T...
IF I...!!
I...
I ABSO-LUTELY...
HATE SPIRITS!!!!

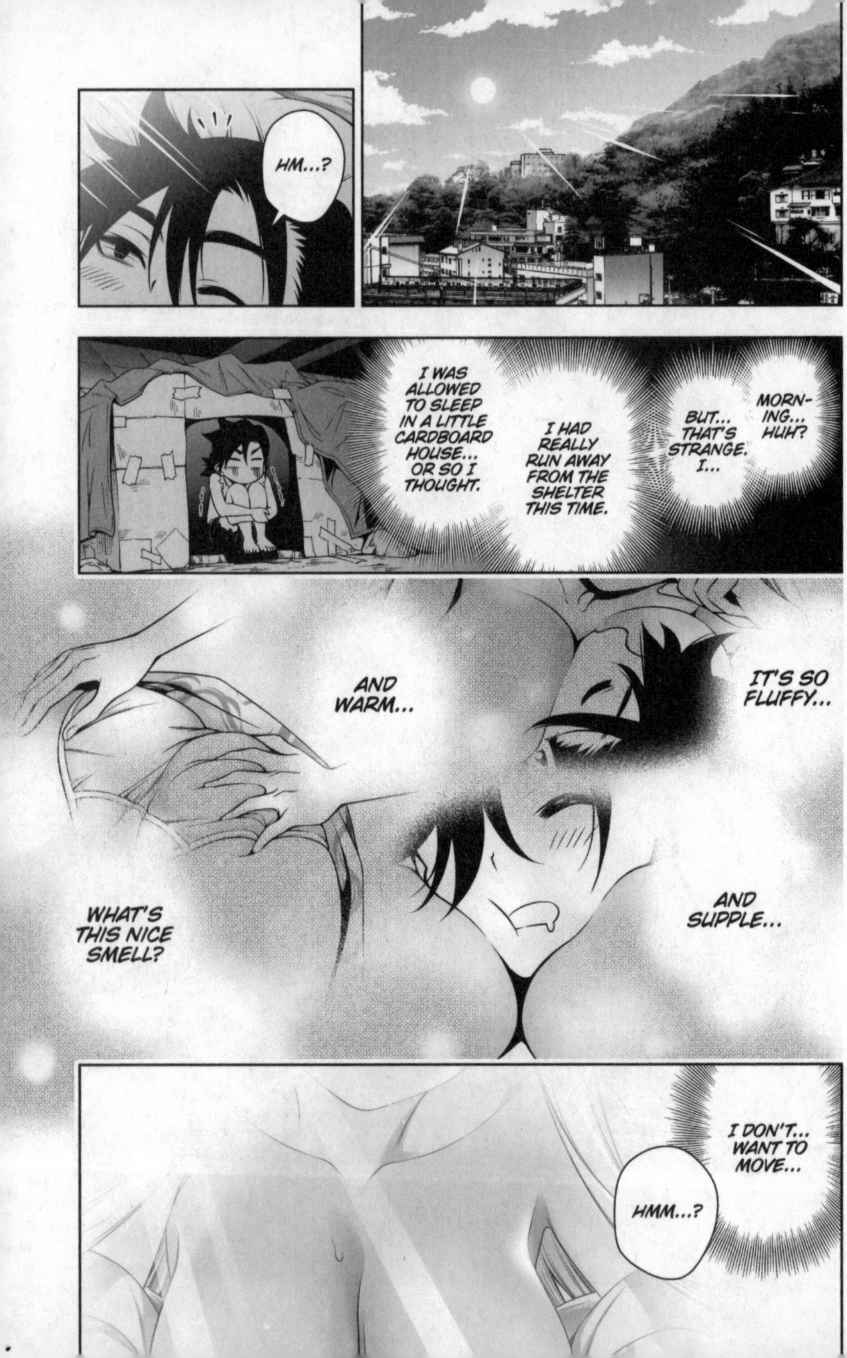
HM...?
MORN-ING... HUH?
BUT... THAT'S STRANGE. I...
I HAD REALLY RUN AWAY FROM THE SHELTER THIS TIME.
I WAS ALLOWED TO SLEEP IN A LITTLE CARDBOARD HOUSE... OR SO I THOUGHT.
IT'S SO FLUFFY...
AND WARM...
AND SUPPLE...
WHAT'S THIS NICE SMELL?
I DON'T... WANT TO MOVE...
HMM...?

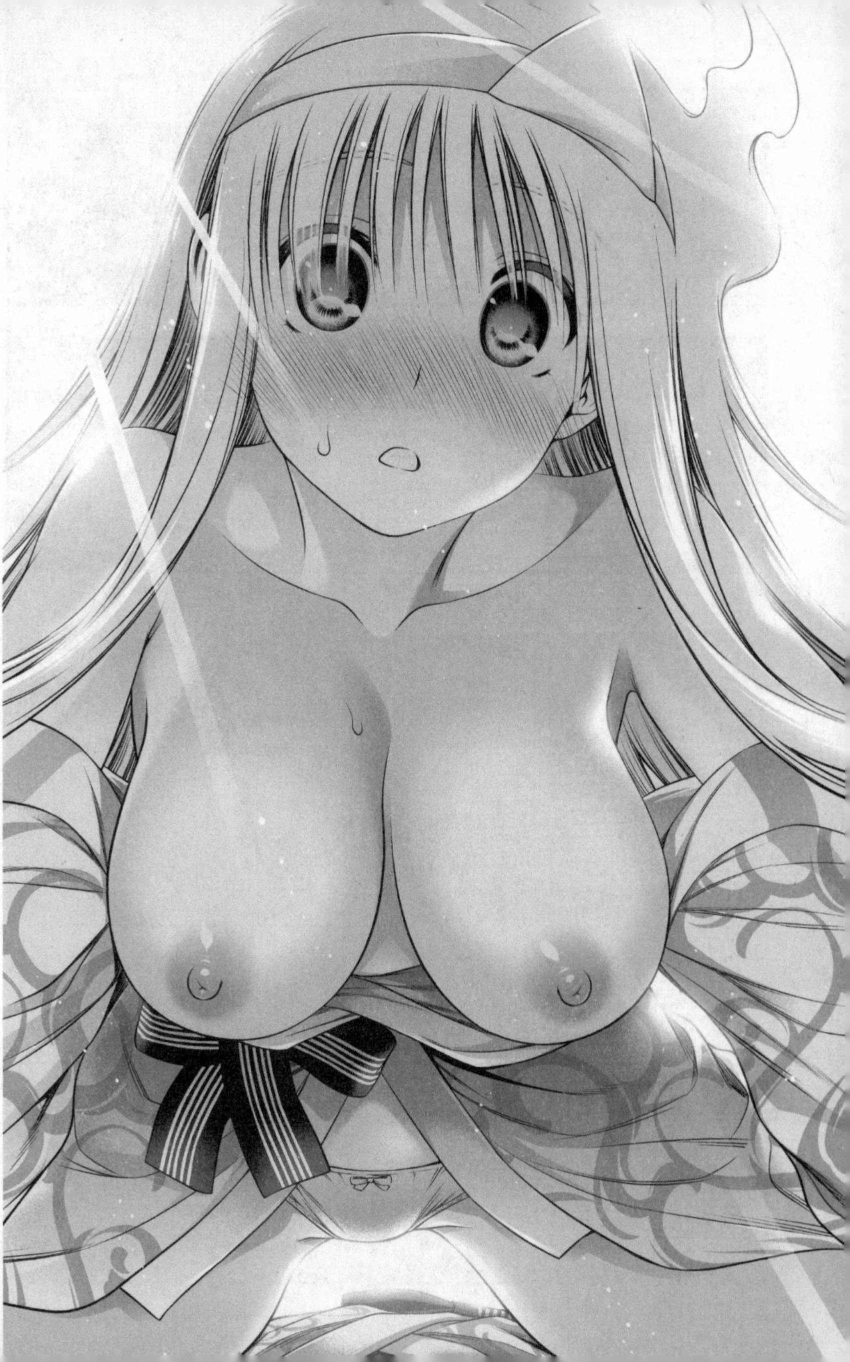

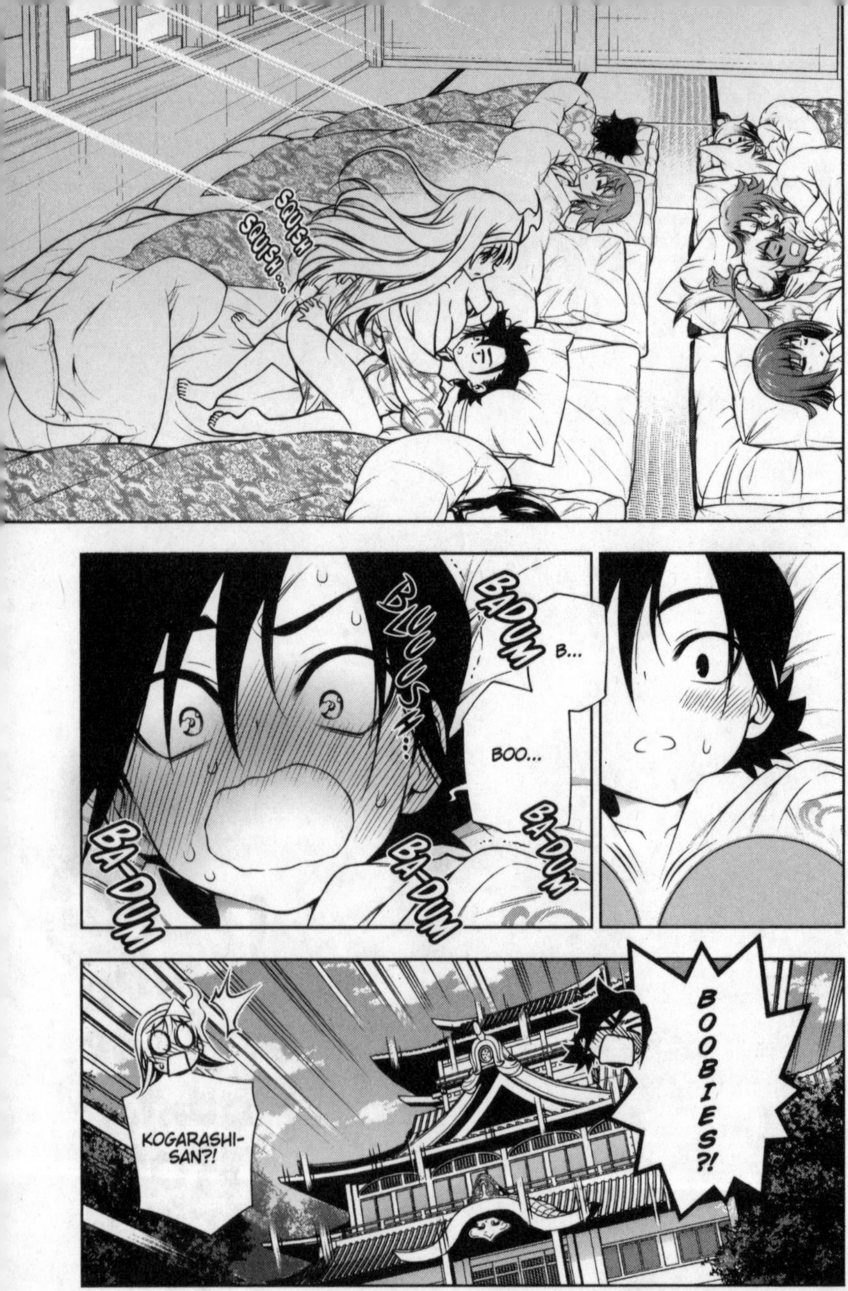
SQUISH
SQUISH...
BADUM
BLUUUSH...
B...
BOO...
BA-DUM
BA-DUM
BA-DUM
BOOBIES?!
KOGARASHI-SAN?!

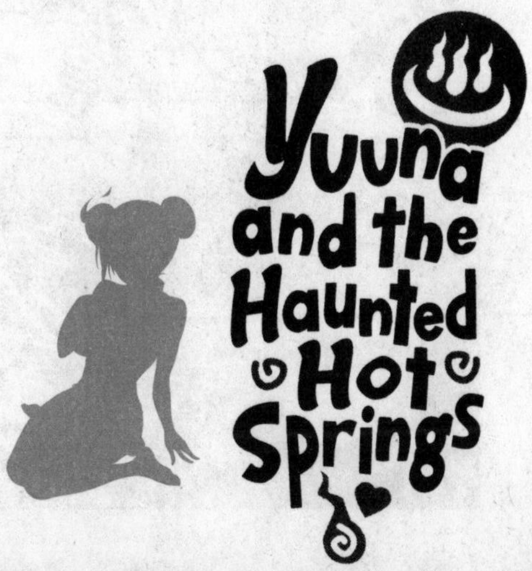

Yuuna and the Haunted Hot Springs

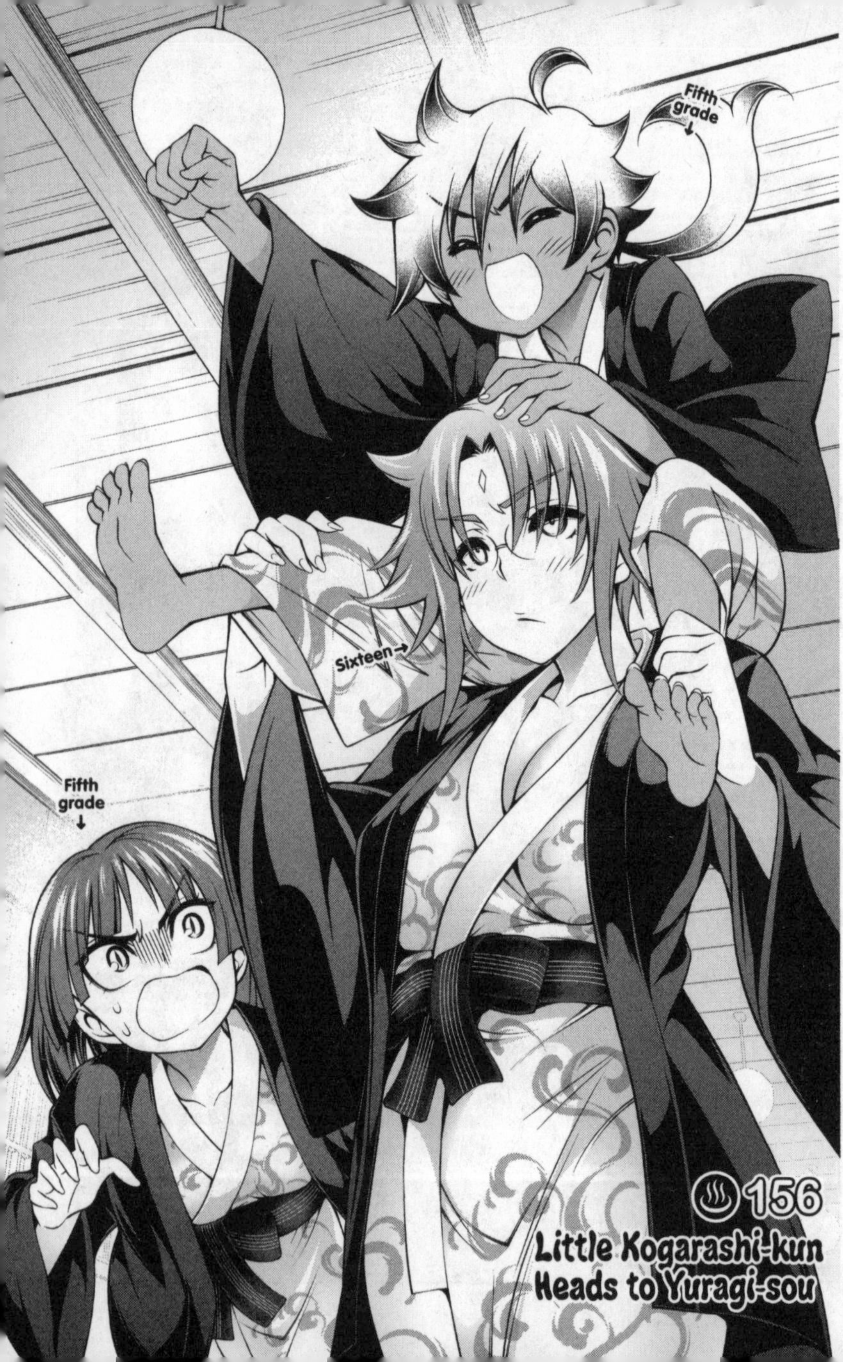
Fifth grade ↓
Sixteen →
Fifth grade ↓
156
Little Kogarashi-kun Heads to Yuragi-sou

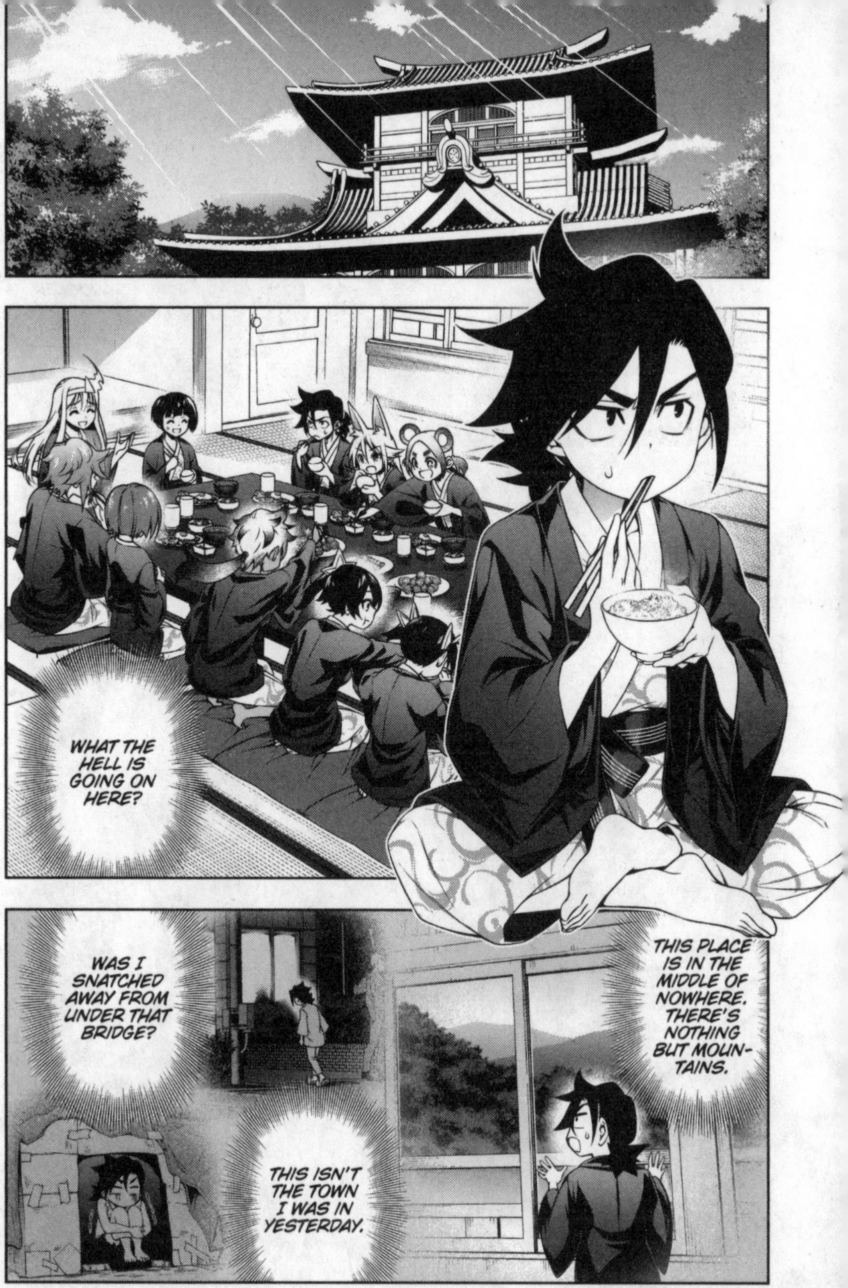
WHAT THE HELL IS GOING ON HERE?
THIS PLACE IS IN THE MIDDLE OF NOWHERE. THERE'S NOTHING BUT MOUN-TAINS.
THIS ISN'T THE TOWN I WAS IN YESTERDAY.
WAS I SNATCHED AWAY FROM UNDER THAT BRIDGE?

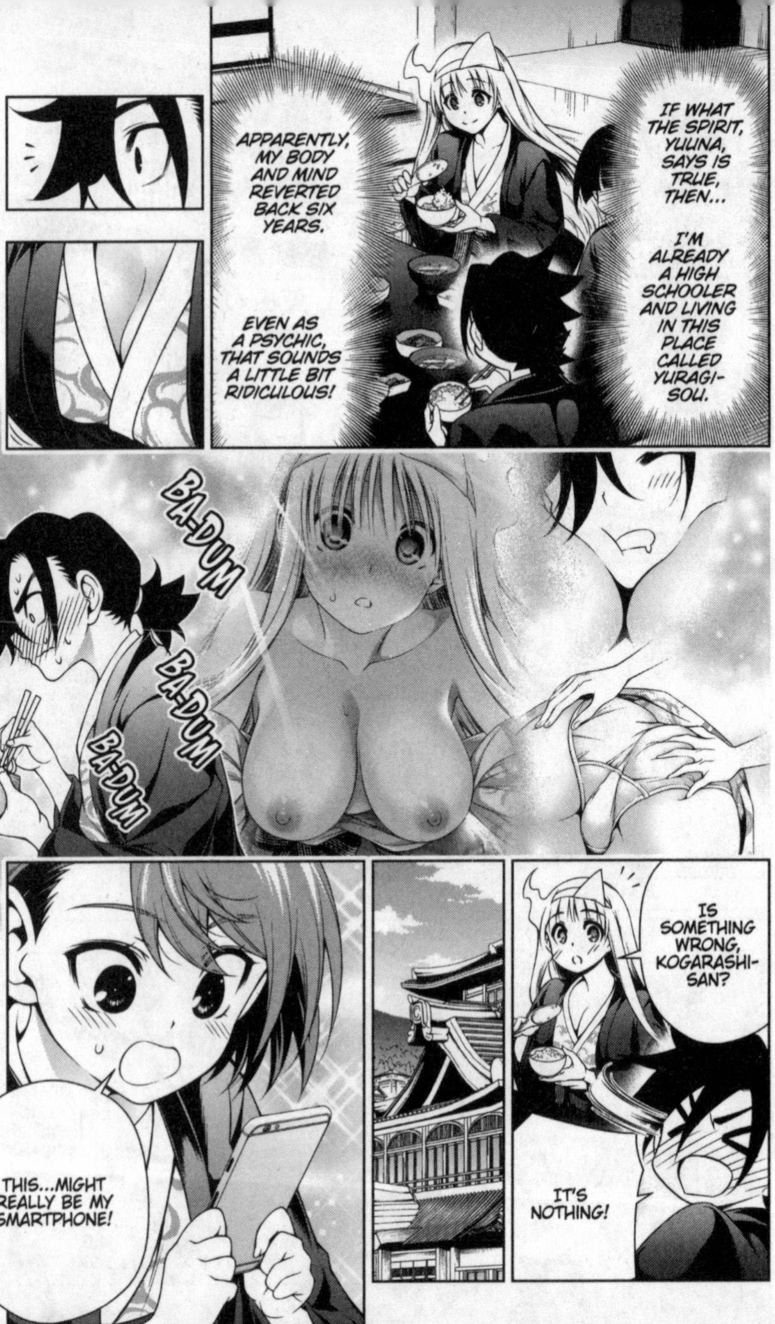
IF WHAT THE SPIRIT, YUUNA, SAYS IS TRUE, THEN...
I'M ALREADY A HIGH SCHOOLER AND LIVING IN THIS PLACE CALLED YURAGI-SOU.
APPARENTLY, MY BODY AND MIND REVERTED BACK SIX YEARS.
EVEN AS A PSYCHIC, THAT SOUNDS A LITTLE BIT RIDICULOUS!
BA-DUM
BA-DUM
BA-DUM
IS SOMETHING WRONG, KOGARASHI-SAN?
IT'S NOTHING!
THIS...MIGHT REALLY BE MY SMARTPHONE!

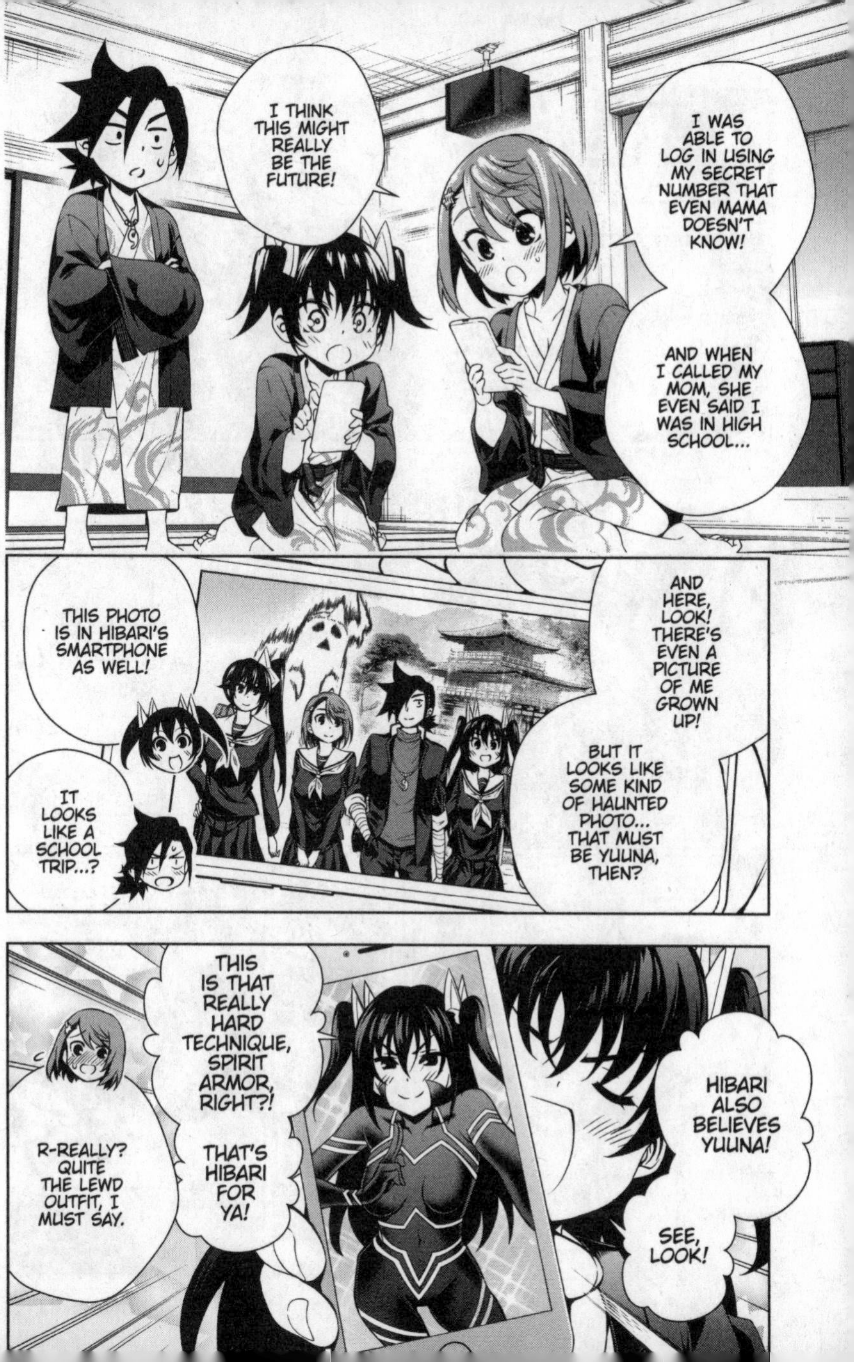
I WAS ABLE TO LOG IN USING MY SECRET NUMBER THAT EVEN MAMA DOESN'T KNOW!
AND WHEN I CALLED MY MOM, SHE EVEN SAID I WAS IN HIGH SCHOOL...
I THINK THIS MIGHT REALLY BE THE FUTURE!
AND HERE, LOOK! THERE'S EVEN A PICTURE OF ME GROWN UP!
BUT IT LOOKS LIKE SOME KIND OF HAUNTED PHOTO... THAT MUST BE YUUNA, THEN?
THIS PHOTO IS IN HIBARI'S SMARTPHONE AS WELL!
IT LOOKS LIKE A SCHOOL TRIP...?
HIBARI ALSO BELIEVES YUUNA!
SEE, LOOK!
THIS IS THAT REALLY HARD TECHNIQUE, SPIRIT ARMOR, RIGHT?!
THAT'S HIBARI FOR YA!
R-REALLY? QUITE THE LEWD OUTFIT, I MUST SAY.

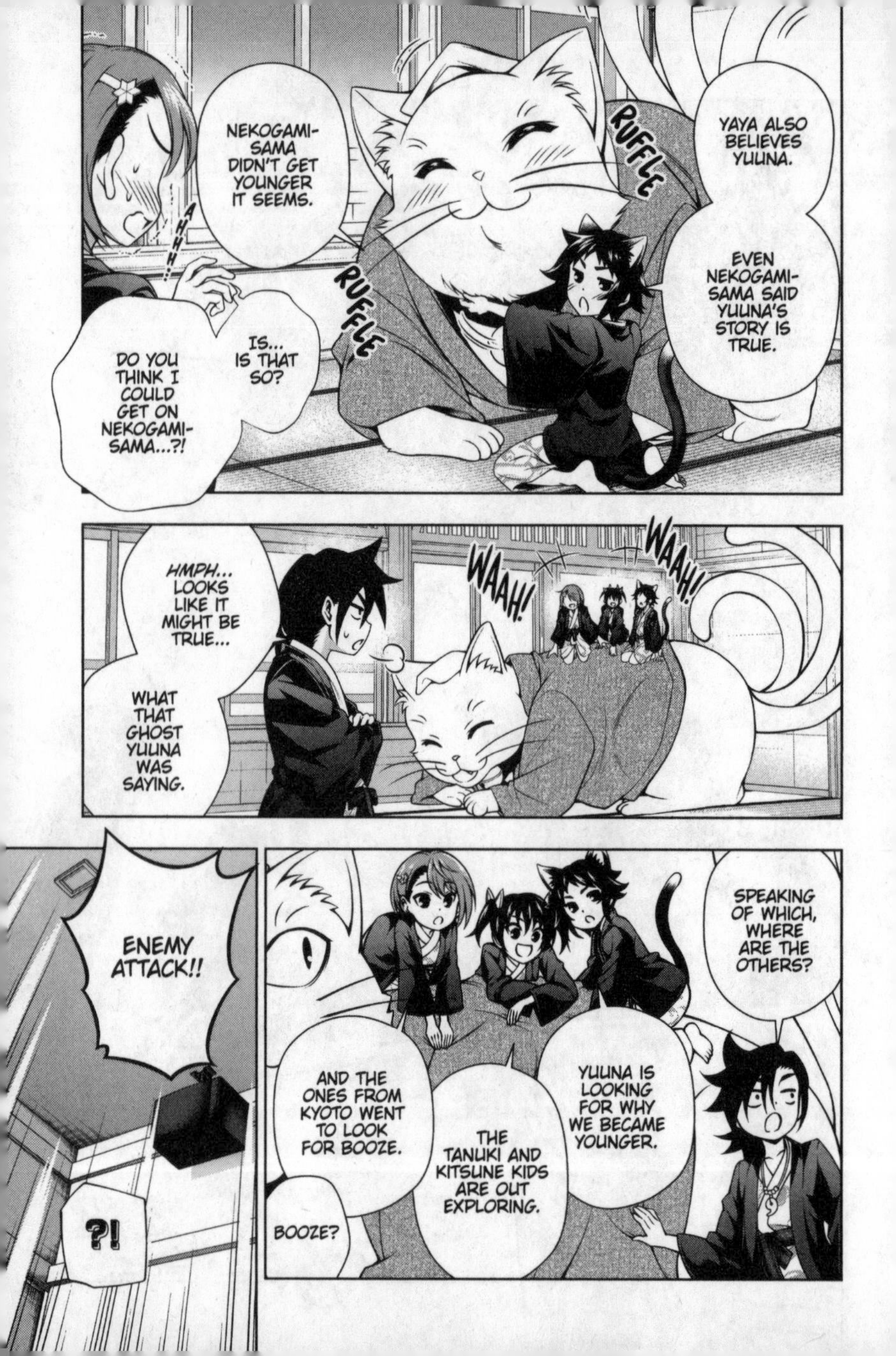
YAYA ALSO BELIEVES YUUNA.
EVEN NEKOGAMI-SAMA SAID YUUNA'S STORY IS TRUE.
RUFFLE
RUFFLE
NEKOGAMI-SAMA DIDN'T GET YOUNGER IT SEEMS.
AHHH!!
IS... IS THAT SO?
DO YOU THINK I COULD GET ON NEKOGAMI-SAMA...?!
WAAH!
WAAH!
HMPH... LOOKS LIKE IT MIGHT BE TRUE...
WHAT THAT GHOST YUUNA WAS SAYING.
SPEAKING OF WHICH, WHERE ARE THE OTHERS?
YUUNA IS LOOKING FOR WHY WE BECAME YOUNGER.
THE TANUKI AND KITSUNE KIDS ARE OUT EXPLORING.
AND THE ONES FROM KYOTO WENT TO LOOK FOR BOOZE.
BOOZE?
ENEMY ATTACK!!
?!

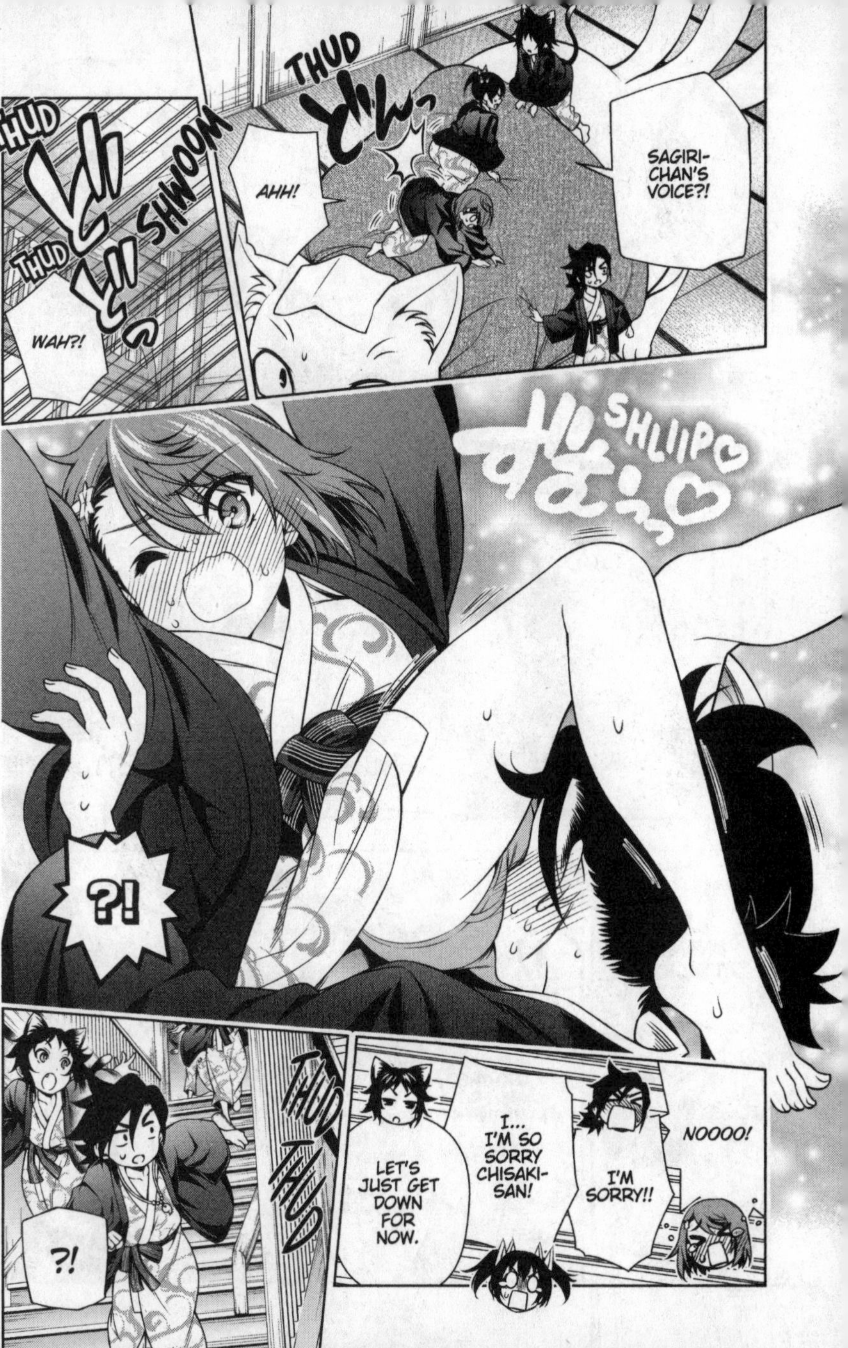

SAGIRI-CHAN'S VOICE?!
THUD
AHH!
THUD
THUD
SHWOOM
WAH?!
SHLIIP
?!
NOOOO!
I'M SORRY!!
I... I'M SO SORRY CHISAKI-SAN!
LET'S JUST GET DOWN FOR NOW.
THUD THUD
?!

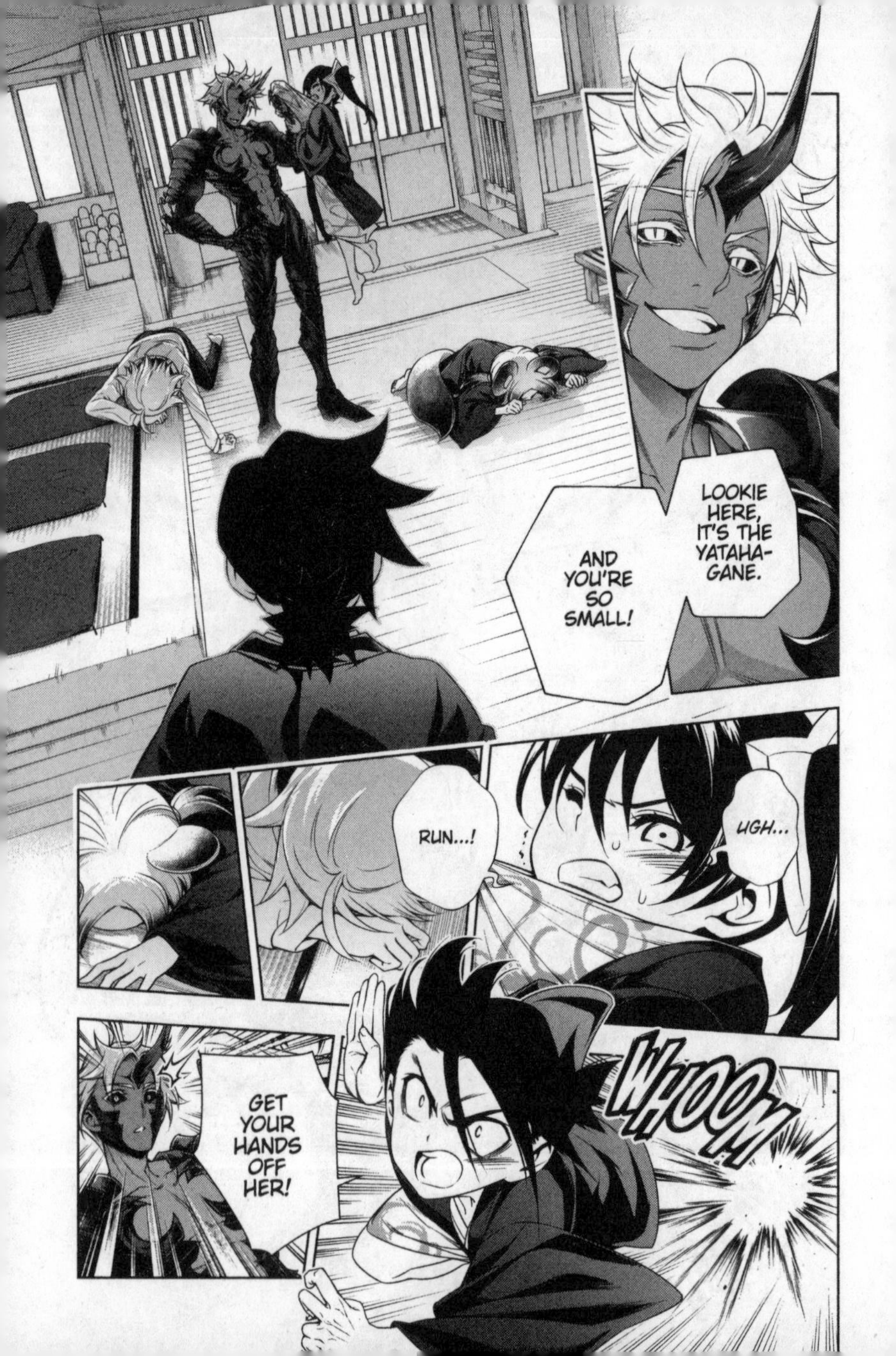
LOOKIE HERE, IT'S THE YATAHA-GANE.
AND YOU'RE SO SMALL!
UGH...
RUN...!
WHOOM
GET YOUR HANDS OFF HER!

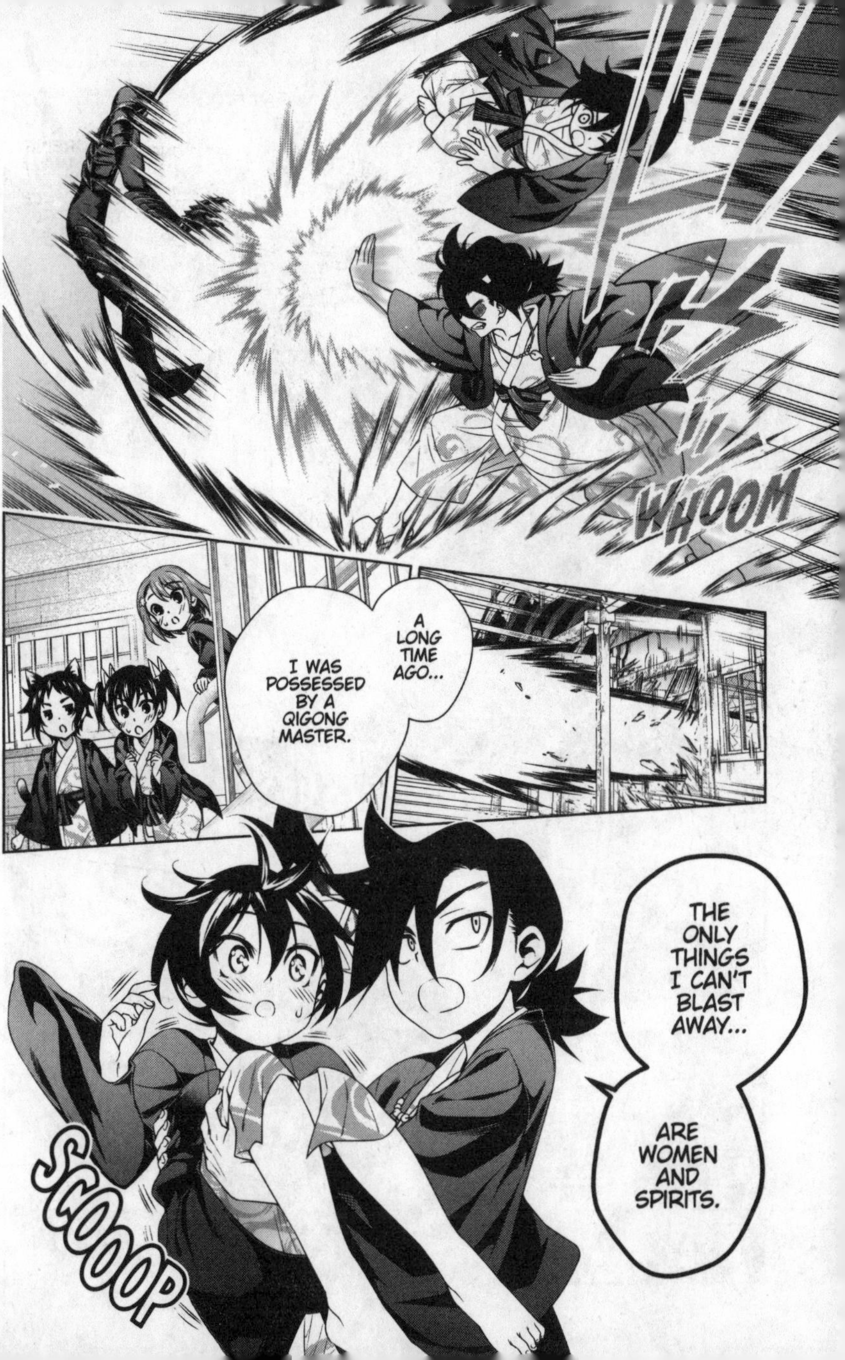
WHOOM
A LONG TIME AGO...
I WAS POSSESSED BY A QIGONG MASTER.
THE ONLY THINGS I CAN'T BLAST AWAY...
ARE WOMEN AND SPIRITS.
SCOOOP

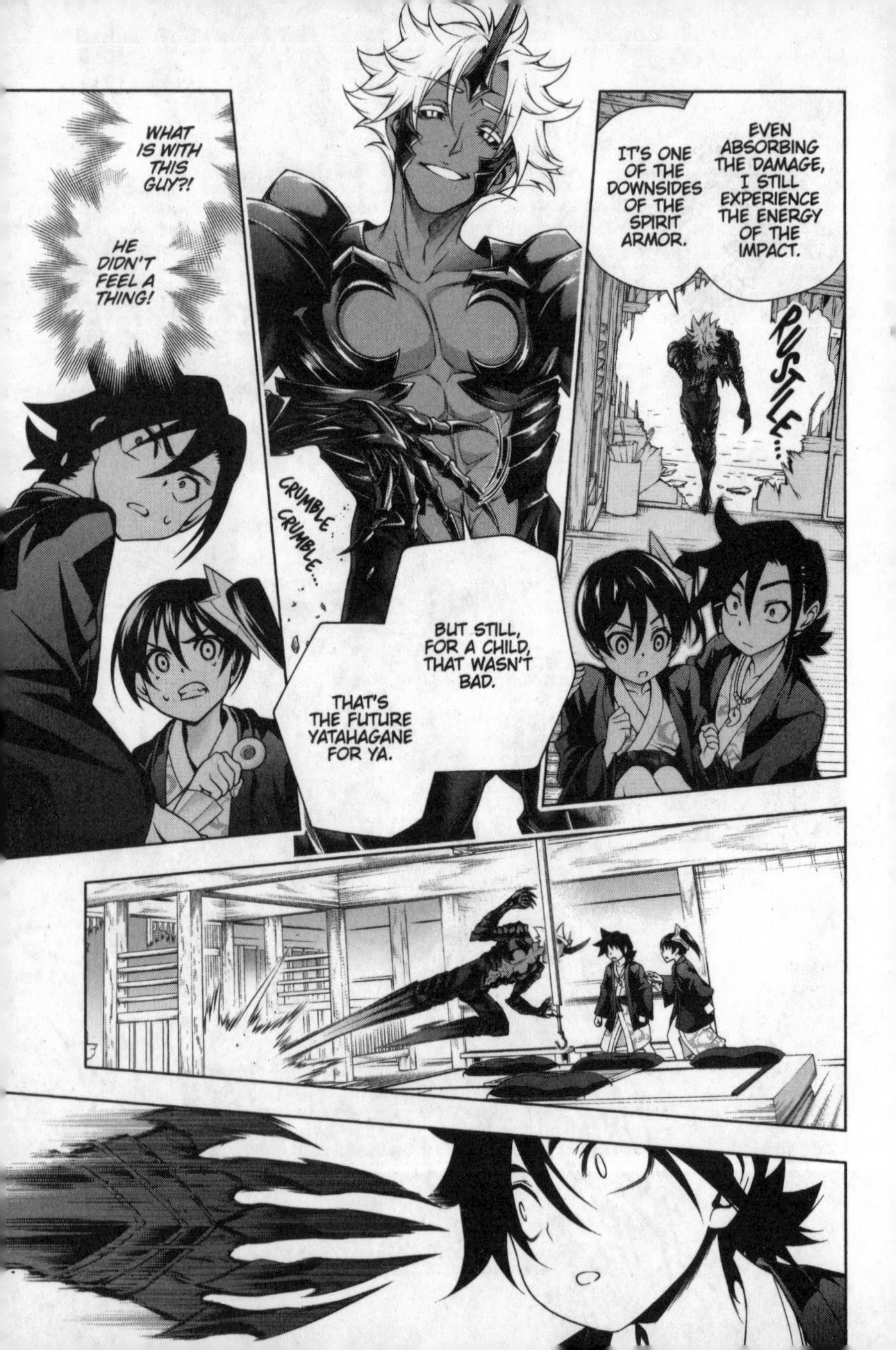
EVEN ABSORBING THE DAMAGE, I STILL EXPERIENCE THE ENERGY OF THE IMPACT.
IT'S ONE OF THE DOWNSIDES OF THE SPIRIT ARMOR.
RUSTLE...
BUT STILL, FOR A CHILD, THAT WASN'T BAD.
THAT'S THE FUTURE YATAHAGANE FOR YA.
CRUMBLE CRUMBLE...
WHAT IS WITH THIS GUY?!
HE DIDN'T FEEL A THING!

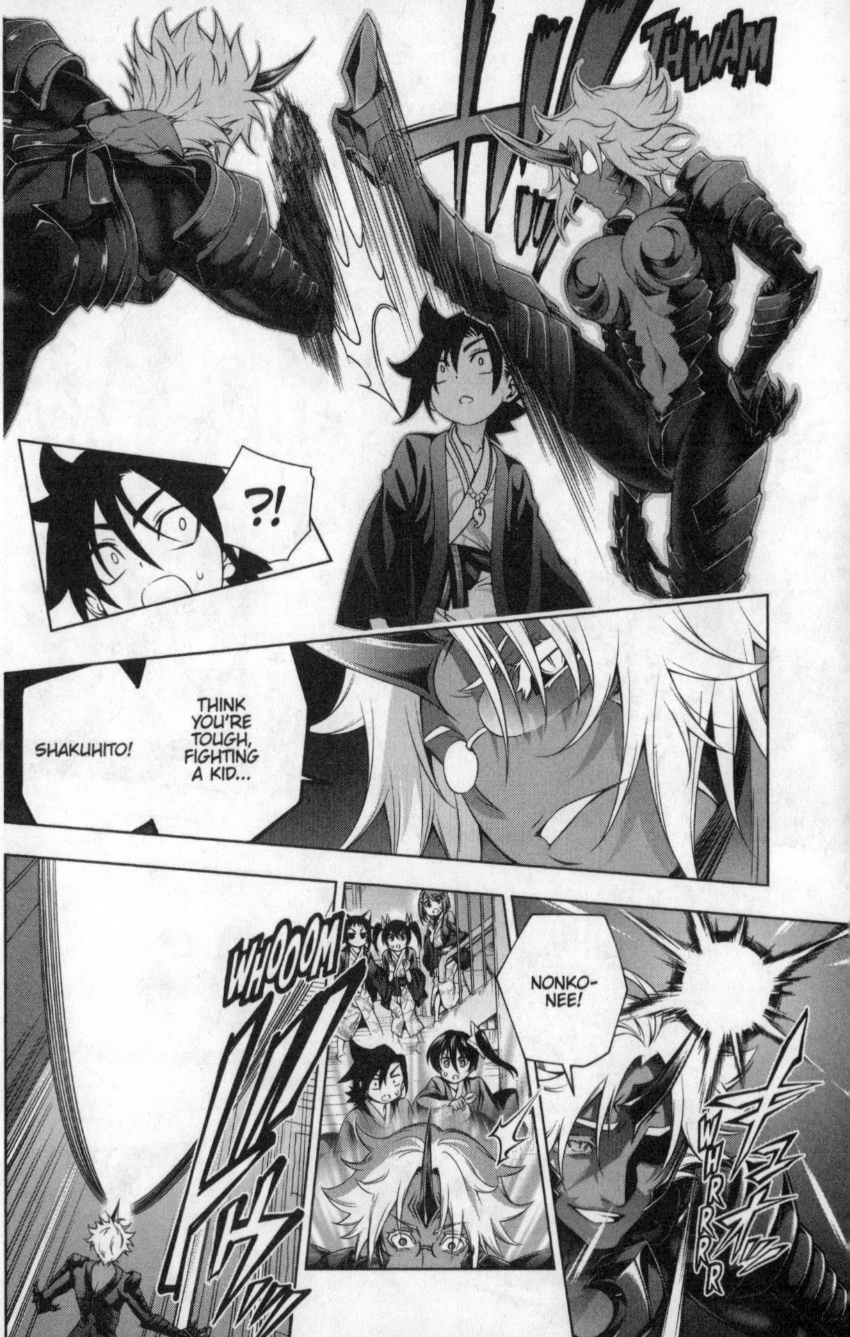
THWAM
?!
THINK YOU'RE TOUGH, FIGHTING A KID...
SHAKUHITO!
NONKO-NEE!
WHRRRRR
WHOOOM

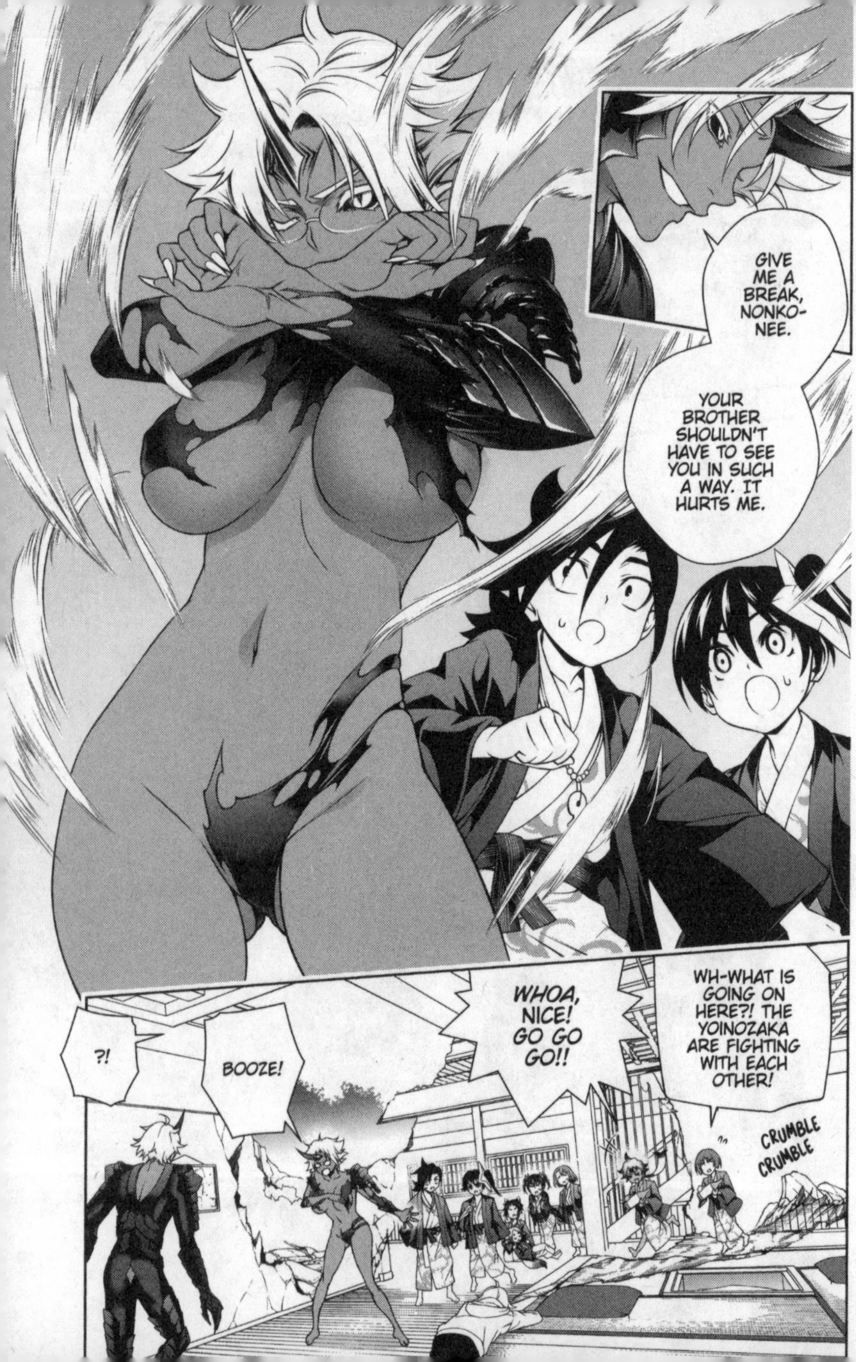
GIVE ME A BREAK, NONKO-NEE.
YOUR BROTHER SHOULDN'T HAVE TO SEE YOU IN SUCH A WAY. IT HURTS ME.
WH-WHAT IS GOING ON HERE?! THE YOINOZAKA ARE FIGHTING WITH EACH OTHER!
CRUMBLE CRUMBLE
WHOA, NICE! GO GO GO!!
BOOZE!
?!

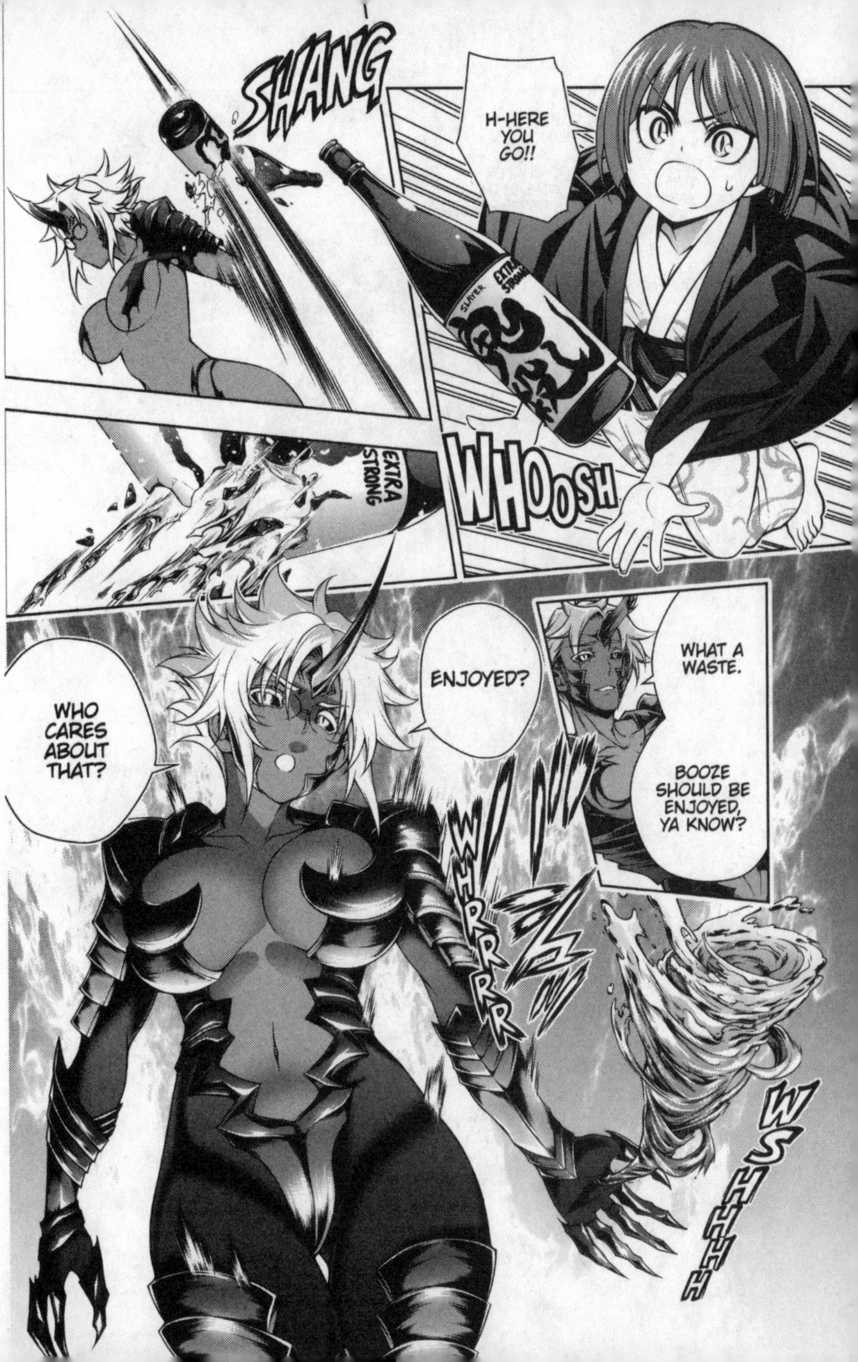
H-HERE YOU GO!!
SHANG
SLAYER
EXTRA STRONG
WHOOSH
EXTRA STRONG
WHAT A WASTE.
BOOZE SHOULD BE ENJOYED, YA KNOW?
ENJOYED?
WHO CARES ABOUT THAT?
WHRRRR
WSHHHHH

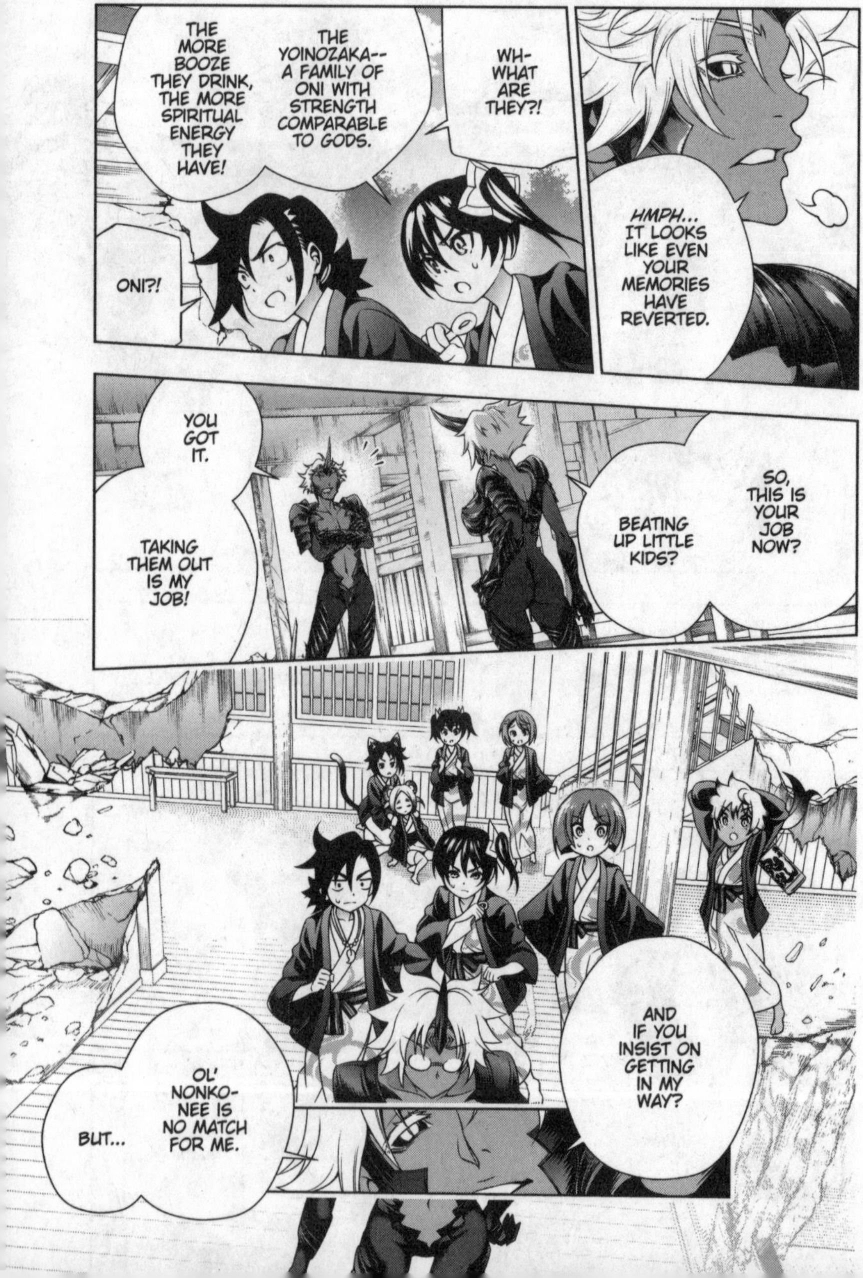
HMPH... IT LOOKS LIKE EVEN YOUR MEMORIES HAVE REVERTED.
WH- WHAT ARE THEY?!
THE YOINOZAKA-- A FAMILY OF ONI WITH STRENGTH COMPARABLE TO GODS.
THE MORE BOOZE THEY DRINK, THE MORE SPIRITUAL ENERGY THEY HAVE!
ONI?!
SO, THIS IS YOUR JOB NOW?
BEATING UP LITTLE KIDS?
YOU GOT IT.
TAKING THEM OUT IS MY JOB!
AND IF YOU INSIST ON GETTING IN MY WAY?
OL' NONKO-NEE IS NO MATCH FOR ME.
BUT...

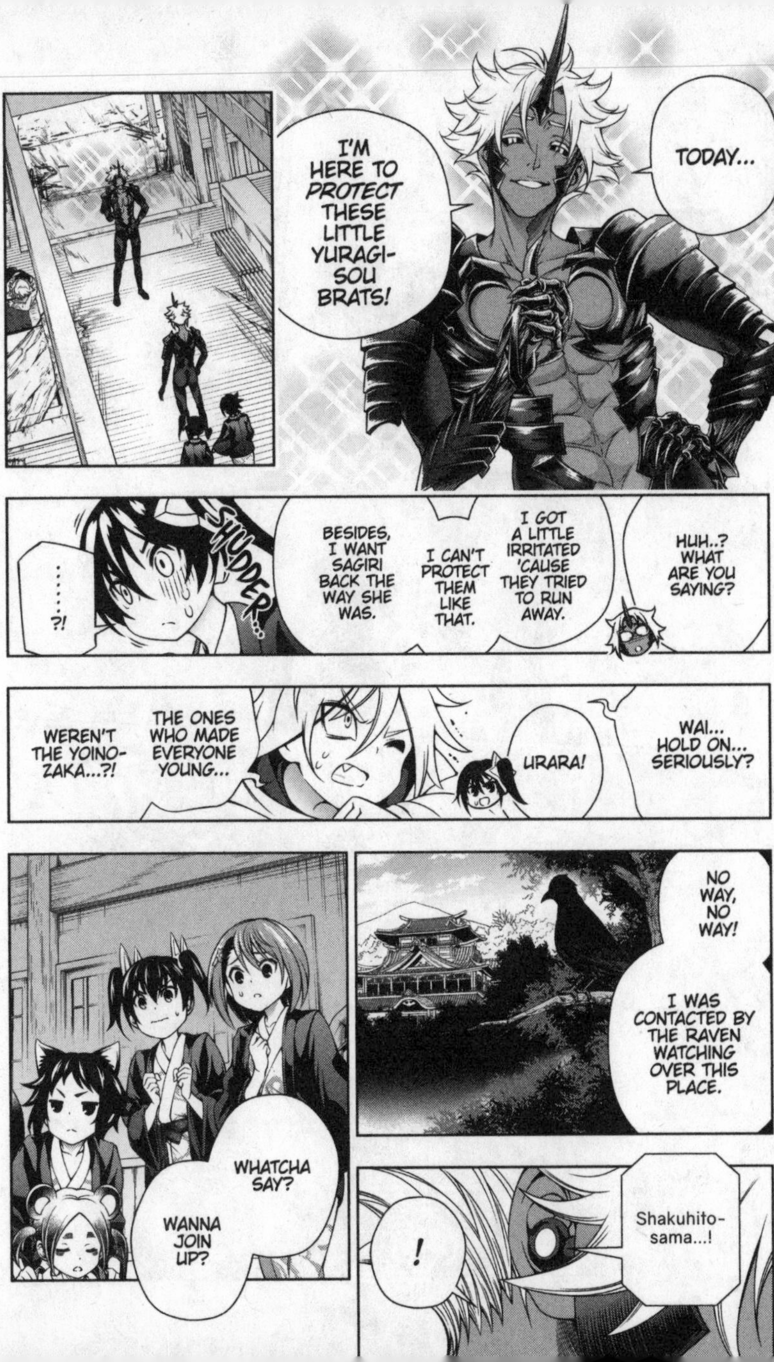
TODAY...
I'M HERE TO *PROTECT* THESE LITTLE YURAGI-SOU BRATS!
HUH..? WHAT ARE YOU SAYING?
I GOT A LITTLE IRRITATED 'CAUSE THEY TRIED TO RUN AWAY.
I CAN'T PROTECT THEM LIKE THAT.
BESIDES, I WANT SAGIRI BACK THE WAY SHE WAS.
SHUDDER...
......?!
WAI... HOLD ON... SERIOUSLY?
URARA!
THE ONES WHO MADE EVERYONE YOUNG...
WEREN'T THE YOINO-ZAKA...?!
NO WAY, NO WAY!
I WAS CONTACTED BY THE RAVEN WATCHING OVER THIS PLACE.
Shakuhito-sama...!
!
WHATCHA SAY?
WANNA JOIN UP?

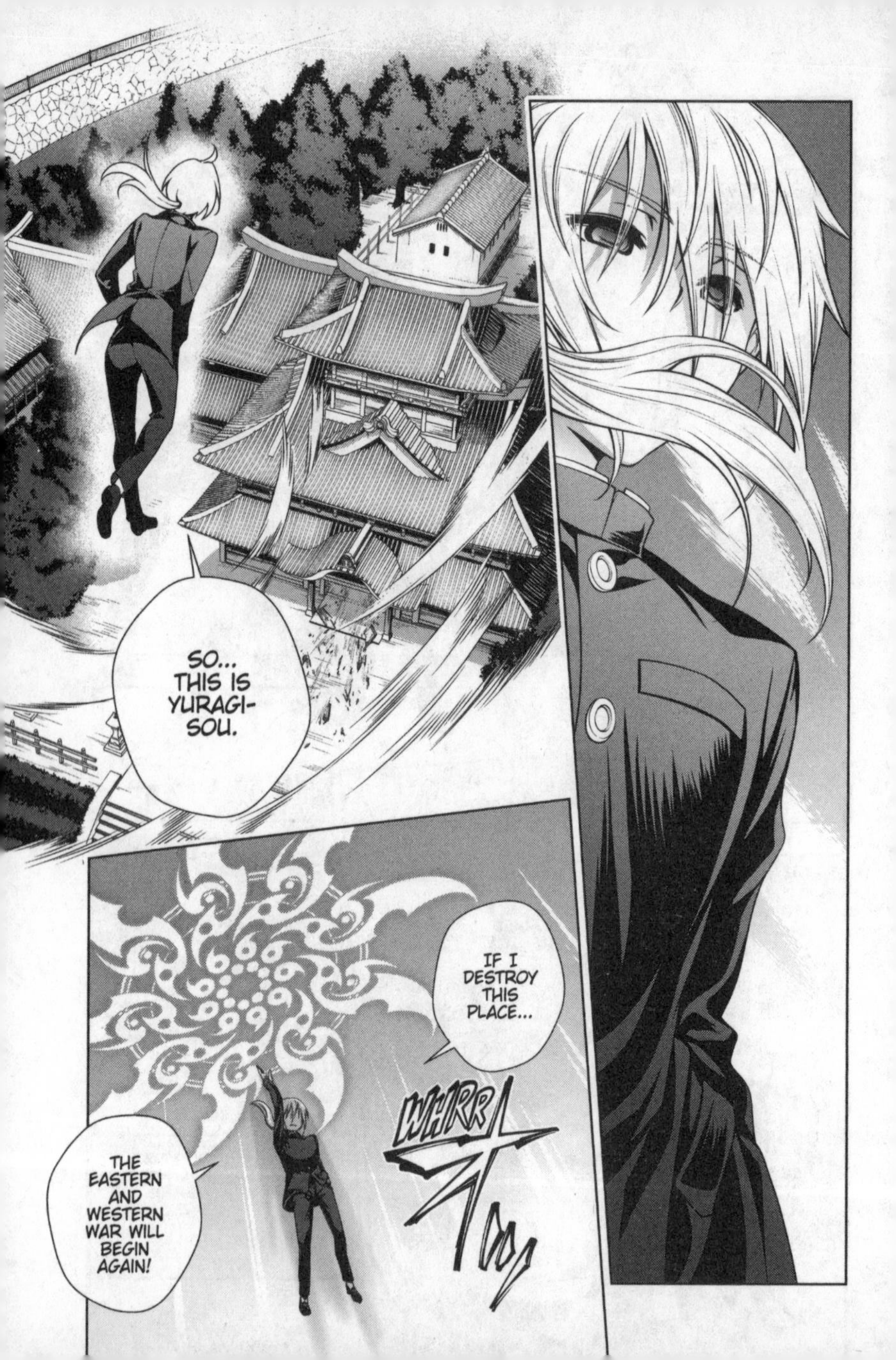

SO... THIS IS YURAGI-SOU.
IF I DESTROY THIS PLACE...
WHRR
THE EASTERN AND WESTERN WAR WILL BEGIN AGAIN!

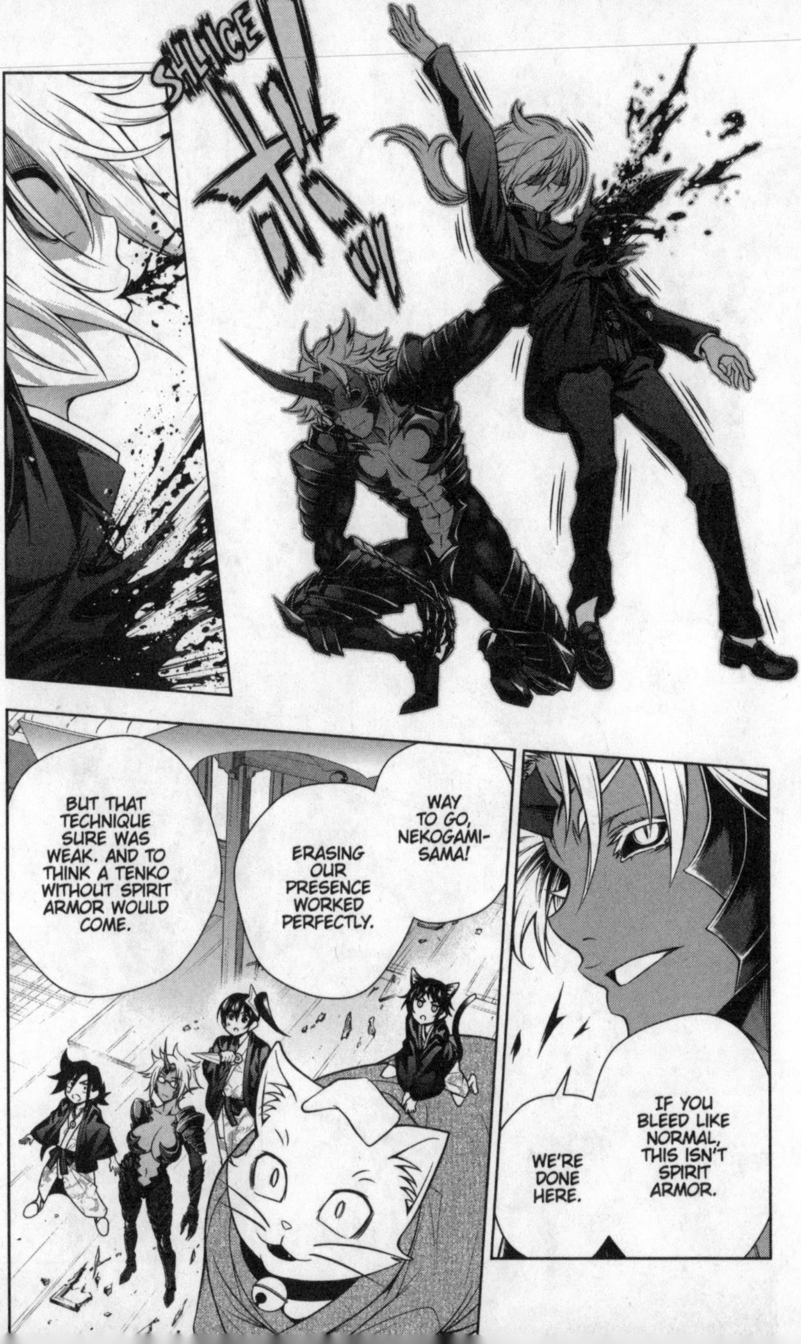
SHLICE!!
IF YOU BLEED LIKE NORMAL, THIS ISN'T SPIRIT ARMOR.
WE'RE DONE HERE.
WAY TO GO, NEKOGAMI-SAMA!
ERASING OUR PRESENCE WORKED PERFECTLY.
BUT THAT TECHNIQUE SURE WAS WEAK. AND TO THINK A TENKO WITHOUT SPIRIT ARMOR WOULD COME.

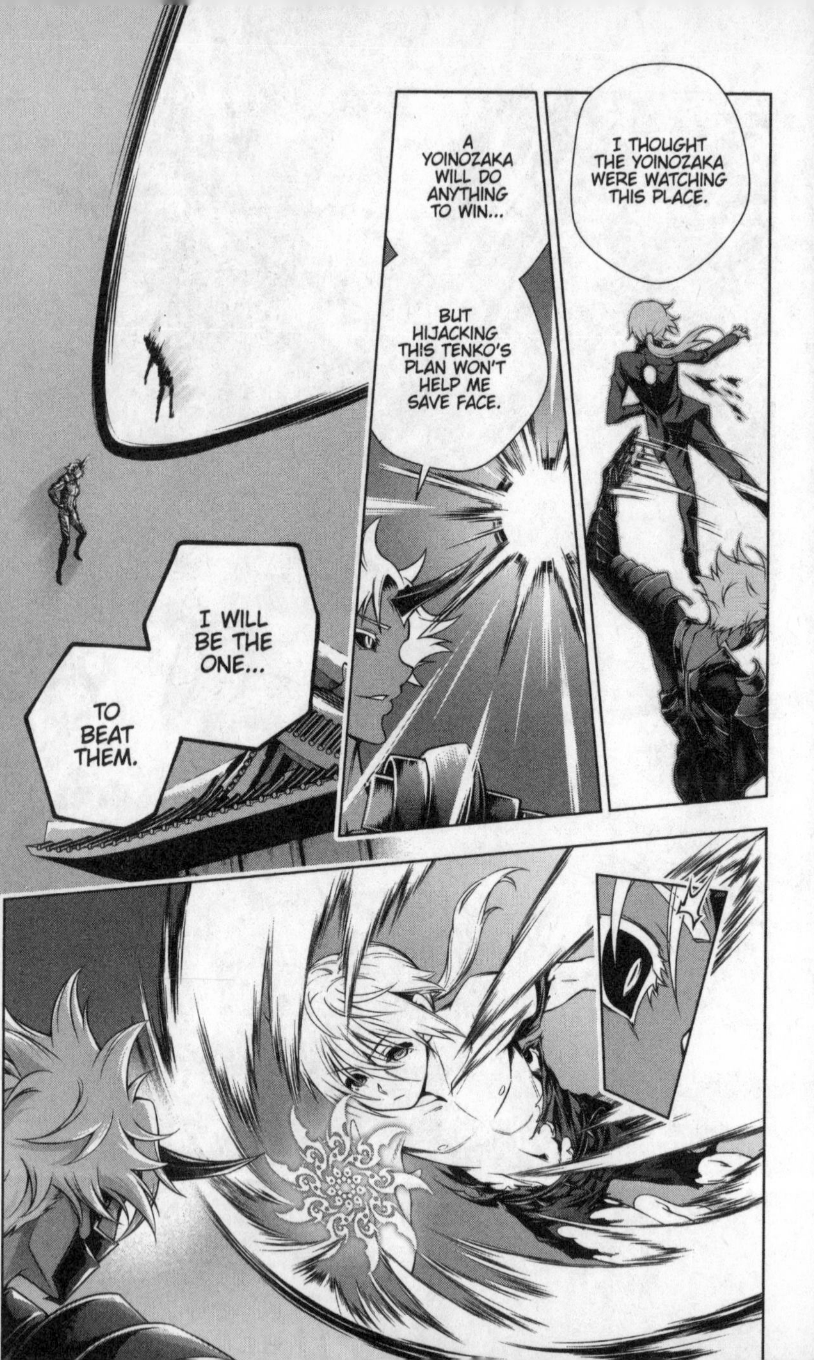
I THOUGHT THE YOINOZAKA WERE WATCHING THIS PLACE.
A YOINOZAKA WILL DO ANYTHING TO WIN...
BUT HIJACKING THIS TENKO'S PLAN WON'T HELP ME SAVE FACE.
I WILL BE THE ONE...
TO BEAT THEM.

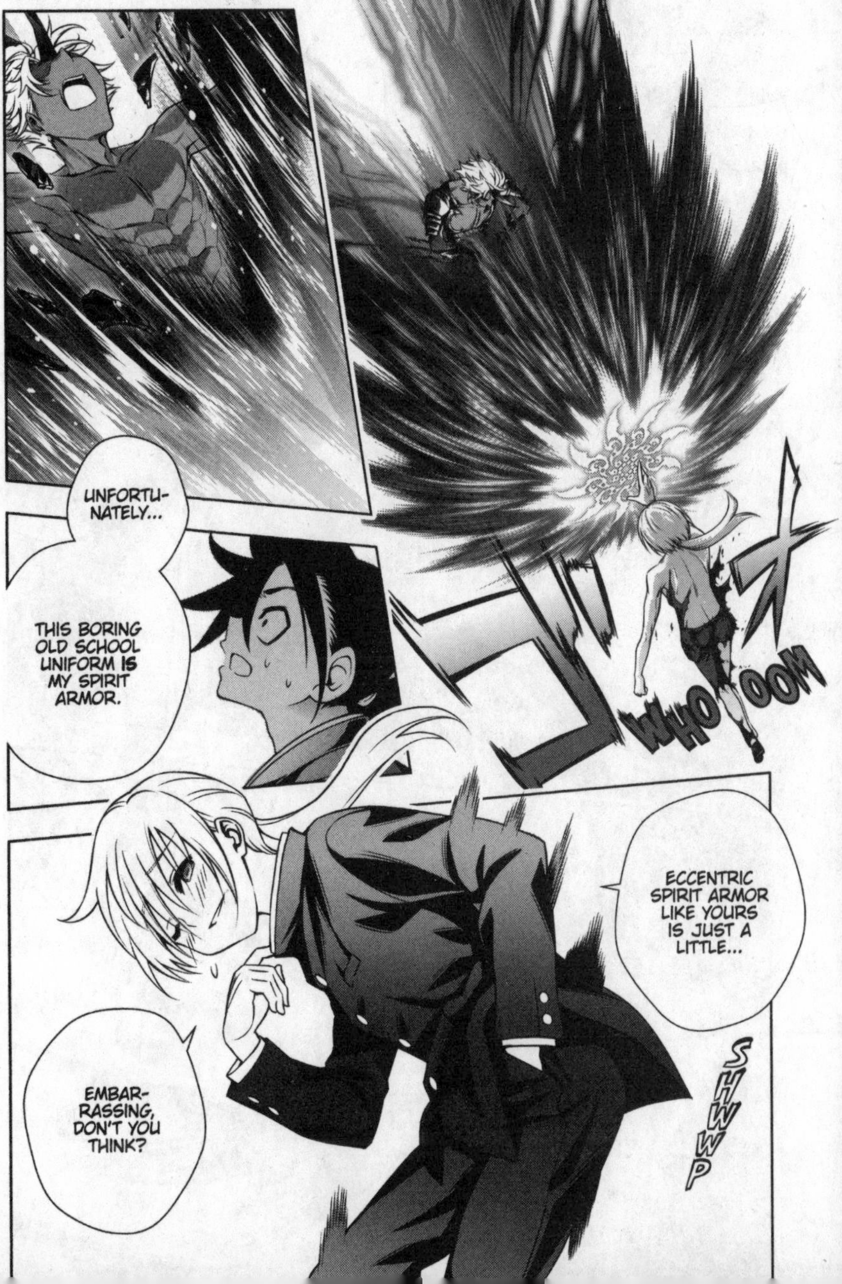
WHOOOM
UNFORTUNATELY...
THIS BORING OLD SCHOOL UNIFORM IS MY SPIRIT ARMOR.
ECCENTRIC SPIRIT ARMOR LIKE YOURS IS JUST A LITTLE...
EMBARRASSING, DON'T YOU THINK?
SHWWP

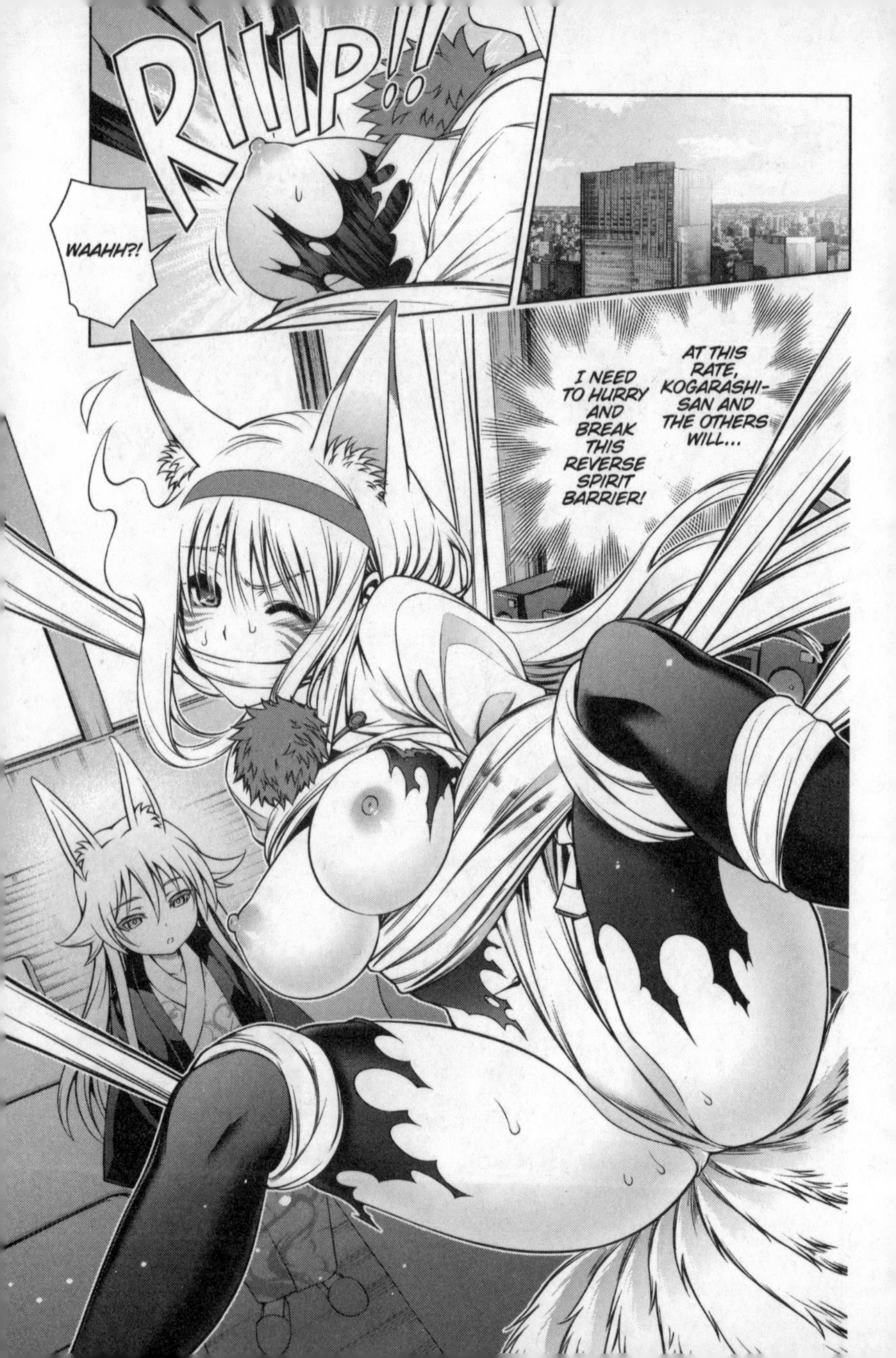
RIIIP!!
WAAHH?!
AT THIS RATE, KOGARASHI-SAN AND THE OTHERS WILL...
I NEED TO HURRY AND BREAK THIS REVERSE SPIRIT BARRIER!

Yuuna and the Haunted Hot Springs

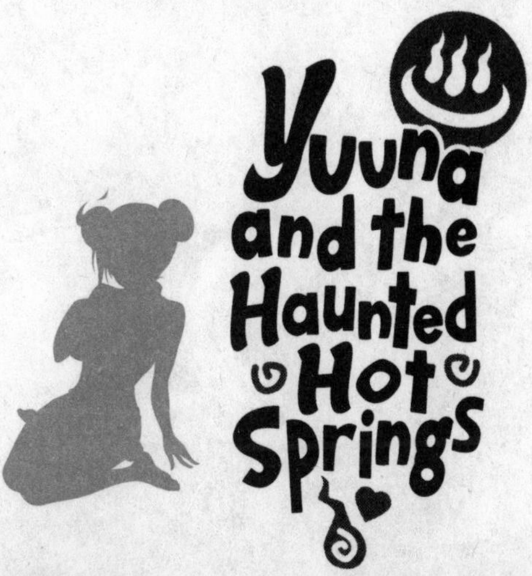

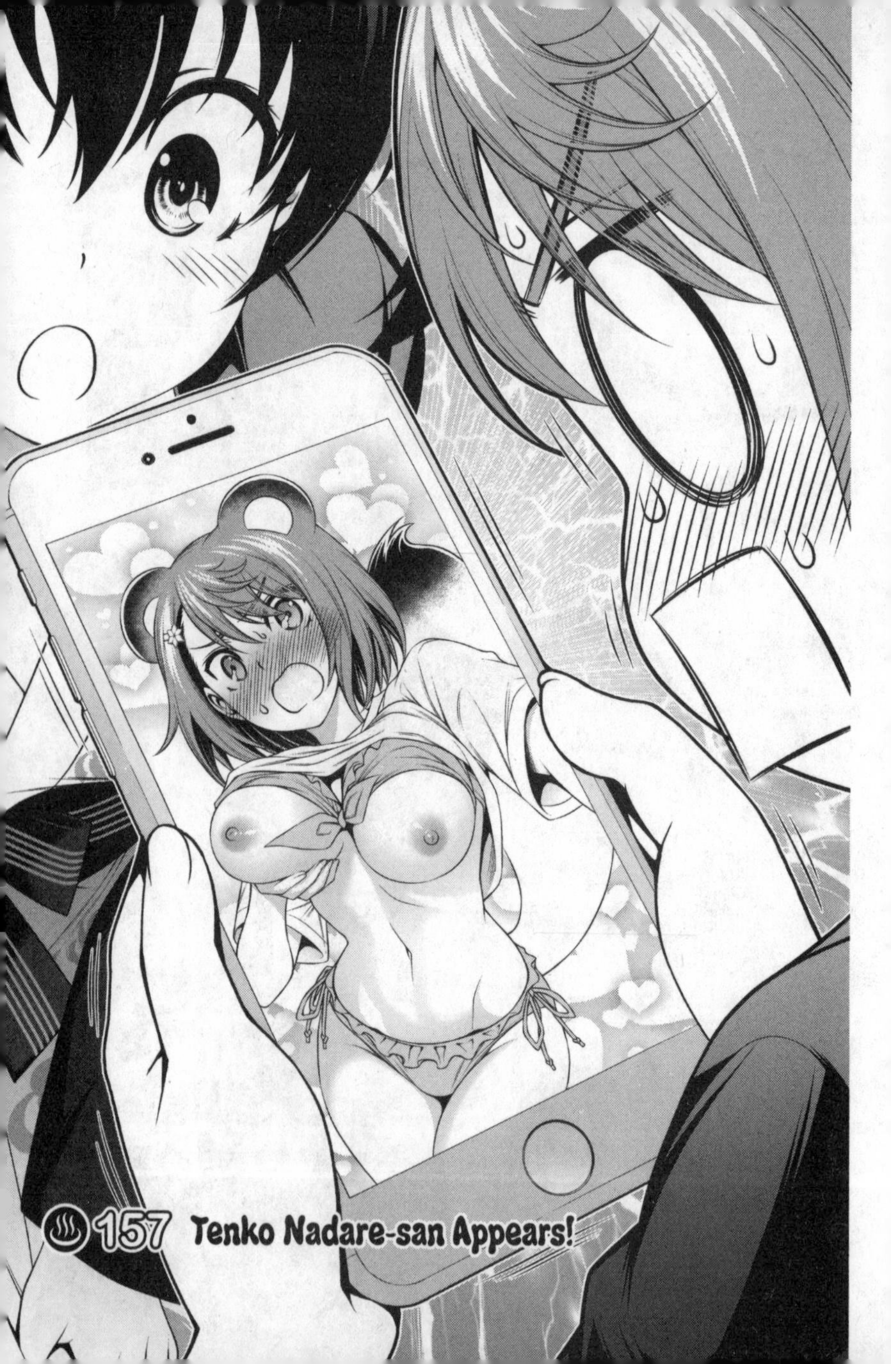
157 Tenko Nadare-san Appears!

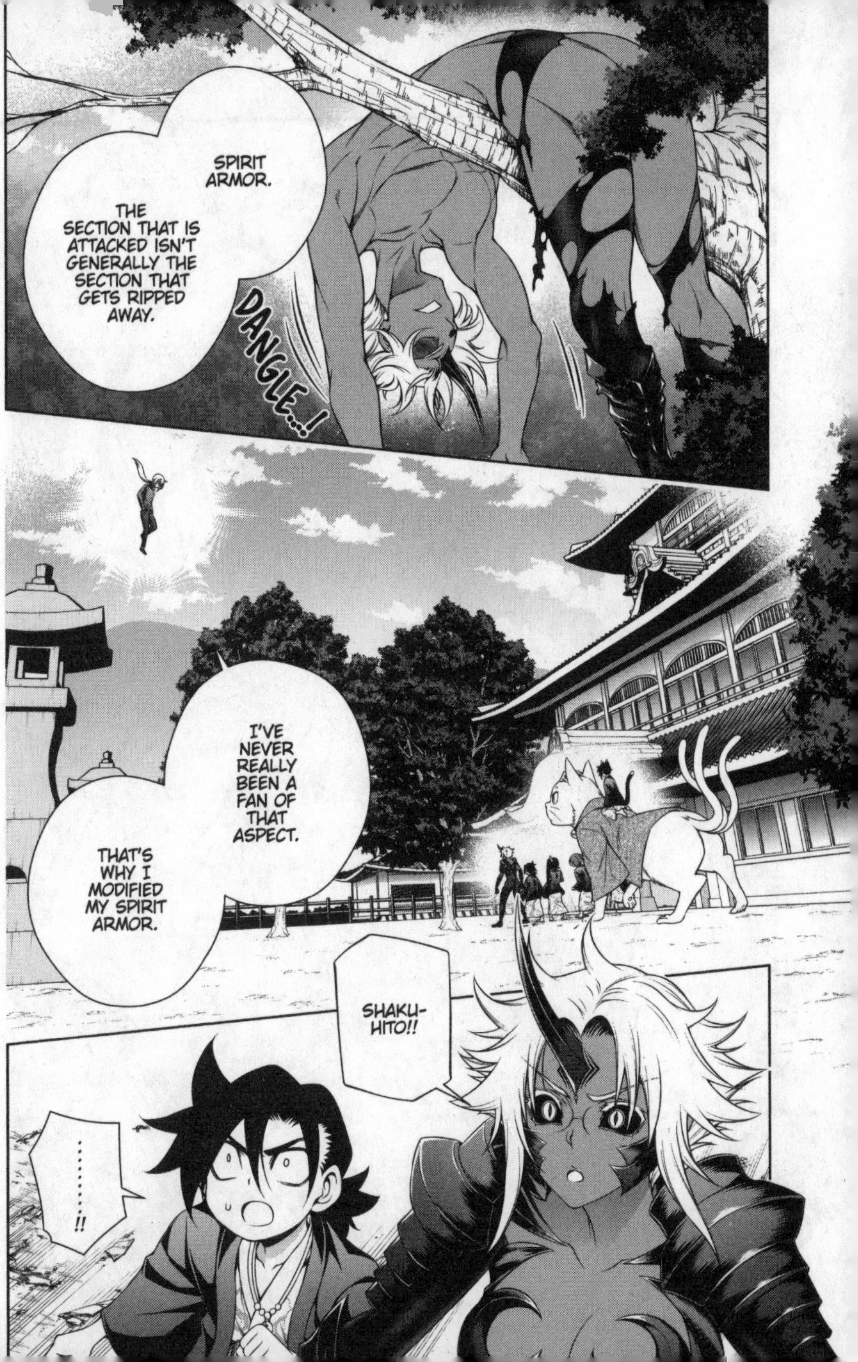

SPIRIT ARMOR.
THE SECTION THAT IS ATTACKED ISN'T GENERALLY THE SECTION THAT GETS RIPPED AWAY.
DANGLE...!
I'VE NEVER REALLY BEEN A FAN OF THAT ASPECT.
THAT'S WHY I MODIFIED MY SPIRIT ARMOR.
SHAKU-HITO!!
.........!!

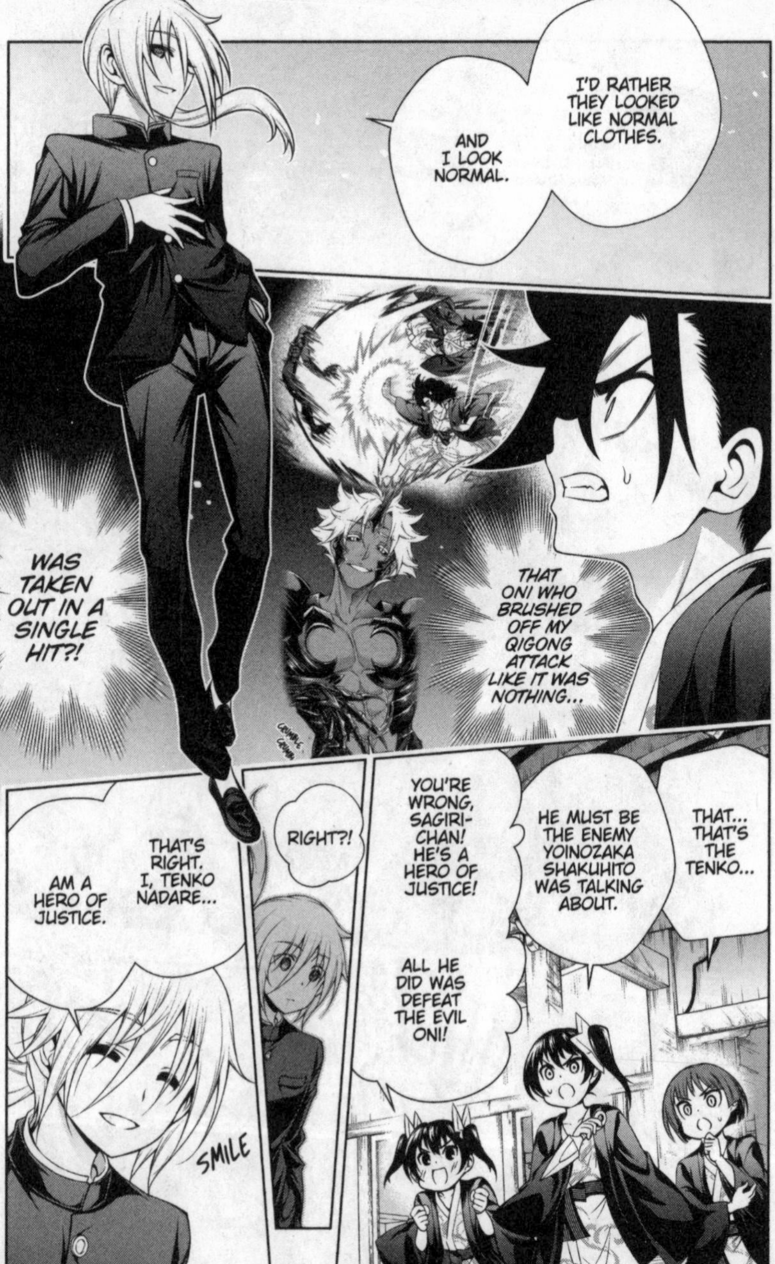
I'D RATHER THEY LOOKED LIKE NORMAL CLOTHES.
AND I LOOK NORMAL.
THAT ONI WHO BRUSHED OFF MY QIGONG ATTACK LIKE IT WAS NOTHING...
WAS TAKEN OUT IN A SINGLE HIT?!
THAT... THAT'S THE TENKO...
HE MUST BE THE ENEMY YOINOZAKA SHAKUHITO WAS TALKING ABOUT.
YOU'RE WRONG, SAGIRI-CHAN! HE'S A HERO OF JUSTICE!
ALL HE DID WAS DEFEAT THE EVIL ONI!
RIGHT?!
THAT'S RIGHT. I, TENKO NADARE...
AM A HERO OF JUSTICE.
SMILE

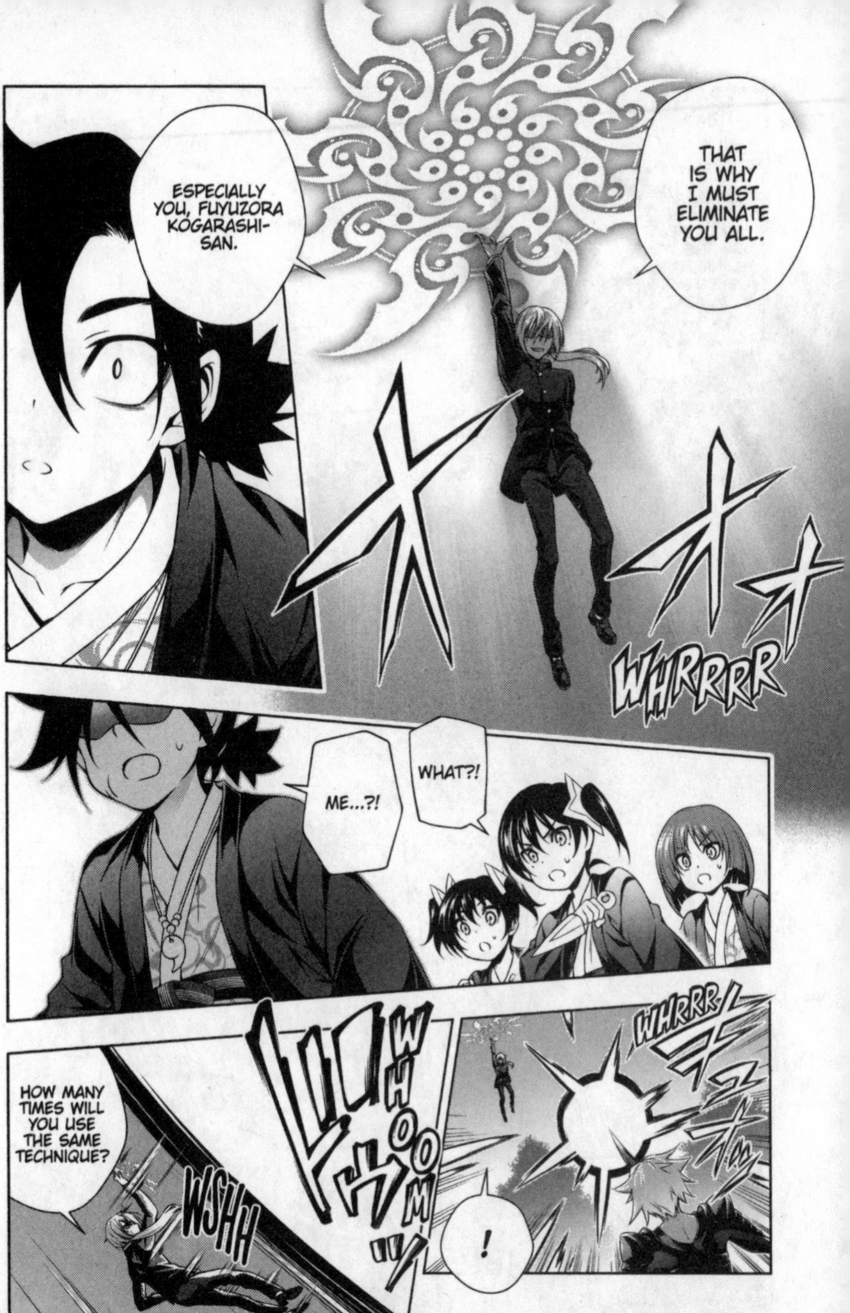
THAT IS WHY I MUST ELIMINATE YOU ALL.
ESPECIALLY YOU, FUYUZORA KOGARASHI-SAN.
WHRRRR
WHAT?!
ME...?!
WHRRR
!
WHOOOM
HOW MANY TIMES WILL YOU USE THE SAME TECHNIQUE?
WSHH

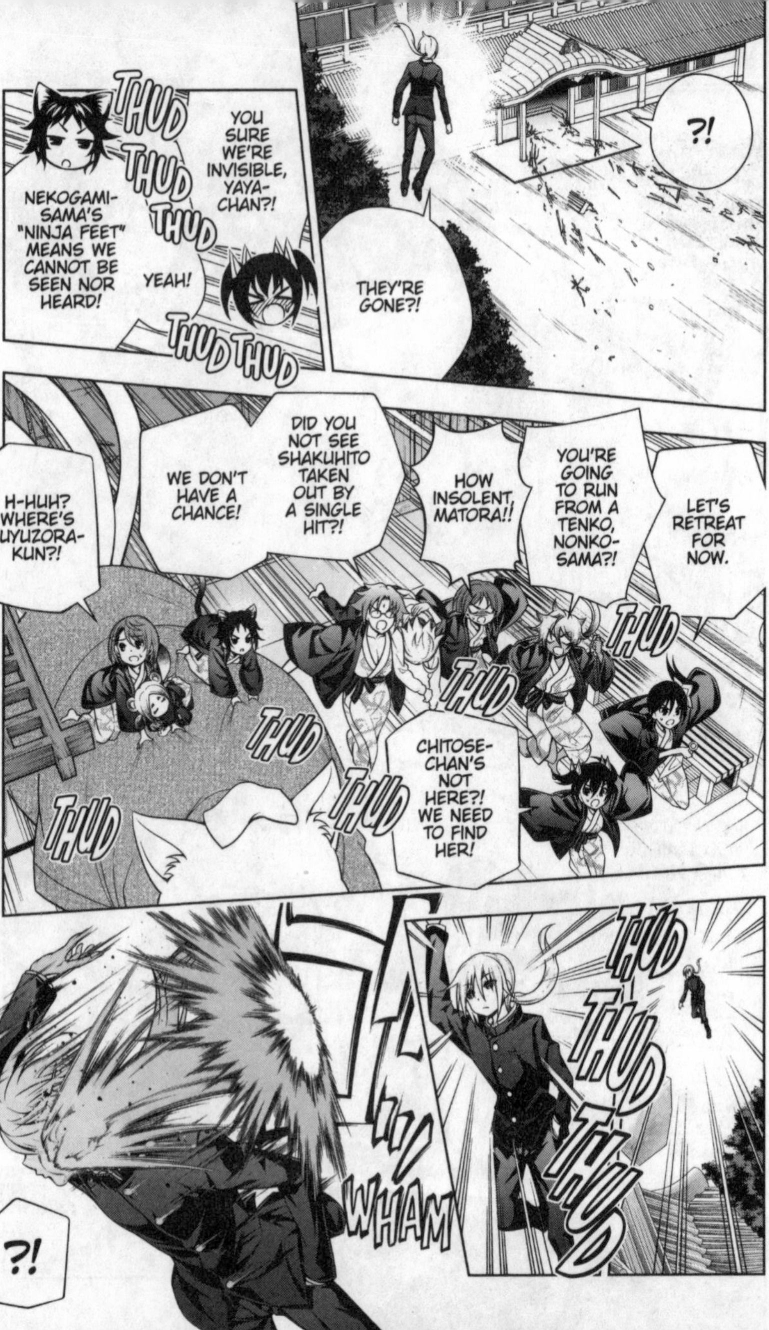
?!
THEY'RE GONE?!
THUD THUD THUD
YOU SURE WE'RE INVISIBLE, YAYA-CHAN?!
YEAH!
NEKOGAMI-SAMA'S "NINJA FEET" MEANS WE CANNOT BE SEEN NOR HEARD!
THUD THUD
LET'S RETREAT FOR NOW.
YOU'RE GOING TO RUN FROM A TENKO, NONKO-SAMA?!
HOW INSOLENT, MATORA!!
DID YOU NOT SEE SHAKUHITO TAKEN OUT BY A SINGLE HIT?!
WE DON'T HAVE A CHANCE!
H-HUH? WHERE'S FUYUZORA-KUN?!
THUD
THUD
CHITOSE-CHAN'S NOT HERE?! WE NEED TO FIND HER!
THUD
THUD
THUD
THUD THUD THUD
WHAM
?!

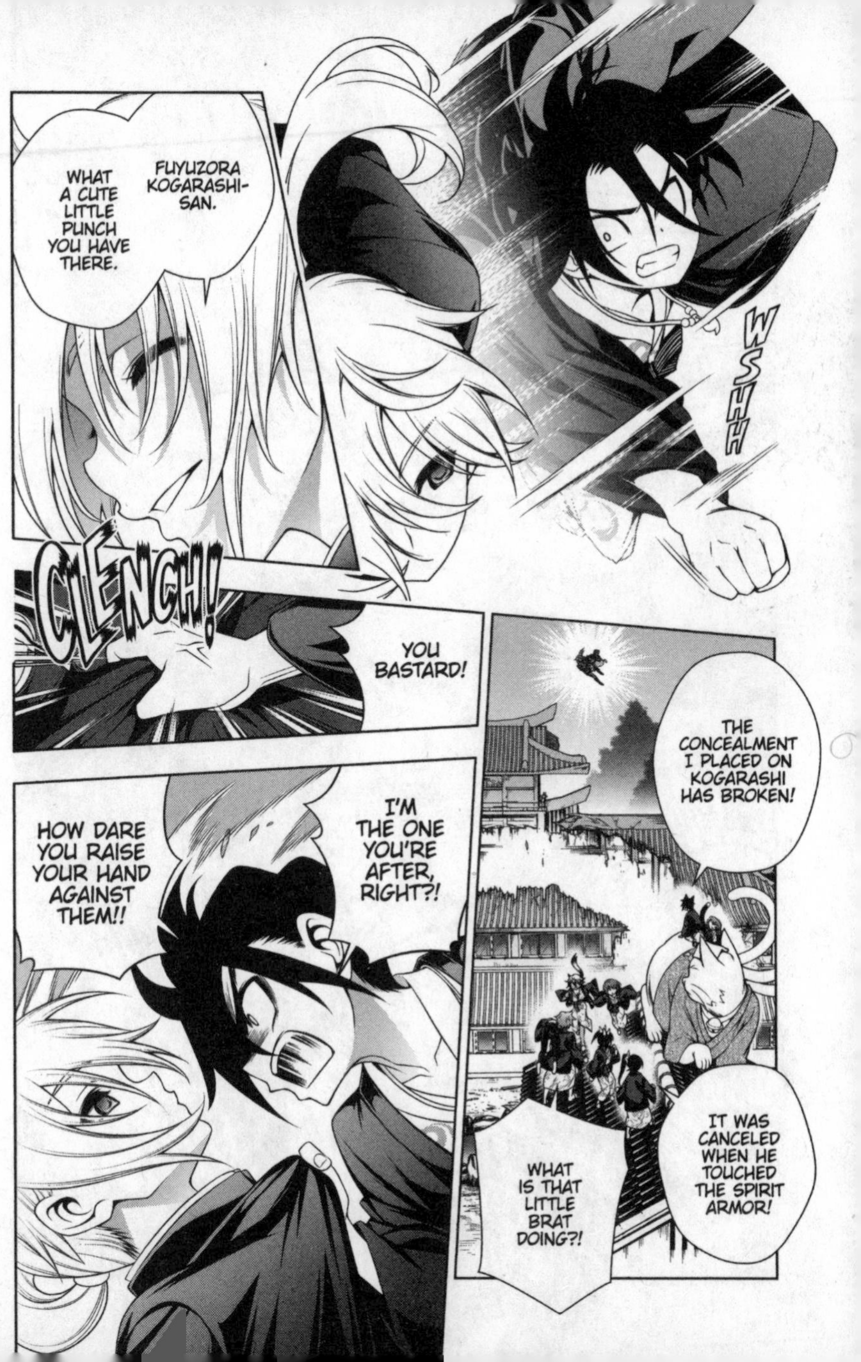
FUYUZORA KOGARASHI-SAN.
WHAT A CUTE LITTLE PUNCH YOU HAVE THERE.
WSHH
CLENCH!
THE CONCEALMENT I PLACED ON KOGARASHI HAS BROKEN!
IT WAS CANCELED WHEN HE TOUCHED THE SPIRIT ARMOR!
WHAT IS THAT LITTLE BRAT DOING?!
YOU BASTARD!
I'M THE ONE YOU'RE AFTER, RIGHT?!
HOW DARE YOU RAISE YOUR HAND AGAINST THEM!!

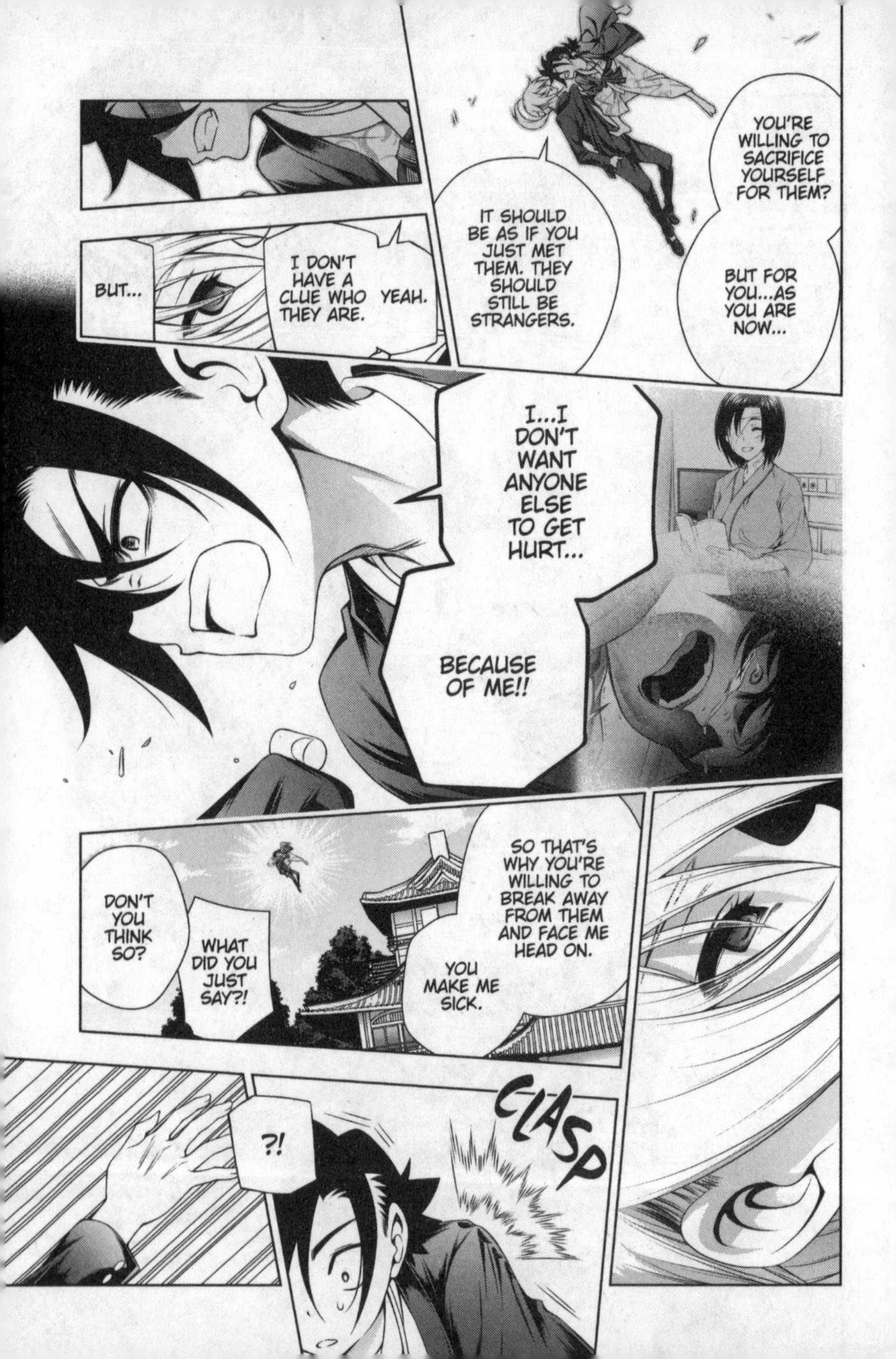
YOU'RE WILLING TO SACRIFICE YOURSELF FOR THEM?
BUT FOR YOU...AS YOU ARE NOW...
IT SHOULD BE AS IF YOU JUST MET THEM. THEY SHOULD STILL BE STRANGERS.
YEAH.
I DON'T HAVE A CLUE WHO THEY ARE.
BUT...
I...I DON'T WANT ANYONE ELSE TO GET HURT...
BECAUSE OF ME!!
SO THAT'S WHY YOU'RE WILLING TO BREAK AWAY FROM THEM AND FACE ME HEAD ON.
YOU MAKE ME SICK.
WHAT DID YOU JUST SAY?!
DON'T YOU THINK SO?
CLASP
?!

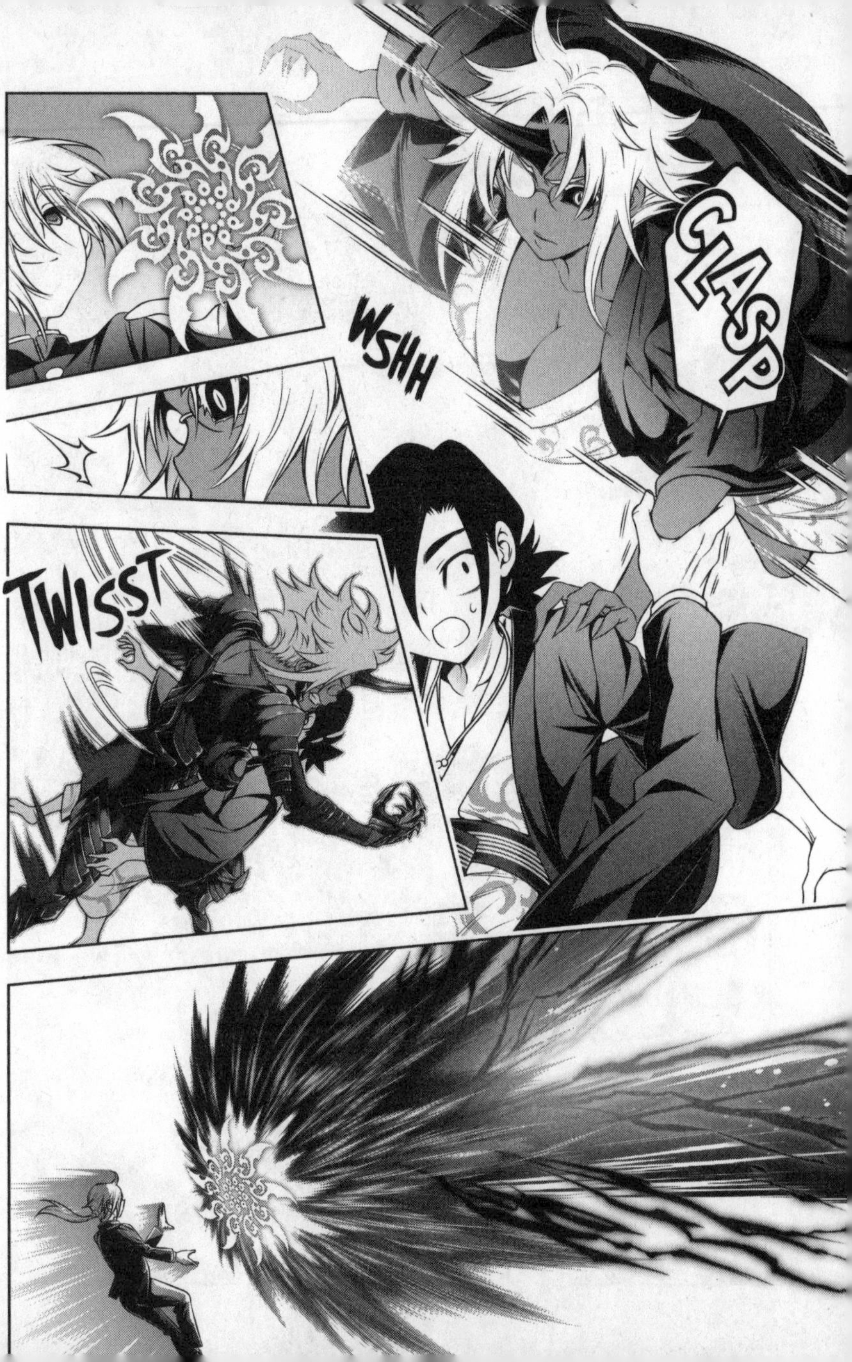
CLASP
WSHH
TWISST

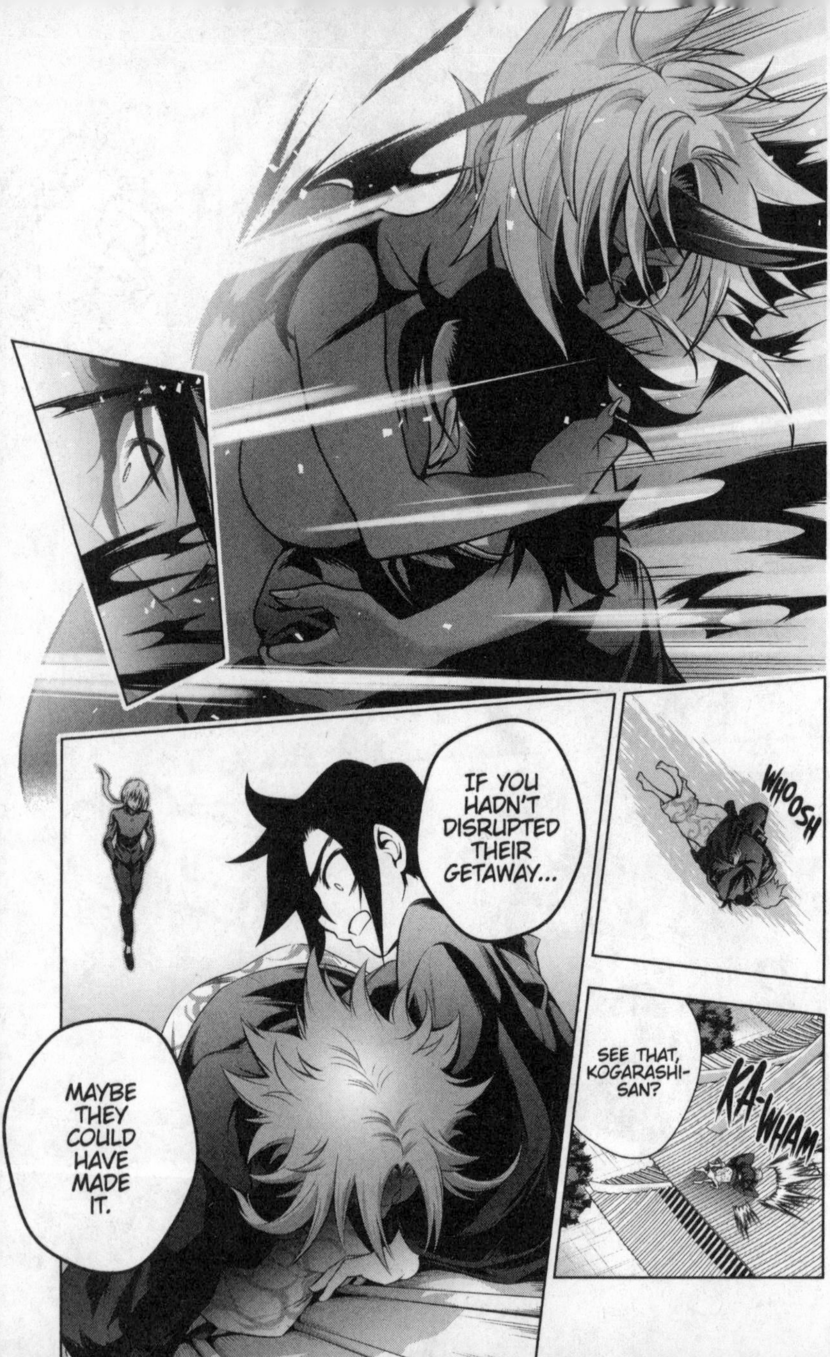
WHOOSH
SEE THAT, KOGARASHI-SAN?
KA-WHAM
IF YOU HADN'T DISRUPTED THEIR GETAWAY...
MAYBE THEY COULD HAVE MADE IT.

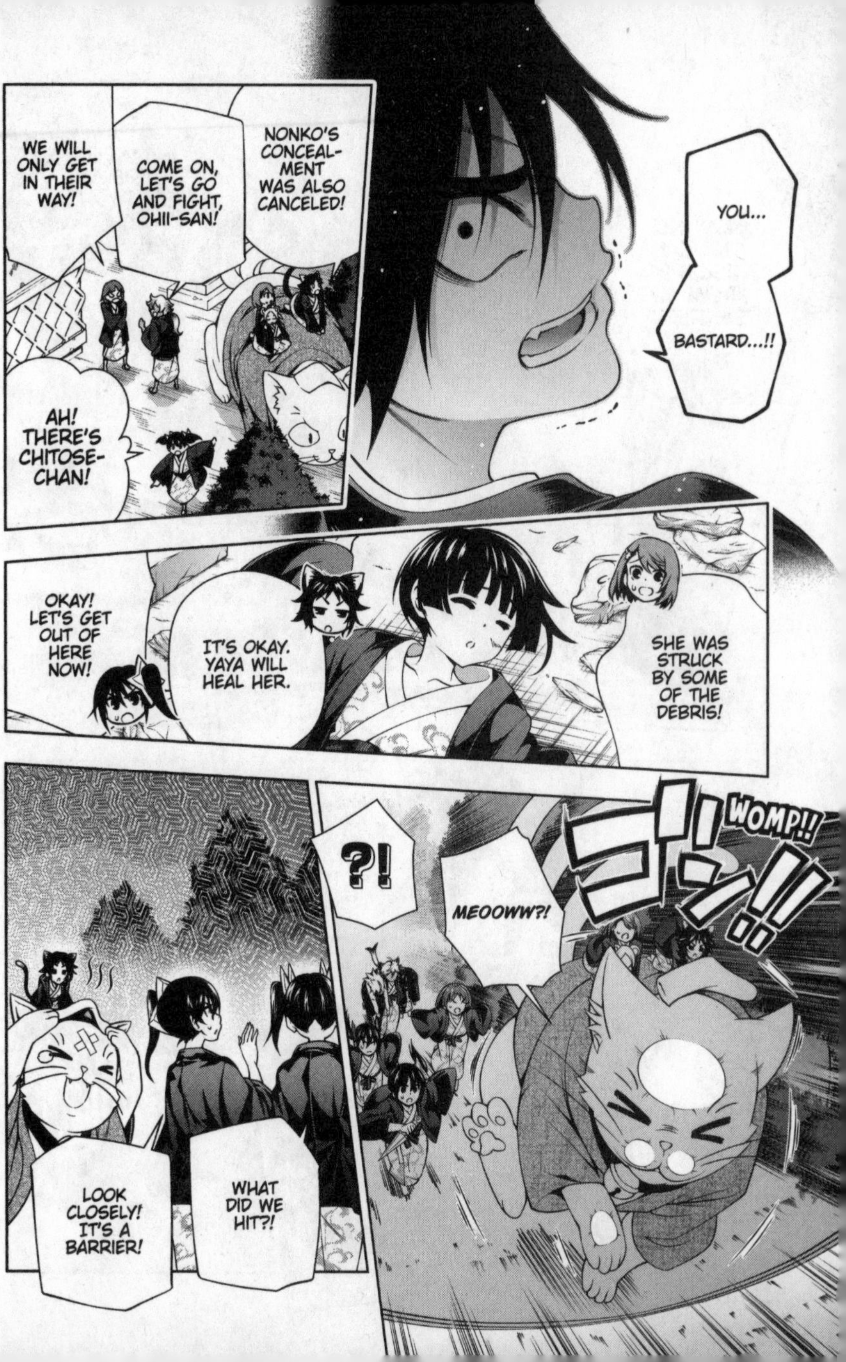
YOU...
BASTARD...!!
NONKO'S CONCEAL-MENT WAS ALSO CANCELED!
COME ON, LET'S GO AND FIGHT, OHII-SAN!
WE WILL ONLY GET IN THEIR WAY!
AH! THERE'S CHITOSE-CHAN!
SHE WAS STRUCK BY SOME OF THE DEBRIS!
IT'S OKAY. YAYA WILL HEAL HER.
OKAY! LET'S GET OUT OF HERE NOW!
WOMP!!
MEOOWW?!
?!
WHAT DID WE HIT?!
LOOK CLOSELY! IT'S A BARRIER!

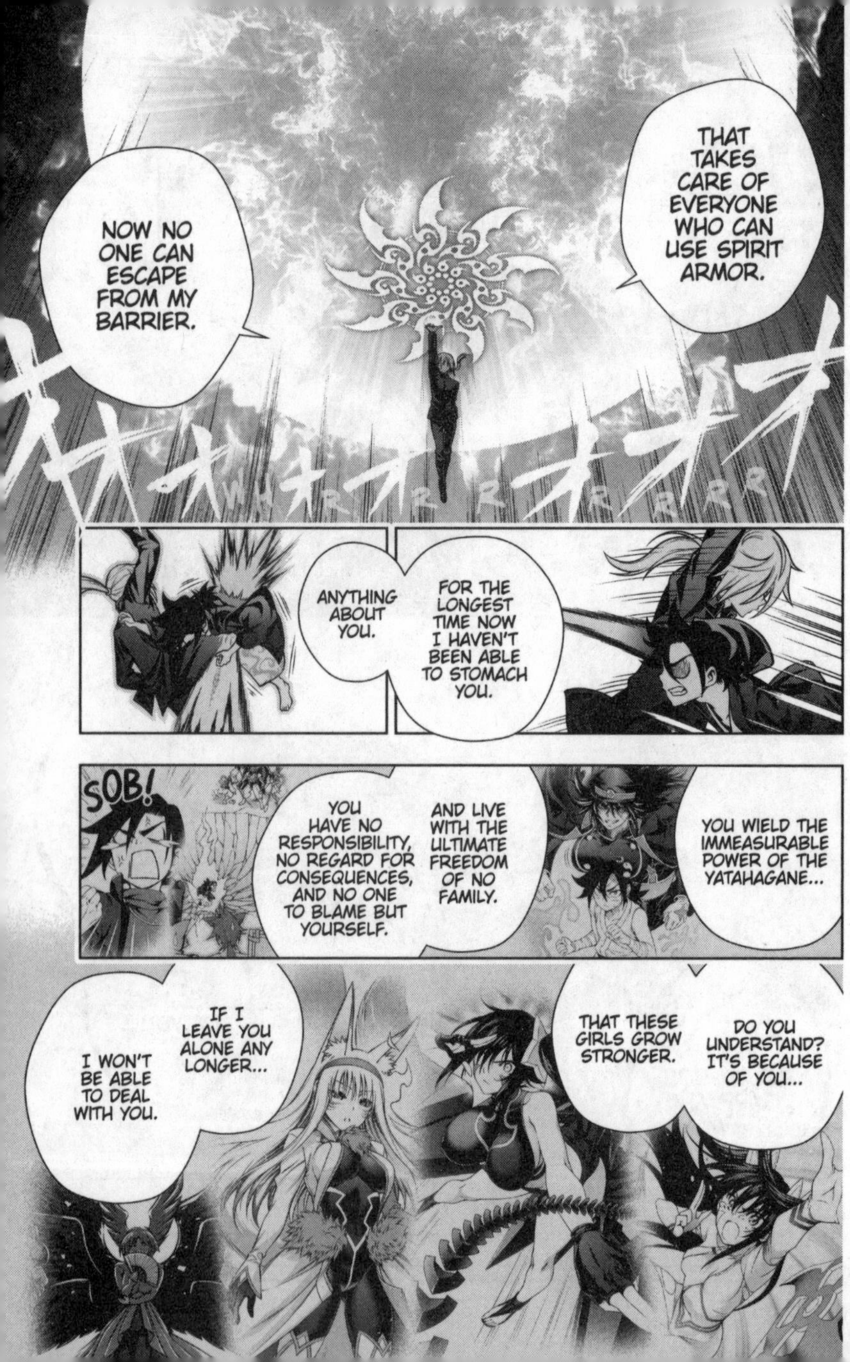
THAT TAKES CARE OF EVERYONE WHO CAN USE SPIRIT ARMOR.
NOW NO ONE CAN ESCAPE FROM MY BARRIER.
FOR THE LONGEST TIME NOW I HAVEN'T BEEN ABLE TO STOMACH YOU.
ANYTHING ABOUT YOU.
YOU WIELD THE IMMEASURABLE POWER OF THE YATAHAGANE...
AND LIVE WITH THE ULTIMATE FREEDOM OF NO FAMILY.
YOU HAVE NO RESPONSIBILITY, NO REGARD FOR CONSEQUENCES, AND NO ONE TO BLAME BUT YOURSELF.
SOB!
DO YOU UNDERSTAND? IT'S BECAUSE OF YOU...
THAT THESE GIRLS GROW STRONGER.
IF I LEAVE YOU ALONE ANY LONGER...
I WON'T BE ABLE TO DEAL WITH YOU.

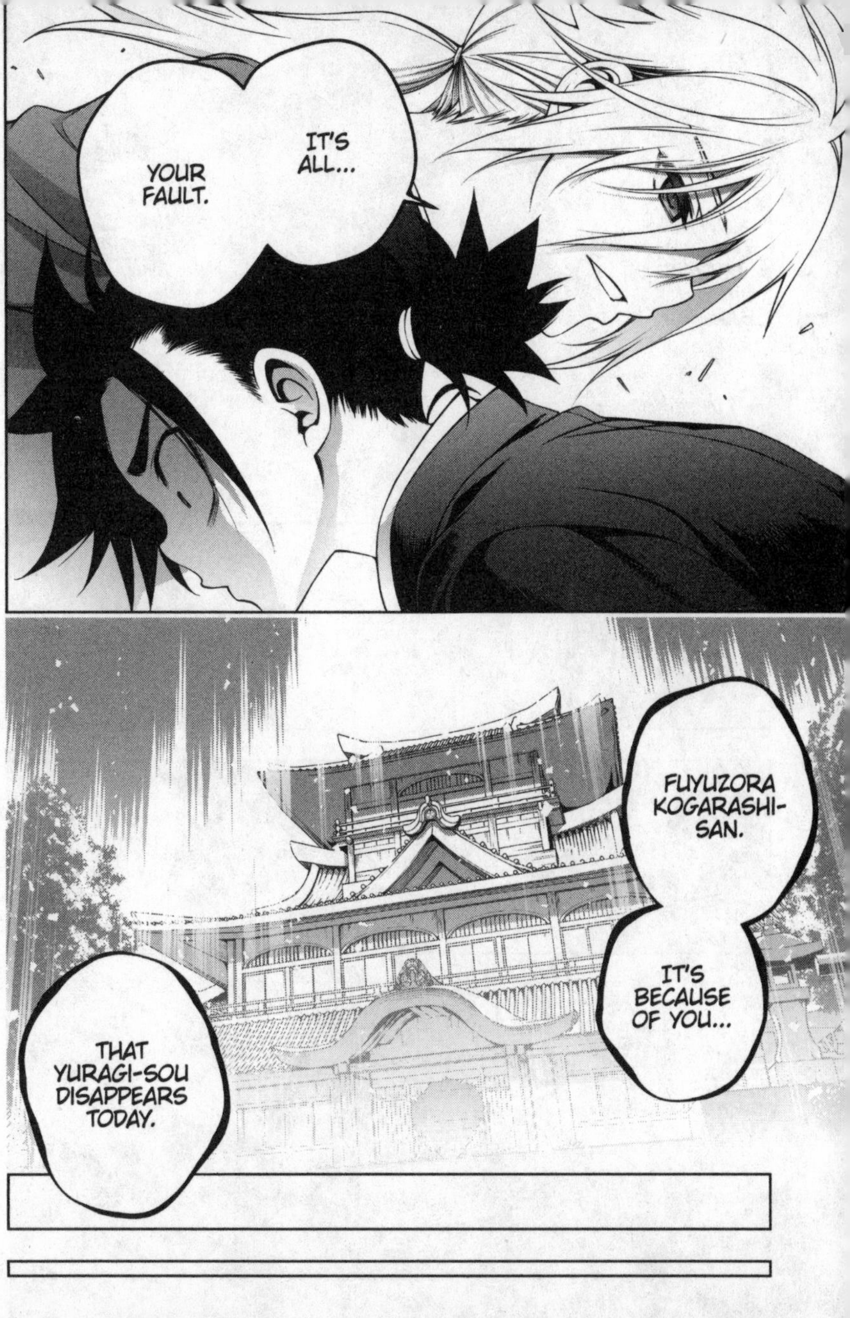
IT'S ALL...
YOUR FAULT.
FUYUZORA KOGARASHI-SAN.
IT'S BECAUSE OF YOU...
THAT YURAGI-SOU DISAPPEARS TODAY.

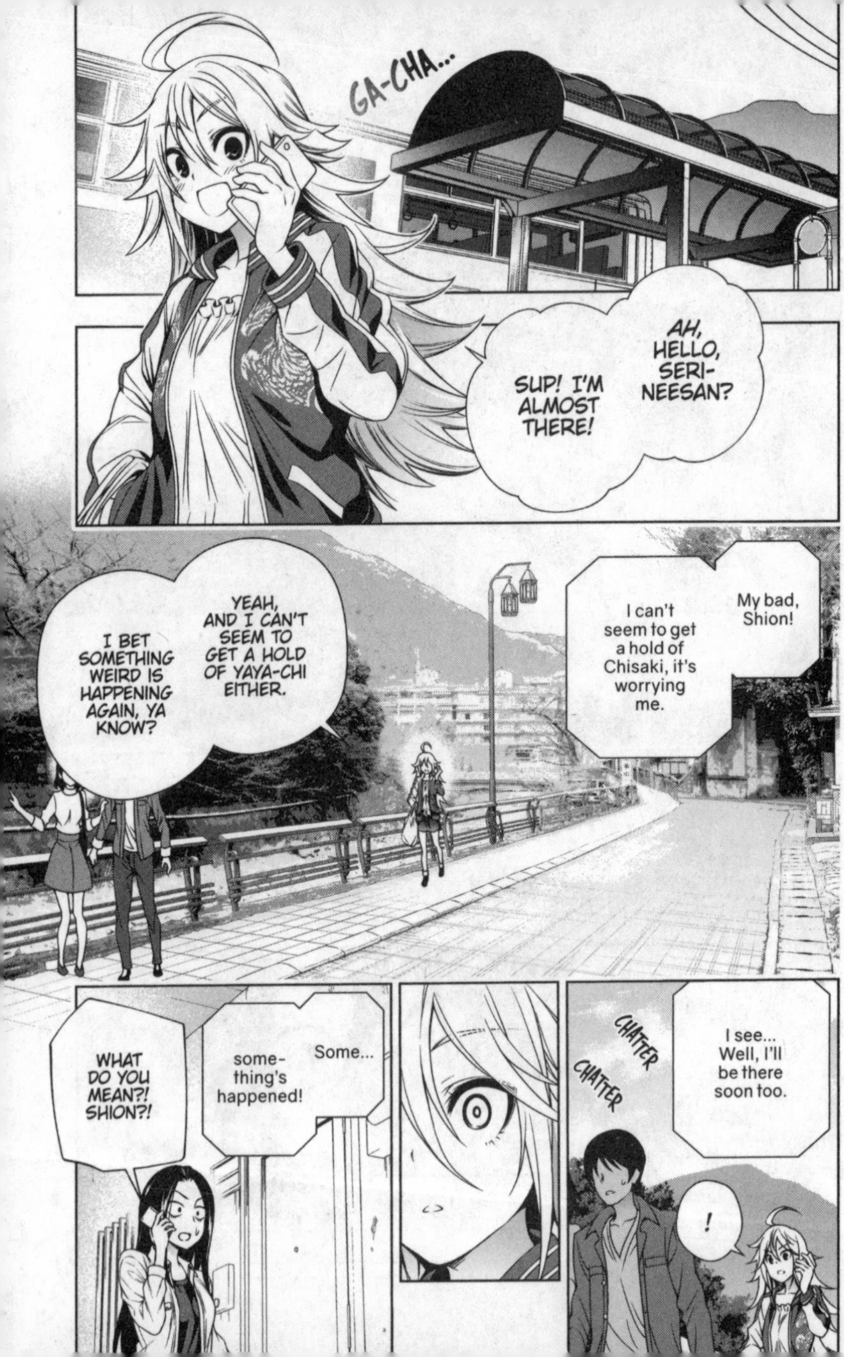
GA-CHA...
AH, HELLO, SERI-NEESAN?
SUP! I'M ALMOST THERE!
My bad, Shion!
I can't seem to get a hold of Chisaki, it's worrying me.
YEAH, AND I CAN'T SEEM TO GET A HOLD OF YAYA-CHI EITHER.
I BET SOMETHING WEIRD IS HAPPENING AGAIN, YA KNOW?
I see... Well, I'll be there soon too.
CHATTER
CHATTER
!
Some...
some-thing's happened!
WHAT DO YOU MEAN?! SHION?!

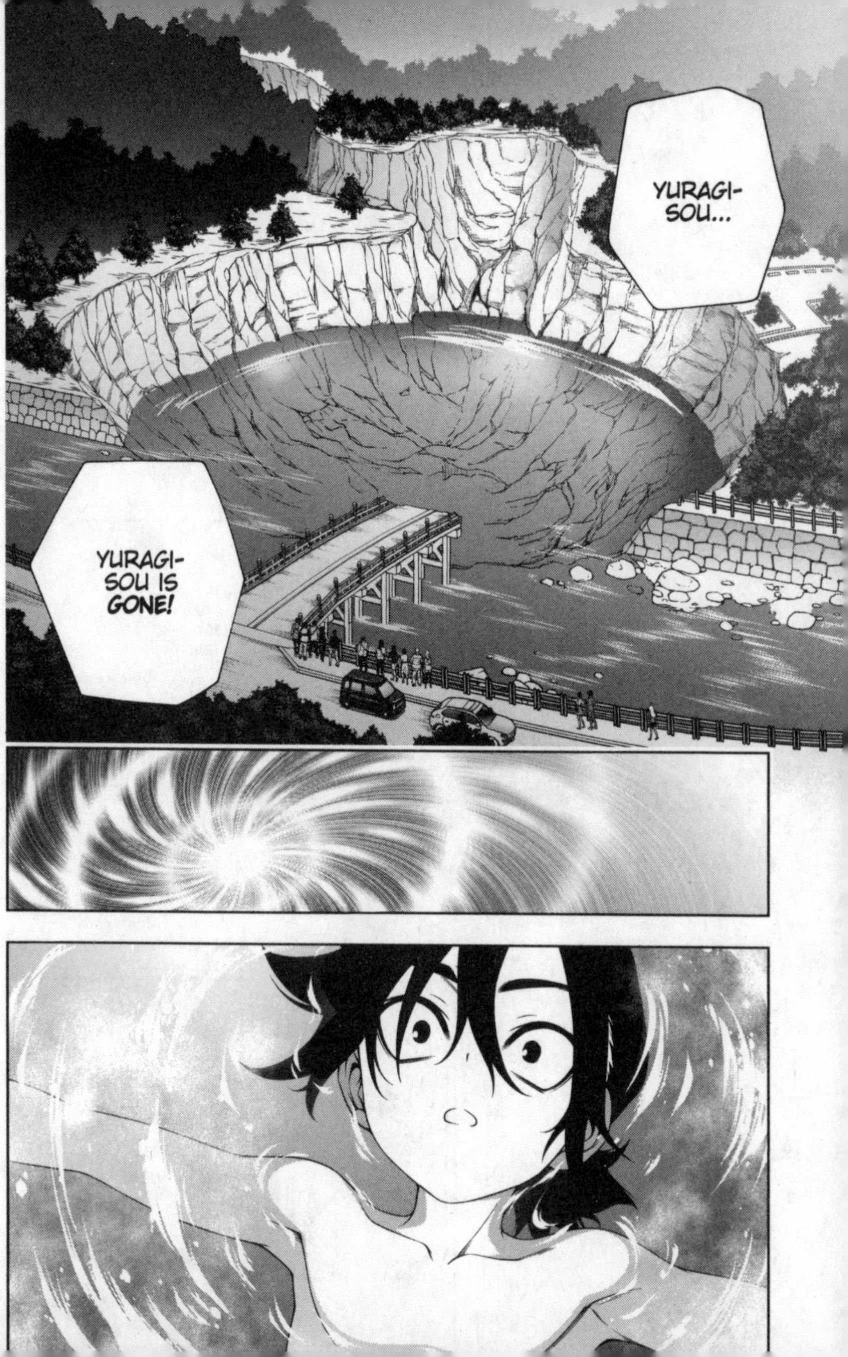
YURAGI-SOU...
YURAGI-SOU IS GONE!

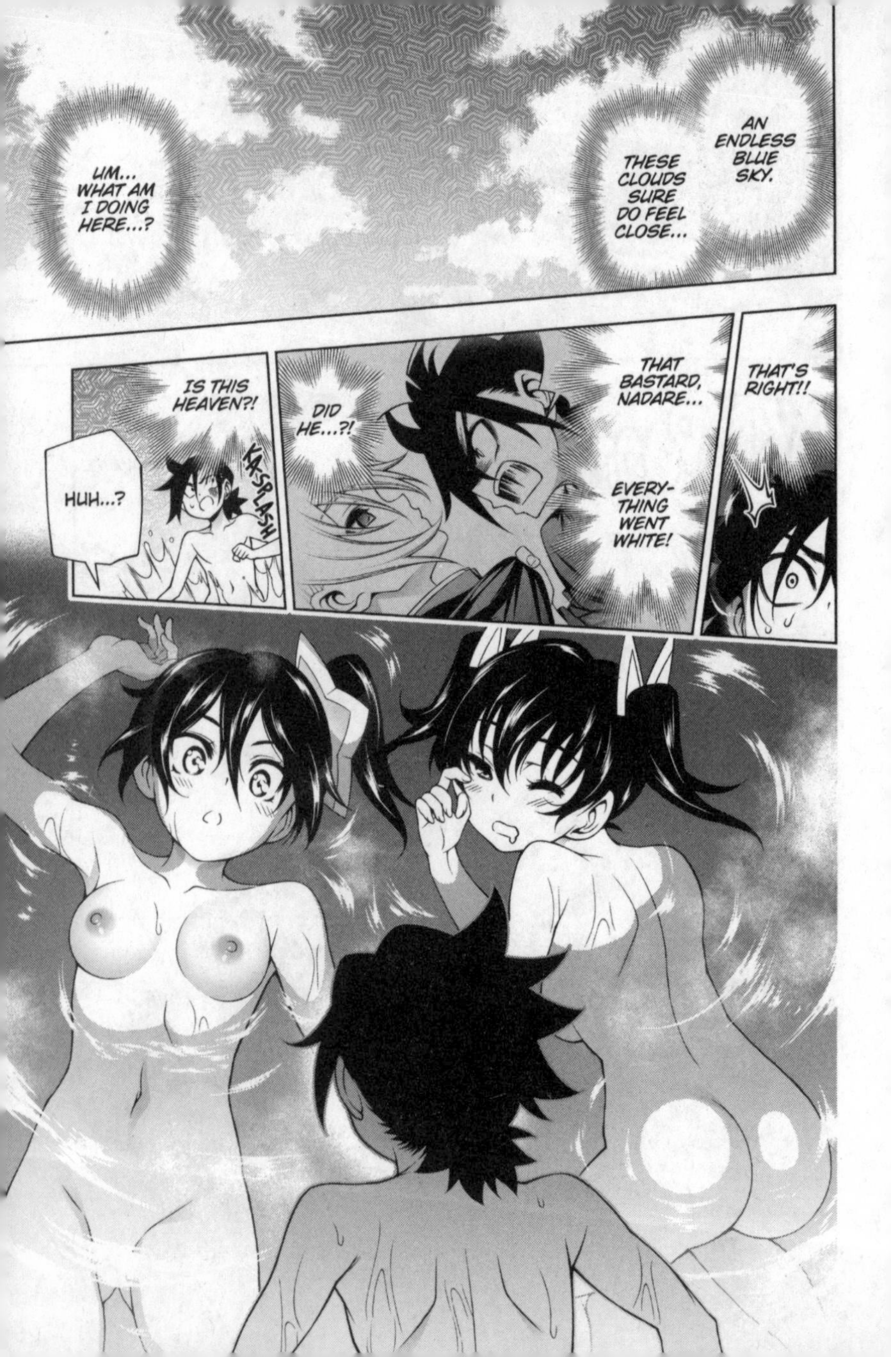
AN ENDLESS BLUE SKY.
THESE CLOUDS SURE DO FEEL CLOSE...
UM... WHAT AM I DOING HERE...?
THAT'S RIGHT!!
THAT BASTARD, NADARE...
EVERY-THING WENT WHITE!
DID HE...?!
IS THIS HEAVEN?!
KA-SPLASH
HUH...?

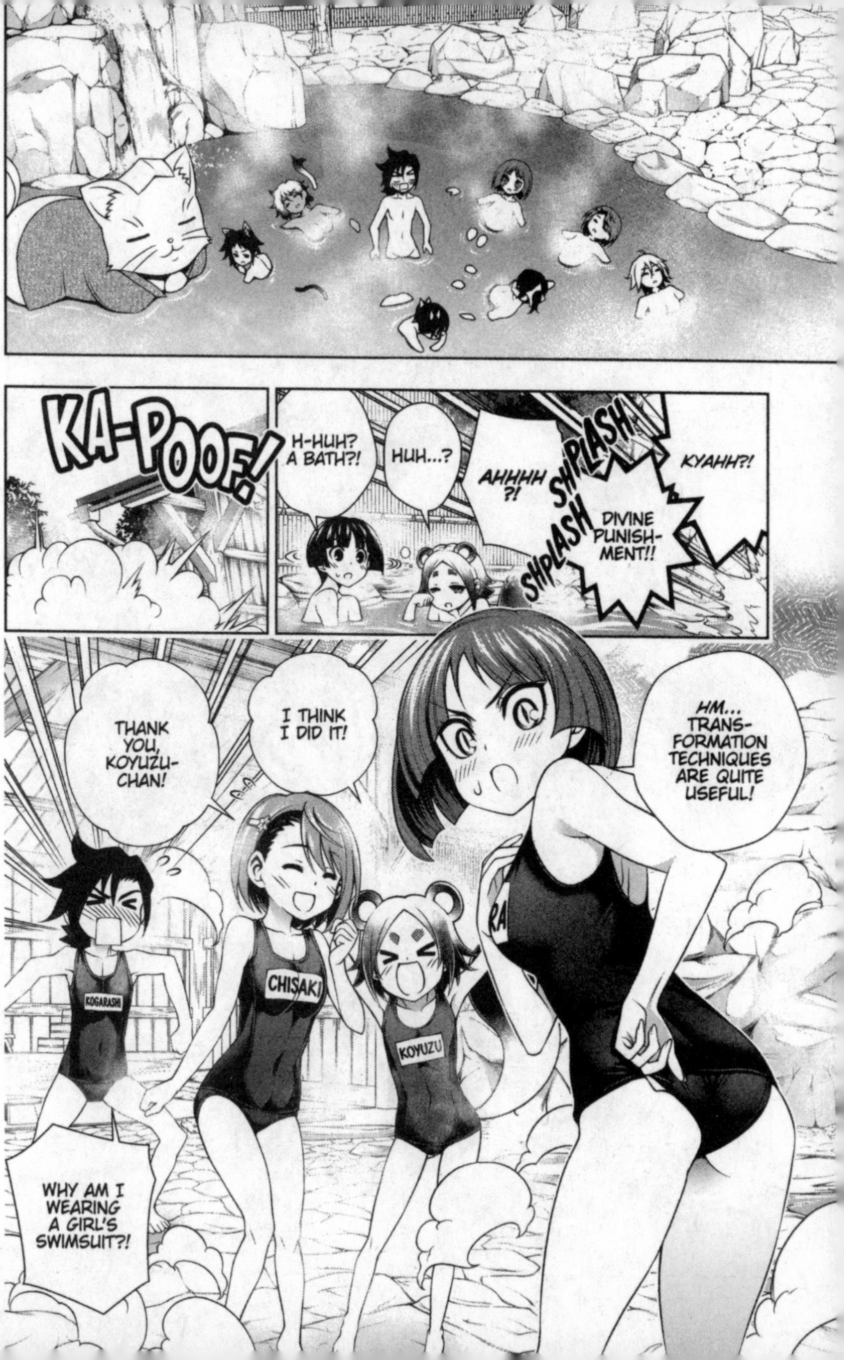
KYAHH?!
SHPLASH
SHPLASH
SHPLASH
DIVINE PUNISH-MENT!!
AHHHH?!
HUH...?
H-HUH? A BATH?!
KA-POOF!
HM... TRANS-FORMATION TECHNIQUES ARE QUITE USEFUL!
I THINK I DID IT!
THANK YOU, KOYUZU-CHAN!
KOYUZU
CHISAKI
KOGARASHI
WHY AM I WEARING A GIRL'S SWIMSUIT?!

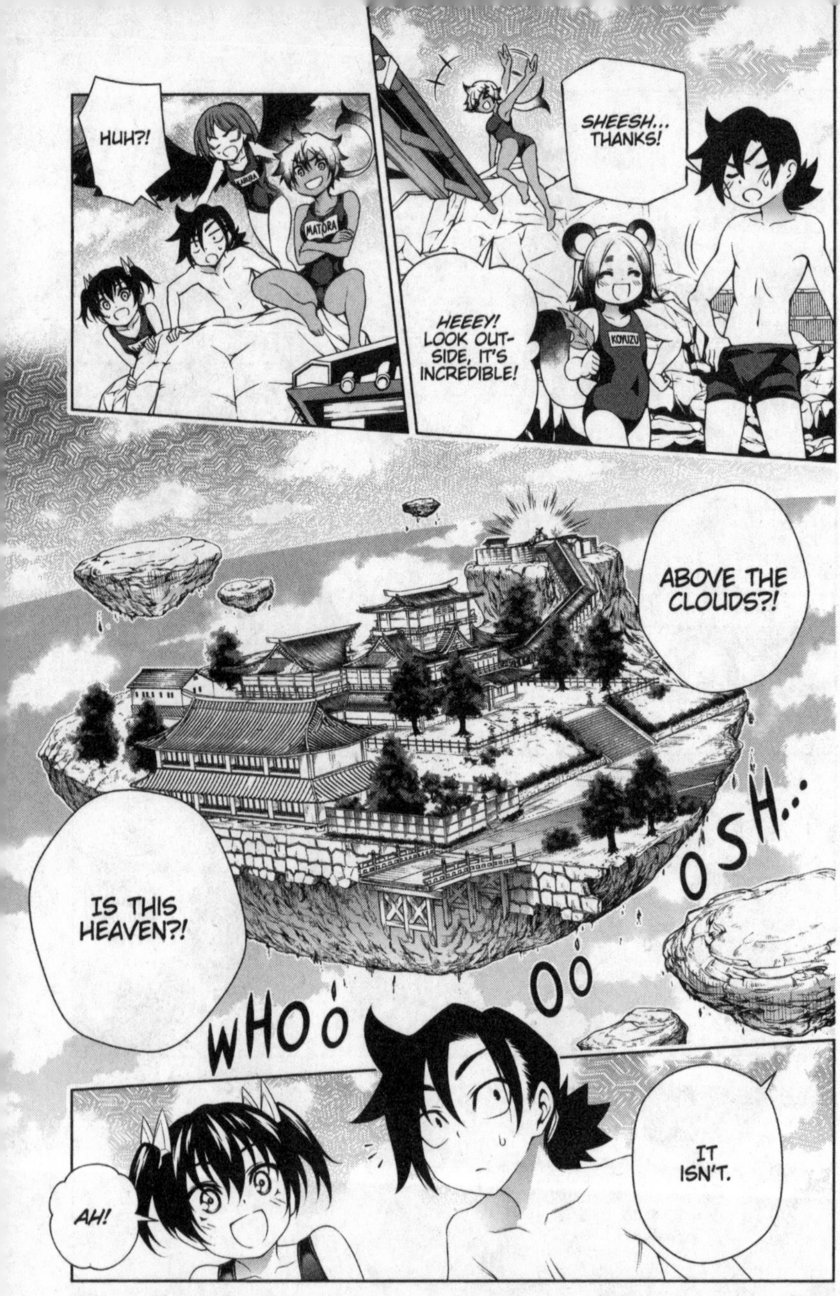
SHEESH... THANKS!
HEEEY! LOOK OUT-SIDE, IT'S INCREDIBLE!
KOYUZU
HUH?!
MATORA
ABOVE THE CLOUDS?!
IS THIS HEAVEN?!
WHOOOOSH...
IT ISN'T.
AH!

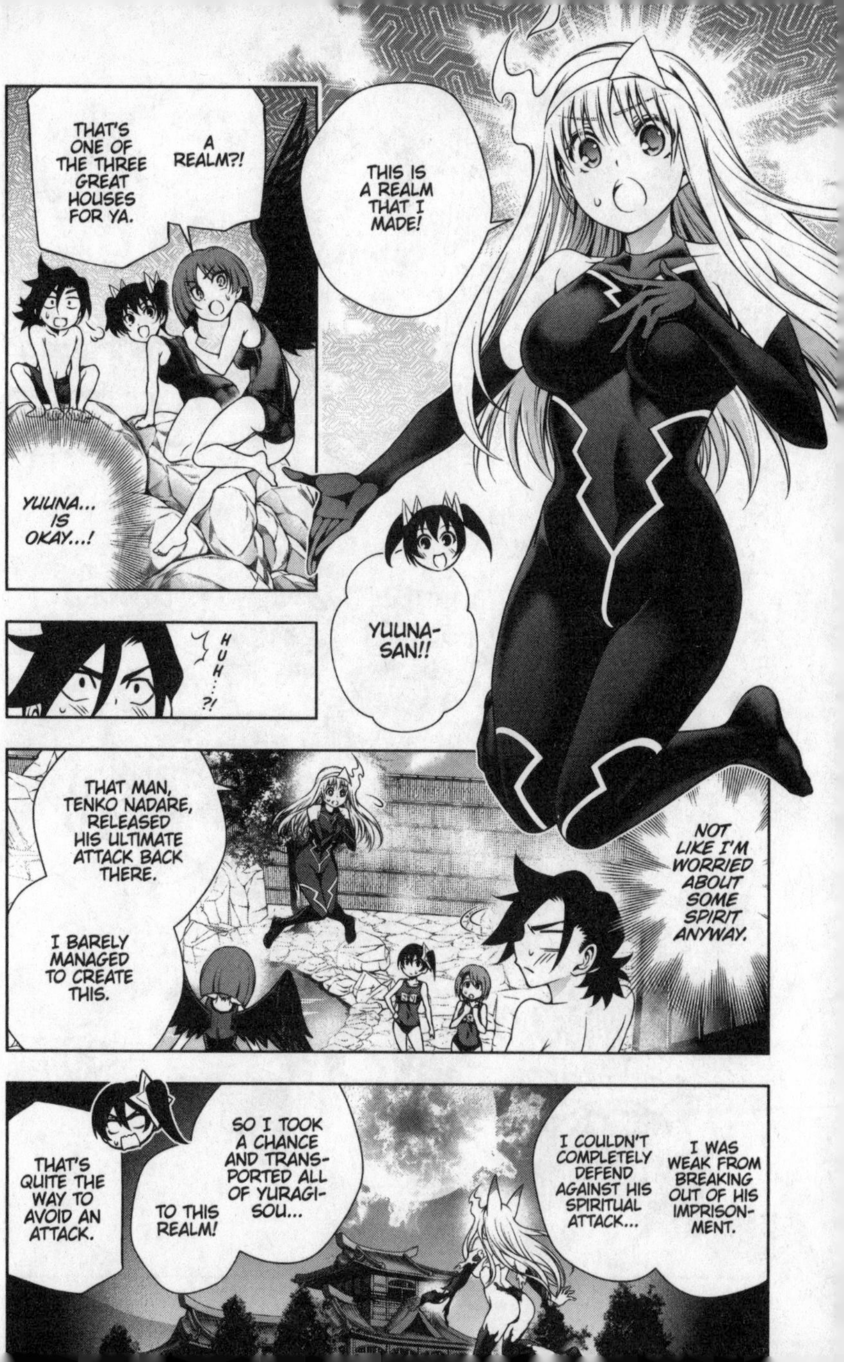
THIS IS A REALM THAT I MADE!
A REALM?!
THAT'S ONE OF THE THREE GREAT HOUSES FOR YA.
YUUNA... IS OKAY...!
YUUNA-SAN!!
HUH...?!
NOT LIKE I'M WORRIED ABOUT SOME SPIRIT ANYWAY.
THAT MAN, TENKO NADARE, RELEASED HIS ULTIMATE ATTACK BACK THERE.
I BARELY MANAGED TO CREATE THIS.
I WAS WEAK FROM BREAKING OUT OF HIS IMPRISONMENT.
I COULDN'T COMPLETELY DEFEND AGAINST HIS SPIRITUAL ATTACK...
SO I TOOK A CHANCE AND TRANSPORTED ALL OF YURAGI-SOU...
TO THIS REALM!
THAT'S QUITE THE WAY TO AVOID AN ATTACK.

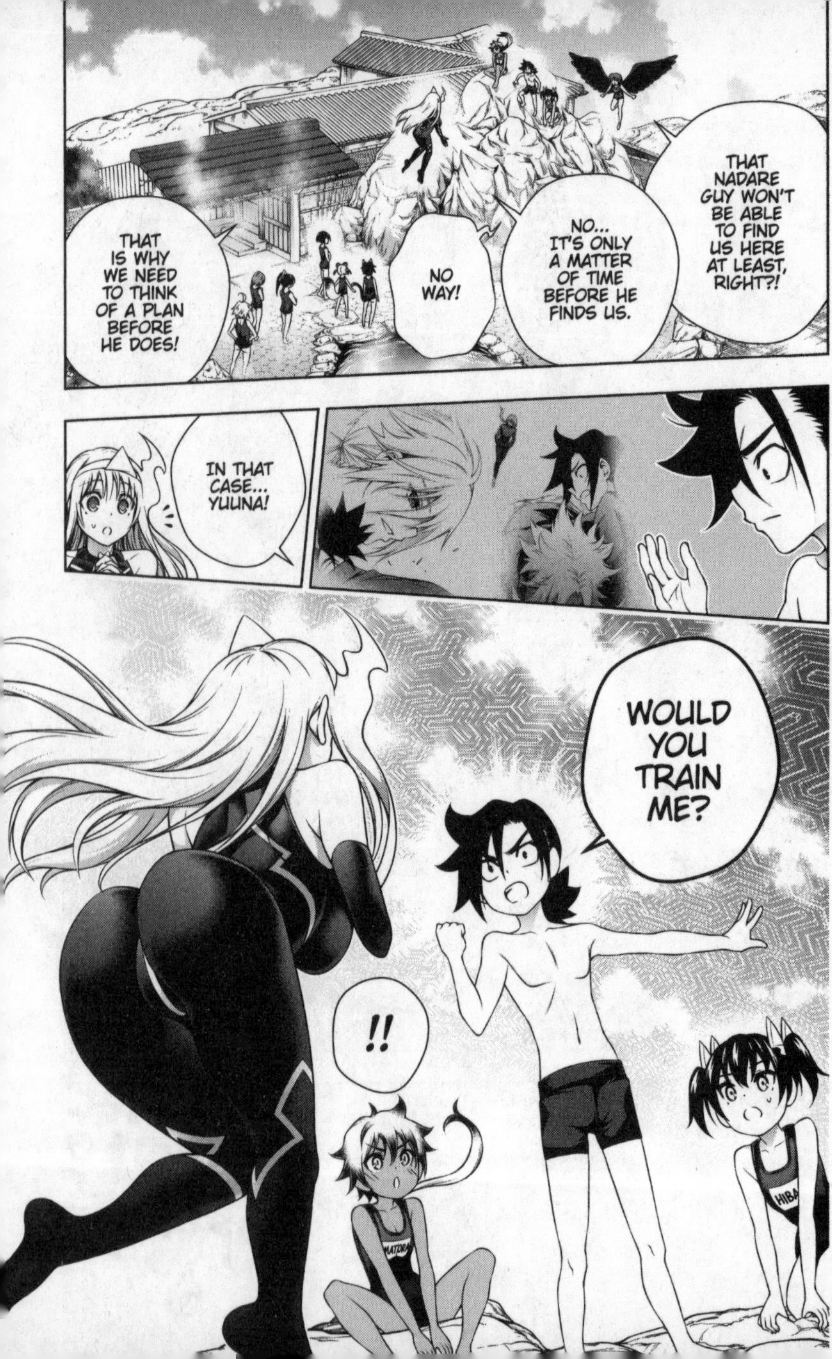
THAT NADARE GUY WON'T BE ABLE TO FIND US HERE AT LEAST, RIGHT?!
NO... IT'S ONLY A MATTER OF TIME BEFORE HE FINDS US.
NO WAY!
THAT IS WHY WE NEED TO THINK OF A PLAN BEFORE HE DOES!
IN THAT CASE... YUUNA!
WOULD YOU TRAIN ME?
!!
MATORA

Yuuna and the Haunted Hot Springs

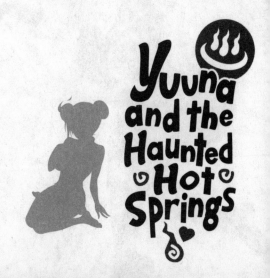

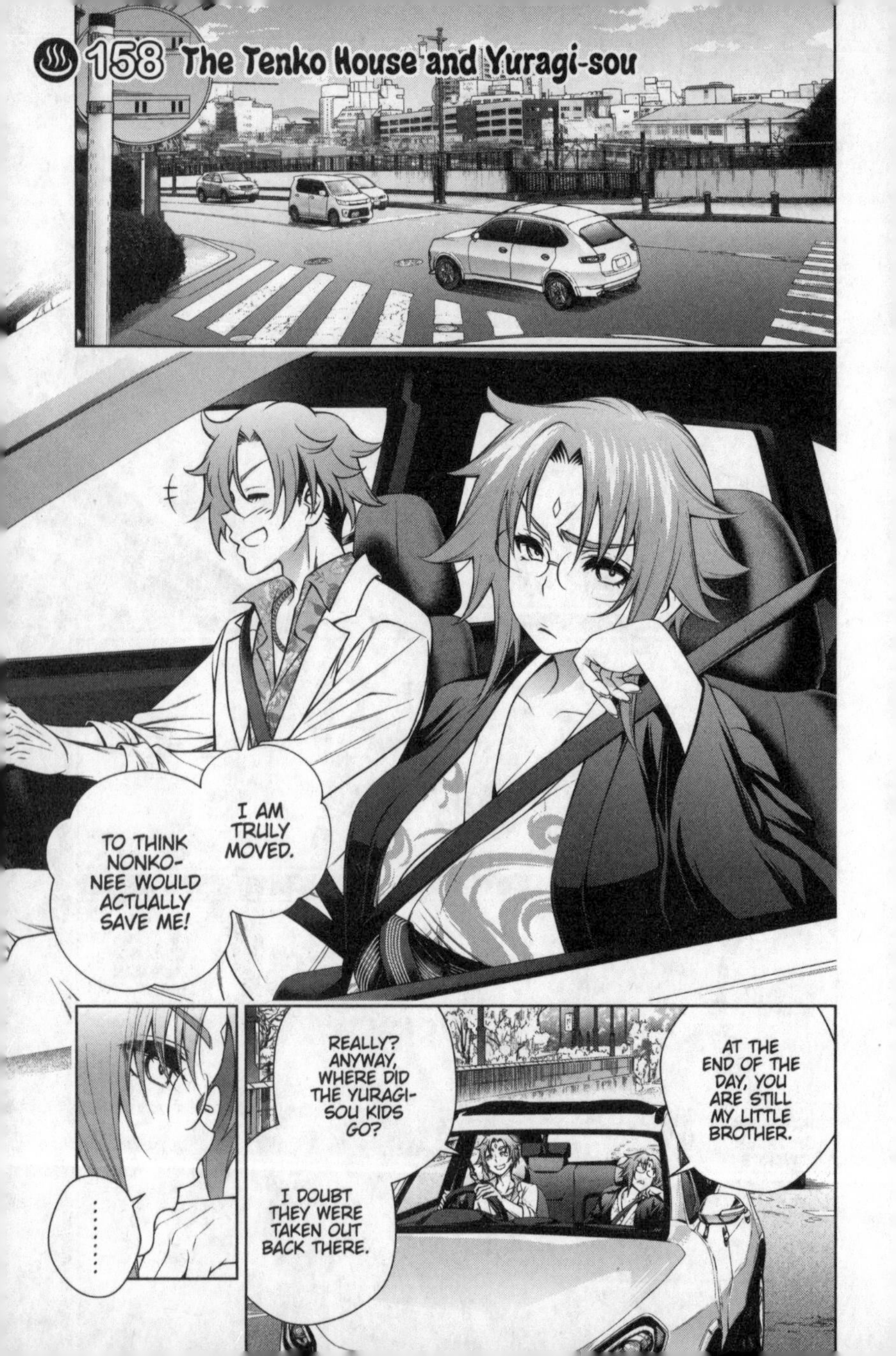
158 The Tenko House and Yuragi-sou
I AM TRULY MOVED.
TO THINK NONKO-NEE WOULD ACTUALLY SAVE ME!
AT THE END OF THE DAY, YOU ARE STILL MY LITTLE BROTHER.
REALLY? ANYWAY, WHERE DID THE YURAGI-SOU KIDS GO?
I DOUBT THEY WERE TAKEN OUT BACK THERE.
......

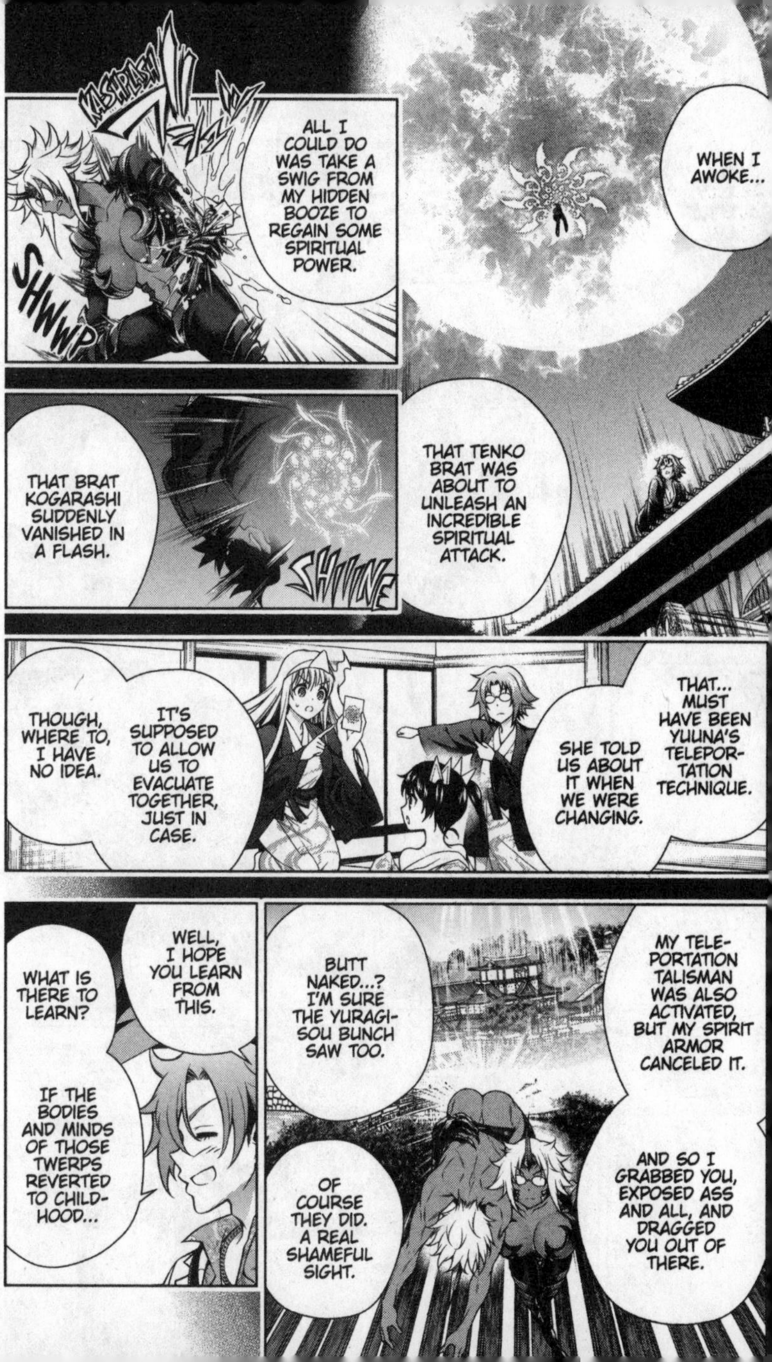

WHEN I AWOKE...
KASHPLASH
SHWWP
ALL I COULD DO WAS TAKE A SWIG FROM MY HIDDEN BOOZE TO REGAIN SOME SPIRITUAL POWER.
THAT TENKO BRAT WAS ABOUT TO UNLEASH AN INCREDIBLE SPIRITUAL ATTACK.
SHIIINE
THAT BRAT KOGARASHI SUDDENLY VANISHED IN A FLASH.
THAT... MUST HAVE BEEN YUUNA'S TELEPORTATION TECHNIQUE.
SHE TOLD US ABOUT IT WHEN WE WERE CHANGING.
IT'S SUPPOSED TO ALLOW US TO EVACUATE TOGETHER, JUST IN CASE.
THOUGH, WHERE TO, I HAVE NO IDEA.
MY TELEPORTATION TALISMAN WAS ALSO ACTIVATED, BUT MY SPIRIT ARMOR CANCELED IT.
BUTT NAKED...? I'M SURE THE YURAGI-SOU BUNCH SAW TOO.
AND SO I GRABBED YOU, EXPOSED ASS AND ALL, AND DRAGGED YOU OUT OF THERE.
OF COURSE THEY DID. A REAL SHAMEFUL SIGHT.
WELL, I HOPE YOU LEARN FROM THIS.
WHAT IS THERE TO LEARN?
IF THE BODIES AND MINDS OF THOSE TWERPS REVERTED TO CHILDHOOD...

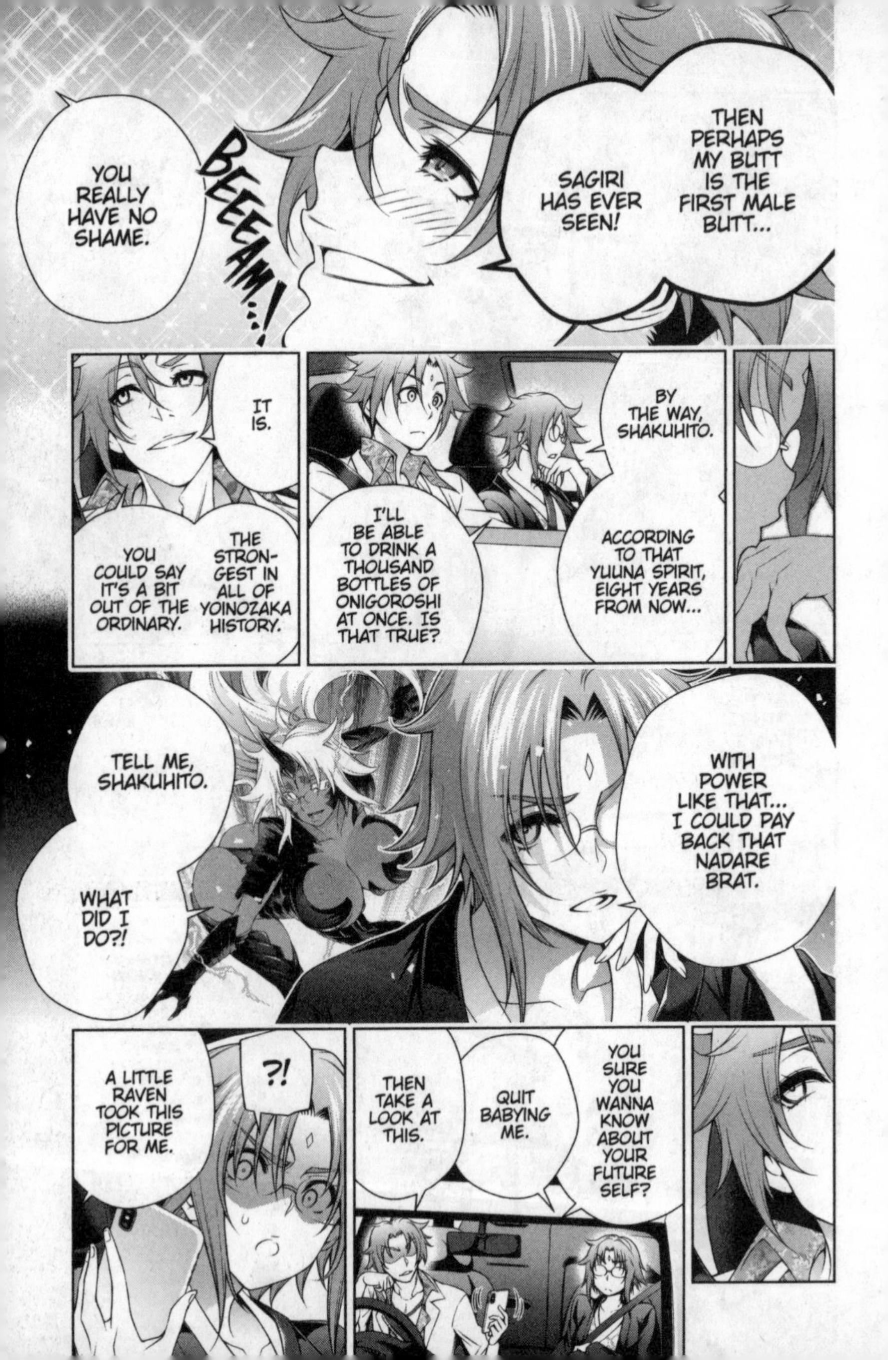
THEN PERHAPS MY BUTT IS THE FIRST MALE BUTT...
SAGIRI HAS EVER SEEN!
BEEEAM...!
YOU REALLY HAVE NO SHAME.
BY THE WAY, SHAKUHITO.
ACCORDING TO THAT YUUNA SPIRIT, EIGHT YEARS FROM NOW...
I'LL BE ABLE TO DRINK A THOUSAND BOTTLES OF ONIGOROSHI AT ONCE. IS THAT TRUE?
IT IS.
THE STRONGEST IN ALL OF YOINOZAKA HISTORY.
YOU COULD SAY IT'S A BIT OUT OF THE ORDINARY.
WITH POWER LIKE THAT... I COULD PAY BACK THAT NADARE BRAT.
TELL ME, SHAKUHITO.
WHAT DID I DO?!
YOU SURE YOU WANNA KNOW ABOUT YOUR FUTURE SELF?
QUIT BABYING ME.
THEN TAKE A LOOK AT THIS.
?!
A LITTLE RAVEN TOOK THIS PICTURE FOR ME.

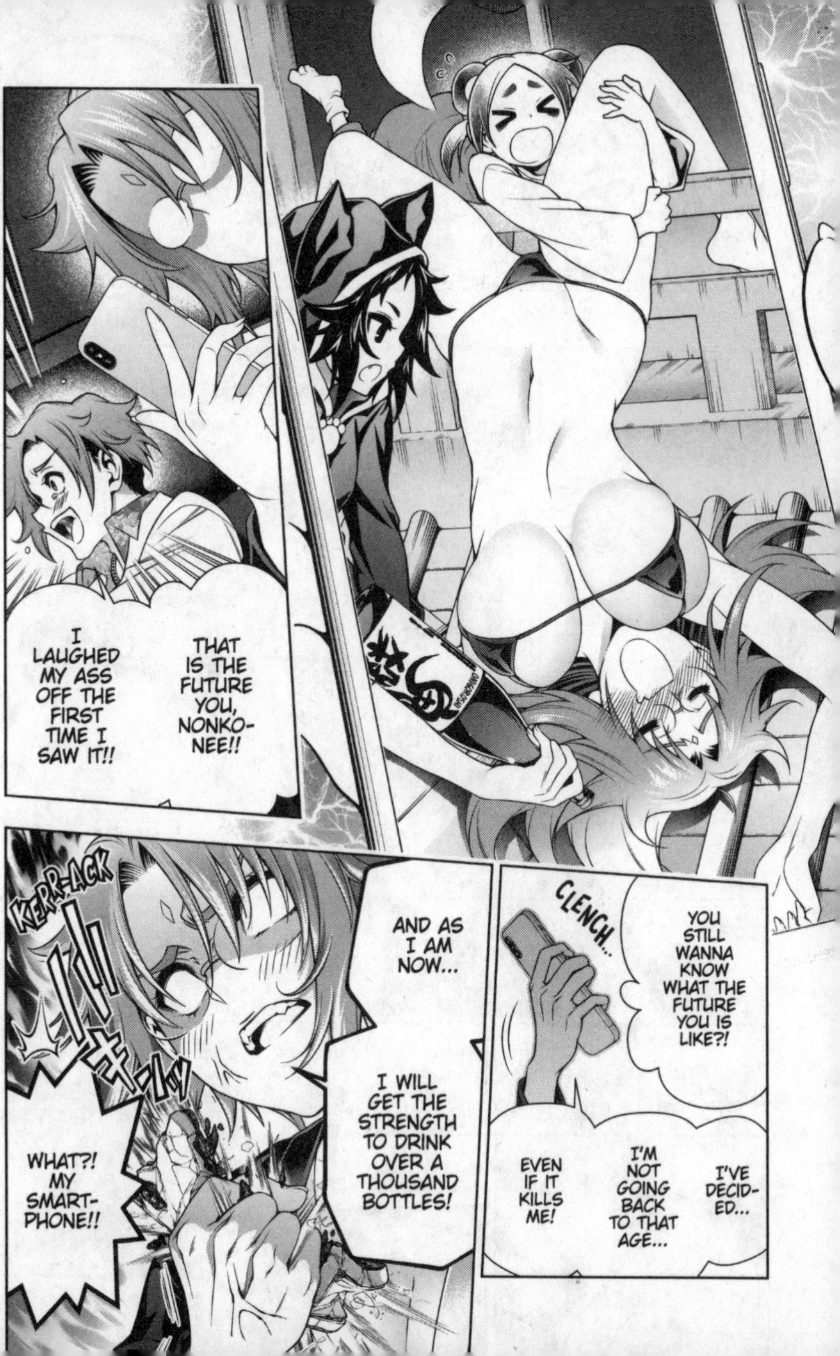
THAT IS THE FUTURE YOU, NONKO-NEE!!
I LAUGHED MY ASS OFF THE FIRST TIME I SAW IT!!
YOU STILL WANNA KNOW WHAT THE FUTURE YOU IS LIKE?!
CLENCH...
I'VE DECID-ED...
I'M NOT GOING BACK TO THAT AGE...
EVEN IF IT KILLS ME!
AND AS I AM NOW...
I WILL GET THE STRENGTH TO DRINK OVER A THOUSAND BOTTLES!
KERR-ACK
WHAT?! MY SMART-PHONE!!

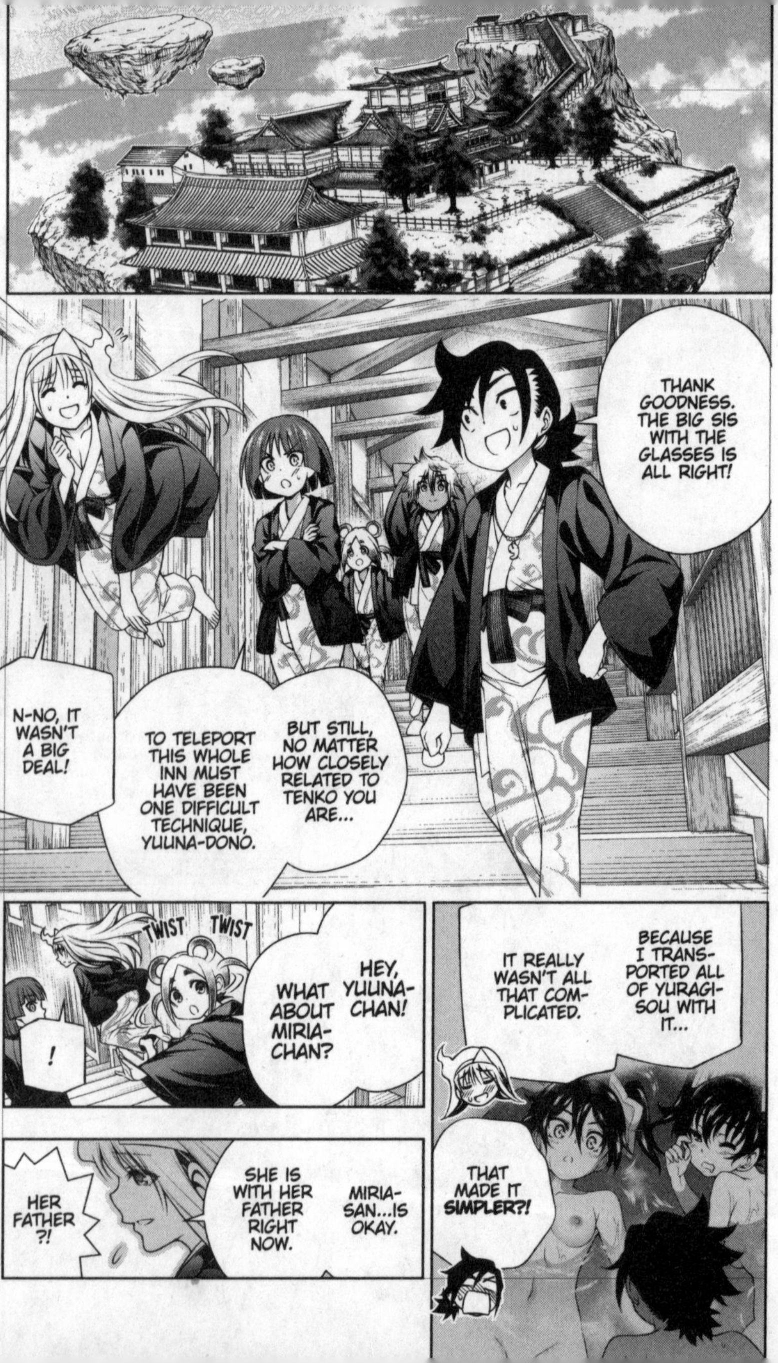
THANK GOODNESS. THE BIG SIS WITH THE GLASSES IS ALL RIGHT!
BUT STILL, NO MATTER HOW CLOSELY RELATED TO TENKO YOU ARE...
TO TELEPORT THIS WHOLE INN MUST HAVE BEEN ONE DIFFICULT TECHNIQUE, YUUNA-DONO.
N-NO, IT WASN'T A BIG DEAL!
BECAUSE I TRANS-PORTED ALL OF YURAGI-SOU WITH IT...
IT REALLY WASN'T ALL THAT COM-PLICATED.
THAT MADE IT SIMPLER?!
TWIST TWIST
HEY, YUUNA-CHAN!
WHAT ABOUT MIRIA-CHAN?
!
MIRIA-SAN...IS OKAY.
SHE IS WITH HER FATHER RIGHT NOW.
HER FATHER?!

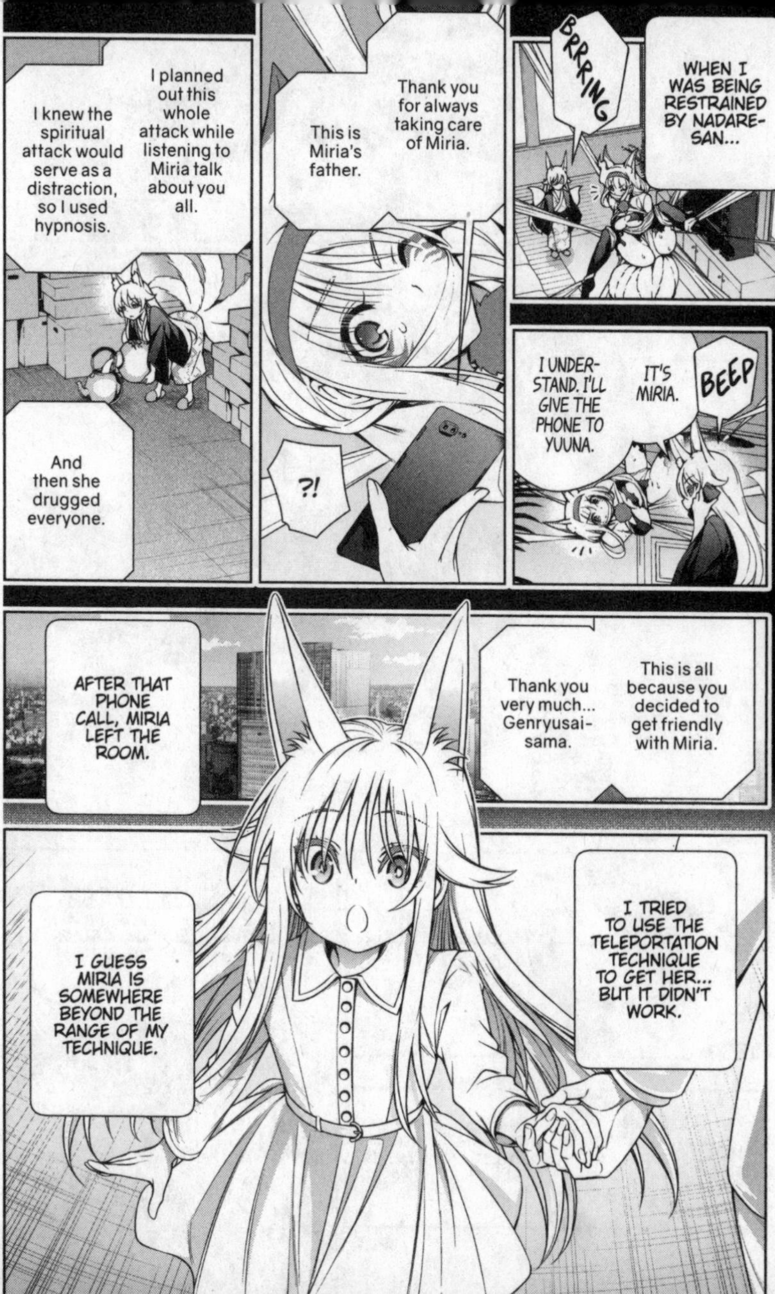

WHEN I WAS BEING RESTRAINED BY NADARE-SAN...
BRRRING
BEEP
IT'S MIRIA.
I UNDERSTAND. I'LL GIVE THE PHONE TO YUUNA.
Thank you for always taking care of Miria.
This is Miria's father.
?!
I planned out this whole attack while listening to Miria talk about you all.
I knew the spiritual attack would serve as a distraction, so I used hypnosis.
And then she drugged everyone.
This is all because you decided to get friendly with Miria.
Thank you very much... Genryusai-sama.
AFTER THAT PHONE CALL, MIRIA LEFT THE ROOM.
I TRIED TO USE THE TELEPORTATION TECHNIQUE TO GET HER... BUT IT DIDN'T WORK.
I GUESS MIRIA IS SOMEWHERE BEYOND THE RANGE OF MY TECHNIQUE.

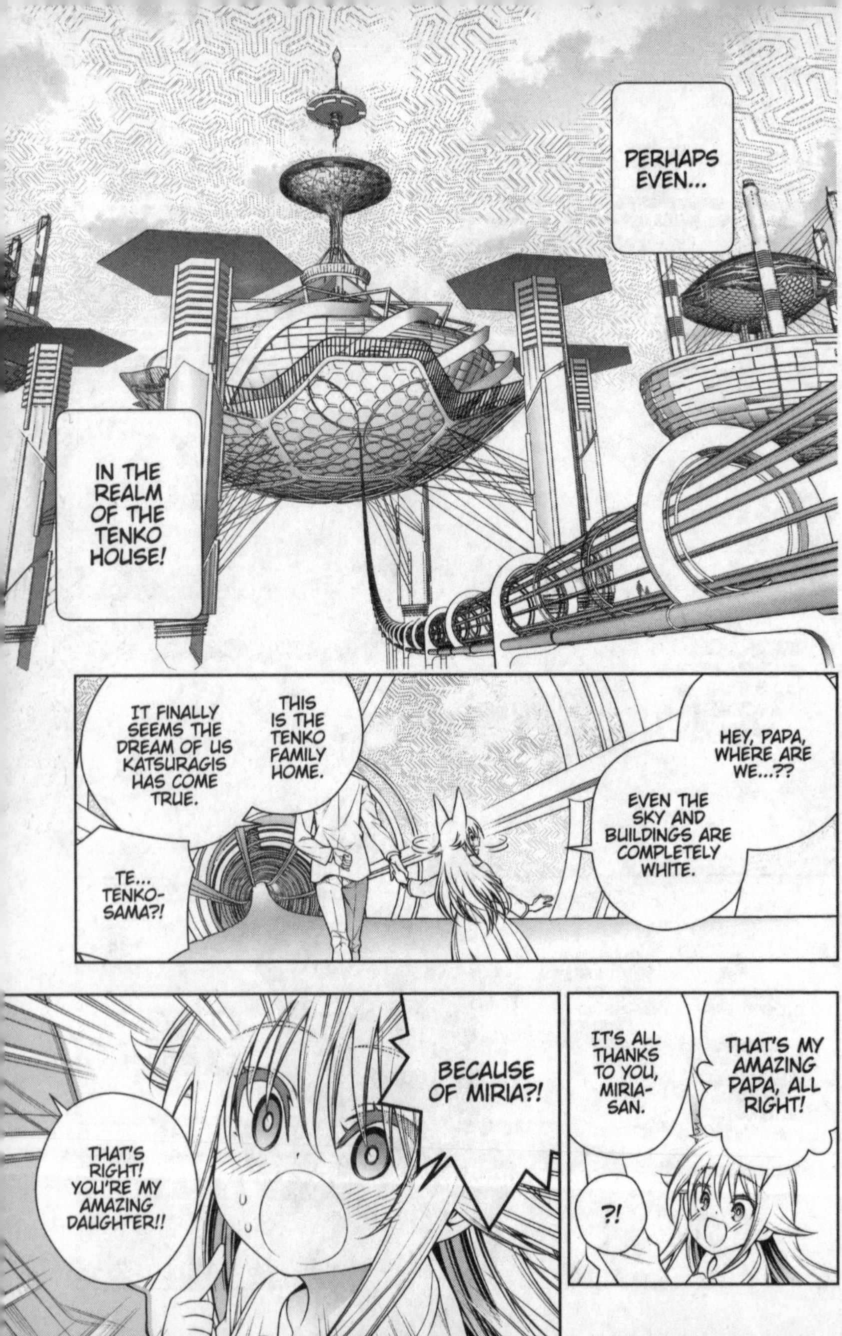

PERHAPS EVEN...
IN THE REALM OF THE TENKO HOUSE!
HEY, PAPA, WHERE ARE WE...??
EVEN THE SKY AND BUILDINGS ARE COMPLETELY WHITE.
THIS IS THE TENKO FAMILY HOME.
IT FINALLY SEEMS THE DREAM OF US KATSURAGIS HAS COME TRUE.
TE... TENKO-SAMA?!
THAT'S MY AMAZING PAPA, ALL RIGHT!
IT'S ALL THANKS TO YOU, MIRIA-SAN.
?!
BECAUSE OF MIRIA?!
THAT'S RIGHT! YOU'RE MY AMAZING DAUGHTER!!

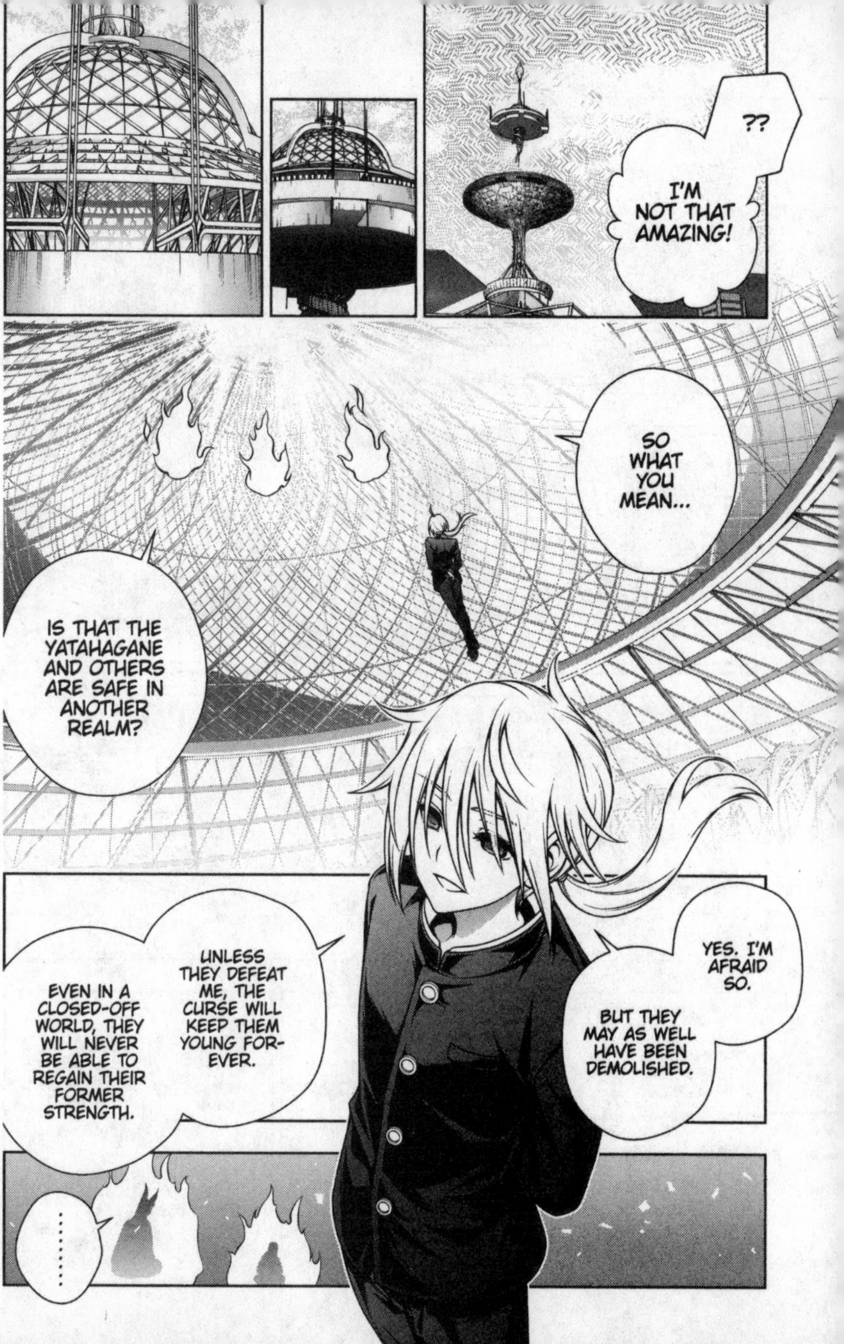
??
I'M NOT THAT AMAZING!
SO WHAT YOU MEAN...
IS THAT THE YATAHAGANE AND OTHERS ARE SAFE IN ANOTHER REALM?
YES. I'M AFRAID SO.
BUT THEY MAY AS WELL HAVE BEEN DEMOLISHED.
UNLESS THEY DEFEAT ME, THE CURSE WILL KEEP THEM YOUNG FOREVER.
EVEN IN A CLOSED-OFF WORLD, THEY WILL NEVER BE ABLE TO REGAIN THEIR FORMER STRENGTH.
......

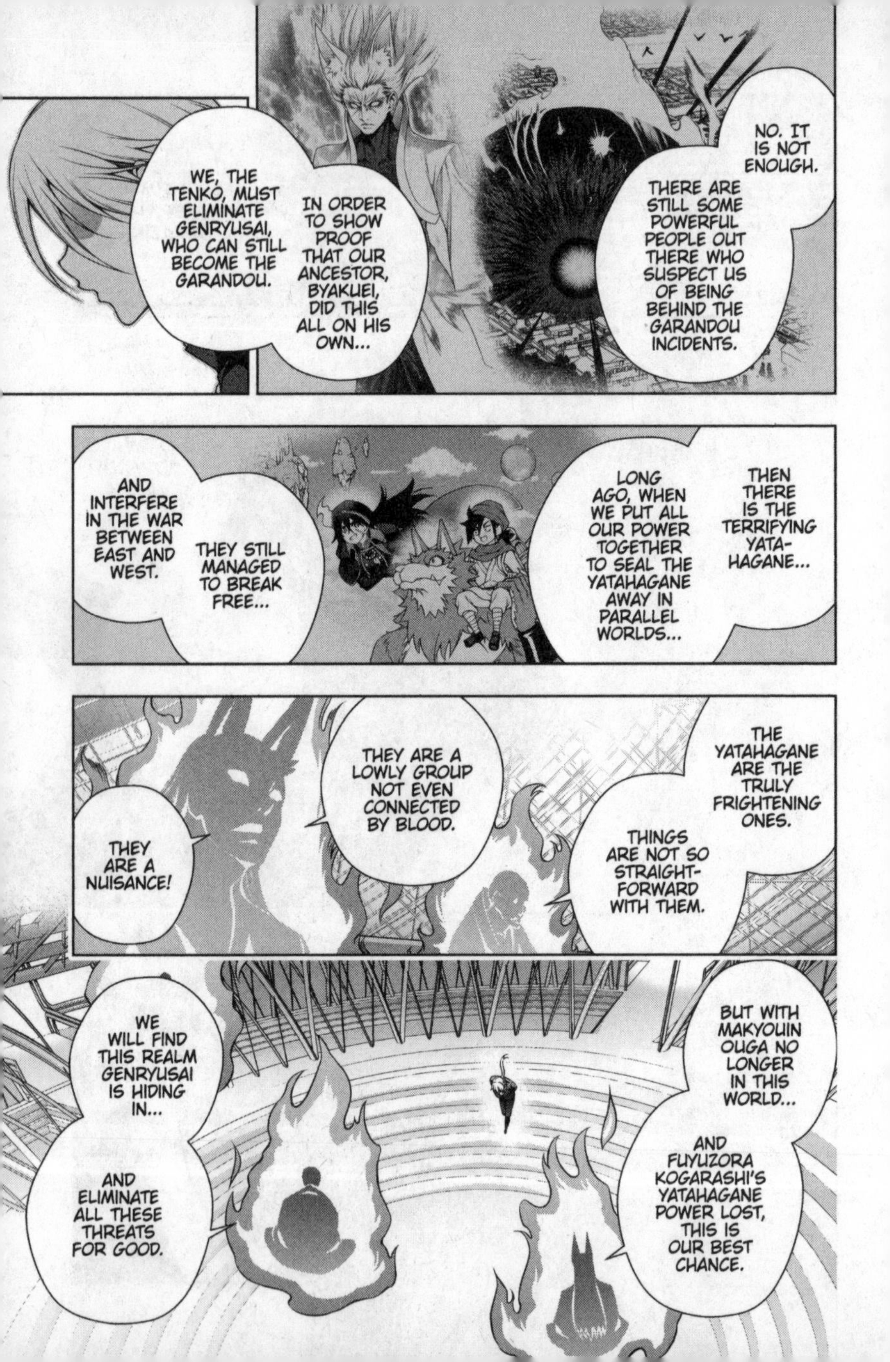
NO. IT IS NOT ENOUGH.
THERE ARE STILL SOME POWERFUL PEOPLE OUT THERE WHO SUSPECT US OF BEING BEHIND THE GARANDOU INCIDENTS.
IN ORDER TO SHOW PROOF THAT OUR ANCESTOR, BYAKUEI, DID THIS ALL ON HIS OWN...
WE, THE TENKO, MUST ELIMINATE GENRYUSAI, WHO CAN STILL BECOME THE GARANDOU.
THEN THERE IS THE TERRIFYING YATA-HAGANE...
LONG AGO, WHEN WE PUT ALL OUR POWER TOGETHER TO SEAL THE YATAHAGANE AWAY IN PARALLEL WORLDS...
THEY STILL MANAGED TO BREAK FREE...
AND INTERFERE IN THE WAR BETWEEN EAST AND WEST.
THE YATAHAGANE ARE THE TRULY FRIGHTENING ONES.
THINGS ARE NOT SO STRAIGHT-FORWARD WITH THEM.
THEY ARE A LOWLY GROUP NOT EVEN CONNECTED BY BLOOD.
THEY ARE A NUISANCE!
BUT WITH MAKYOUIN OUGA NO LONGER IN THIS WORLD...
AND FUYUZORA KOGARASHI'S YATAHAGANE POWER LOST, THIS IS OUR BEST CHANCE.
WE WILL FIND THIS REALM GENRYUSAI IS HIDING IN...
AND ELIMINATE ALL THESE THREATS FOR GOOD.

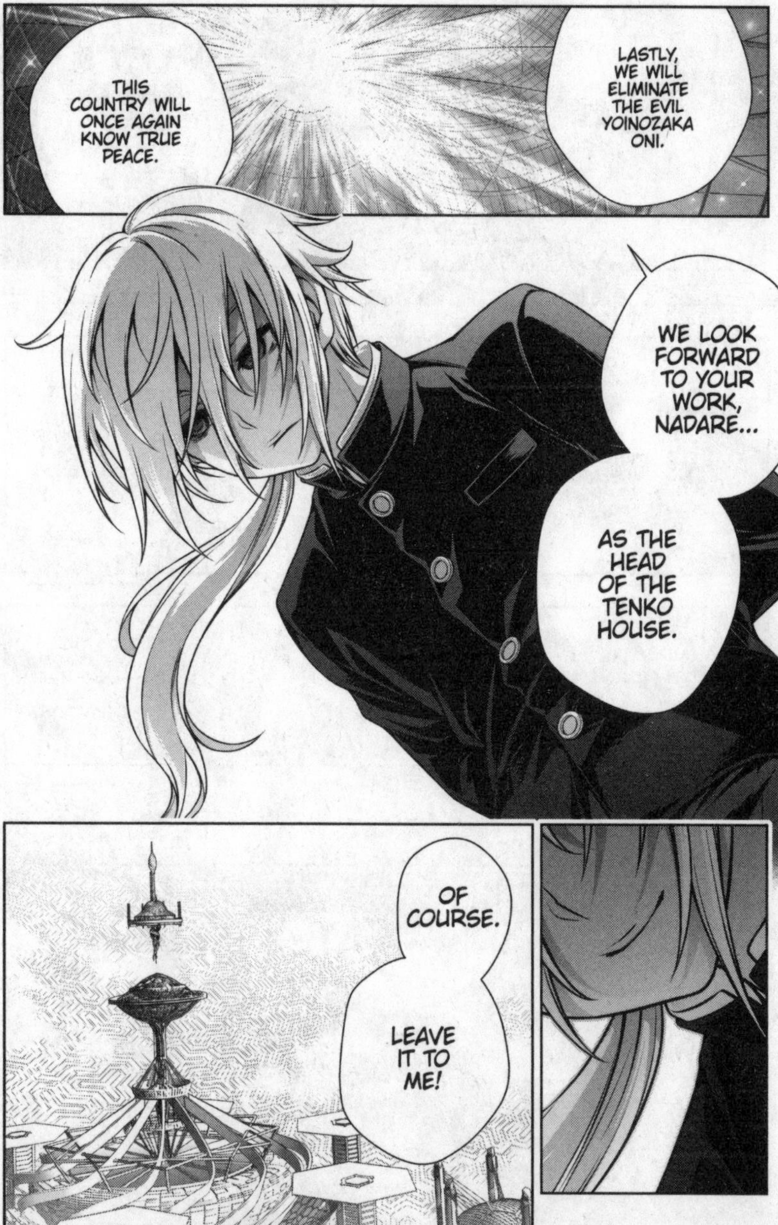
LASTLY, WE WILL ELIMINATE THE EVIL YOINOZAKA ONI.
THIS COUNTRY WILL ONCE AGAIN KNOW TRUE PEACE.
WE LOOK FORWARD TO YOUR WORK, NADARE...
AS THE HEAD OF THE TENKO HOUSE.
OF COURSE.
LEAVE IT TO ME!

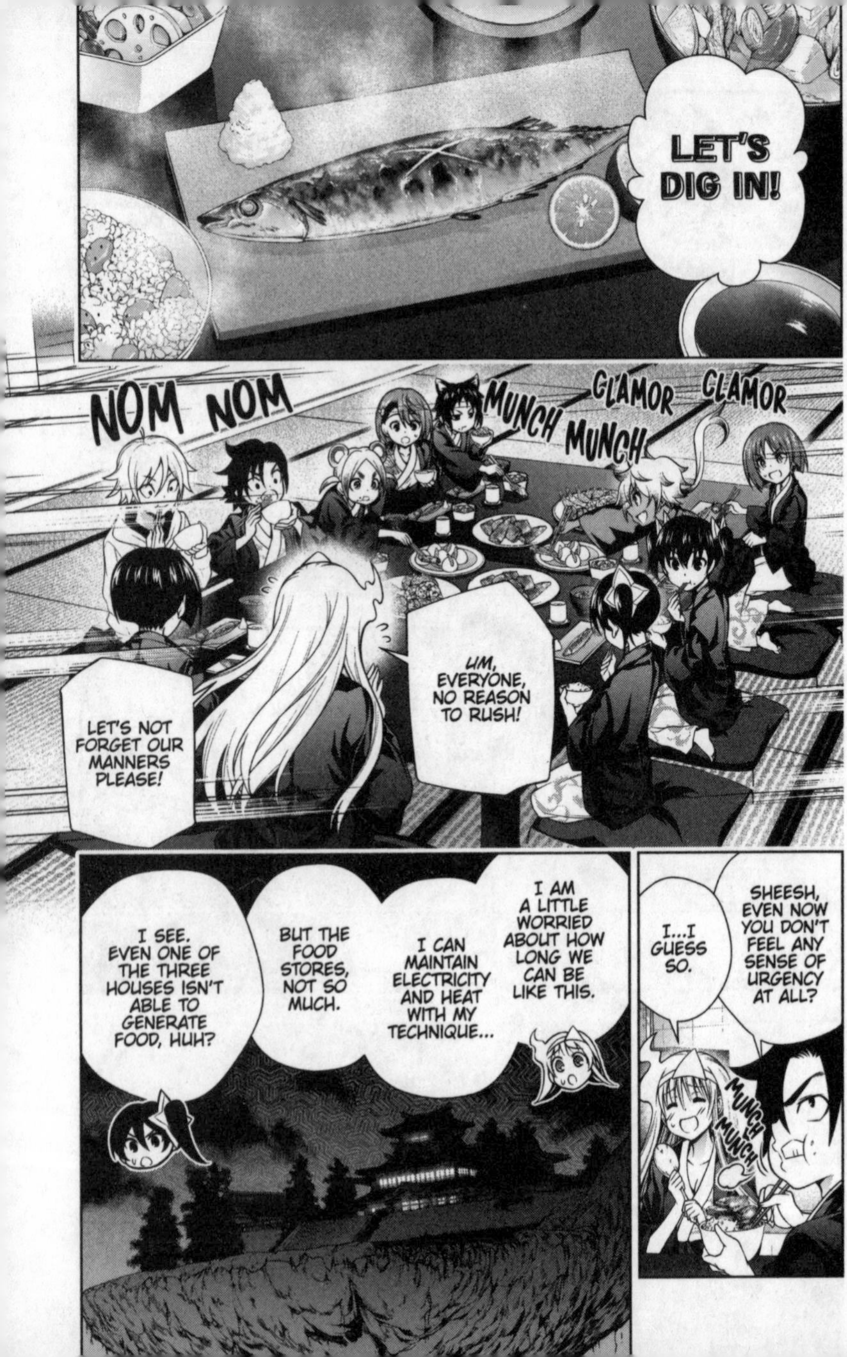

LET'S DIG IN!
CLAMOR CLAMOR
MUNCH MUNCH
NOM NOM
UM, EVERYONE, NO REASON TO RUSH!
LET'S NOT FORGET OUR MANNERS PLEASE!
SHEESH, EVEN NOW YOU DON'T FEEL ANY SENSE OF URGENCY AT ALL?
I...I GUESS SO.
MUNCH MUNCH
I AM A LITTLE WORRIED ABOUT HOW LONG WE CAN BE LIKE THIS.
I CAN MAINTAIN ELECTRICITY AND HEAT WITH MY TECHNIQUE...
BUT THE FOOD STORES, NOT SO MUCH.
I SEE. EVEN ONE OF THE THREE HOUSES ISN'T ABLE TO GENERATE FOOD, HUH?

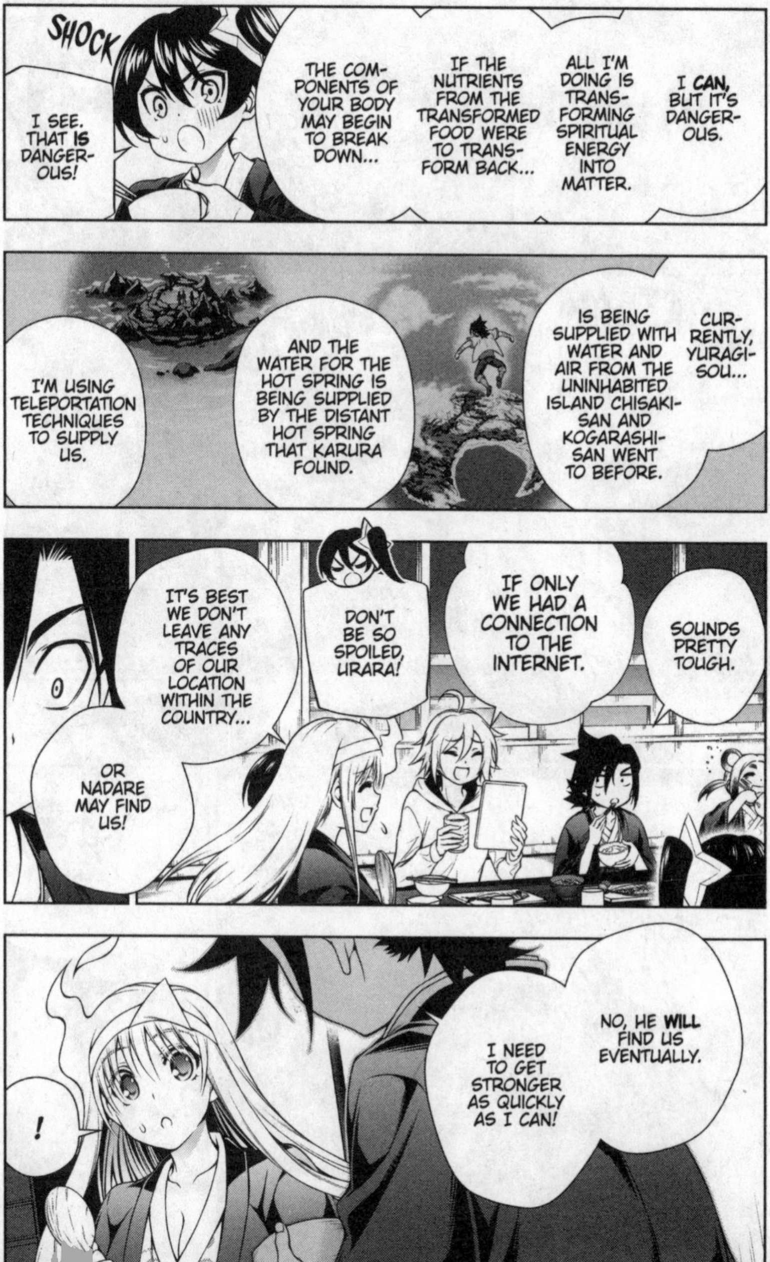
I **CAN**, BUT IT'S DANGEROUS.
ALL I'M DOING IS TRANSFORMING SPIRITUAL ENERGY INTO MATTER.
IF THE NUTRIENTS FROM THE TRANSFORMED FOOD WERE TO TRANSFORM BACK...
THE COMPONENTS OF YOUR BODY MAY BEGIN TO BREAK DOWN...
SHOCK
I SEE. THAT **IS** DANGEROUS!
CURRENTLY, YURAGI-SOU...
IS BEING SUPPLIED WITH WATER AND AIR FROM THE UNINHABITED ISLAND CHISAKI-SAN AND KOGARASHI-SAN WENT TO BEFORE.
AND THE WATER FOR THE HOT SPRING IS BEING SUPPLIED BY THE DISTANT HOT SPRING THAT KARURA FOUND.
I'M USING TELEPORTATION TECHNIQUES TO SUPPLY US.
SOUNDS PRETTY TOUGH.
IF ONLY WE HAD A CONNECTION TO THE INTERNET.
DON'T BE SO SPOILED, URARA!
IT'S BEST WE DON'T LEAVE ANY TRACES OF OUR LOCATION WITHIN THE COUNTRY...
OR NADARE MAY FIND US!
NO, HE **WILL** FIND US EVENTUALLY.
I NEED TO GET STRONGER AS QUICKLY AS I CAN!
!

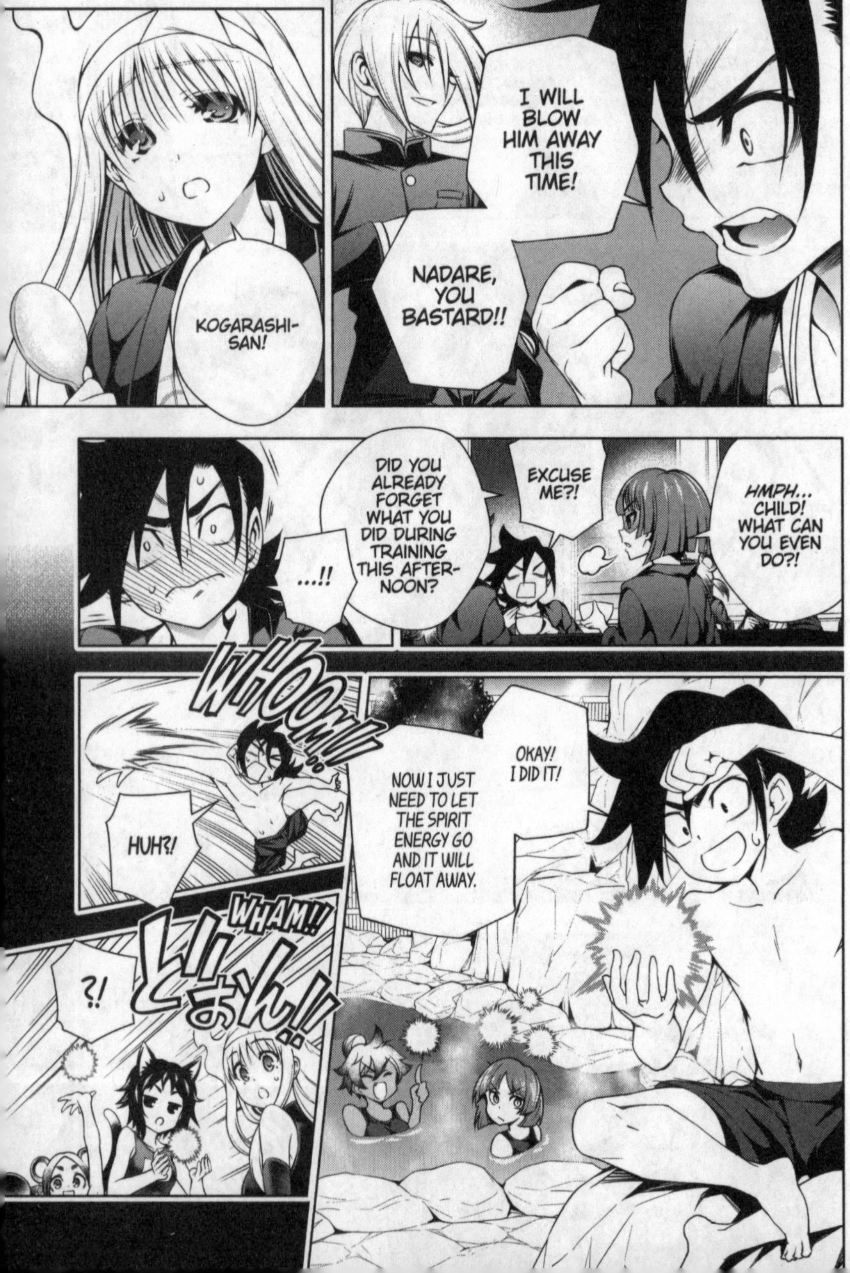
I WILL BLOW HIM AWAY THIS TIME!
NADARE, YOU BASTARD!!
KOGARASHI-SAN!
HMPH... CHILD! WHAT CAN YOU EVEN DO?!
EXCUSE ME?!
DID YOU ALREADY FORGET WHAT YOU DID DURING TRAINING THIS AFTERNOON?
...!!
OKAY! I DID IT!
NOW I JUST NEED TO LET THE SPIRIT ENERGY GO AND IT WILL FLOAT AWAY.
WHOOM!!
HUH?!
WHAM!!
どぉん!!
?!

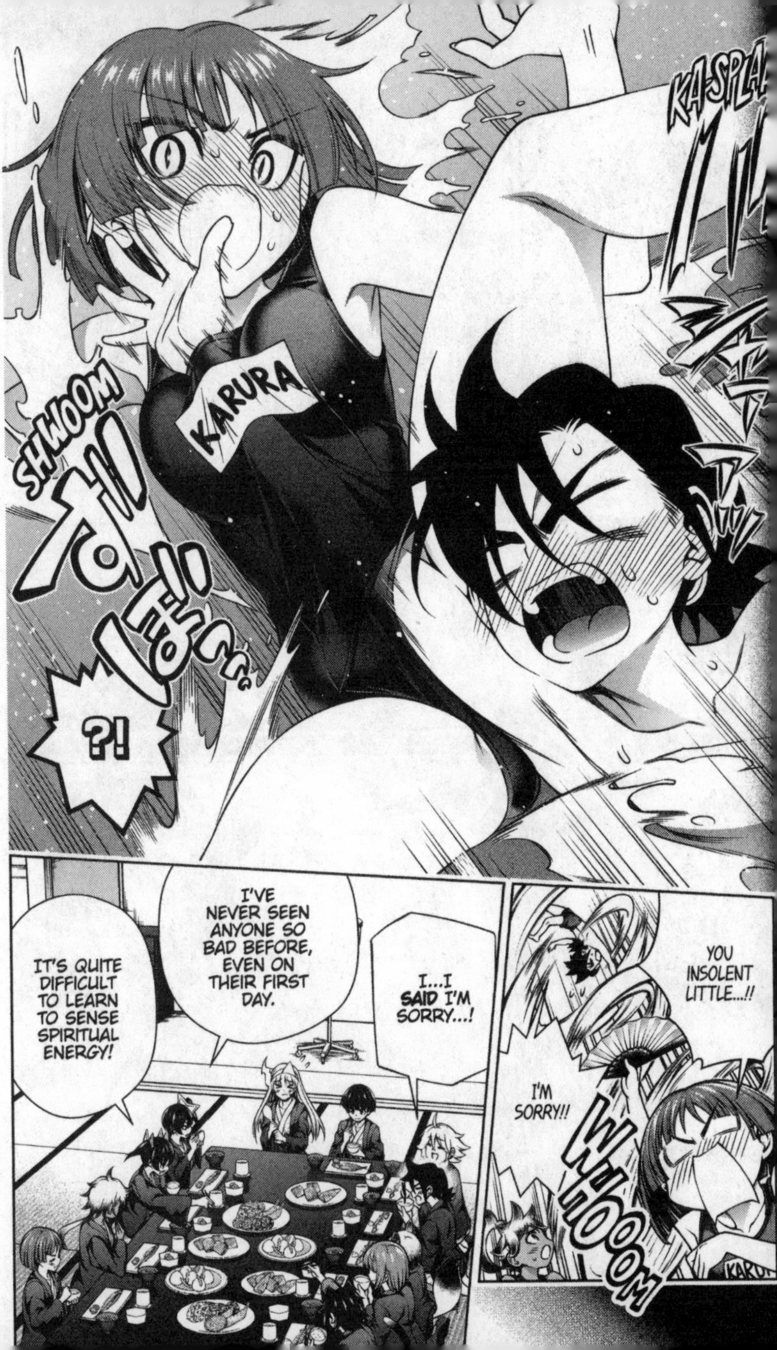
KARURA
SHWOOM
?!
YOU INSOLENT LITTLE...!!
I'M SORRY!!
WHOOOM
I...I SAID I'M SORRY...!
I'VE NEVER SEEN ANYONE SO BAD BEFORE, EVEN ON THEIR FIRST DAY.
IT'S QUITE DIFFICULT TO LEARN TO SENSE SPIRITUAL ENERGY!

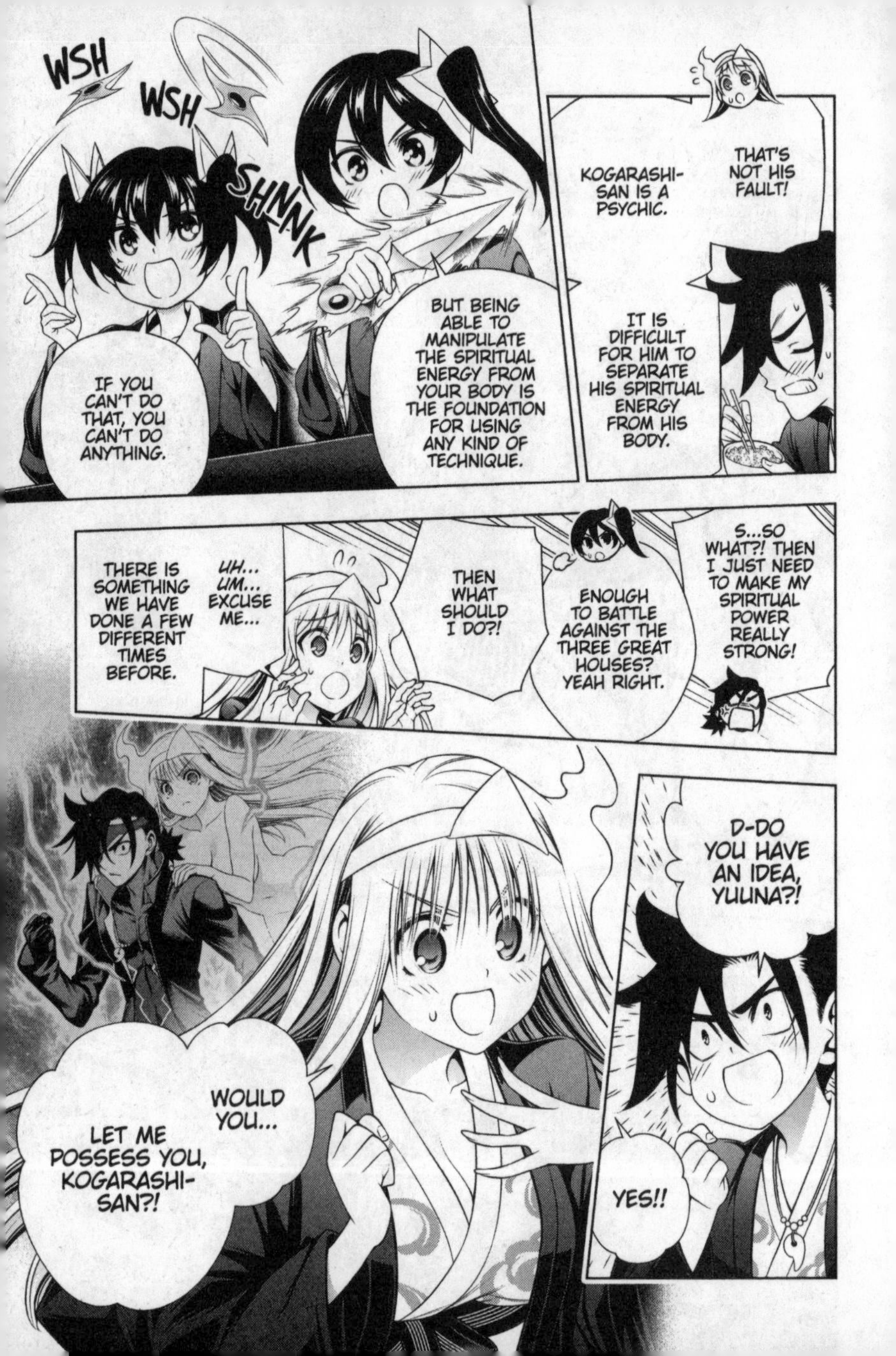
THAT'S NOT HIS FAULT!
KOGARASHI-SAN IS A PSYCHIC.
IT IS DIFFICULT FOR HIM TO SEPARATE HIS SPIRITUAL ENERGY FROM HIS BODY.
WSH
WSH
SHNNK
BUT BEING ABLE TO MANIPULATE THE SPIRITUAL ENERGY FROM YOUR BODY IS THE FOUNDATION FOR USING ANY KIND OF TECHNIQUE.
IF YOU CAN'T DO THAT, YOU CAN'T DO ANYTHING.
S...SO WHAT?! THEN I JUST NEED TO MAKE MY SPIRITUAL POWER REALLY STRONG!
ENOUGH TO BATTLE AGAINST THE THREE GREAT HOUSES? YEAH RIGHT.
THEN WHAT SHOULD I DO?!
UH... UM... EXCUSE ME...
THERE IS SOMETHING WE HAVE DONE A FEW DIFFERENT TIMES BEFORE.
D-DO YOU HAVE AN IDEA, YUUNA?!
YES!!
WOULD YOU...
LET ME POSSESS YOU, KOGARASHI-SAN?!

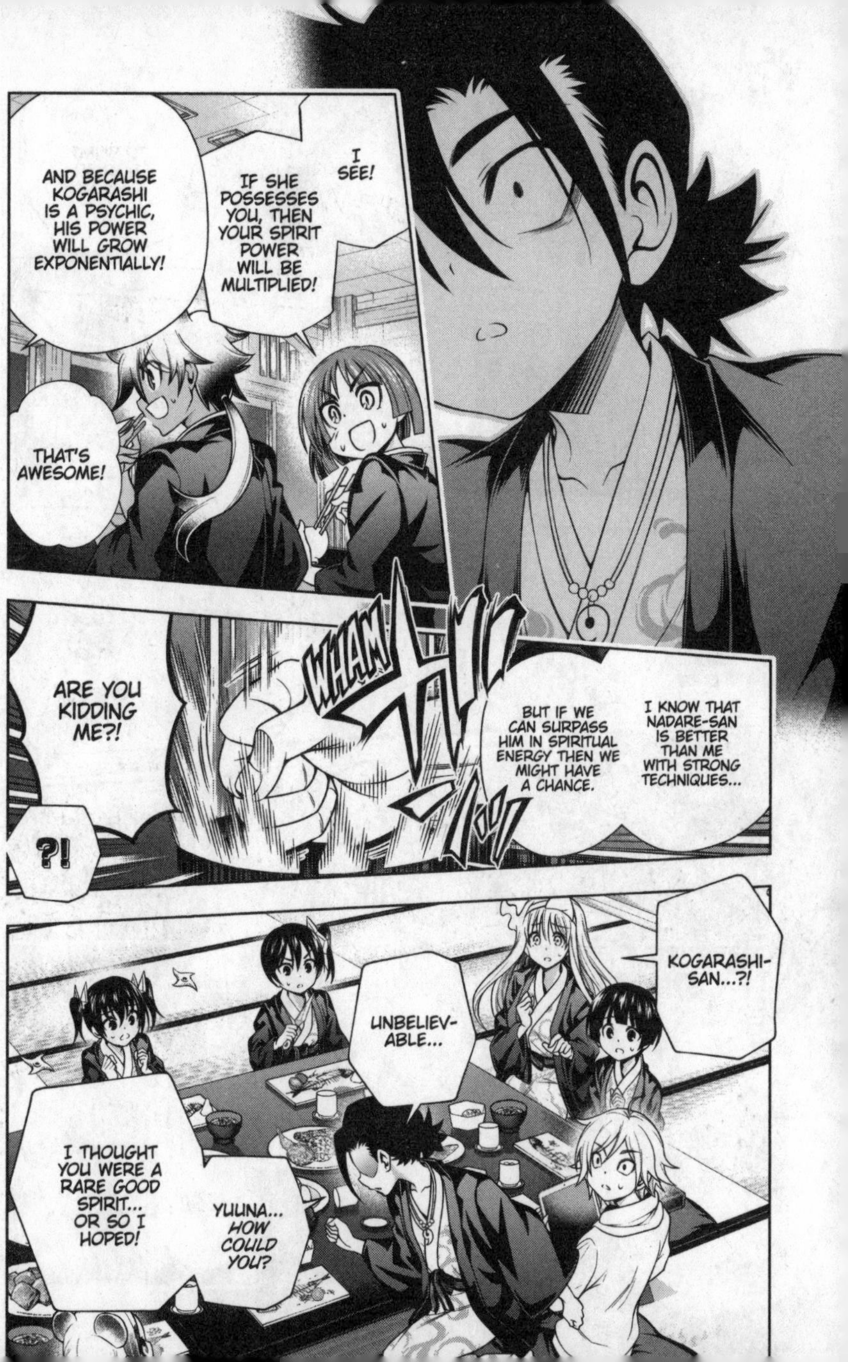
I SEE!
IF SHE POSSESSES YOU, THEN YOUR SPIRIT POWER WILL BE MULTIPLIED!
AND BECAUSE KOGARASHI IS A PSYCHIC, HIS POWER WILL GROW EXPONENTIALLY!
THAT'S AWESOME!
I KNOW THAT NADARE-SAN IS BETTER THAN ME WITH STRONG TECHNIQUES...
BUT IF WE CAN SURPASS HIM IN SPIRITUAL ENERGY THEN WE MIGHT HAVE A CHANCE.
WHAM
ARE YOU KIDDING ME?!
?!
KOGARASHI-SAN...?!
UNBELIEV-ABLE...
YUUNA... HOW COULD YOU?
I THOUGHT YOU WERE A RARE GOOD SPIRIT... OR SO I HOPED!

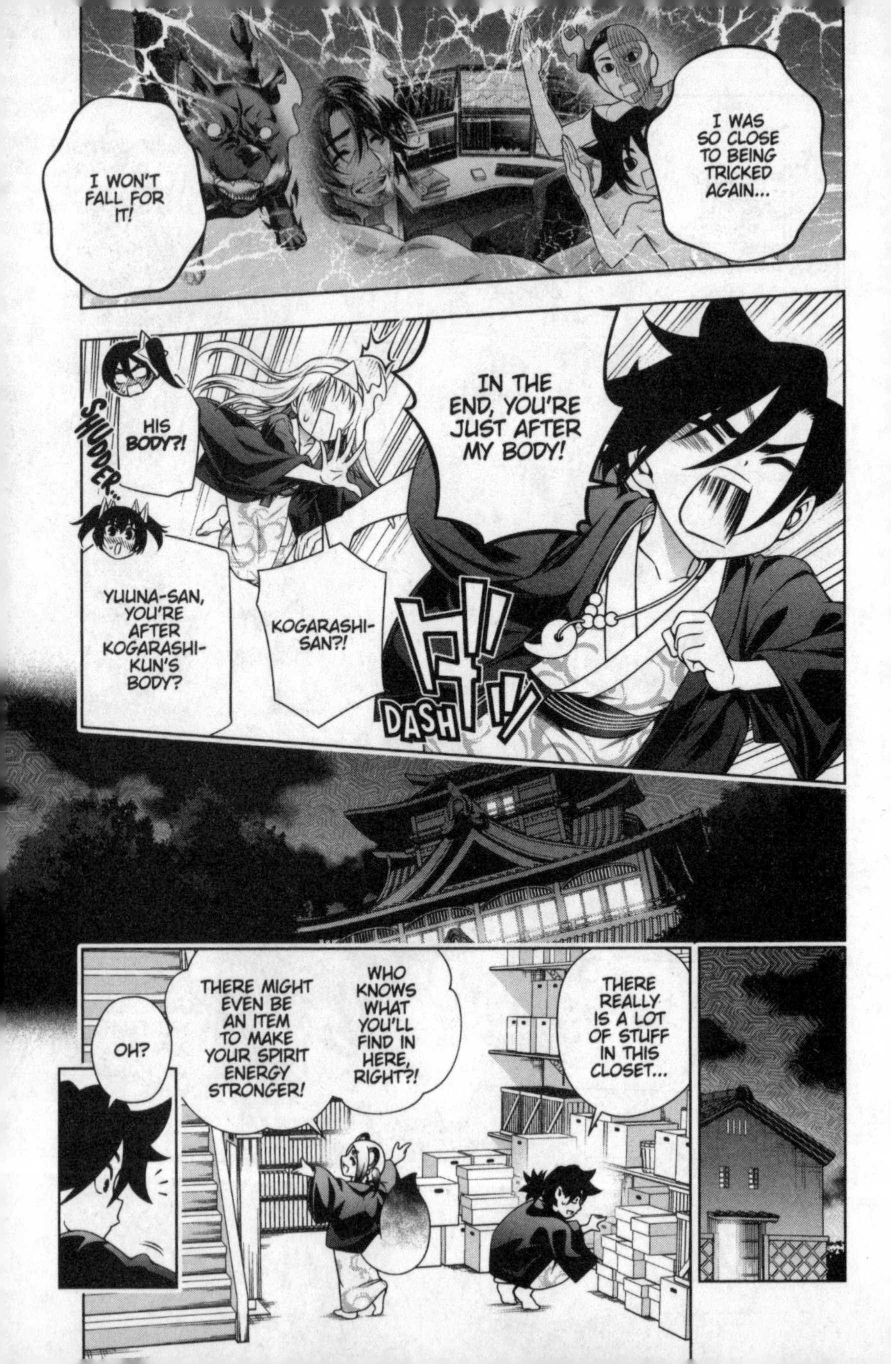
I WAS SO CLOSE TO BEING TRICKED AGAIN...
I WON'T FALL FOR IT!
IN THE END, YOU'RE JUST AFTER MY BODY!
HIS BODY?!
SHUDDER...
KOGARASHI-SAN?!
YUUNA-SAN, YOU'RE AFTER KOGARASHI-KUN'S BODY?
DASH
THERE REALLY IS A LOT OF STUFF IN THIS CLOSET...
WHO KNOWS WHAT YOU'LL FIND IN HERE, RIGHT?!
THERE MIGHT EVEN BE AN ITEM TO MAKE YOUR SPIRIT ENERGY STRONGER!
OH?

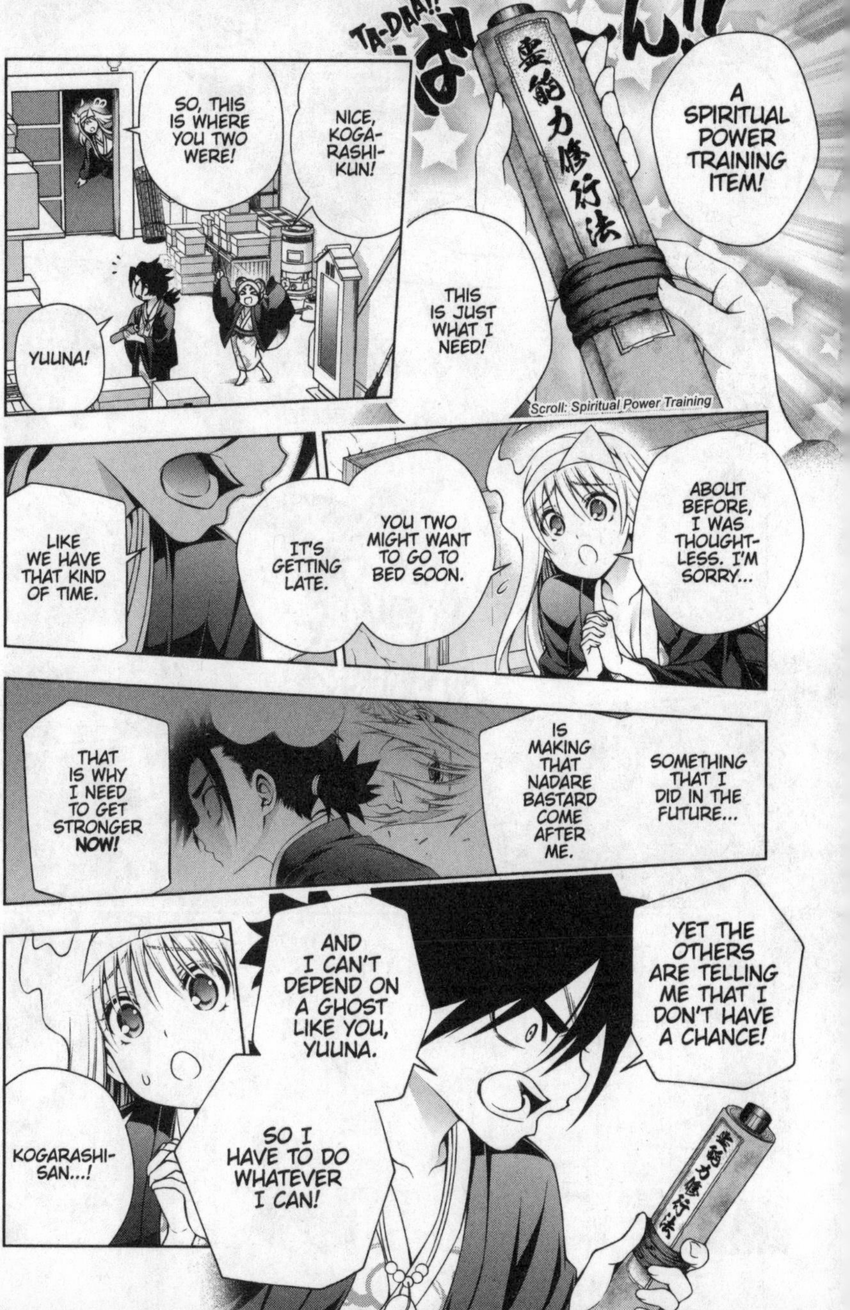
TA-DAA!!
霊能力修行法
A SPIRITUAL POWER TRAINING ITEM!
THIS IS JUST WHAT I NEED!
Scroll: Spiritual Power Training
NICE, KOGA-RASHI-KUN!
SO, THIS IS WHERE YOU TWO WERE!
YUUNA!
ABOUT BEFORE, I WAS THOUGHT-LESS. I'M SORRY...
YOU TWO MIGHT WANT TO GO TO BED SOON.
IT'S GETTING LATE.
LIKE WE HAVE THAT KIND OF TIME.
SOMETHING THAT I DID IN THE FUTURE...
IS MAKING THAT NADARE BASTARD COME AFTER ME.
THAT IS WHY I NEED TO GET STRONGER NOW!
YET THE OTHERS ARE TELLING ME THAT I DON'T HAVE A CHANCE!
AND I CAN'T DEPEND ON A GHOST LIKE YOU, YUUNA.
SO I HAVE TO DO WHATEVER I CAN!
KOGARASHI-SAN...!

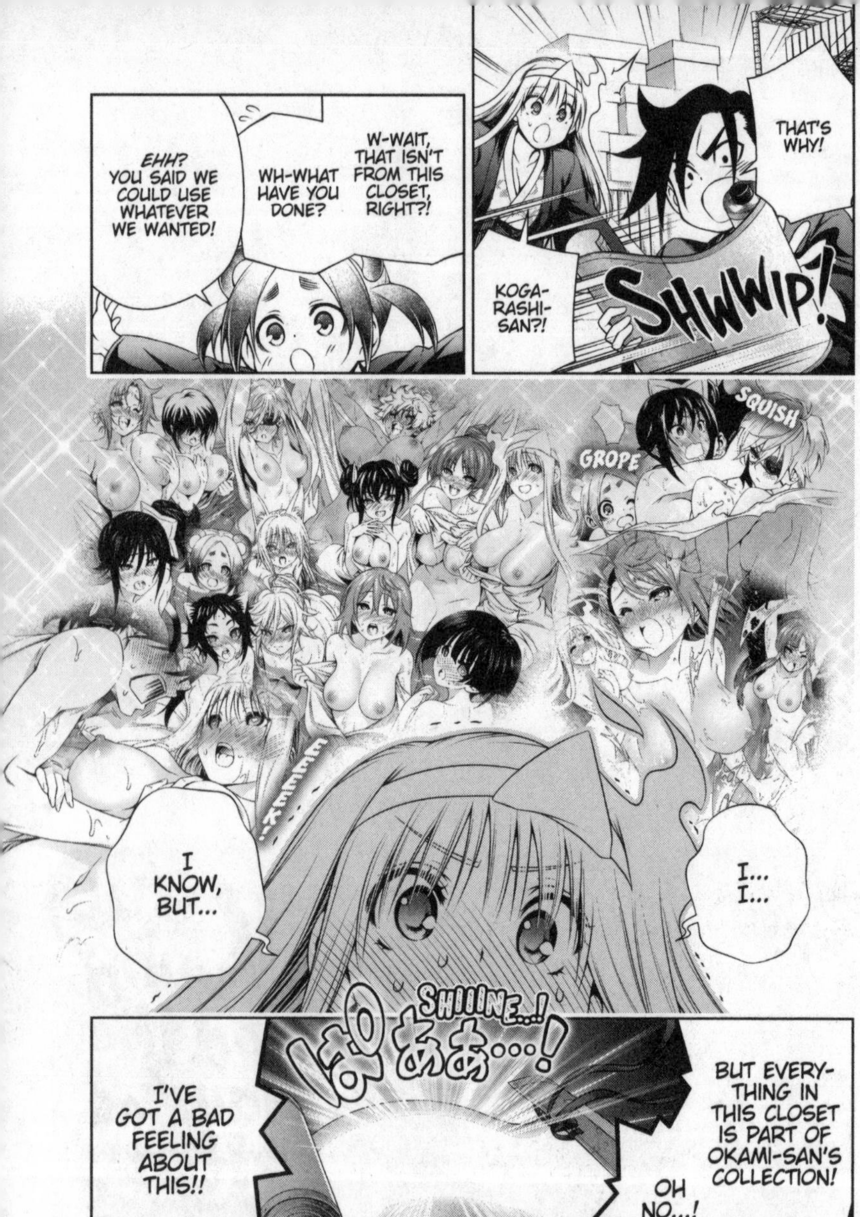

THAT'S WHY!
SHWWIP!
KOGA-RASHI-SAN?!
W-WAIT, THAT ISN'T FROM THIS CLOSET, RIGHT?!
WH-WHAT HAVE YOU DONE?
EHH? YOU SAID WE COULD USE WHATEVER WE WANTED!
SQUISH
GROPE
I... I...
I KNOW, BUT...
SHIIINE...!
はぁあ…!
BUT EVERYTHING IN THIS CLOSET IS PART OF OKAMI-SAN'S COLLECTION!
OH NO...!
I'VE GOT A BAD FEELING ABOUT THIS!!

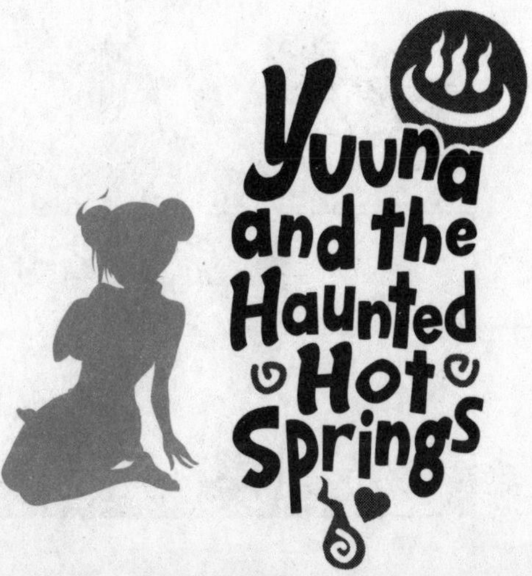

Yuuna and the Haunted Hot Springs

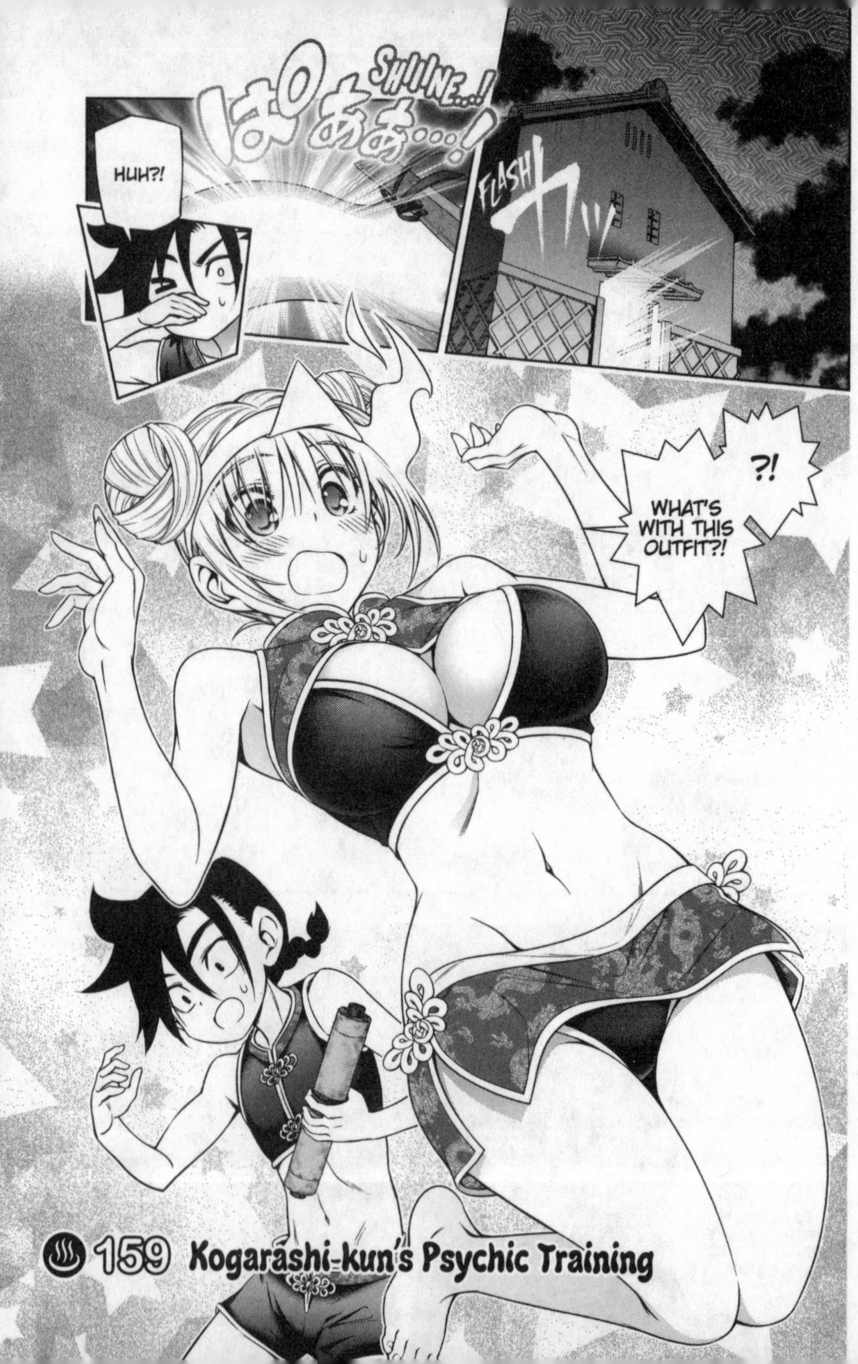
SHIINE...!
FLASH
HUH?!
?!
WHAT'S WITH THIS OUTFIT?!

159 Kogarashi-kun's Psychic Training

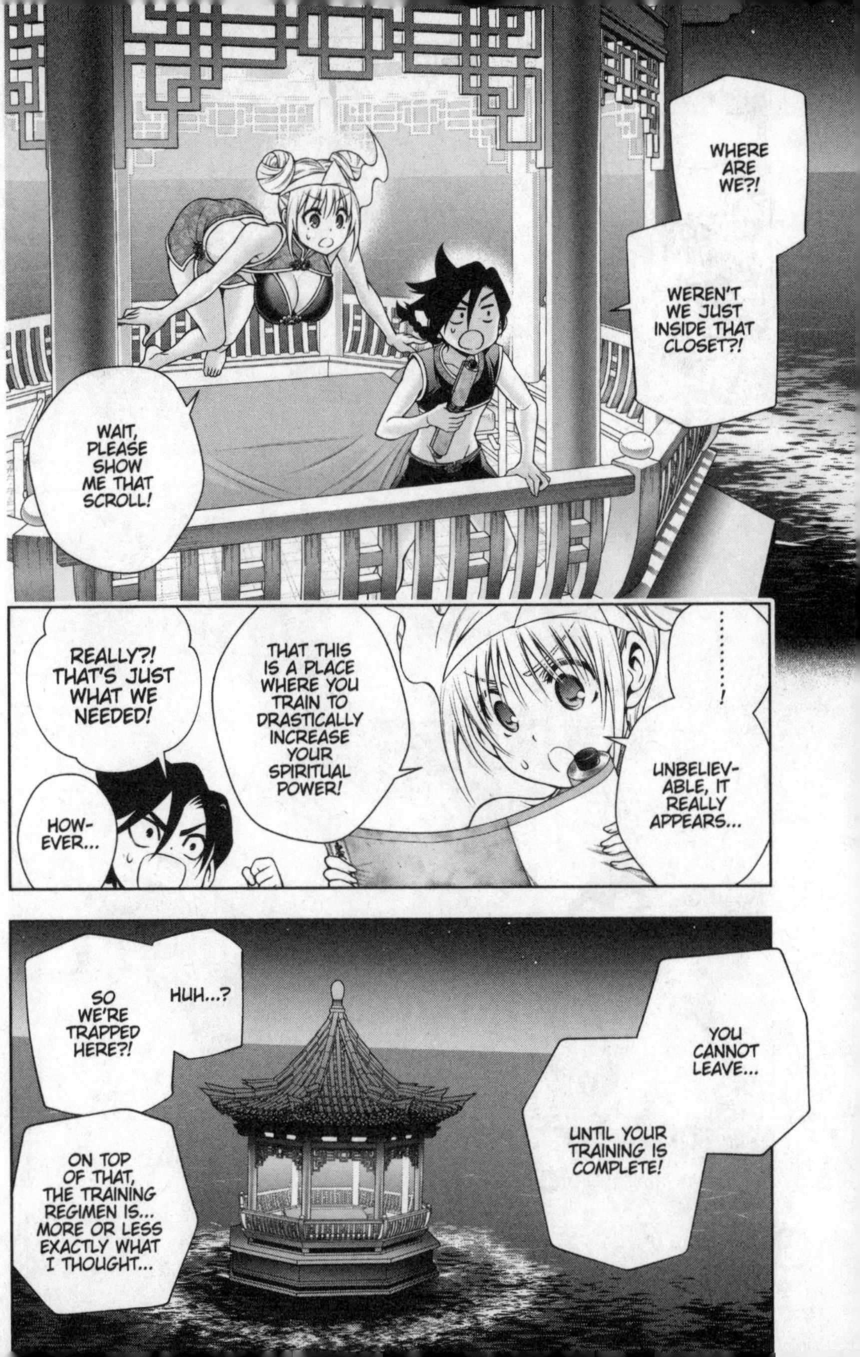
WHERE ARE WE?!
WEREN'T WE JUST INSIDE THAT CLOSET?!
WAIT, PLEASE SHOW ME THAT SCROLL!
......!
UNBELIEV-ABLE, IT REALLY APPEARS...
THAT THIS IS A PLACE WHERE YOU TRAIN TO DRASTICALLY INCREASE YOUR SPIRITUAL POWER!
REALLY?! THAT'S JUST WHAT WE NEEDED!
HOW-EVER...
YOU CANNOT LEAVE...
UNTIL YOUR TRAINING IS COMPLETE!
HUH...?
SO WE'RE TRAPPED HERE?!
ON TOP OF THAT, THE TRAINING REGIMEN IS... MORE OR LESS EXACTLY WHAT I THOUGHT...

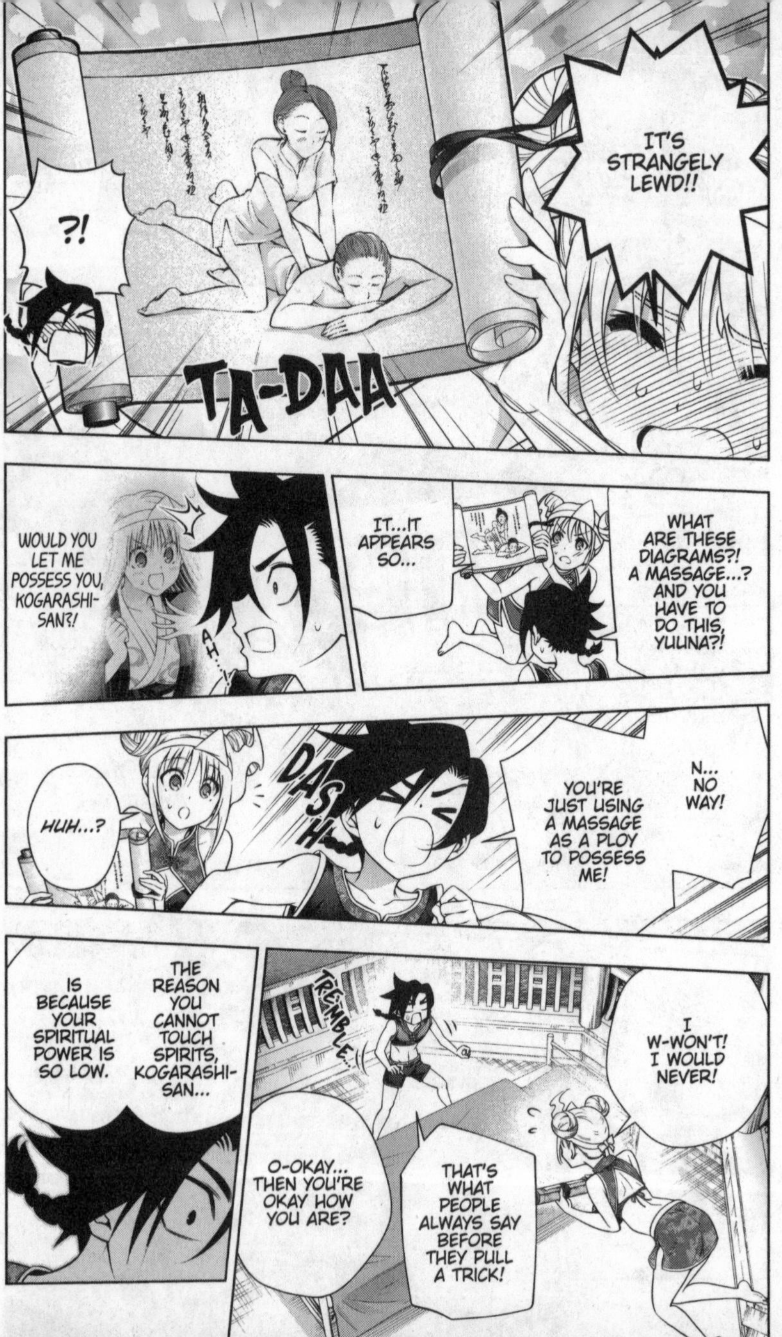
IT'S STRANGELY LEWD!!
TA-DAA
?!
WHAT ARE THESE DIAGRAMS?! A MASSAGE...? AND YOU HAVE TO DO THIS, YUUNA?!
IT...IT APPEARS SO...
WOULD YOU LET ME POSSESS YOU, KOGARASHI-SAN?!
AH...!
N... NO WAY!
YOU'RE JUST USING A MASSAGE AS A PLOY TO POSSESS ME!
DASH
HUH...?
I W-WON'T! I WOULD NEVER!
TREMBLE...
THAT'S WHAT PEOPLE ALWAYS SAY BEFORE THEY PULL A TRICK!
O-OKAY... THEN YOU'RE OKAY HOW YOU ARE?
THE REASON YOU CANNOT TOUCH SPIRITS, KOGARASHI-SAN...
IS BECAUSE YOUR SPIRITUAL POWER IS SO LOW.

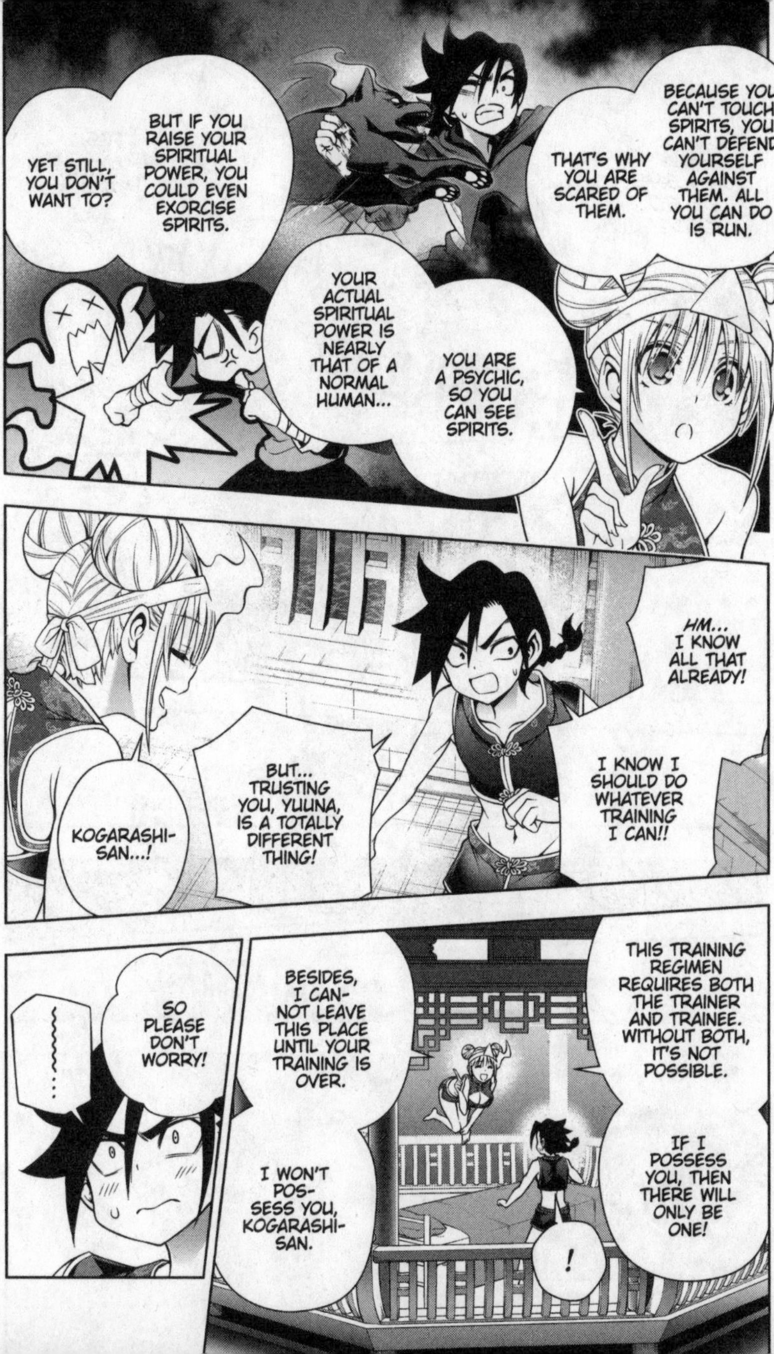
YOU ARE A PSYCHIC, SO YOU CAN SEE SPIRITS.
YOUR ACTUAL SPIRITUAL POWER IS NEARLY THAT OF A NORMAL HUMAN...
BECAUSE YOU CAN'T TOUCH SPIRITS, YOU CAN'T DEFEND YOURSELF AGAINST THEM. ALL YOU CAN DO IS RUN.
THAT'S WHY YOU ARE SCARED OF THEM.
BUT IF YOU RAISE YOUR SPIRITUAL POWER, YOU COULD EVEN EXORCISE SPIRITS.
YET STILL, YOU DON'T WANT TO?
HM... I KNOW ALL THAT ALREADY!
I KNOW I SHOULD DO WHATEVER TRAINING I CAN!!
BUT... TRUSTING YOU, YUUNA, IS A TOTALLY DIFFERENT THING!
KOGARASHI-SAN...!
THIS TRAINING REGIMEN REQUIRES BOTH THE TRAINER AND TRAINEE. WITHOUT BOTH, IT'S NOT POSSIBLE.
IF I POSSESS YOU, THEN THERE WILL ONLY BE ONE!
!
BESIDES, I CAN-NOT LEAVE THIS PLACE UNTIL YOUR TRAINING IS OVER.
I WON'T POS-SESS YOU, KOGARASHI-SAN.
SO PLEASE DON'T WORRY!
......

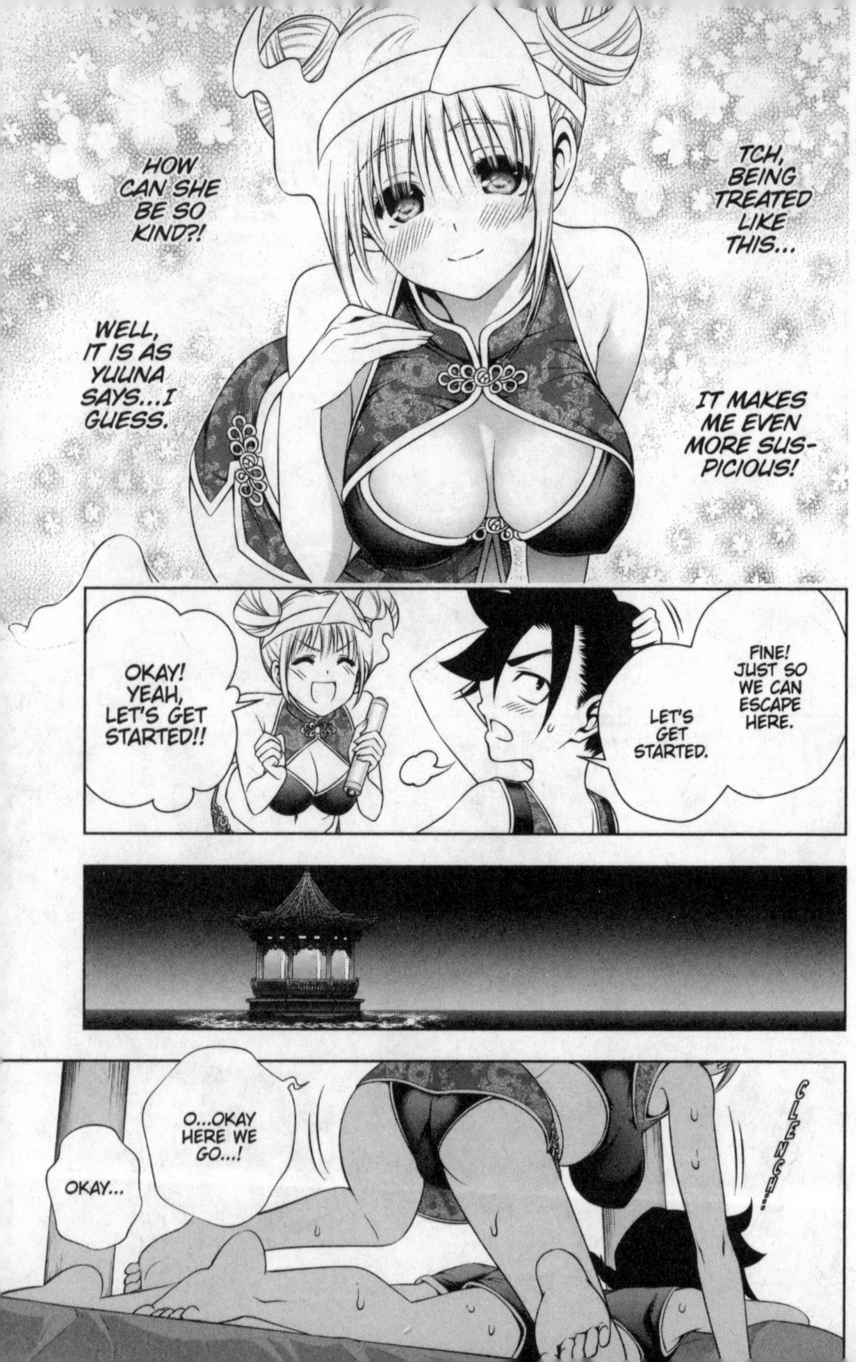
TCH, BEING TREATED LIKE THIS...
IT MAKES ME EVEN MORE SUS-PICIOUS!
HOW CAN SHE BE SO KIND?!
WELL, IT IS AS YUUNA SAYS...I GUESS.
FINE! JUST SO WE CAN ESCAPE HERE.
LET'S GET STARTED.
OKAY! YEAH, LET'S GET STARTED!!
CLENCH...
O...OKAY HERE WE GO...!
OKAY...

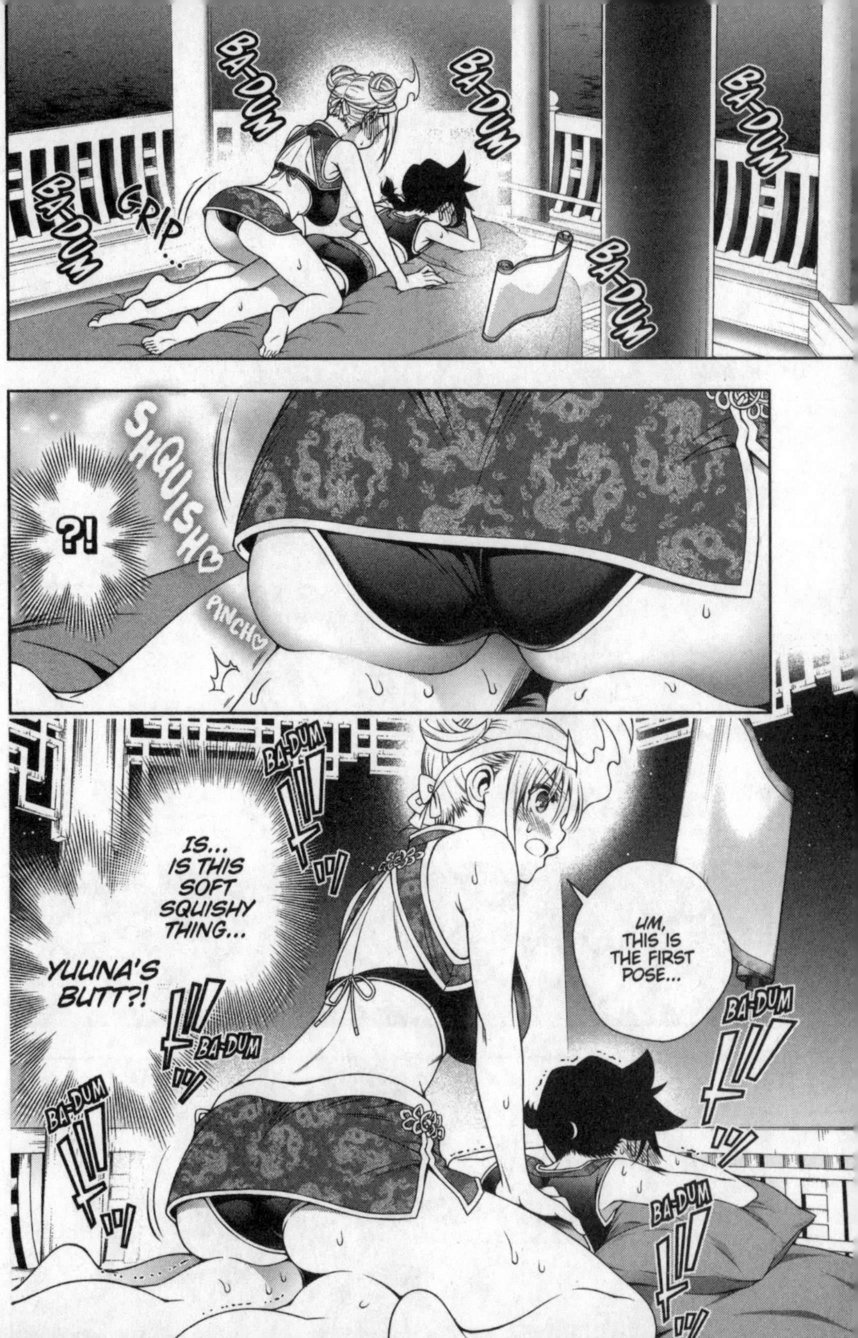
BA-DUM
BA-DUM
BA-DUM
BA-DUM
GRIP...
BA-DUM
SHQUISH♡
?!
PINCH♡
UM, THIS IS THE FIRST POSE...
BA-DUM
BA-DUM
BA-DUM
IS... IS THIS SOFT SQUISHY THING...
YUUNA'S BUTT?!
BA-DUM
BA-DUM

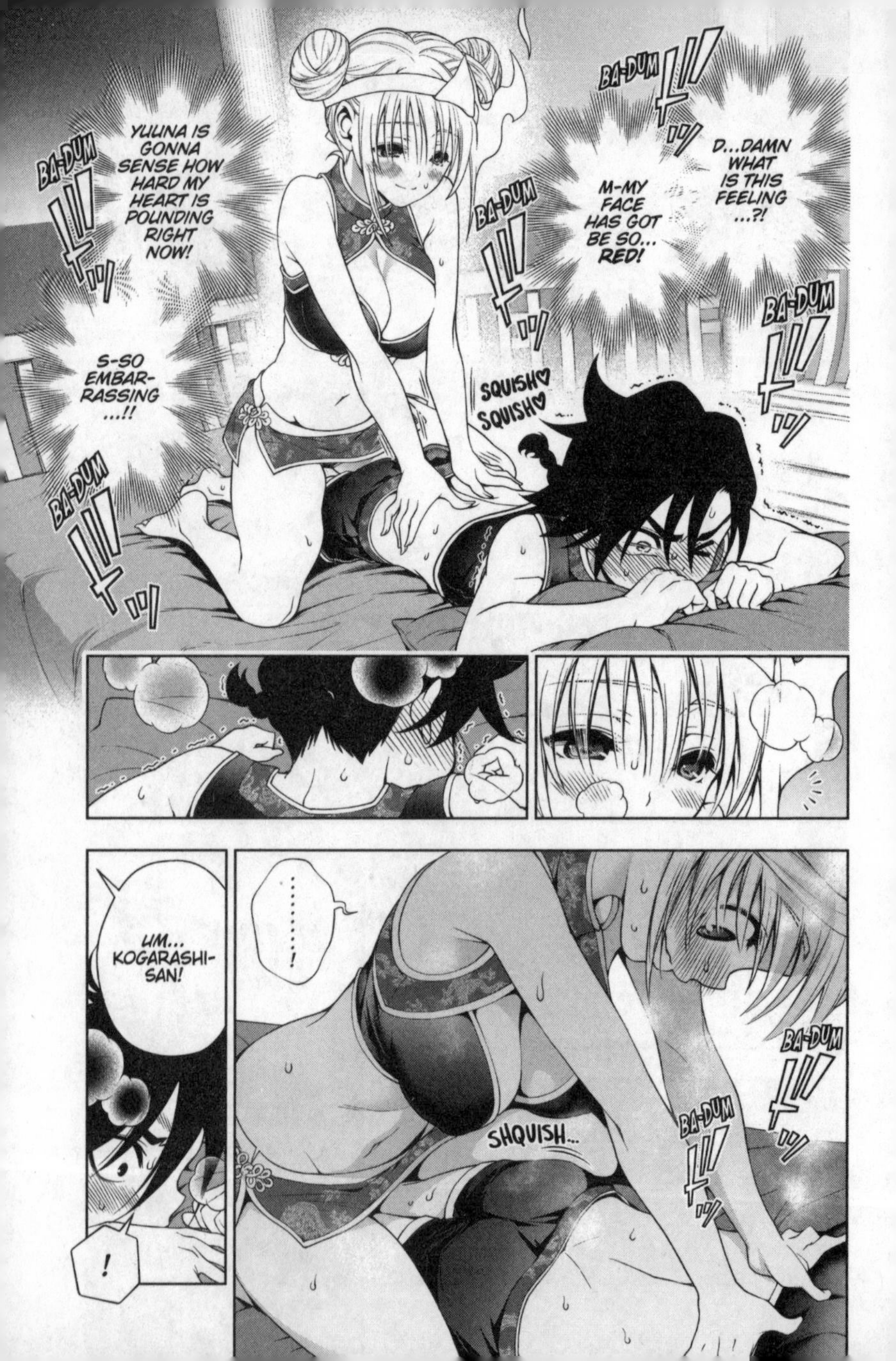
BA-DUM
D...DAMN WHAT IS THIS FEELING ...?!
M-MY FACE HAS GOT BE SO... RED!
BA-DUM
BA-DUM
YUUNA IS GONNA SENSE HOW HARD MY HEART IS POUNDING RIGHT NOW!
BA-DUM
S-SO EMBAR-RASSING ...!!
SQUISH♡
SQUISH♡
BA-DUM
......!
UM... KOGARASHI-SAN!
BA-DUM
BA-DUM
SHQUISH...
!

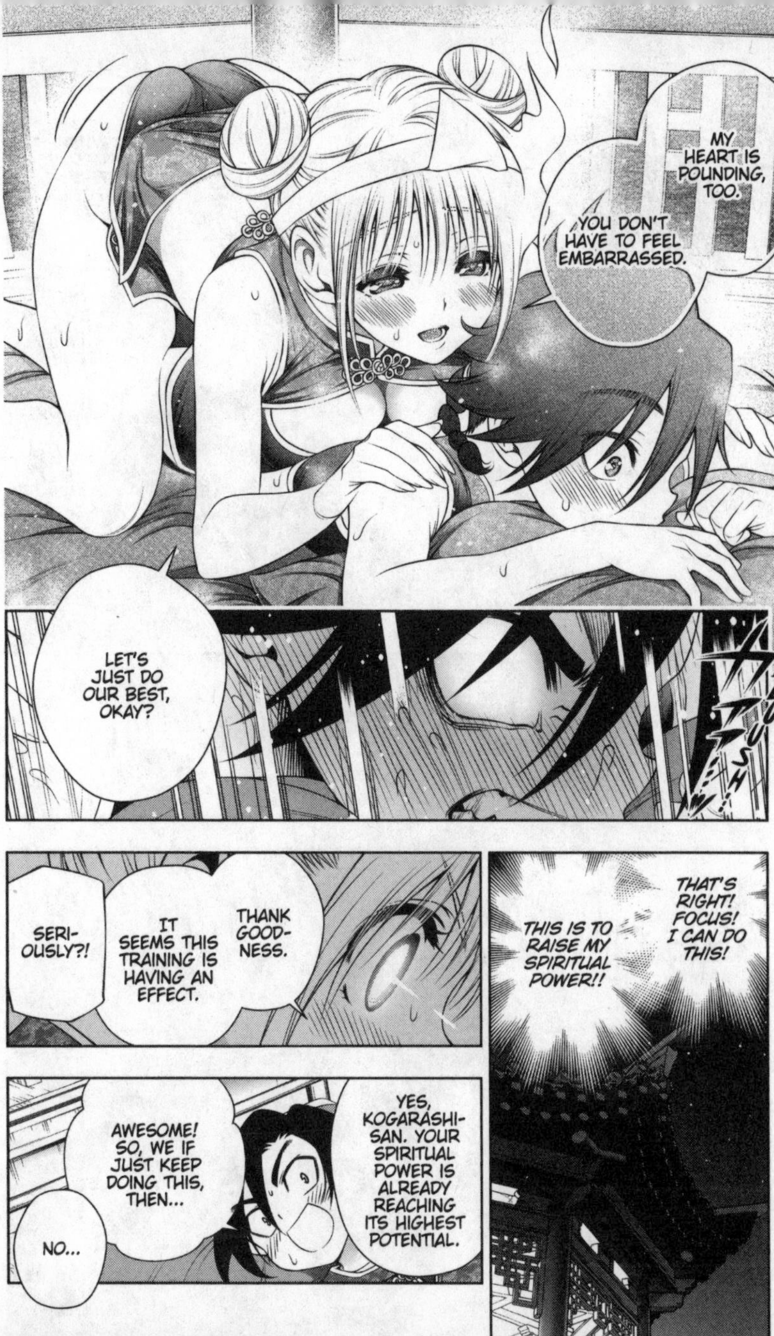
MY HEART IS POUNDING, TOO.
YOU DON'T HAVE TO FEEL EMBARRASSED.
LET'S JUST DO OUR BEST, OKAY?
BLUUSH!!
THAT'S RIGHT! FOCUS! I CAN DO THIS!
THIS IS TO RAISE MY SPIRITUAL POWER!!
THANK GOODNESS.
IT SEEMS THIS TRAINING IS HAVING AN EFFECT.
SERI-OUSLY?!
YES, KOGARASHI-SAN. YOUR SPIRITUAL POWER IS ALREADY REACHING ITS HIGHEST POTENTIAL.
AWESOME! SO, WE IF JUST KEEP DOING THIS, THEN...
NO...

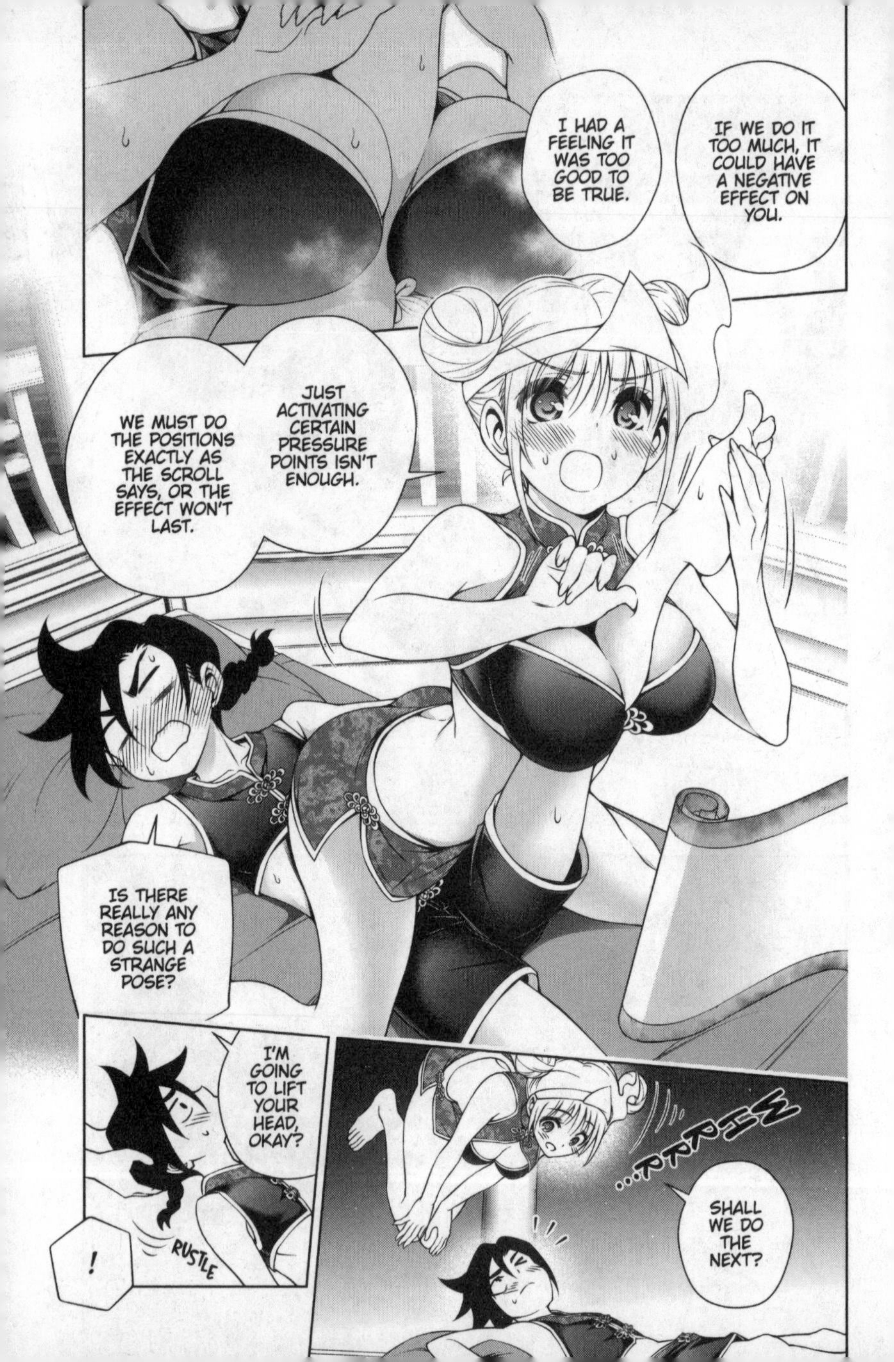
IF WE DO IT TOO MUCH, IT COULD HAVE A NEGATIVE EFFECT ON YOU.
I HAD A FEELING IT WAS TOO GOOD TO BE TRUE.
JUST ACTIVATING CERTAIN PRESSURE POINTS ISN'T ENOUGH.
WE MUST DO THE POSITIONS EXACTLY AS THE SCROLL SAYS, OR THE EFFECT WON'T LAST.
IS THERE REALLY ANY REASON TO DO SUCH A STRANGE POSE?
...RRRISW
SHALL WE DO THE NEXT?
I'M GOING TO LIFT YOUR HEAD, OKAY?
RUSTLE
!

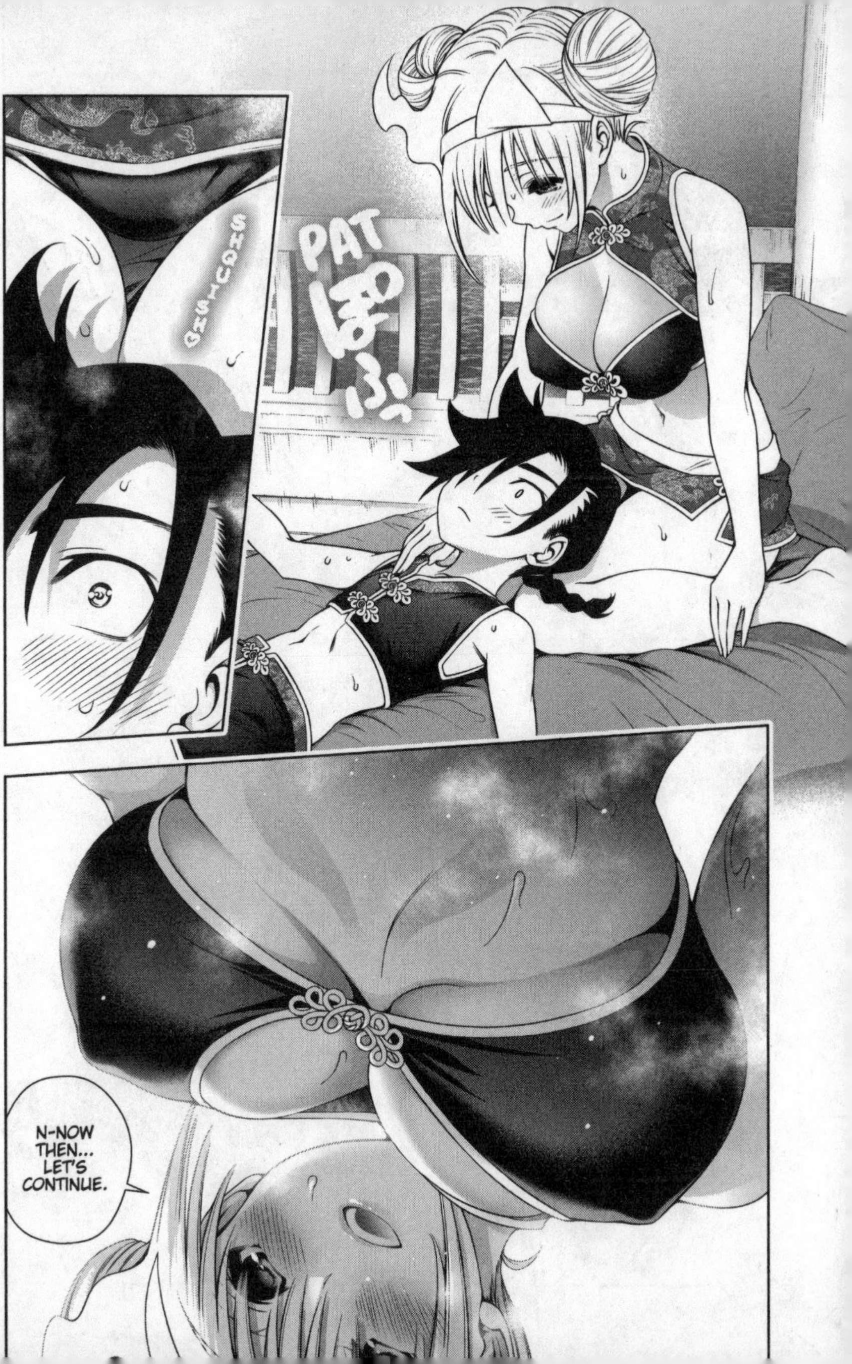
PAT
ぽふっ
SHQUISH
N-NOW THEN... LET'S CONTINUE.

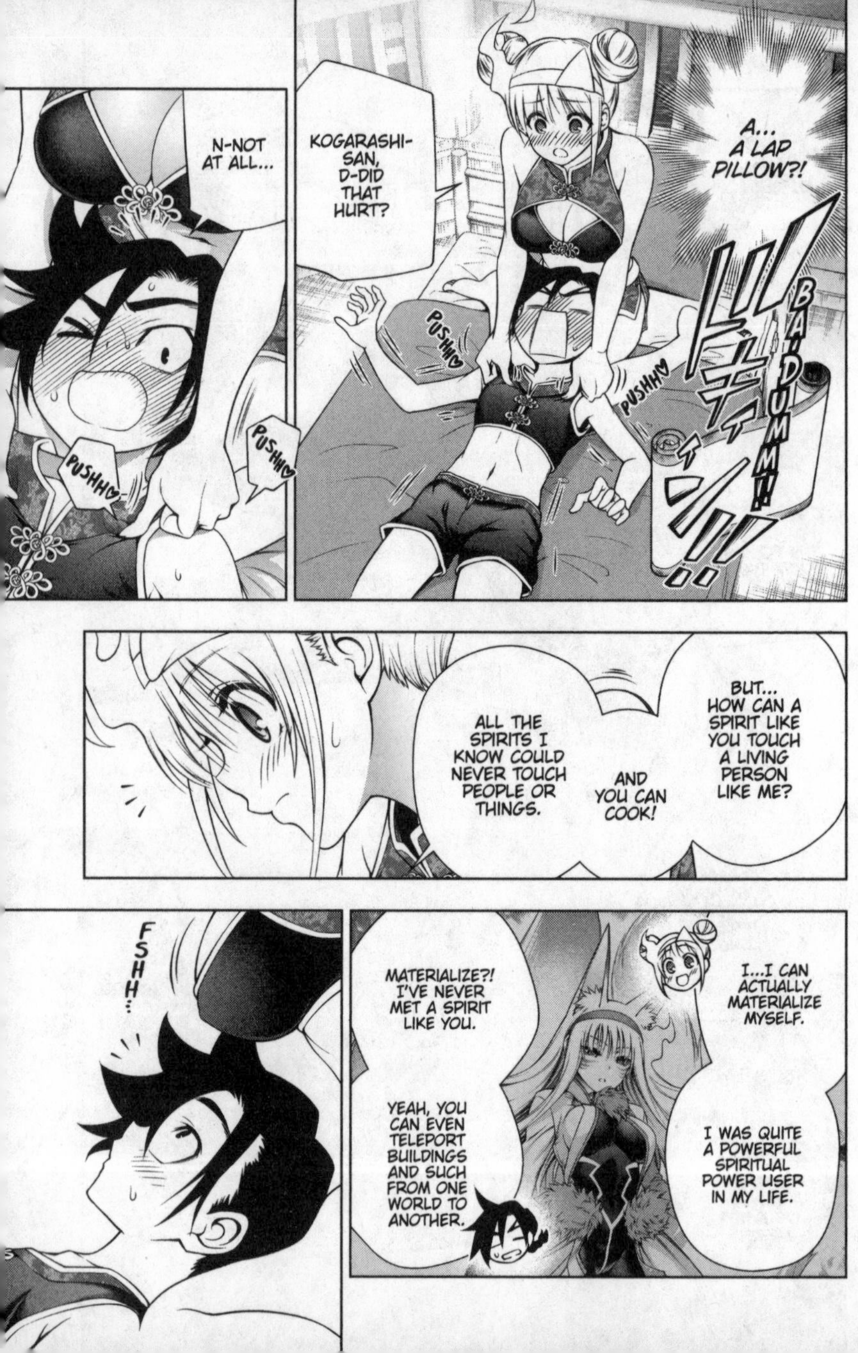
A... A LAP PILLOW?!
BA-DUMM!
KOGARASHI-SAN, D-DID THAT HURT?
PUSHH♡
PUSHH♡
N-NOT AT ALL...
PUSHH♡
PUSHH♡
BUT... HOW CAN A SPIRIT LIKE YOU TOUCH A LIVING PERSON LIKE ME?
AND YOU CAN COOK!
ALL THE SPIRITS I KNOW COULD NEVER TOUCH PEOPLE OR THINGS.
I...I CAN ACTUALLY MATERIALIZE MYSELF.
MATERIALIZE?! I'VE NEVER MET A SPIRIT LIKE YOU.
I WAS QUITE A POWERFUL SPIRITUAL POWER USER IN MY LIFE.
YEAH, YOU CAN EVEN TELEPORT BUILDINGS AND SUCH FROM ONE WORLD TO ANOTHER.
FSHH...

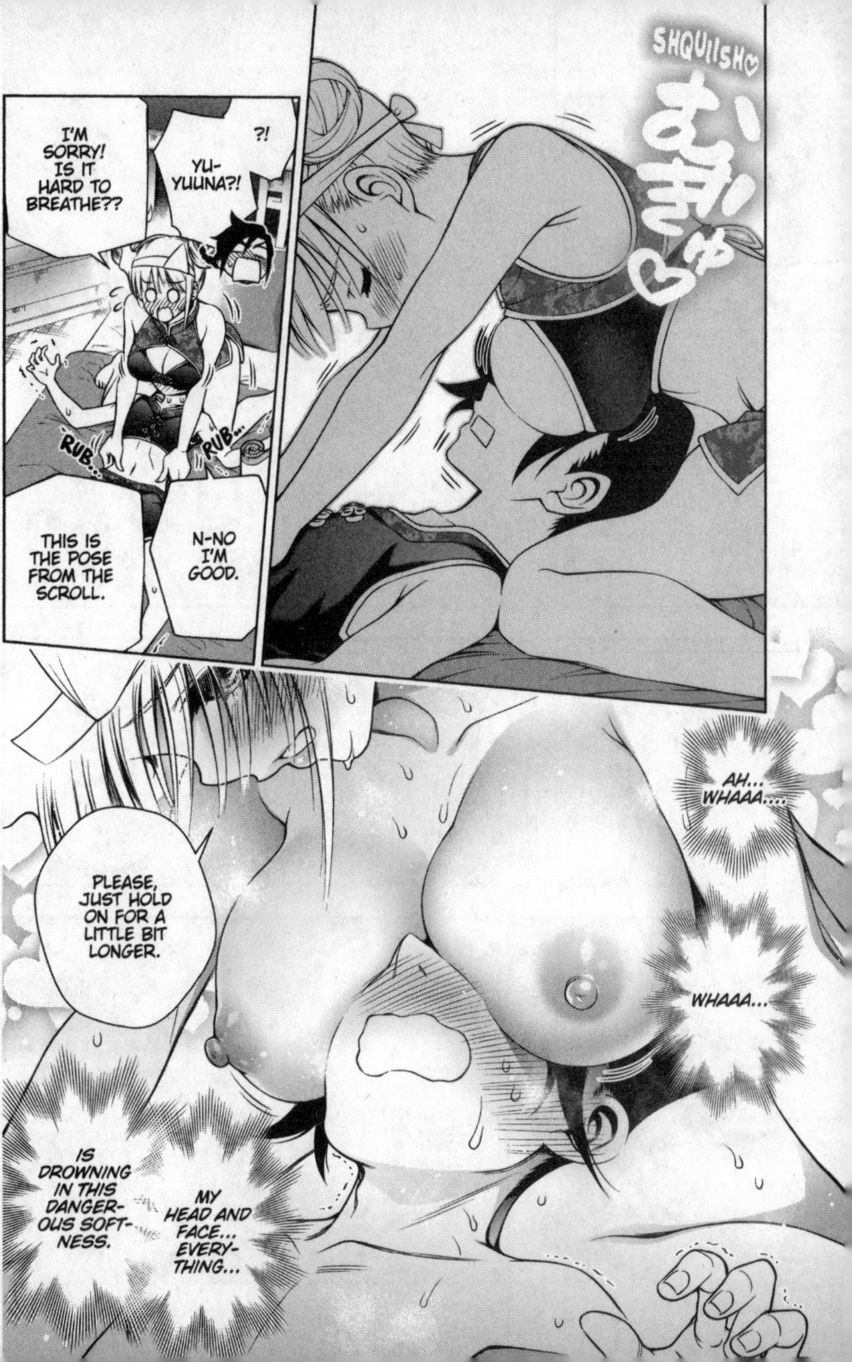
SHQUIISH♡
むぎゅ♡
?!
YU-YUUNA?!
I'M SORRY! IS IT HARD TO BREATHE??
RUB...
RUB...
N-NO I'M GOOD.
THIS IS THE POSE FROM THE SCROLL.
AH... WHAAA...
PLEASE, JUST HOLD ON FOR A LITTLE BIT LONGER.
WHAAA...
MY HEAD AND FACE... EVERYTHING...
IS DROWNING IN THIS DANGEROUS SOFT-NESS.

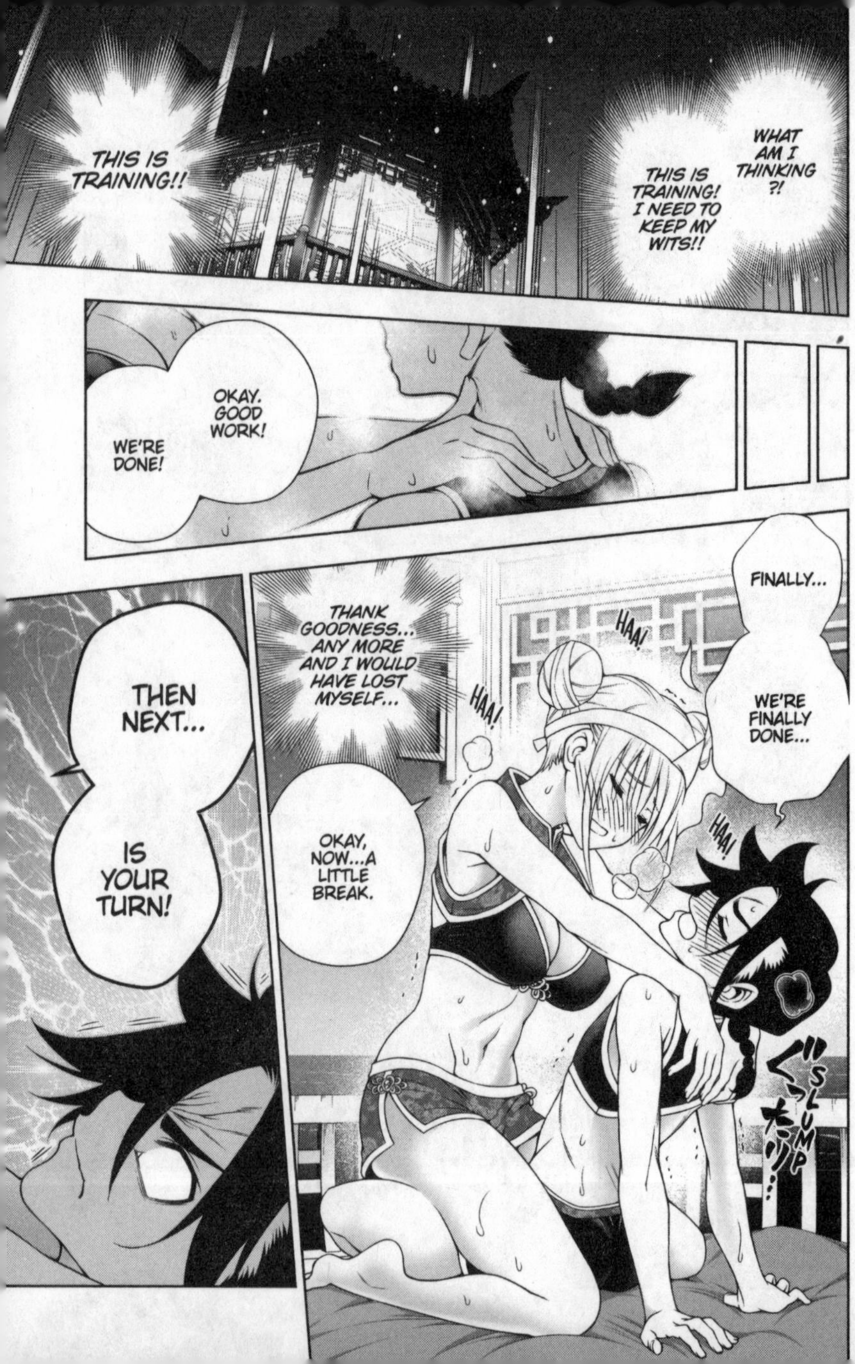
WHAT AM I THINKING?!
THIS IS TRAINING! I NEED TO KEEP MY WITS!!
THIS IS TRAINING!!
OKAY. GOOD WORK!
WE'RE DONE!
FINALLY...
WE'RE FINALLY DONE...
HAA!
HAA!
HAA!
THANK GOODNESS... ANY MORE AND I WOULD HAVE LOST MYSELF...
OKAY, NOW...A LITTLE BREAK.
SLUMP
THEN NEXT...
IS YOUR TURN!

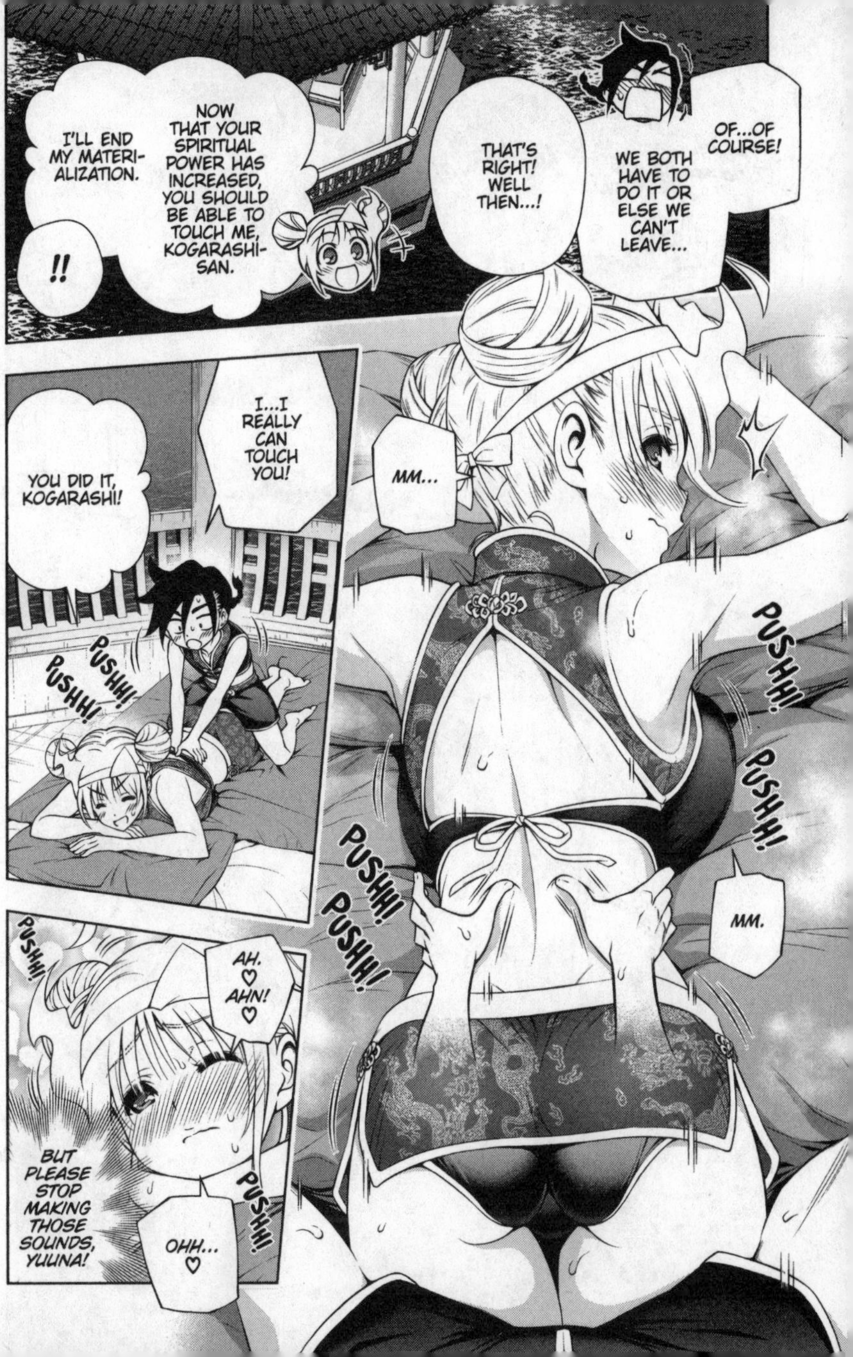
OF...OF COURSE!
WE BOTH HAVE TO DO IT OR ELSE WE CAN'T LEAVE...
THAT'S RIGHT! WELL THEN...!
NOW THAT YOUR SPIRITUAL POWER HAS INCREASED, YOU SHOULD BE ABLE TO TOUCH ME, KOGARASHI-SAN.
I'LL END MY MATERIALIZATION.
!!
MM...
PUSHH!
PUSHH!
MM.
I...I REALLY CAN TOUCH YOU!
YOU DID IT, KOGARASHI!
PUSHH!
PUSHH!
PUSHH!
PUSHH!
AH. ♡ AHN! ♡
PUSHH!
PUSHH!
OHH... ♡
BUT PLEASE STOP MAKING THOSE SOUNDS, YUUNA!

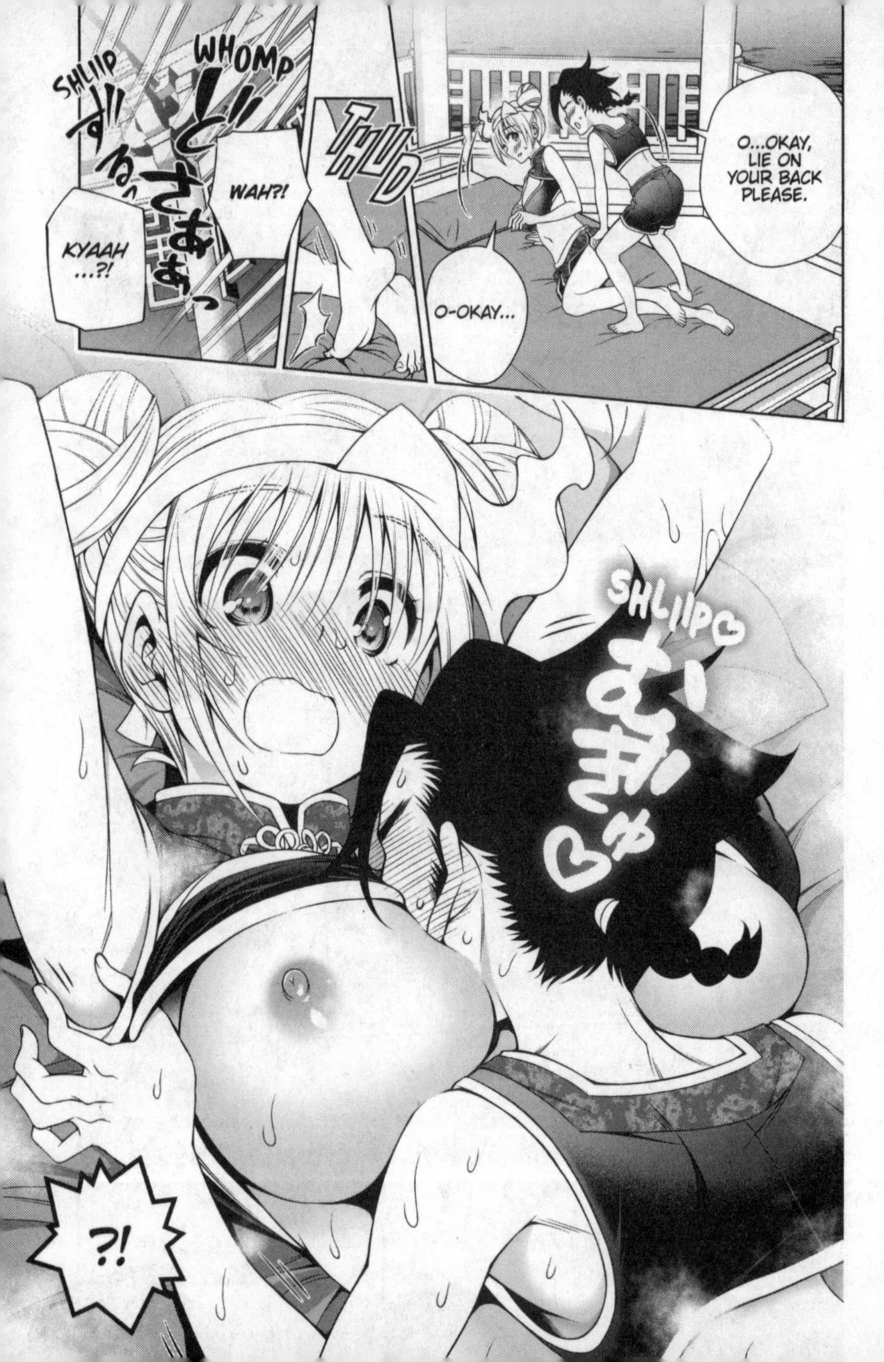
O...OKAY, LIE ON YOUR BACK PLEASE.
O-OKAY...
THUD
WAH?!
WHOMP
SHLIIP
KYAAH ...?!
SHLIIP♡
?!

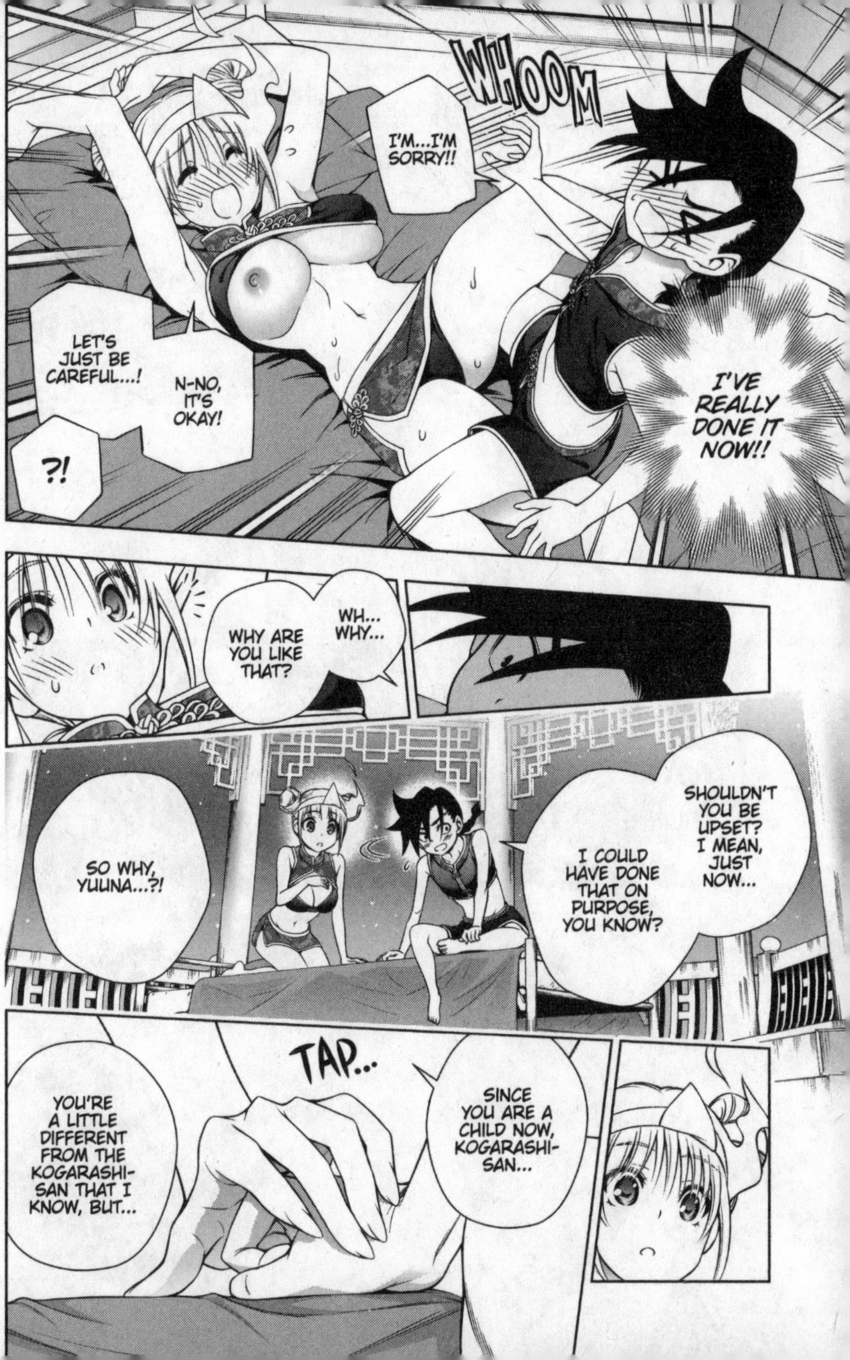
WHOOM
I'M...I'M SORRY!!
I'VE REALLY DONE IT NOW!!
N-NO, IT'S OKAY!
LET'S JUST BE CAREFUL...!
?!
WH... WHY...
WHY ARE YOU LIKE THAT?
SHOULDN'T YOU BE UPSET? I MEAN, JUST NOW...
I COULD HAVE DONE THAT ON PURPOSE, YOU KNOW?
SO WHY, YUUNA...?!
SINCE YOU ARE A CHILD NOW, KOGARASHI-SAN...
TAP...
YOU'RE A LITTLE DIFFERENT FROM THE KOGARASHI-SAN THAT I KNOW, BUT...

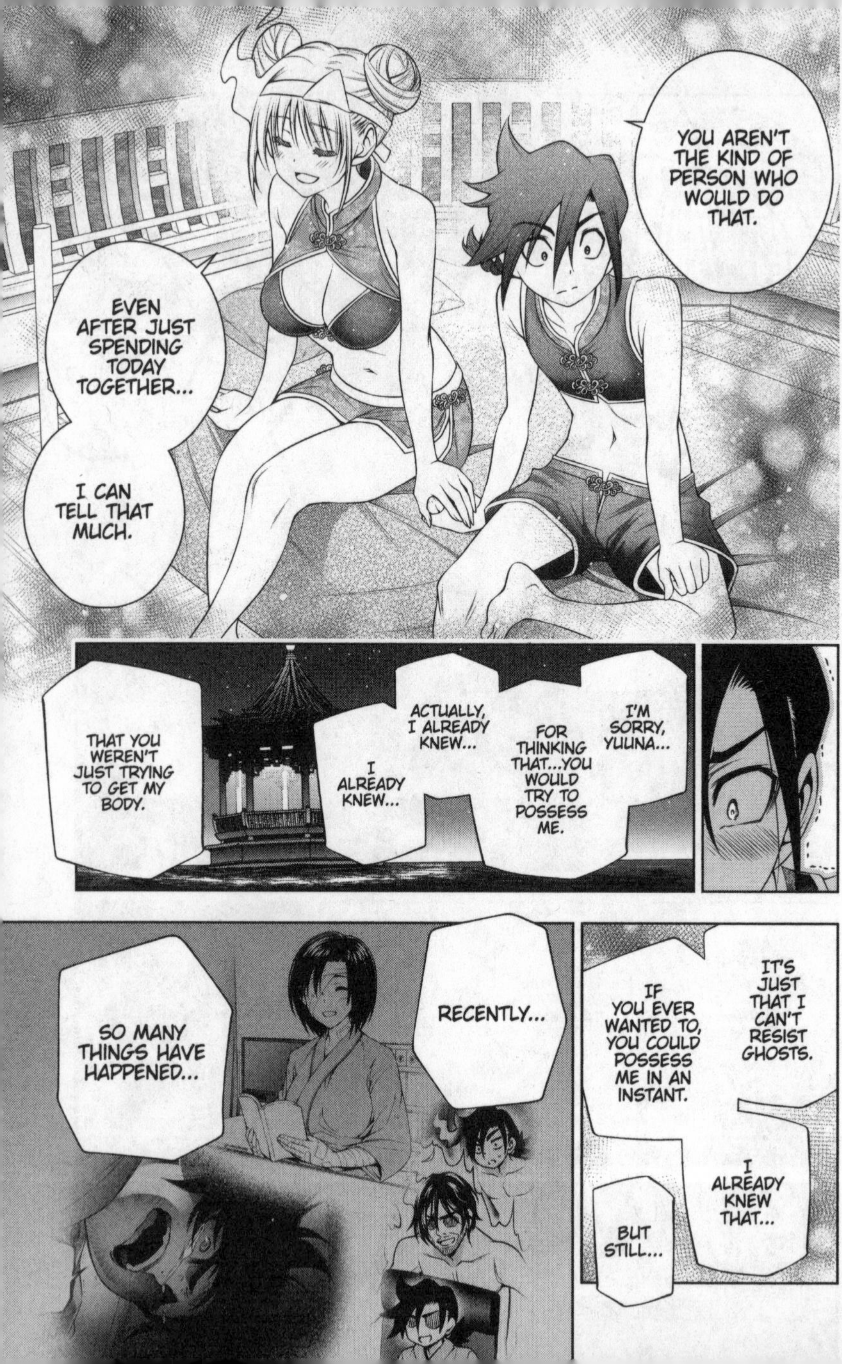
YOU AREN'T THE KIND OF PERSON WHO WOULD DO THAT.
EVEN AFTER JUST SPENDING TODAY TOGETHER...
I CAN TELL THAT MUCH.
I'M SORRY, YUUNA...
FOR THINKING THAT...YOU WOULD TRY TO POSSESS ME.
ACTUALLY, I ALREADY KNEW...
I ALREADY KNEW...
THAT YOU WEREN'T JUST TRYING TO GET MY BODY.
IT'S JUST THAT I CAN'T RESIST GHOSTS.
IF YOU EVER WANTED TO, YOU COULD POSSESS ME IN AN INSTANT.
I ALREADY KNEW THAT...
BUT STILL...
RECENTLY...
SO MANY THINGS HAVE HAPPENED...

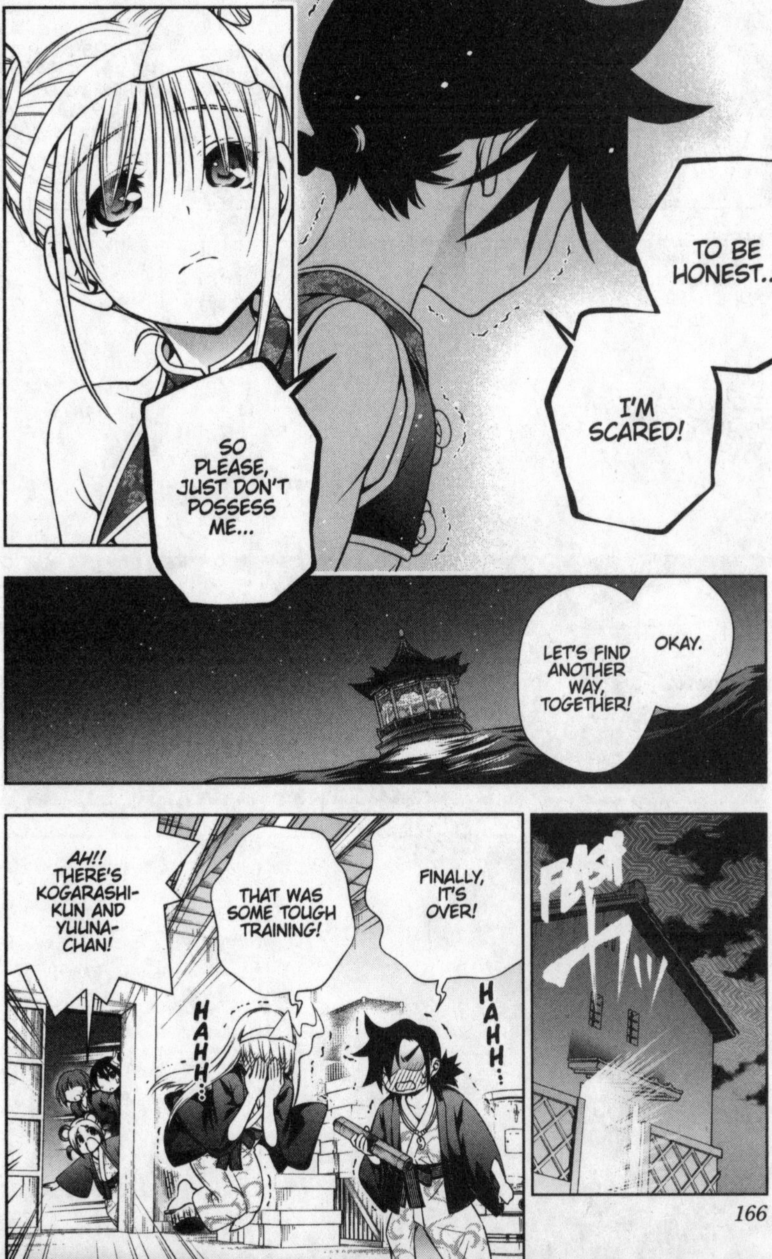
TO BE HONEST...
I'M SCARED!
SO PLEASE, JUST DON'T POSSESS ME...
OKAY.
LET'S FIND ANOTHER WAY, TOGETHER!
FLASH
FINALLY, IT'S OVER!
HAHH HAHH...
THAT WAS SOME TOUGH TRAINING!
HAHH HAHH...
AH!! THERE'S KOGARASHI-KUN AND YUUNA-CHAN!

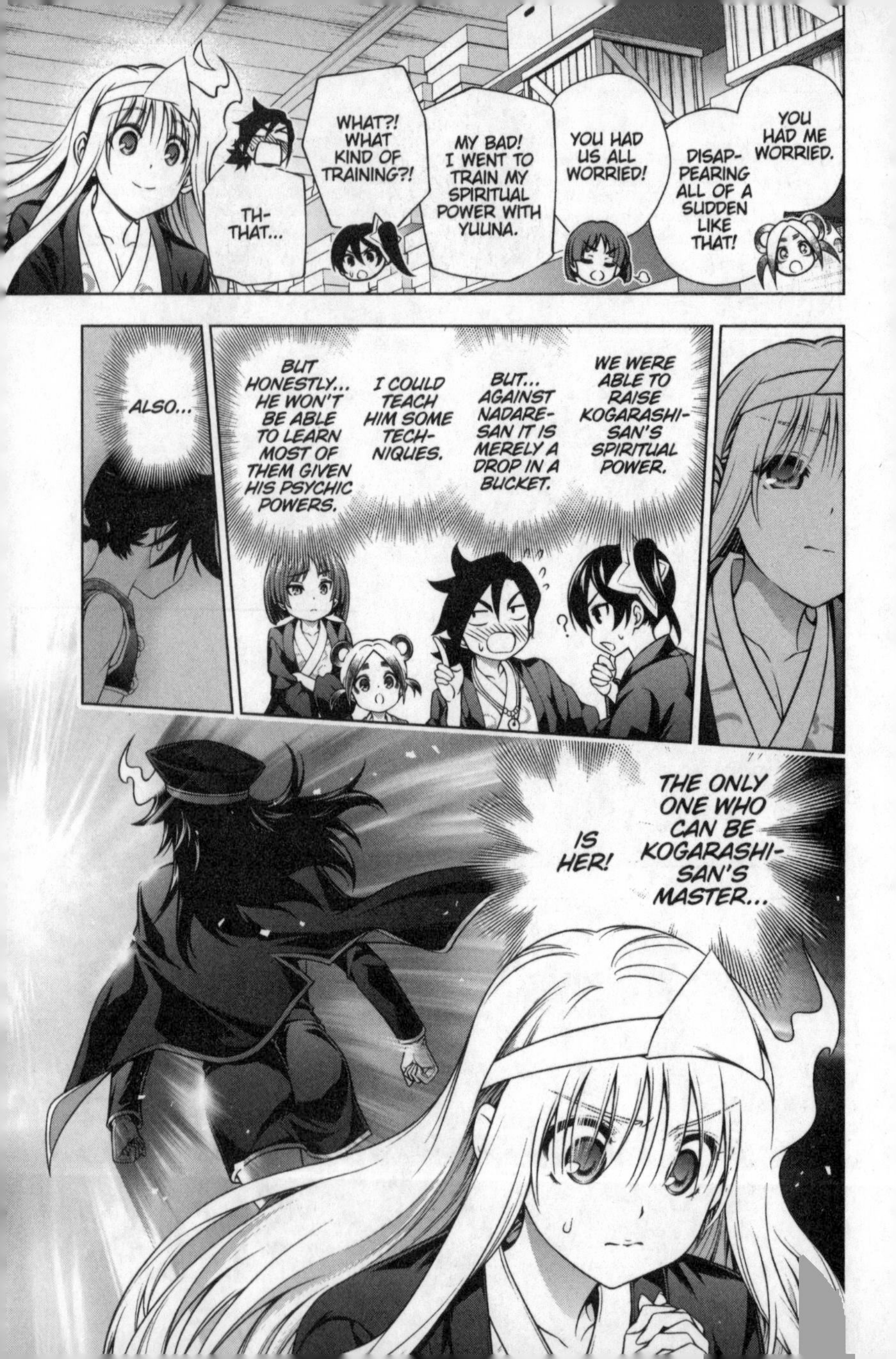
YOU HAD ME WORRIED.
DISAP-PEARING ALL OF A SUDDEN LIKE THAT!
YOU HAD US ALL WORRIED!
MY BAD! I WENT TO TRAIN MY SPIRITUAL POWER WITH YUUNA.
WHAT?! WHAT KIND OF TRAINING?!
TH-THAT...
WE WERE ABLE TO RAISE KOGARASHI-SAN'S SPIRITUAL POWER.
BUT... AGAINST NADARE-SAN IT IS MERELY A DROP IN A BUCKET.
I COULD TEACH HIM SOME TECH-NIQUES.
BUT HONESTLY... HE WON'T BE ABLE TO LEARN MOST OF THEM GIVEN HIS PSYCHIC POWERS.
ALSO...
THE ONLY ONE WHO CAN BE KOGARASHI-SAN'S MASTER...
IS HER!

Yuuna and the Haunted Hot Springs

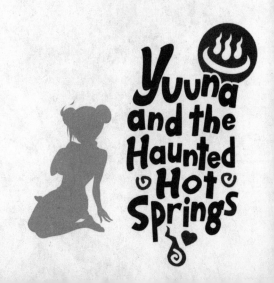

♨ 160 Everyone's Psychic Training

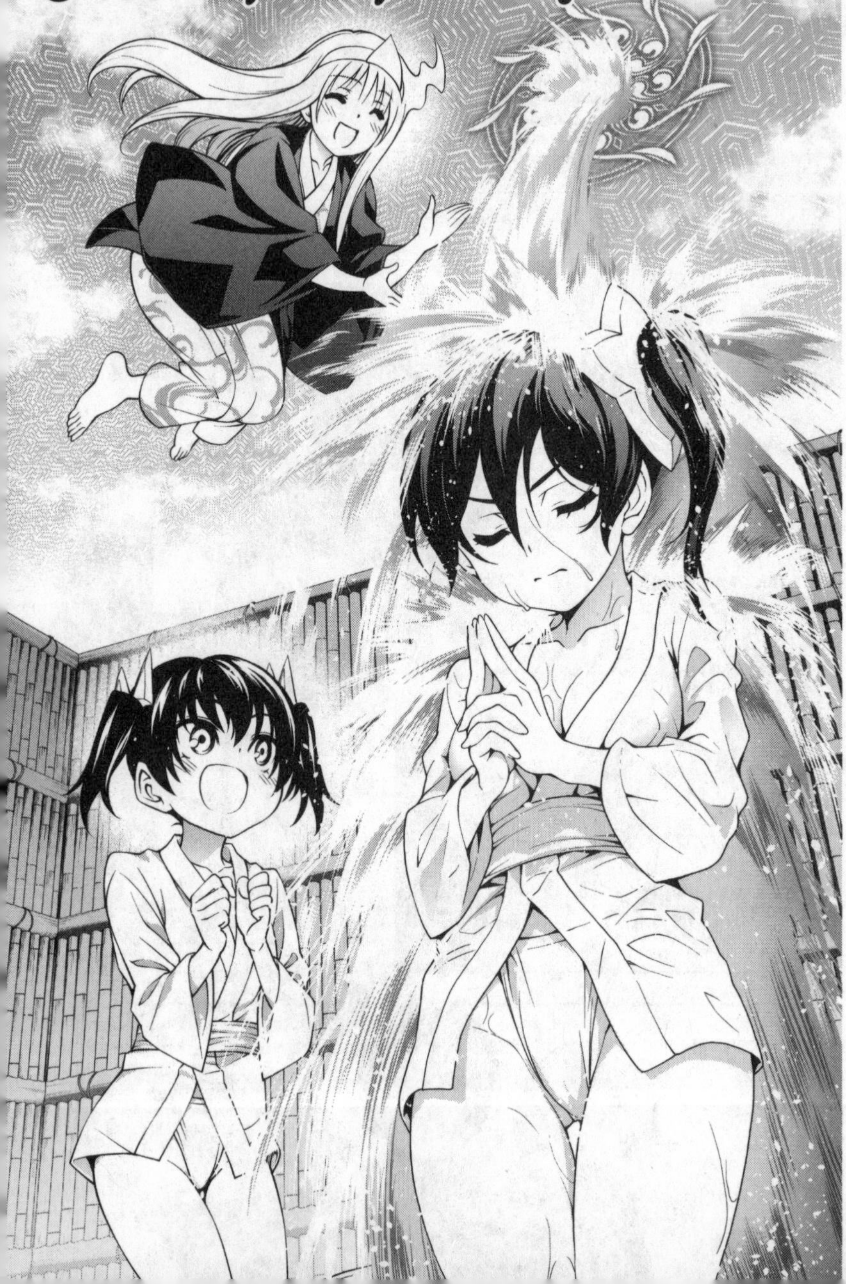

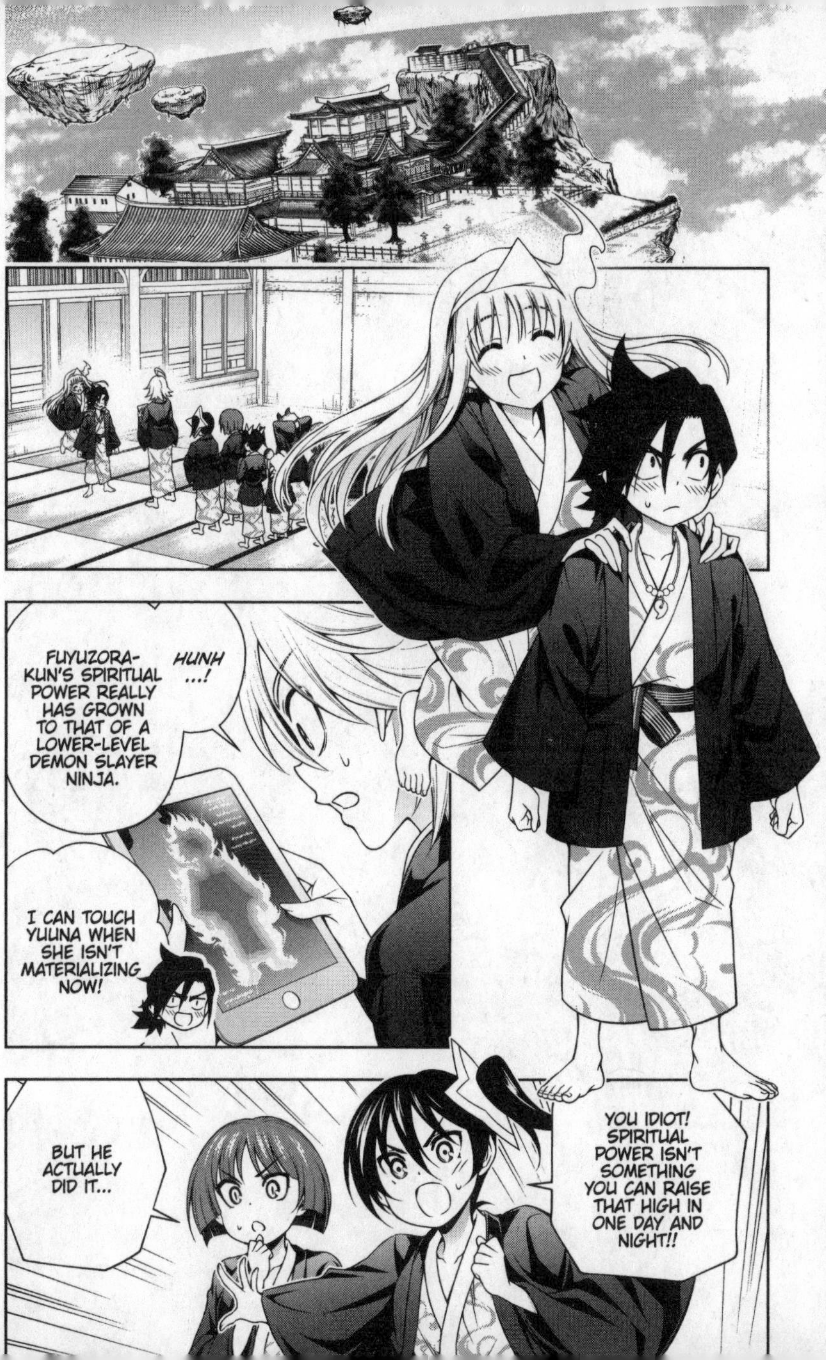
HUNH ...!
FUYUZORA-KUN'S SPIRITUAL POWER REALLY HAS GROWN TO THAT OF A LOWER-LEVEL DEMON SLAYER NINJA.
I CAN TOUCH YUUNA WHEN SHE ISN'T MATERIALIZING NOW!
YOU IDIOT! SPIRITUAL POWER ISN'T SOMETHING YOU CAN RAISE THAT HIGH IN ONE DAY AND NIGHT!!
BUT HE ACTUALLY DID IT...

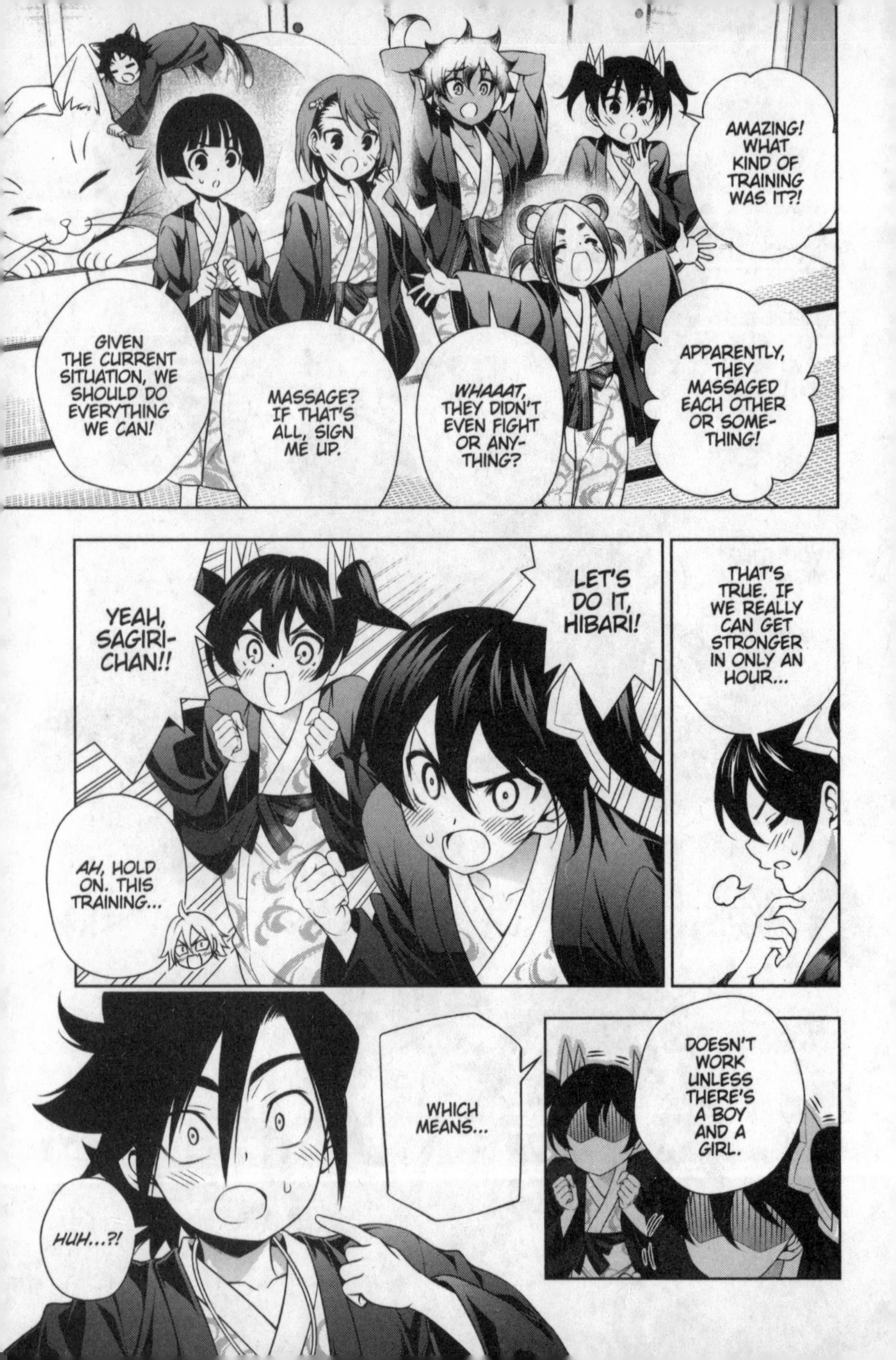
AMAZING! WHAT KIND OF TRAINING WAS IT?!
APPARENTLY, THEY MASSAGED EACH OTHER OR SOME-THING!
WHAAAT, THEY DIDN'T EVEN FIGHT OR ANY-THING?
MASSAGE? IF THAT'S ALL, SIGN ME UP.
GIVEN THE CURRENT SITUATION, WE SHOULD DO EVERYTHING WE CAN!
THAT'S TRUE. IF WE REALLY CAN GET STRONGER IN ONLY AN HOUR...
LET'S DO IT, HIBARI!
YEAH, SAGIRI-CHAN!!
AH, HOLD ON. THIS TRAINING...
DOESN'T WORK UNLESS THERE'S A BOY AND A GIRL.
WHICH MEANS...
HUH...?!

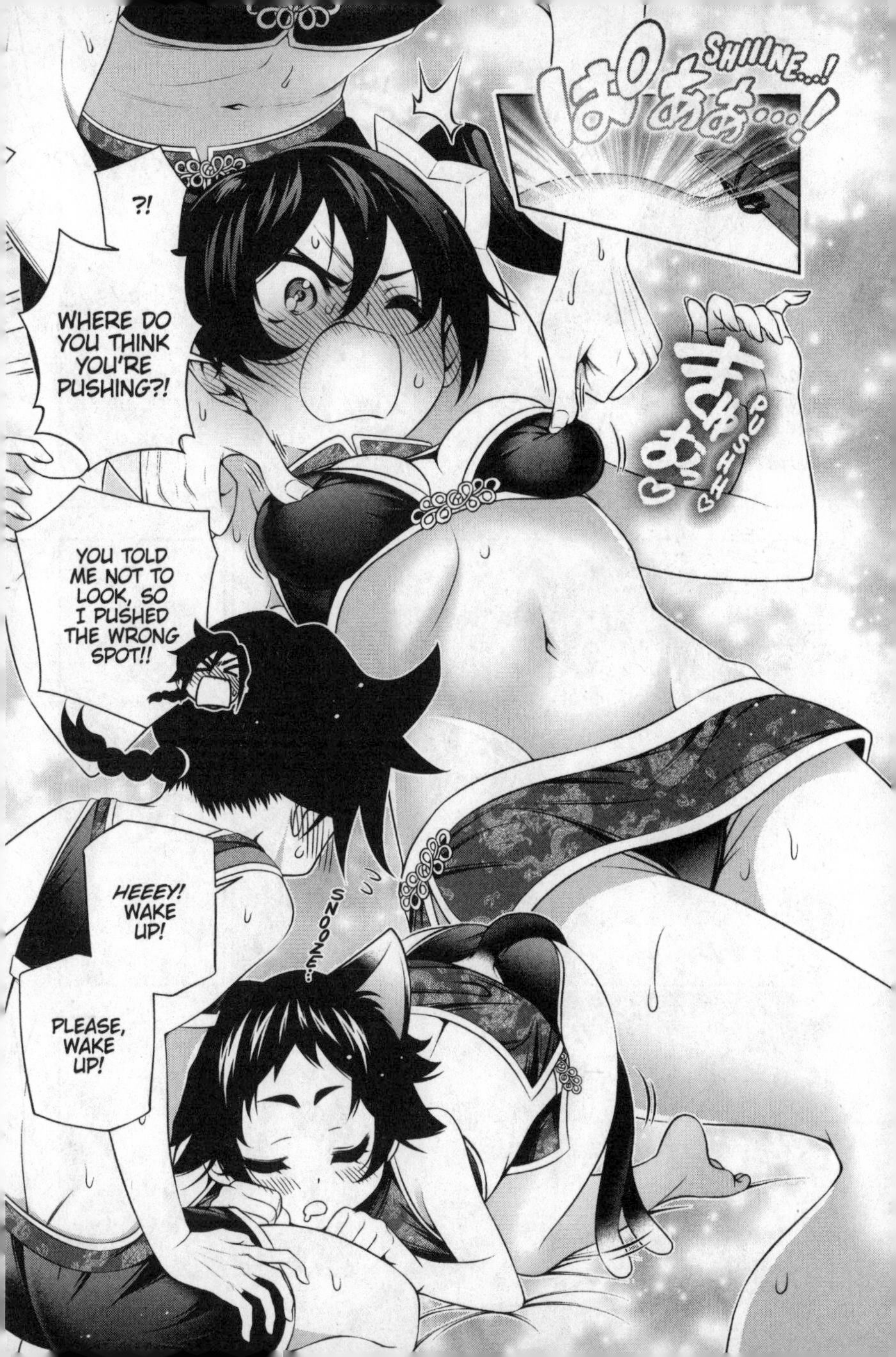
SHIIINE...!
?!
WHERE DO YOU THINK YOU'RE PUSHING?!
PUSHH♡
YOU TOLD ME NOT TO LOOK, SO I PUSHED THE WRONG SPOT!!
HEEEY! WAKE UP!
SNOOZE...
PLEASE, WAKE UP!

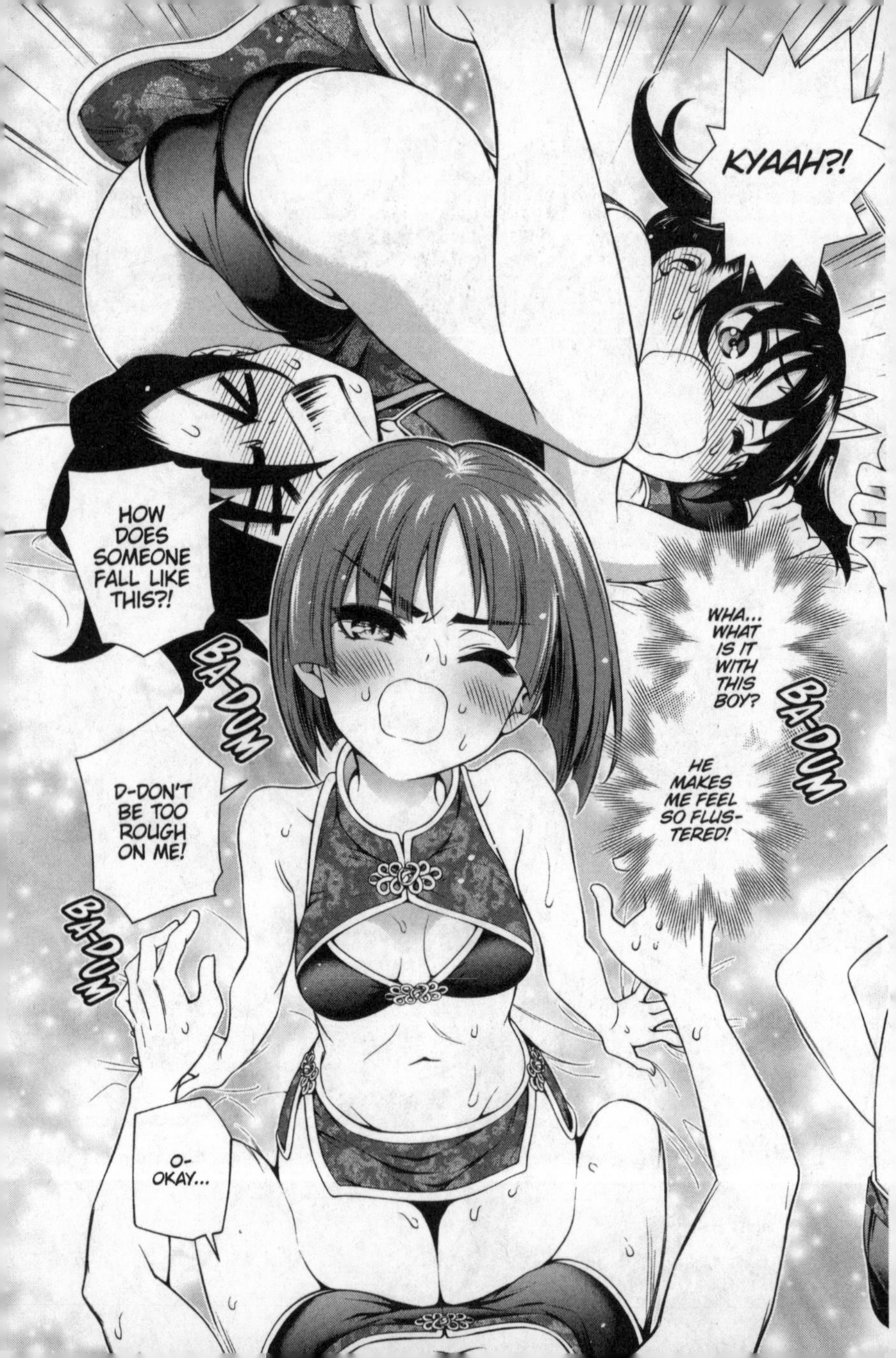
KYAAH?!
HOW DOES SOMEONE FALL LIKE THIS?!
WHA... WHAT IS IT WITH THIS BOY?
BA-DUM
HE MAKES ME FEEL SO FLUS-TERED!
BA-DUM
D-DON'T BE TOO ROUGH ON ME!
BA-DUM
O-OKAY...

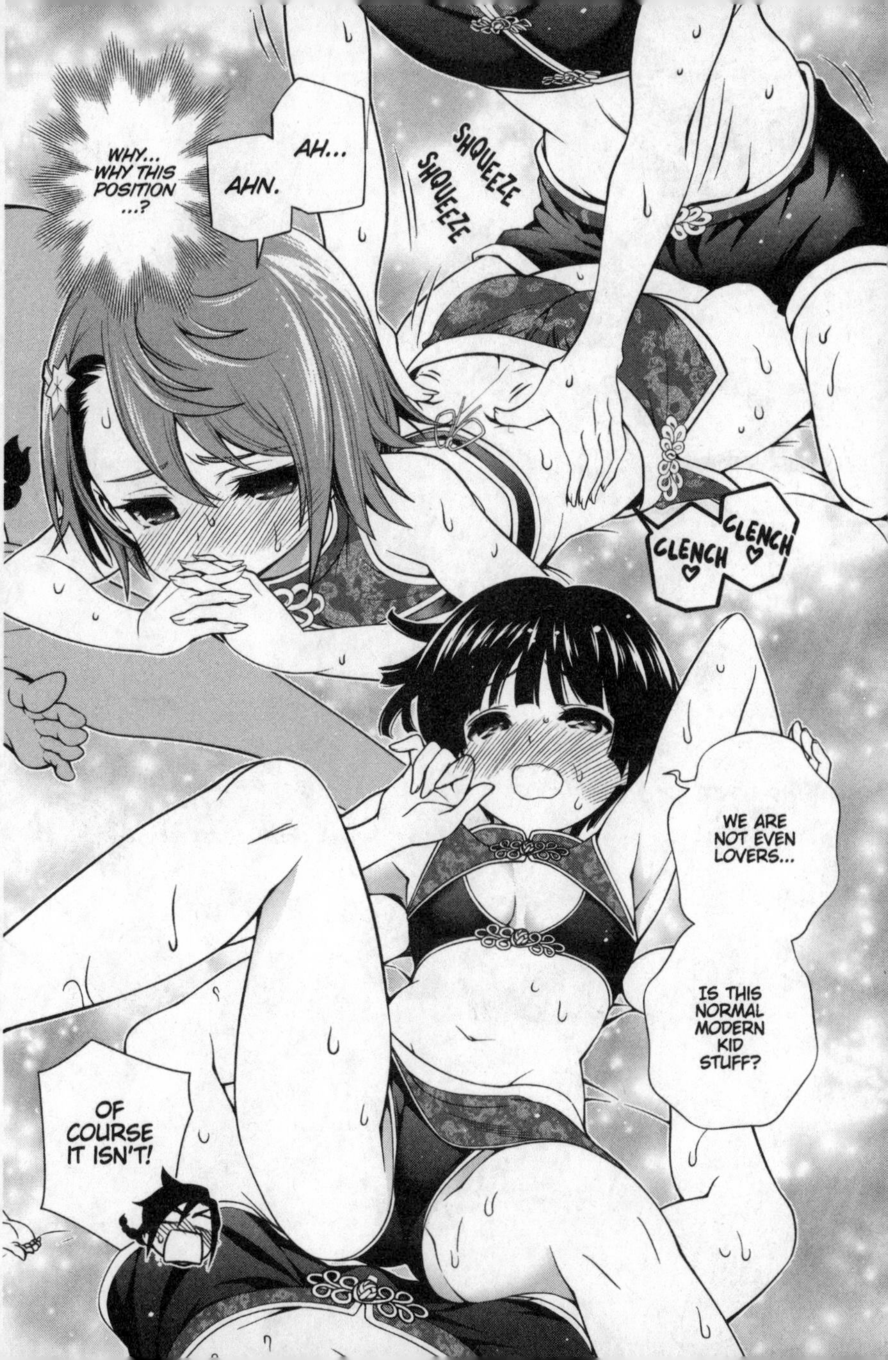
SHQUEEZE
SHQUEEZE
AH...
AHN.
WHY... WHY THIS POSITION ...?
CLENCH ♡
CLENCH ♡
WE ARE NOT EVEN LOVERS...
IS THIS NORMAL MODERN KID STUFF?
OF COURSE IT ISN'T!

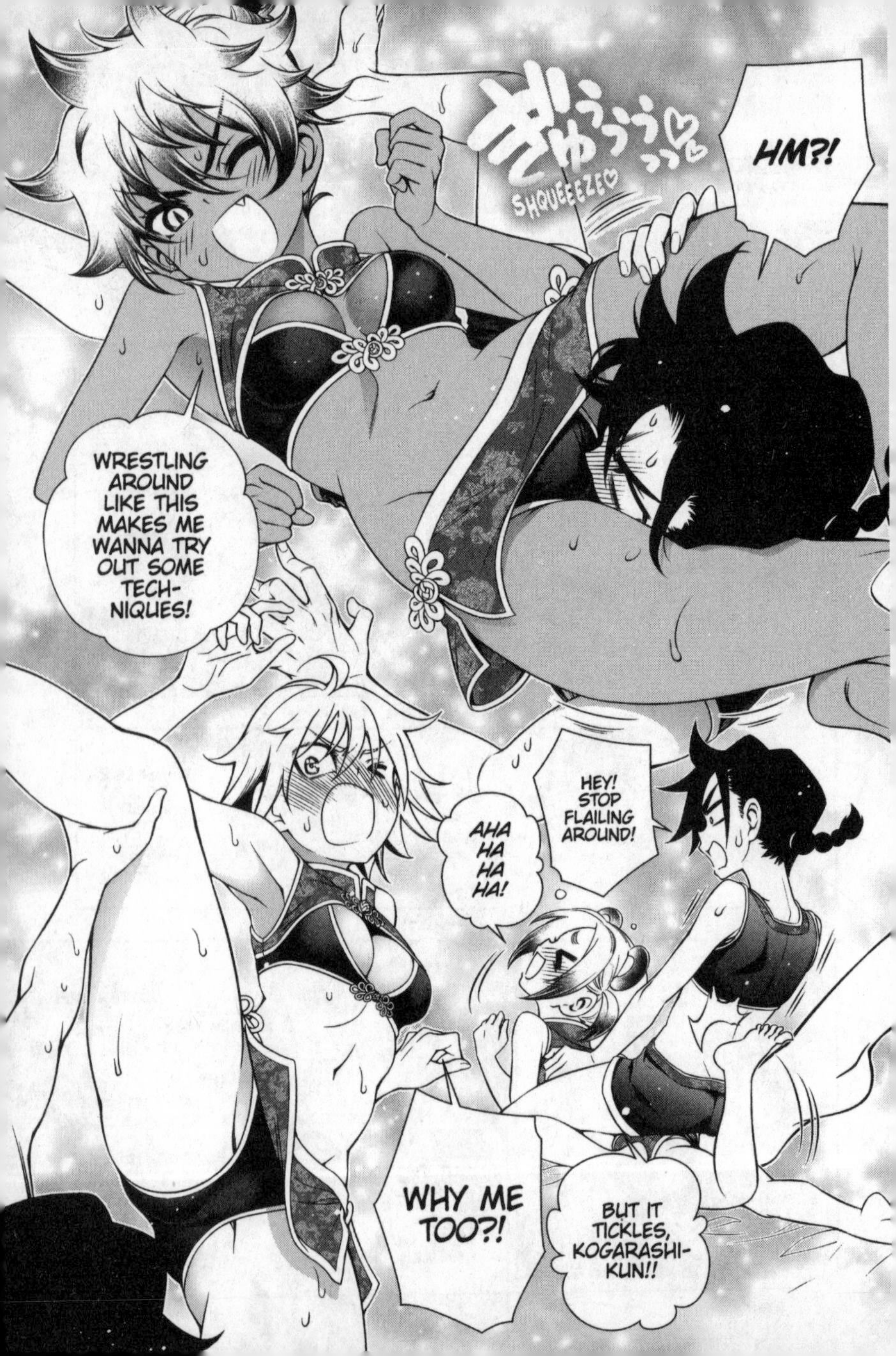
HM?!
SHQUEEEZE♡
WRESTLING AROUND LIKE THIS MAKES ME WANNA TRY OUT SOME TECH-NIQUES!
HEY! STOP FLAILING AROUND!
AHA HA HA HA!
BUT IT TICKLES, KOGARASHI-KUN!!
WHY ME TOO?!

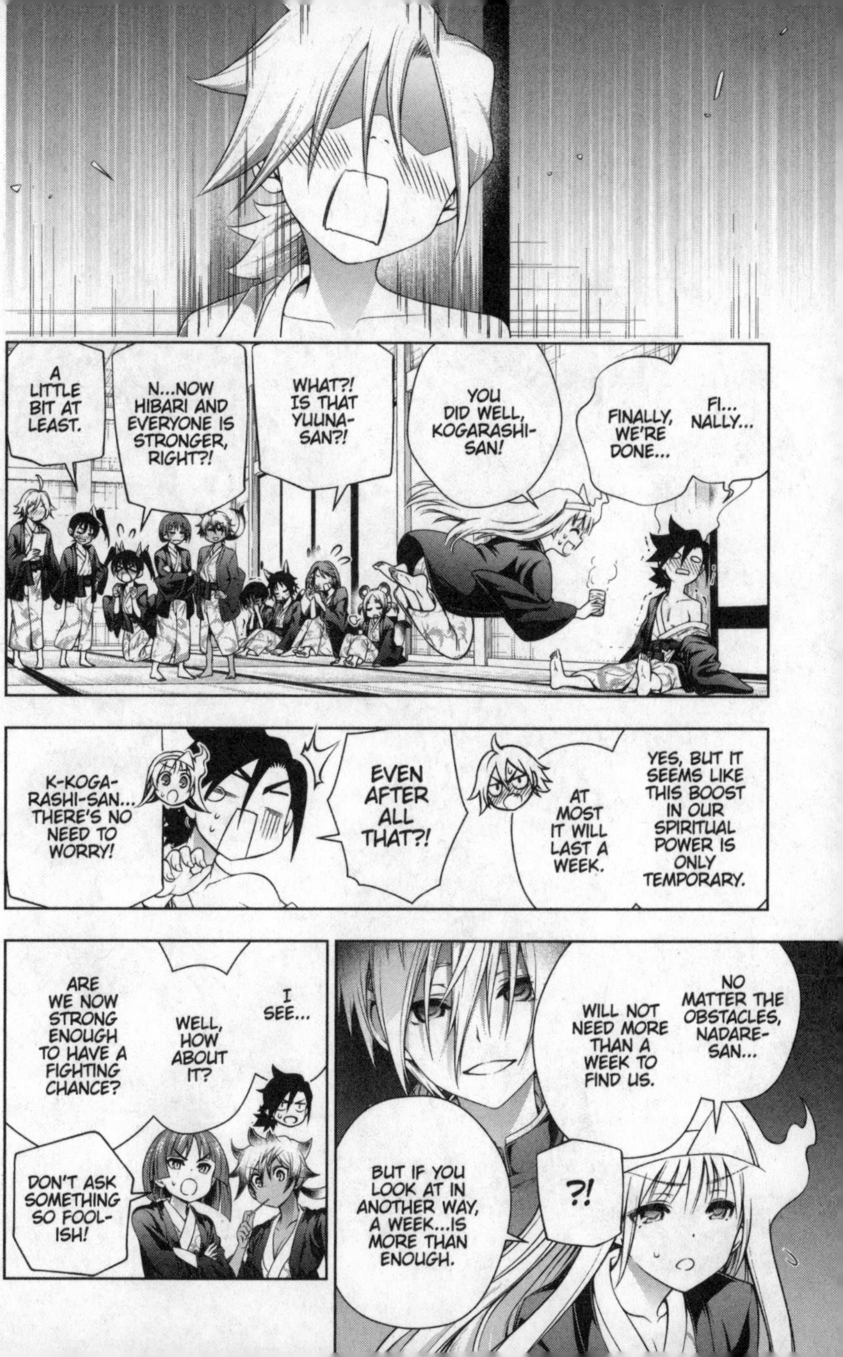
FI... NALLY...
FINALLY, WE'RE DONE...
YOU DID WELL, KOGARASHI-SAN!
WHAT?! IS THAT YUUNA-SAN?!
N...NOW HIBARI AND EVERYONE IS STRONGER, RIGHT?!
A LITTLE BIT AT LEAST.
YES, BUT IT SEEMS LIKE THIS BOOST IN OUR SPIRITUAL POWER IS ONLY TEMPORARY.
AT MOST IT WILL LAST A WEEK.
EVEN AFTER ALL THAT?!
K-KOGARASHI-SAN... THERE'S NO NEED TO WORRY!
NO MATTER THE OBSTACLES, NADARE-SAN...
WILL NOT NEED MORE THAN A WEEK TO FIND US.
?!
BUT IF YOU LOOK AT IN ANOTHER WAY, A WEEK...IS MORE THAN ENOUGH.
I SEE...
WELL, HOW ABOUT IT?
ARE WE NOW STRONG ENOUGH TO HAVE A FIGHTING CHANCE?
DON'T ASK SOMETHING SO FOOL-ISH!

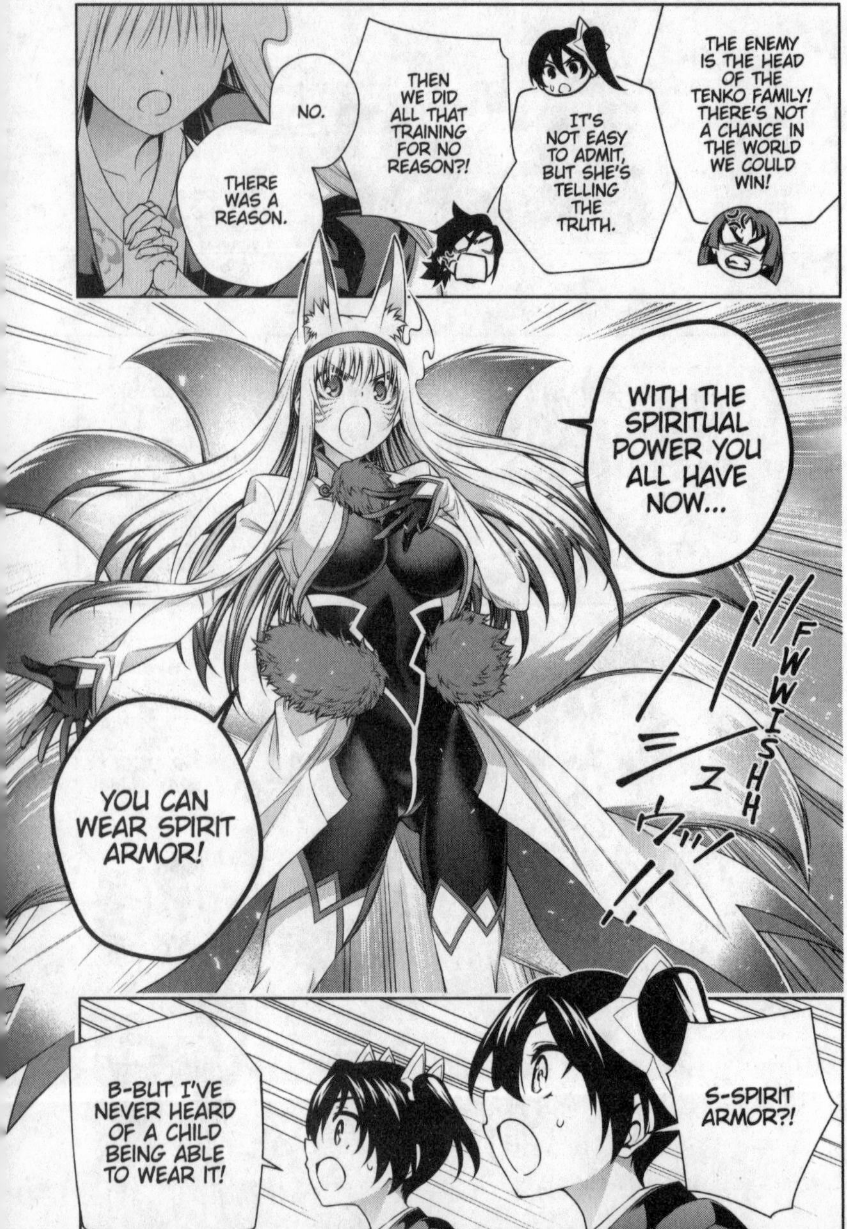
THE ENEMY IS THE HEAD OF THE TENKO FAMILY! THERE'S NOT A CHANCE IN THE WORLD WE COULD WIN!
IT'S NOT EASY TO ADMIT, BUT SHE'S TELLING THE TRUTH.
THEN WE DID ALL THAT TRAINING FOR NO REASON?!
NO.
THERE WAS A REASON.
WITH THE SPIRITUAL POWER YOU ALL HAVE NOW...
FWWISHH
YOU CAN WEAR SPIRIT ARMOR!
S-SPIRIT ARMOR?!
B-BUT I'VE NEVER HEARD OF A CHILD BEING ABLE TO WEAR IT!

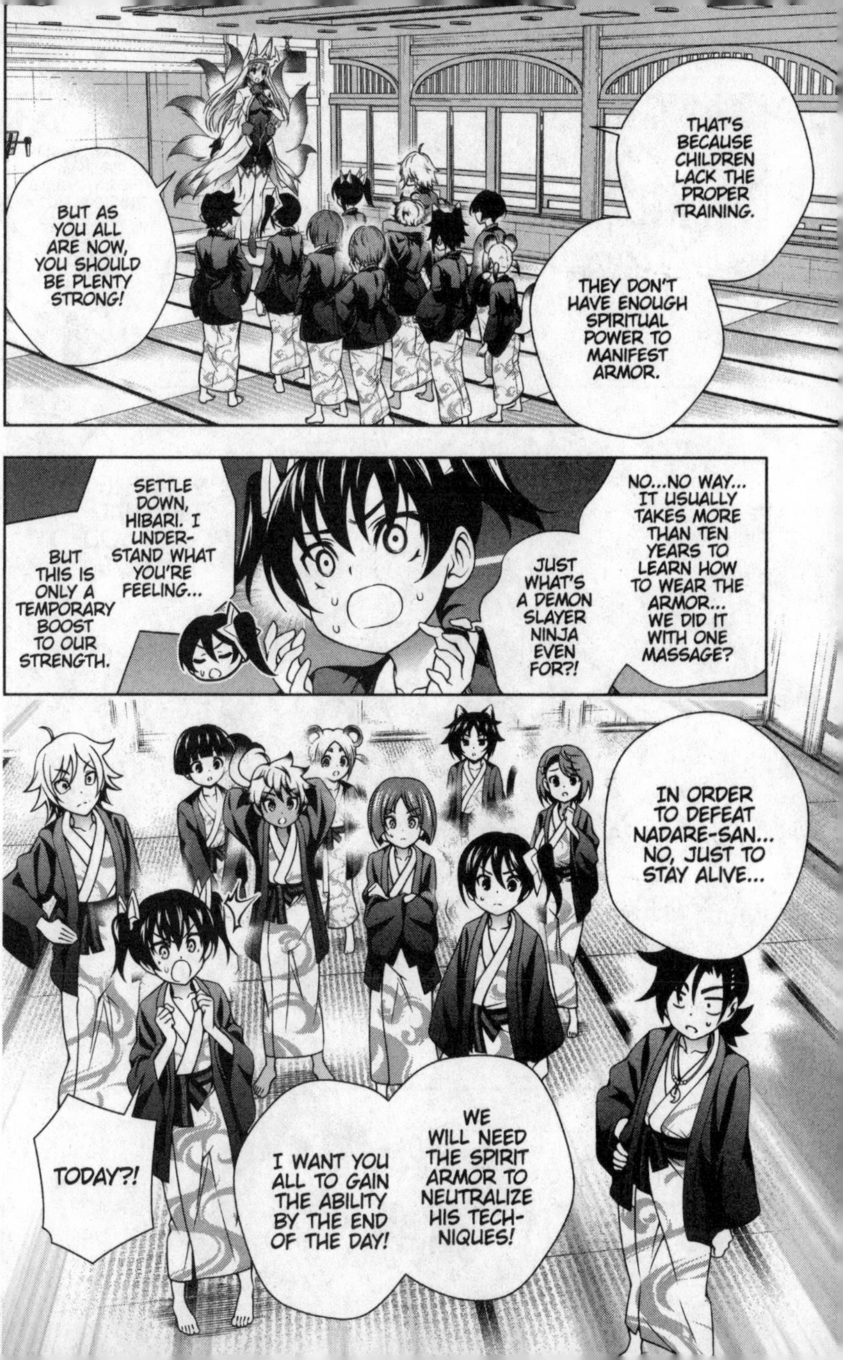
THAT'S BECAUSE CHILDREN LACK THE PROPER TRAINING.
THEY DON'T HAVE ENOUGH SPIRITUAL POWER TO MANIFEST ARMOR.
BUT AS YOU ALL ARE NOW, YOU SHOULD BE PLENTY STRONG!
NO...NO WAY... IT USUALLY TAKES MORE THAN TEN YEARS TO LEARN HOW TO WEAR THE ARMOR... WE DID IT WITH ONE MASSAGE?
JUST WHAT'S A DEMON SLAYER NINJA EVEN FOR?!
SETTLE DOWN, HIBARI. I UNDER-STAND WHAT YOU'RE FEELING...
BUT THIS IS ONLY A TEMPORARY BOOST TO OUR STRENGTH.
IN ORDER TO DEFEAT NADARE-SAN... NO, JUST TO STAY ALIVE...
WE WILL NEED THE SPIRIT ARMOR TO NEUTRALIZE HIS TECH-NIQUES!
I WANT YOU ALL TO GAIN THE ABILITY BY THE END OF THE DAY!
TODAY?!

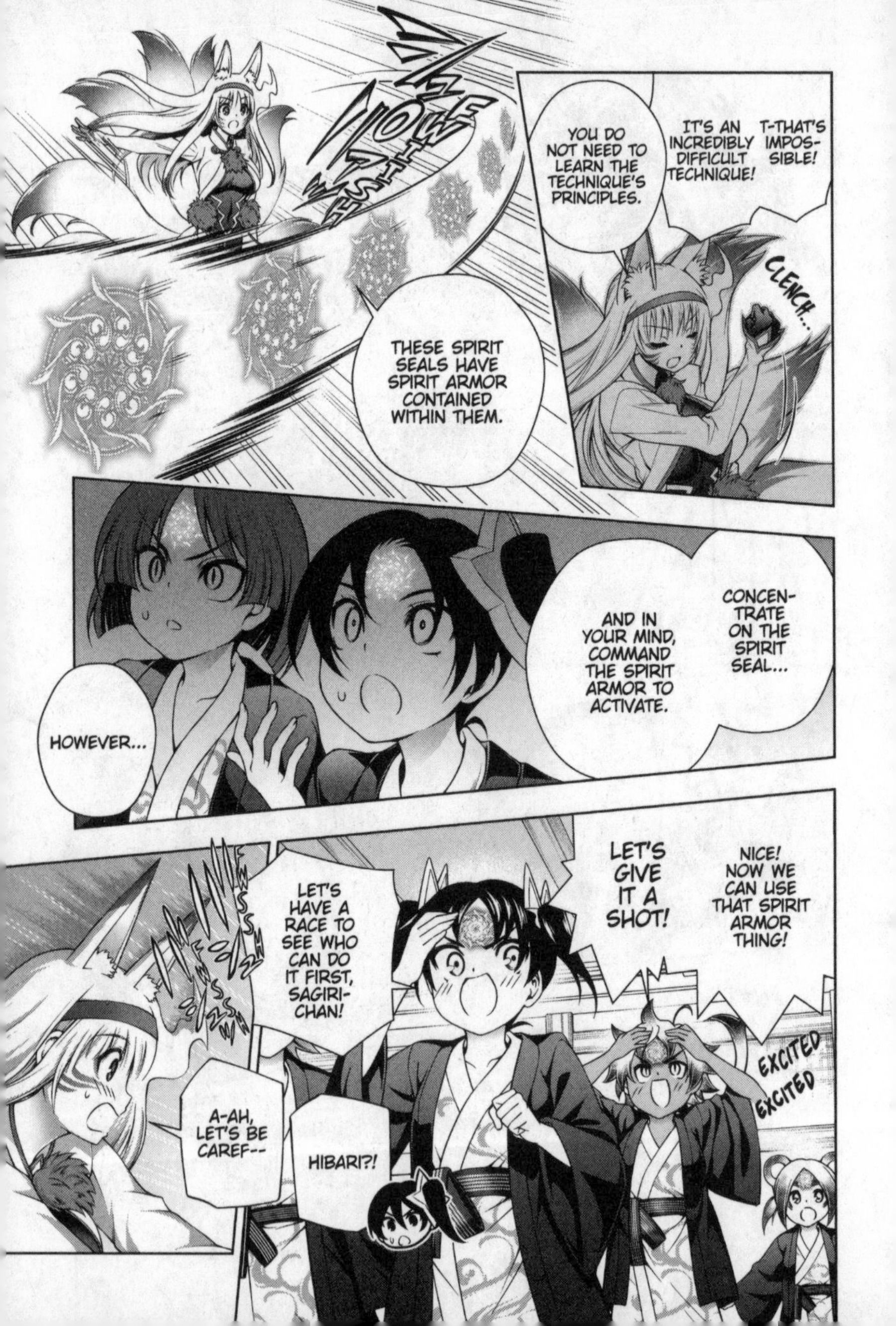
T-THAT'S IMPOS-SIBLE!
IT'S AN INCREDIBLY DIFFICULT TECHNIQUE!
YOU DO NOT NEED TO LEARN THE TECHNIQUE'S PRINCIPLES.
CLENCH...
THESE SPIRIT SEALS HAVE SPIRIT ARMOR CONTAINED WITHIN THEM.
CONCEN-TRATE ON THE SPIRIT SEAL...
AND IN YOUR MIND, COMMAND THE SPIRIT ARMOR TO ACTIVATE.
HOWEVER...
NICE! NOW WE CAN USE THAT SPIRIT ARMOR THING!
LET'S GIVE IT A SHOT!
LET'S HAVE A RACE TO SEE WHO CAN DO IT FIRST, SAGIRI-CHAN!
EXCITED
EXCITED
HIBARI?!
A-AH, LET'S BE CAREF--

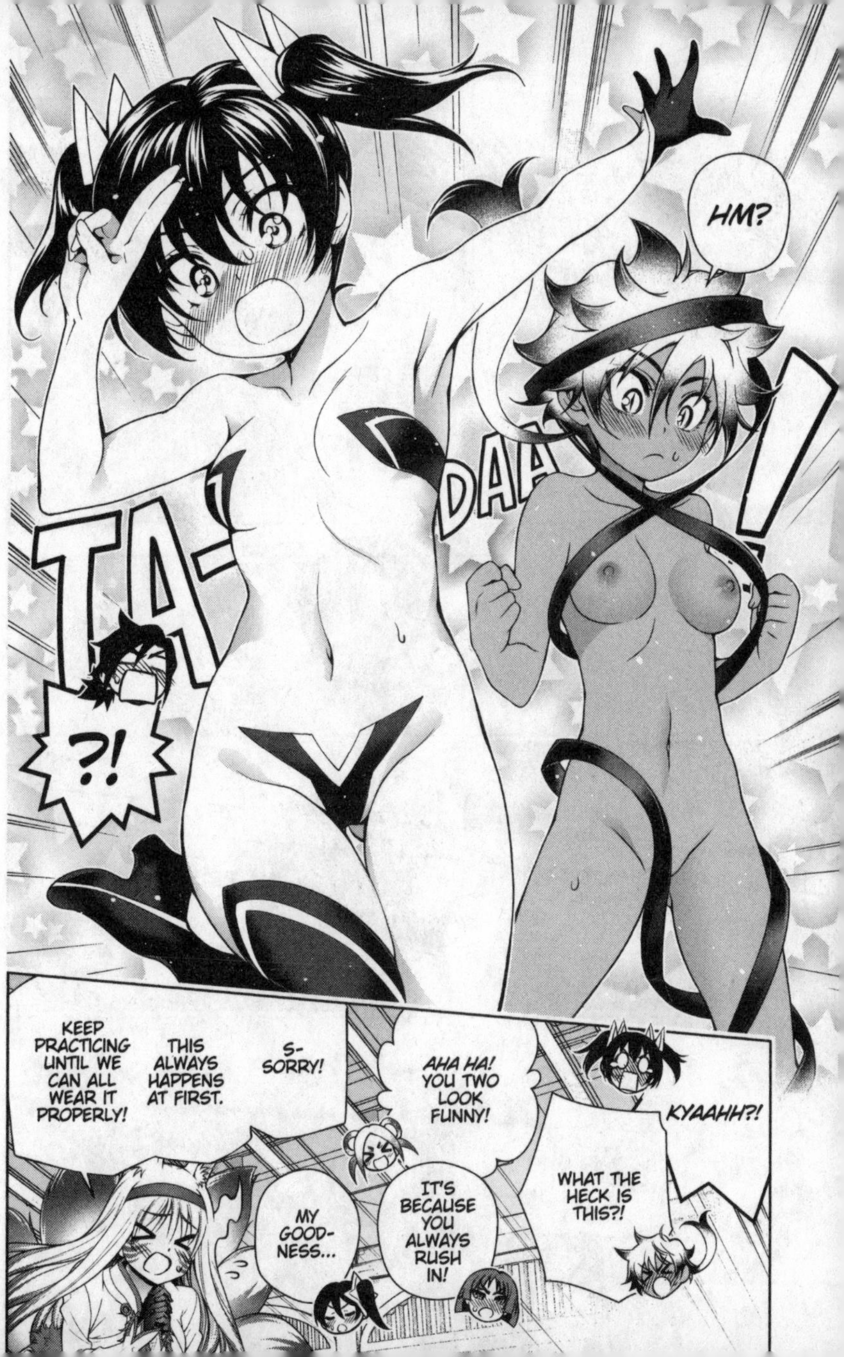
HM?
TA-DAA!
?!
KYAAHH?!
AHA HA! YOU TWO LOOK FUNNY!
S- SORRY!
THIS ALWAYS HAPPENS AT FIRST.
KEEP PRACTICING UNTIL WE CAN ALL WEAR IT PROPERLY!
WHAT THE HECK IS THIS?!
IT'S BECAUSE YOU ALWAYS RUSH IN!
MY GOODNESS...

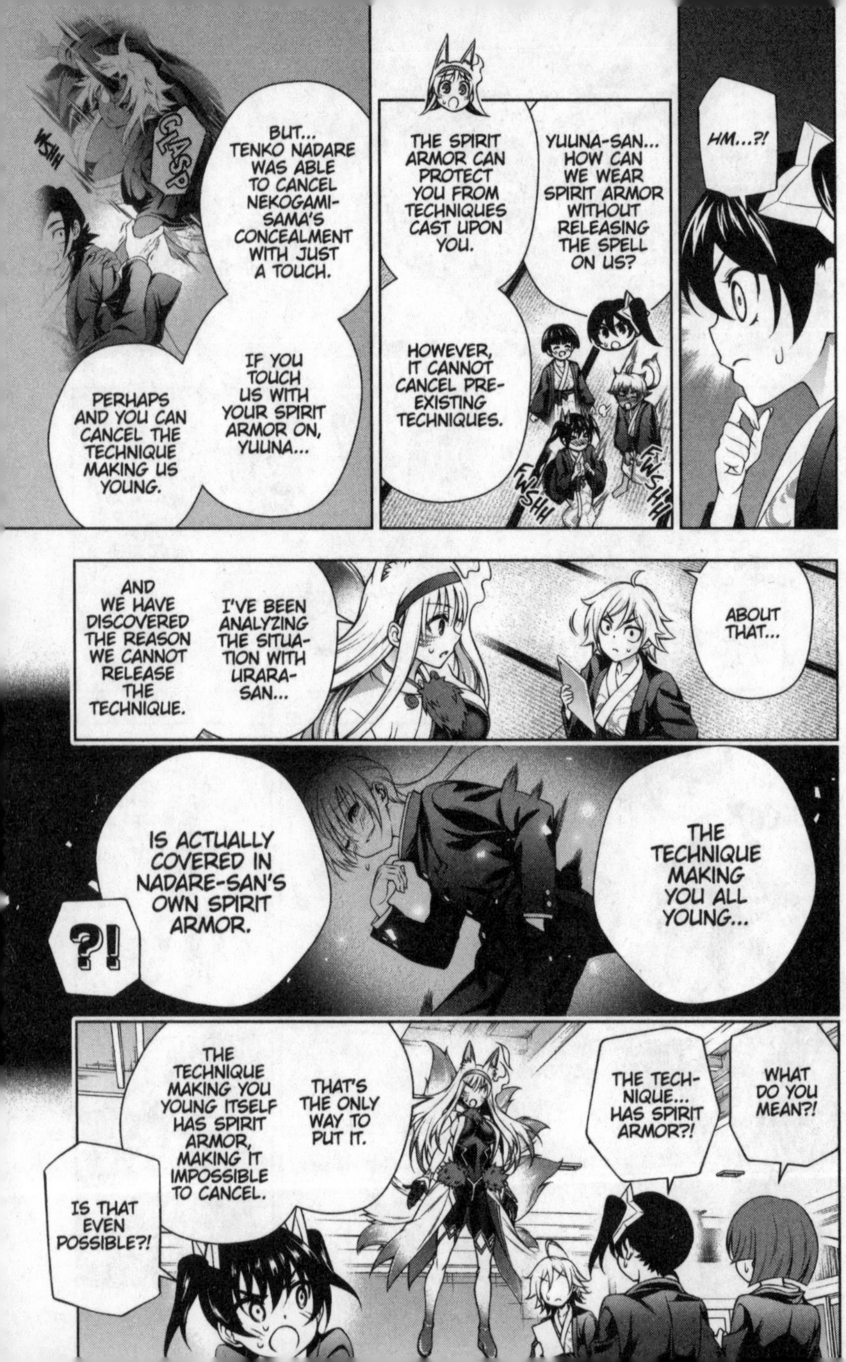
HM...?!
YUUNA-SAN... HOW CAN WE WEAR SPIRIT ARMOR WITHOUT RELEASING THE SPELL ON US?
THE SPIRIT ARMOR CAN PROTECT YOU FROM TECHNIQUES CAST UPON YOU.
HOWEVER, IT CANNOT CANCEL PRE-EXISTING TECHNIQUES.
FWSHH
FWSHH
BUT... TENKO NADARE WAS ABLE TO CANCEL NEKOGAMI-SAMA'S CONCEALMENT WITH JUST A TOUCH.
CLASP
WSHH
IF YOU TOUCH US WITH YOUR SPIRIT ARMOR ON, YUUNA...
PERHAPS AND YOU CAN CANCEL THE TECHNIQUE MAKING US YOUNG.
ABOUT THAT...
I'VE BEEN ANALYZING THE SITUA-TION WITH URARA-SAN...
AND WE HAVE DISCOVERED THE REASON WE CANNOT RELEASE THE TECHNIQUE.
THE TECHNIQUE MAKING YOU ALL YOUNG...
IS ACTUALLY COVERED IN NADARE-SAN'S OWN SPIRIT ARMOR.
?!
WHAT DO YOU MEAN?!
THE TECH-NIQUE... HAS SPIRIT ARMOR?!
THAT'S THE ONLY WAY TO PUT IT.
THE TECHNIQUE MAKING YOU YOUNG ITSELF HAS SPIRIT ARMOR, MAKING IT IMPOSSIBLE TO CANCEL.
IS THAT EVEN POSSIBLE?!

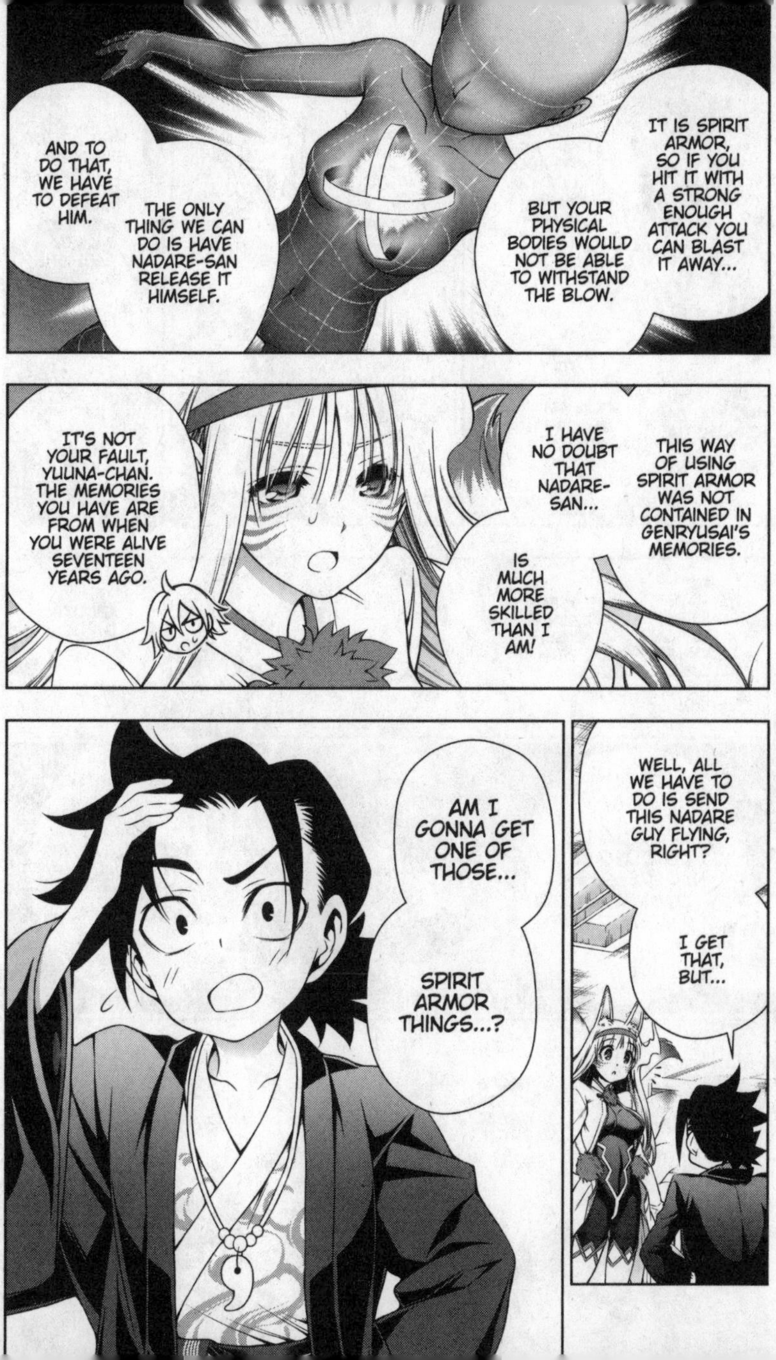
IT IS SPIRIT ARMOR, SO IF YOU HIT IT WITH A STRONG ENOUGH ATTACK YOU CAN BLAST IT AWAY...
BUT YOUR PHYSICAL BODIES WOULD NOT BE ABLE TO WITHSTAND THE BLOW.
THE ONLY THING WE CAN DO IS HAVE NADARE-SAN RELEASE IT HIMSELF.
AND TO DO THAT, WE HAVE TO DEFEAT HIM.
THIS WAY OF USING SPIRIT ARMOR WAS NOT CONTAINED IN GENRYUSAI'S MEMORIES.
I HAVE NO DOUBT THAT NADARE-SAN...
IS MUCH MORE SKILLED THAN I AM!
IT'S NOT YOUR FAULT, YUUNA-CHAN. THE MEMORIES YOU HAVE ARE FROM WHEN YOU WERE ALIVE SEVENTEEN YEARS AGO.
WELL, ALL WE HAVE TO DO IS SEND THIS NADARE GUY FLYING, RIGHT?
I GET THAT, BUT...
AM I GONNA GET ONE OF THOSE...
SPIRIT ARMOR THINGS...?

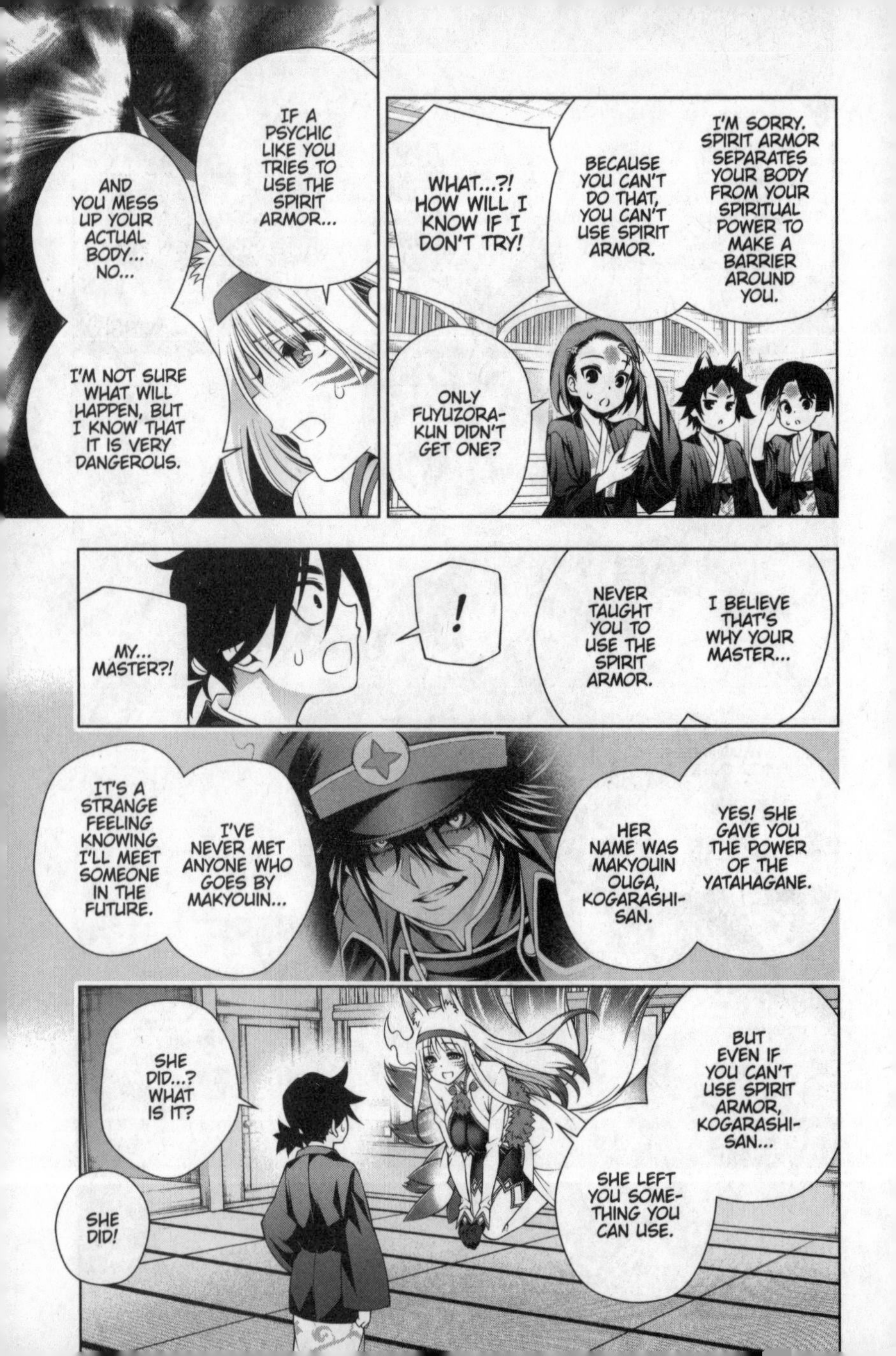

I'M SORRY. SPIRIT ARMOR SEPARATES YOUR BODY FROM YOUR SPIRITUAL POWER TO MAKE A BARRIER AROUND YOU.
BECAUSE YOU CAN'T DO THAT, YOU CAN'T USE SPIRIT ARMOR.
WHAT...?! HOW WILL I KNOW IF I DON'T TRY!
ONLY FUYUZORA-KUN DIDN'T GET ONE?
IF A PSYCHIC LIKE YOU TRIES TO USE THE SPIRIT ARMOR...
AND YOU MESS UP YOUR ACTUAL BODY... NO...
I'M NOT SURE WHAT WILL HAPPEN, BUT I KNOW THAT IT IS VERY DANGEROUS.
I BELIEVE THAT'S WHY YOUR MASTER...
NEVER TAUGHT YOU TO USE THE SPIRIT ARMOR.
!
MY... MASTER?!
YES! SHE GAVE YOU THE POWER OF THE YATAHAGANE.
HER NAME WAS MAKYOUIN OUGA, KOGARASHI-SAN.
I'VE NEVER MET ANYONE WHO GOES BY MAKYOUIN...
IT'S A STRANGE FEELING KNOWING I'LL MEET SOMEONE IN THE FUTURE.
BUT EVEN IF YOU CAN'T USE SPIRIT ARMOR, KOGARASHI-SAN...
SHE LEFT YOU SOME-THING YOU CAN USE.
SHE DID...? WHAT IS IT?
SHE DID!

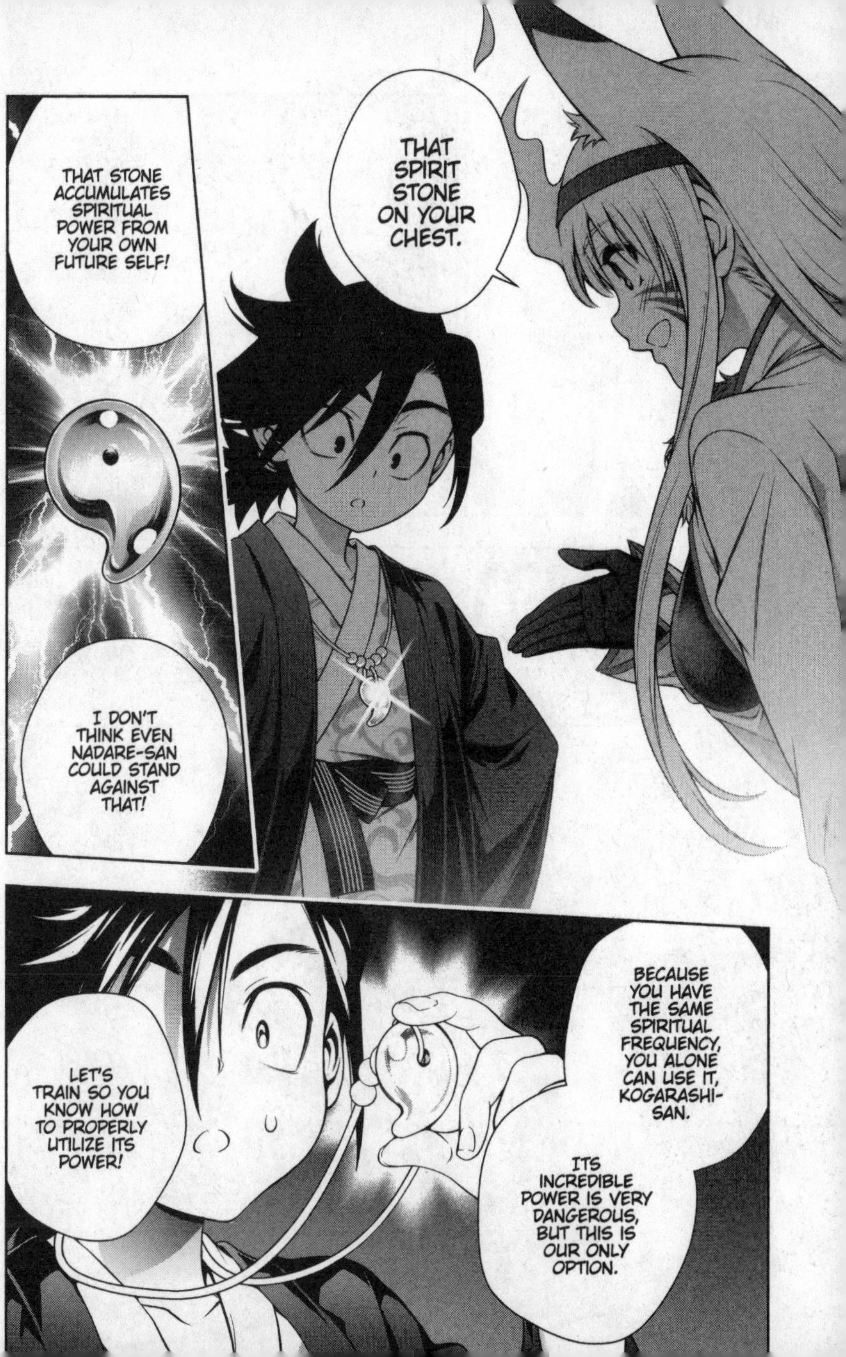
THAT SPIRIT STONE ON YOUR CHEST.
THAT STONE ACCUMULATES SPIRITUAL POWER FROM YOUR OWN FUTURE SELF!
I DON'T THINK EVEN NADARE-SAN COULD STAND AGAINST THAT!
BECAUSE YOU HAVE THE SAME SPIRITUAL FREQUENCY, YOU ALONE CAN USE IT, KOGARASHI-SAN.
ITS INCREDIBLE POWER IS VERY DANGEROUS, BUT THIS IS OUR ONLY OPTION.
LET'S TRAIN SO YOU KNOW HOW TO PROPERLY UTILIZE ITS POWER!

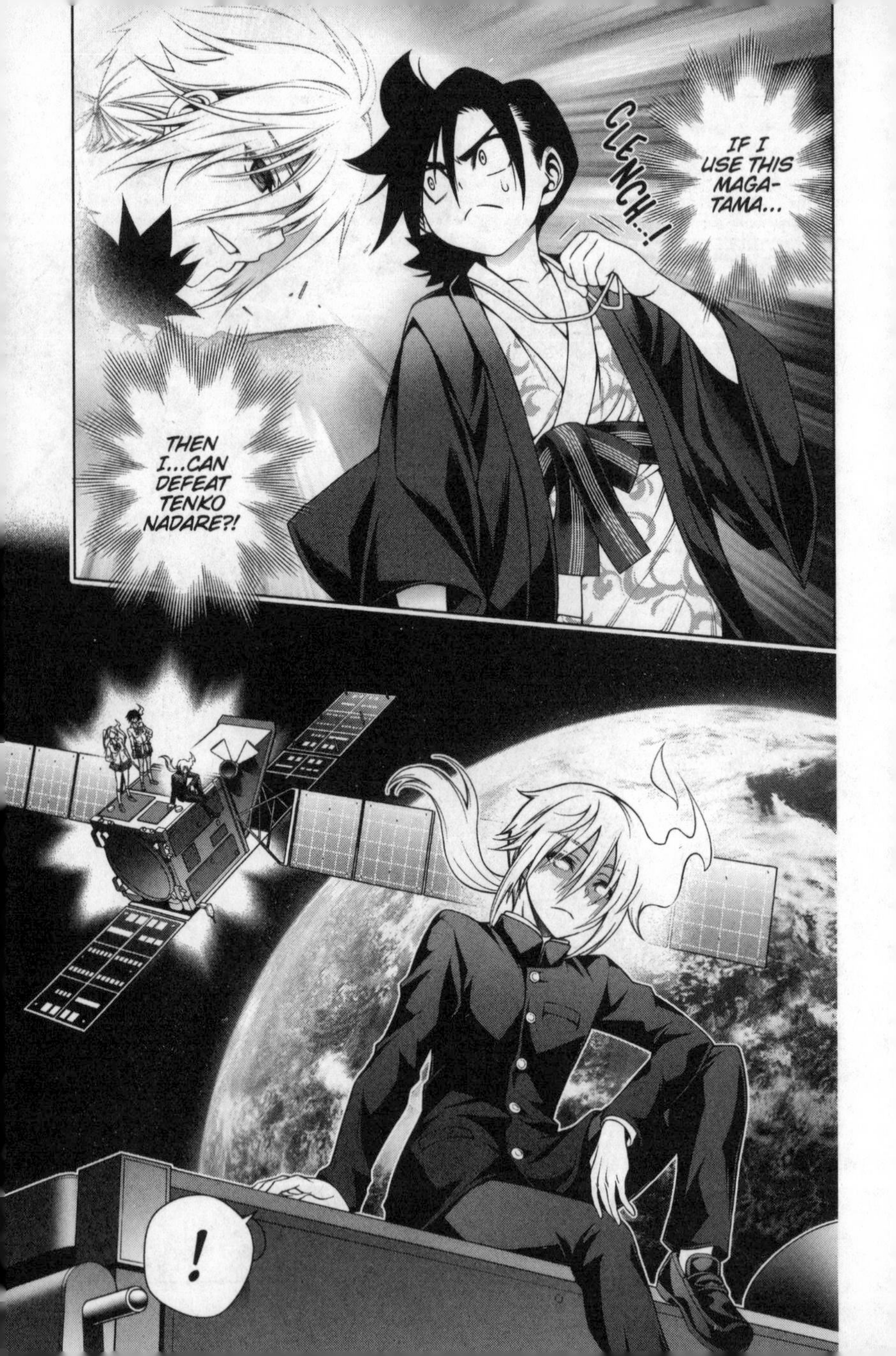
IF I USE THIS MAGA-TAMA...
CLENCH...!
THEN I...CAN DEFEAT TENKO NADARE?!
!

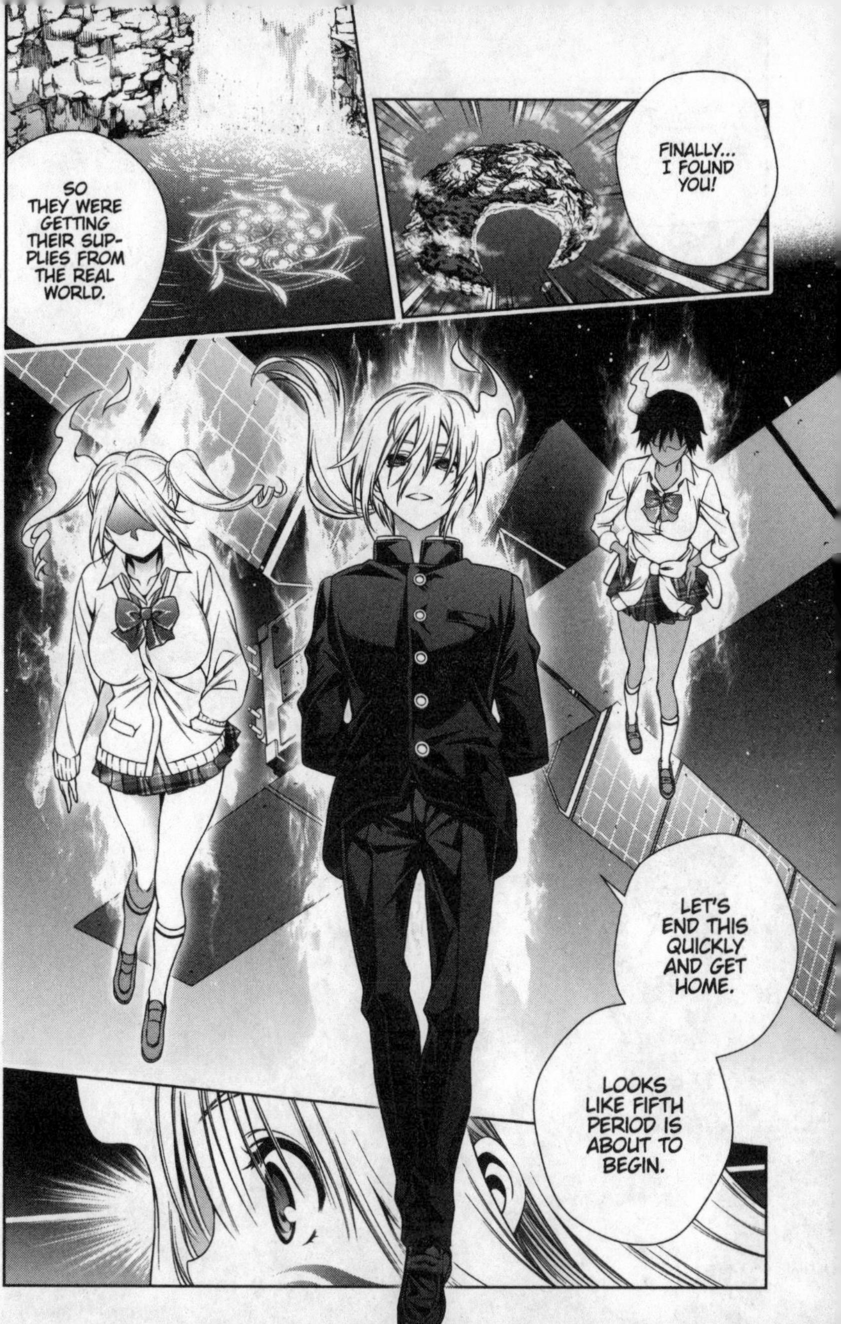
FINALLY... I FOUND YOU!
SO THEY WERE GETTING THEIR SUP-PLIES FROM THE REAL WORLD.
LET'S END THIS QUICKLY AND GET HOME.
LOOKS LIKE FIFTH PERIOD IS ABOUT TO BEGIN.

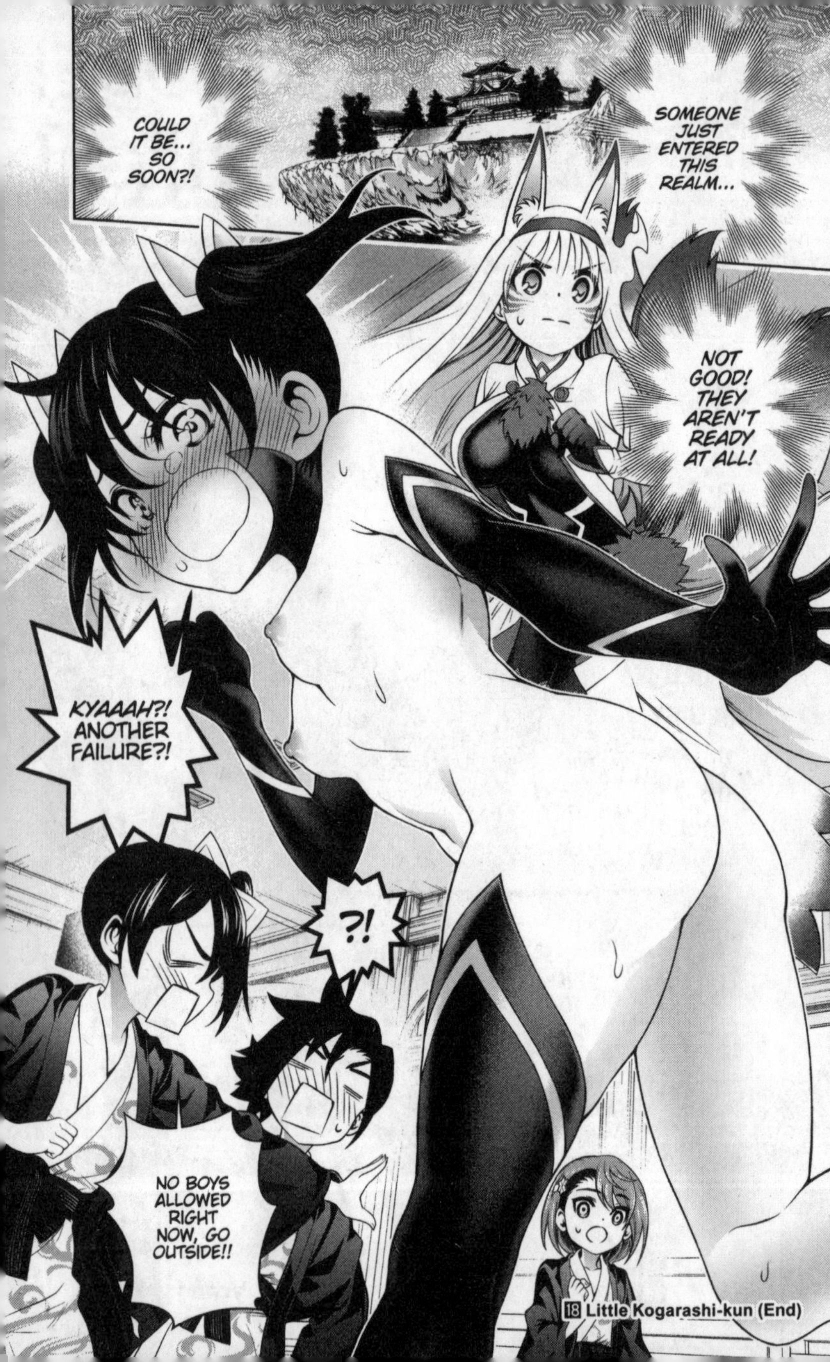
SOMEONE JUST ENTERED THIS REALM...
COULD IT BE... SO SOON?!
NOT GOOD! THEY AREN'T READY AT ALL!
KYAAAH?! ANOTHER FAILURE?!
?!
NO BOYS ALLOWED RIGHT NOW, GO OUTSIDE!!
18 Little Kogarashi-kun (End)

Yuuna and the Haunted Hot Springs

Third anniversary of serialization!

BEST EPISODE Voting Results!!

WJ2019 Vol.11 Voting results announcement!

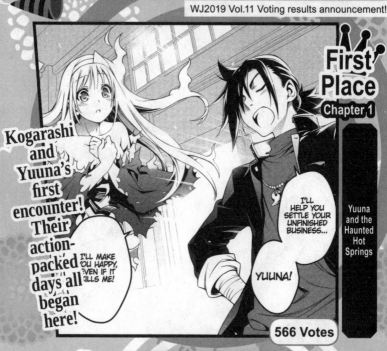

First Place
Chapter 1

Yuuna and the Haunted Hot Springs

Kogarashi and Yuuna's first encounter! Their action-packed days all began here!

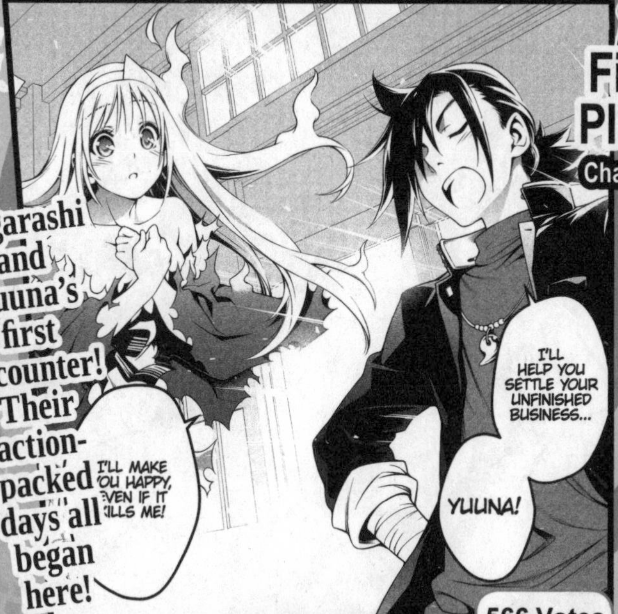
I'LL HELP YOU SETTLE YOUR UNFINISHED BUSINESS...
YUUNA!
I'LL MAKE OU HAPPY, EVEN IF IT ILLS ME!

566 Votes

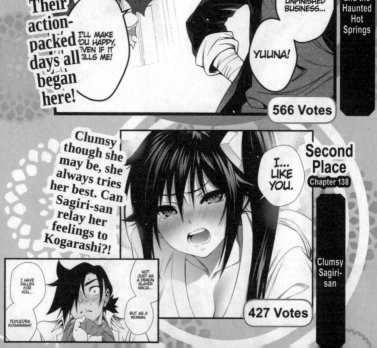

Second Place
Chapter 138

Clumsy Sagiri-san

Clumsy though she may be, she always tries her best. Can Sagiri-san relay her feelings to Kogarashi?!

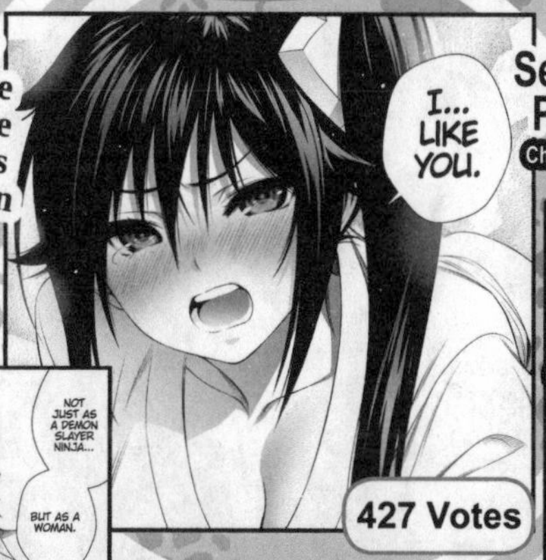
I... LIKE YOU.

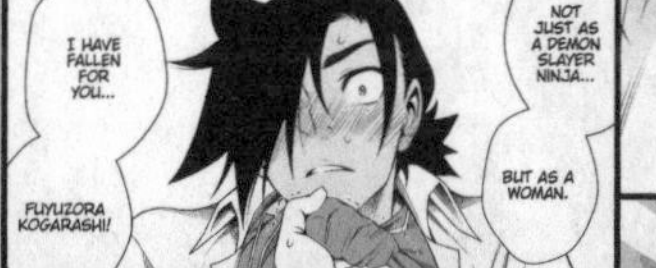
NOT JUST AS A DEMON SLAYER NINJA...
BUT AS A WOMAN.
I HAVE FALLEN FOR YOU...
FUYUZORA KOGARASHI!

427 Votes

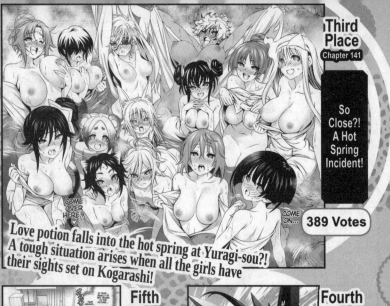

Third Place
Chapter 141

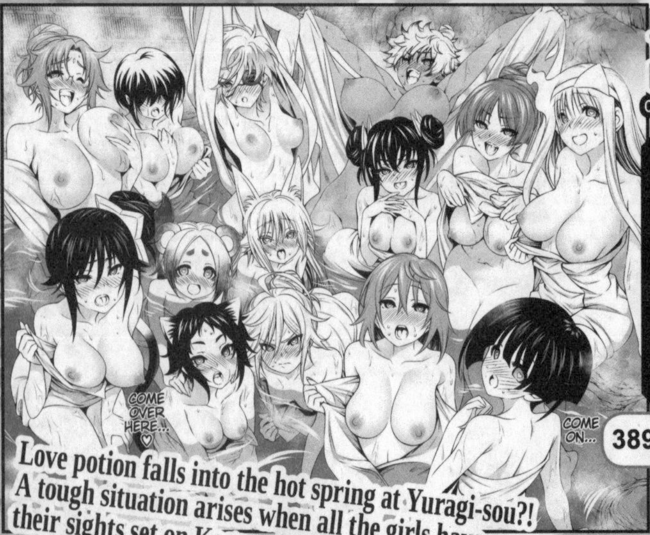
COME OVER HERE...♥
COME ON...

So Close?! A Hot Spring Incident!

389 Votes

Love potion falls into the hot spring at Yuragi-sou?! A tough situation arises when all the girls have their sights set on Kogarashi!

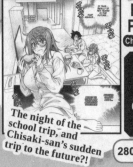

Fifth Place
Chapter 146

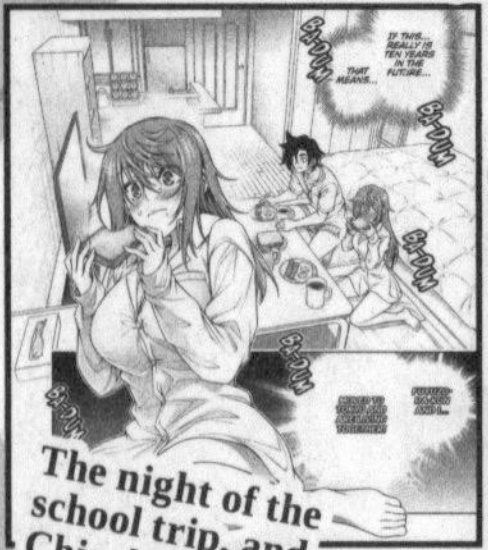

A Future with Chisaki-san

The night of the school trip, and Chisaki-san's sudden trip to the future?!

280 Votes

Fourth Place
Chapter 136

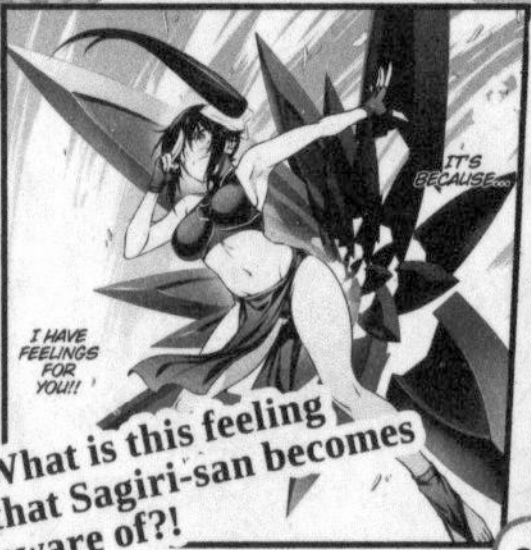
IT'S BECAUSE...
I HAVE FEELINGS FOR YOU!!

Saqiri-san Grows Wary

What is this feeling that Sagiri-san becomes aware of?!

352 Votes

Other High Ranking Chapters all before volume 10!

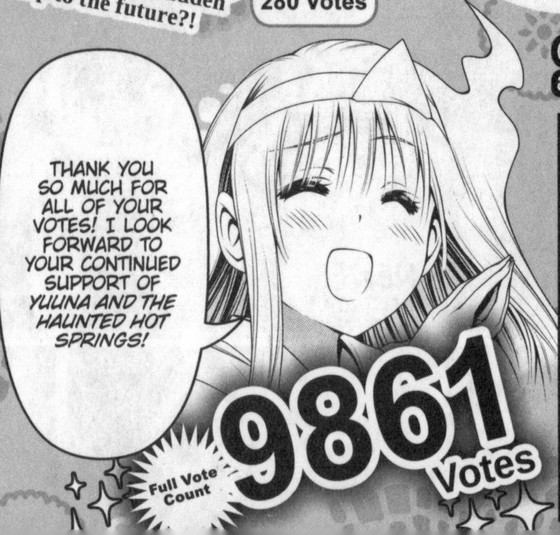
THANK YOU SO MUCH FOR ALL OF YOUR VOTES! I LOOK FORWARD TO YOUR CONTINUED SUPPORT OF *YUUNA AND THE HAUNTED HOT SPRINGS!*

Sixth Place 247 Votes
Chapter 26
Slow Dancing with Yuuna

Seventh Place 228 Votes
Chapter 99
Cursed Kogarashi

Eighth Place 206 Votes
Chapter 77
Casefile: Panties

Ninth Place 185 Votes
Chapter 47
Chisaki and the Blanket of Snow

Chapter 132
I See Chisaki-san.

Full Vote Count **9861 Votes**

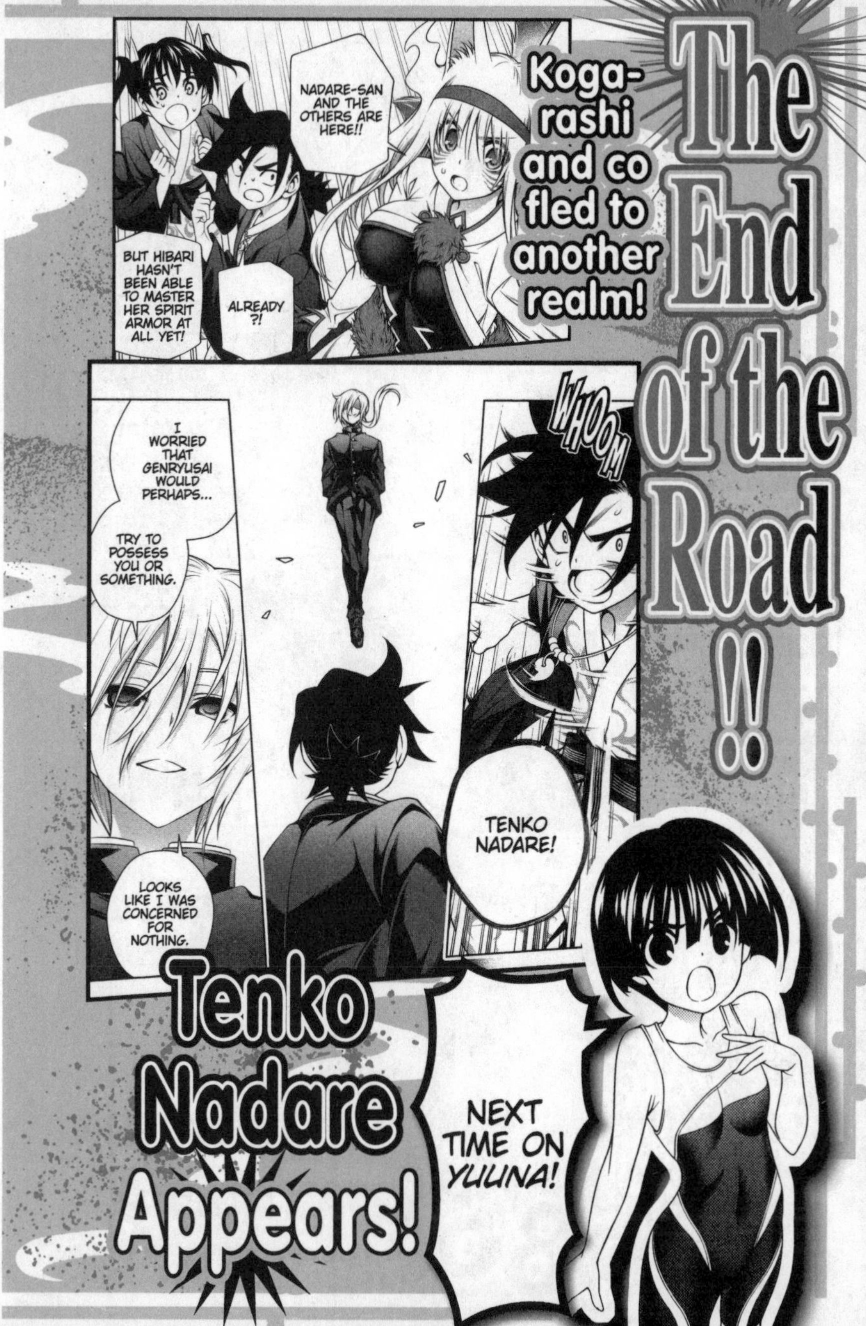
The End of the Road!!
Koga-rashi and co fled to another realm!
NADARE-SAN AND THE OTHERS ARE HERE!!
ALREADY?!
BUT HIBARI HASN'T BEEN ABLE TO MASTER HER SPIRIT ARMOR AT ALL YET!
WHOOM
TENKO NADARE!
I WORRIED THAT GENRYUSAI WOULD PERHAPS...
TRY TO POSSESS YOU OR SOMETHING.
LOOKS LIKE I WAS CONCERNED FOR NOTHING.
NEXT TIME ON YUUNA!
Tenko Nadare Appears!

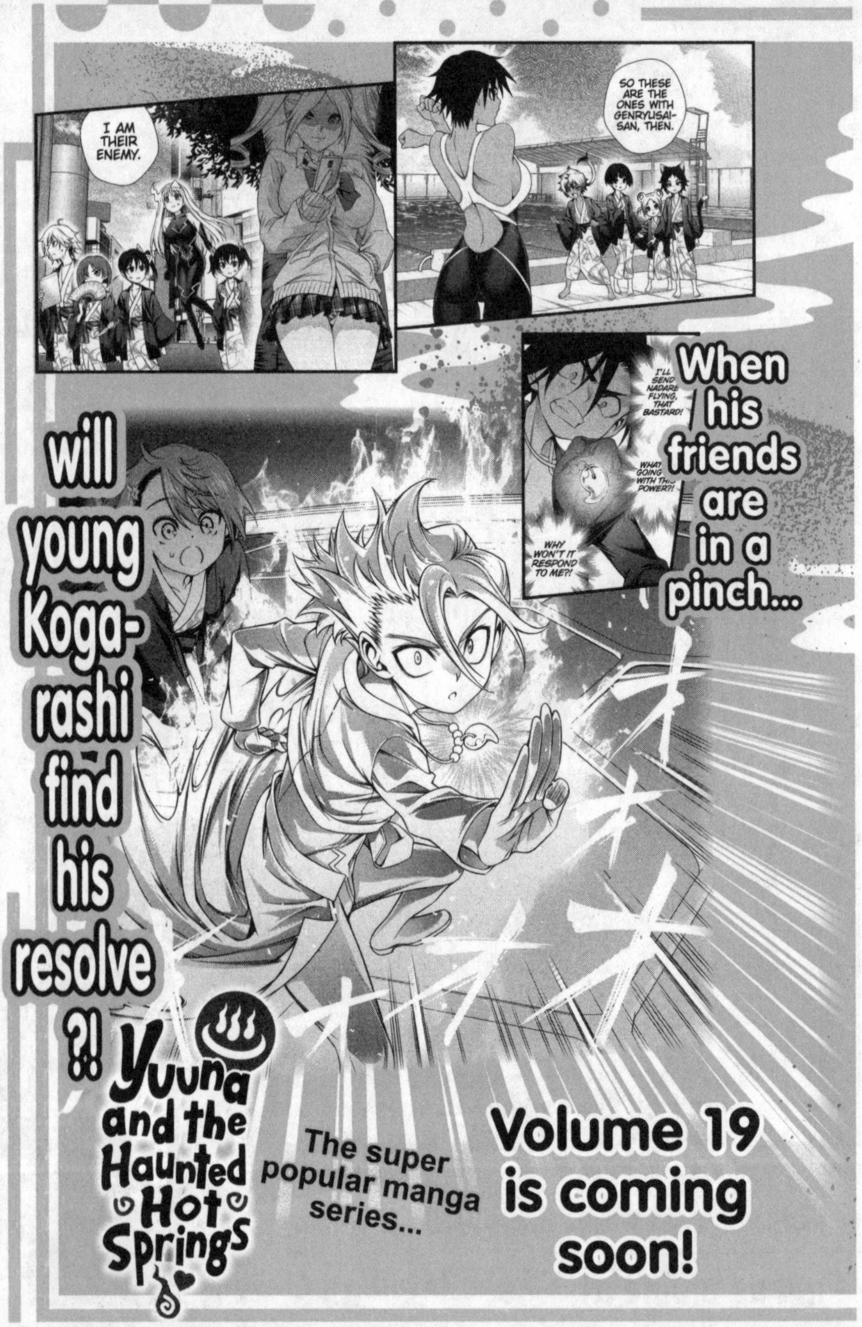
SO THESE ARE THE ONES WITH GENRYUSAI-SAN, THEN.
I AM THEIR ENEMY.
I'LL SEND NADARE FLYING, THAT BASTARD!
WHAT GOING WITH TH POWER?!
WHY WON'T IT RESPOND TO ME?!
When his friends are in a pinch...
will young Koga-rashi find his resolve?!
Yuuna and the Haunted Hot Springs
The super popular manga series...
Volume 19 is coming soon!

Desire Pandora

story & art by
Akira Hizuki

story and art by
MEGURU UENO

1

Does a Hot Elf Live NEXT DOOR to You

MASAHIRO MORIO'S

CALL GIRL in ANOTHER WORLD

1

D1207734

Ghost Ship

Find us online at: GhostShipManga.com